BIBLE MEDITATIONS For Every Day

A GUIDE TO LIVING THE YEAR IN THE SPIRIT OF THE SCRIPTURES

BY JOHN C. KERSTEN, S.V.D.

Dedicated to ST. JOSEPH
Patron of the Universal Church

CATHOLIC BOOK PUBLISHING CO.
NEW YORK

NIHIL OBSTAT: Raymond T. Powers, S.T.D.
Censor Librorum

IMPRIMATUR: ✠ James P Mahoney, D.D.
Vicar General, Archdiocese of New York

The nihil obstat and imprimatur are official declarations that a book or pamphlet is free of doctrinal or moral error. No implication is contained therein that those who have granted the nihil obstat and imprimatur agree with the contents, opinions or statements expressed.

ACKNOWLEDGMENTS

The author and publisher are grateful for permission to quote from the following copyrighted works:

Bhagavad-Gita, translated by Swami Prabhavananda and Christopher Isherwood. A Mentor Book, published by the New American Library of World Literature. Inc. Copyright © 1972 by Vedanta Society of Southern California. Reprinted by permission of the copyright holder.

Moshe Davis and Victor Ratner, *The Stranger Within Ourself* in *The Birthday of the World*. Copyright © 1959 by the Jewish Theological Seminary of America. Reprinted by permission of Farrar, Straus & Giroux, Inc.

Fyodor Dostoevski, *The Brothers Karamazov*. Copyright © by Airmont Publishing Co. Reprinted by permission of the publisher.

Langston Hughes, *Without Benefit of Declaration* in *American Negro Poetry* edited by Anna Bontemps and published by Hill and Wang, Inc. Copyright © 1955, 1963 by Langston Hughes. Reprinted by permission of Harold Ober Associates, Incorporated.

John of the Cross, *The Spiritual Canticle* in *The Collected Works of St. John of the Cross*, translated by Kieran Kavanaugh and Otilio Rodriguez. Copyright © 1964 by Washington Province of Discalced Carmelites, Inc. Paperback edition published by ICS Publications, Washington D.C., U.S.A. Reprinted by permission of the publisher.

Elizabeth Kubler-Ross, *Questions and Answers on Death and Dying*. Copyright © 1974 by Ross Medical Associates S.C. Reprinted by permission of the publisher, Macmillan Publishing Co., Inc.

G. Leibholz, *Memoir* in *The Cost of Discipleship* (2nd ed.) by Dietrich Bonhoeffer. Copyright © 1959 by SCM Press, Ltd. Reprinted by permission of the Macmillan Publishing Co., Inc.

Gabriel Marcel, *Homo Viator—Introduction to a Metaphysic of Hope*. Copyright © 1968 by Harper and Row Publishers. Reprinted by permission of the publisher.

Gabriel Marcel, *Creative Fidelity*. Translated from the French with an Introduction by Robert Rosthal. Copyright © 1964 by Farrar, Straus & Company (now Farrar, Straus & Giroux, Inc.). Reprinted by permission of Farrar, Straus & Giroux, Inc.

Karl Rahner, *Christian Living Formerly and Today* in *Theological Investigations*, vol. 7. Copyright © 1971 by The Seabury Press. Reprinted by permission of the publisher.

(T-277)

CONTENTS

The uncontrolled mind
Does not guess that the Atman
(the Divine in us) is present:
How can it meditate?
Without meditation, where is peace?
Without peace, where is happiness?

—Bhagavad-Gita

The devout Christian of the future will either be a "mystic," one who has "experienced" something, or he will cease to be anything at all.

—Karl Rahner

PREFACE

IN OUR day we observe a widespread interest in meditation. Constantly under stress, we run up our blood pressure and die prematurely of strokes and heart attacks; bored with the daily duties of the home, we have recourse to the psychiatrist; lonesome and alienated, we seek counseling, and have not yet answered the question: "What for?" Is meditation the answer?

Gurus

By the dozens, the gurus (teachers) of the East have been coming to this country to offer their wisdom of the ages. They sell us TM, transcendental (going beyond) meditation, accompanied by mantras (thought-sounds) and the request for "modest fees." Separate from religious attitudes, TM wants to help us find pure awareness and human fulfillment. Other gurus teach yoga discipline or Zen meditation. The meditator sits in a lotus-position as far as possible. Both soul and body are involved in meditation. He should be perfectly relaxed, control his breathing and focus on a physical object like a candle-flame, a sensation, a Zen koan (insoluble philosophical paradox), or an absence of all thought (mental void). Total silence is of paramount importance. And all of this should lead to a mystical, intuitive, direct awareness of the transcendent, inner freedom, and a concomitant mental discipline.

In the West

Religious men and women in the West are more familiar with a form of meditation which practices thinking about meaning. Thinking is our basic procedure for gaining understanding of ourselves and our relationship with God and environment. For centuries we have reserved meditation for priests and religious. Lay people were supposed to say the rosary, recite litanies and prayers which others had made up for them. This book seeks to promote meditation for all—priests, religious, and lay people—as a remedy for the contemporary ailments which we have mentioned above.

Blending

An interesting question is: In meditating, can we learn from the great meditators of the East? The answer is a conditioned yes, with the proviso that we keep in mind that for us Christians the transcendent is not a vague impersonal entity (as it is for the Buddhists), but a personal God who loves us. Moreover, if we adopt the techniques of TM and Zen meditation according to personal taste, we should keep in mind that through these techniques alone we cannot establish union with God. After we have done whatever is humanly possible, we depend totally on God's graciousness. "No one comes to the Father but through me [Jesus Christ]" (John 4:6).

If constant daily meditation, blending Christian tradition with Eastern experience, results in a pure awareness, it should be the awareness of the Ground of my being, as a loving God, in whom I live and move and have my being (Acts 17:28), an encounter of the I with the Absolute Thou, which we call prayer. And this experience should give us the inner freedom, peace of mind, and mental discipline of the children of God.

From Scripture

This is not a meditation book in that it offers pre-meditated material, upon which the reader in his/her turn is invited to meditate. *You are invited to meditate on the suggested Bible passages.* The introductions are not trying to compete with the word of God. Their only purpose is to condition heart and mind for better ingestion of the Divine message.

Out of Business

It sounds strange when a man tries to advertise himself out of business. The author of this book is such a man. Since not all passages of Scripture are equally inviting to prayerful response, I have selected passages which appealed to me or are taken from liturgical readings selected for the Sundays of the year. Though some state that the Church could have done better, on the whole most Scripture scholars are happy with the arrangement. I have introduced the passages with thought-provoking remarks, but I hope that by issuing this book for daily meditation, the reader will learn how to use the Bible itself as a meditation book.

There are passages and even books in the Bible that are not very inspiring for reflective prayer. Skim them, but stop wherever a line provokes reflection. Try to understand the setting (man's word—read footnotes!), apply the passage to your own life situation (God's word), and respond in prayer! Mark those passages with a pencil and return to them! *Your* Bible should be *your* book, through which God speaks to you.

Meditation-Contemplation

Biblical meditations are discursive (through images, forms and figures). When to abandon them and pass on to the state of contemplation? St. John of the Cross advises us to go on with making discursive meditation as long as we can do so with satisfaction. Only when dryness and disinclination to fix the imagination upon extraneous things enters the picture, and one likes to remain alone in the loving awareness of God without the acts of intellect, memory, and will, should one gradually make the transition.[1]

Catholics But Not Christians

During a workshop on Bible reading, I made the remark: "We have plenty of Catholics, but too many of them are not Christians." I received a lot of flack on that. But aren't many Catholics primarily committed to the Institution with only a weak commitment to the heart of the matter: Jesus Christ? Being a Christian means being spellbound by the Lord Jesus and what he stands for. Being part of the Institution (the Roman Catholic Church) is essential but not to be severed from attachment to Christ. I am pessimistic about the future of the Church if Catholics are not going to change. Daily, prayerful Bible reading can bring that change about.

1 *The Ascent of Mount Carmel, Collected Works,* pp. 140-141.

HOW TO USE THIS BOOK

Prepare

Quiet down. Forget about your daily duties. Find a quiet place and complete silence. Preferably meditate with an empty stomach. Ask the Holy Spirit to guide your meditation!

Ponder

1. Read Introduction and Bible passage. Visualize the original Bible setting.

2. Read the Scripture passage again, now slowly, and with a pencil mark words/ideas that strike you.

3. Sit in a position that fits you. If it is your taste, take the lotus position as far as possible. Breathe deeply several times and be completely relaxed. Both body and mind should be involved. Close your eyes and think of God, in whom you live and move and have your being. He is love. He abides in you and you in him. (See Acts 17:28; 1 John 4:16.)

Pray

Let your thoughts flow and bring in the ideas/words that strike you in the Bible reading. Apply them to your own life situation and respond to God, who is present to you. Your prayer does not have to be verbal. Often mental prayer does better.

Do this daily for 15-20 minutes!

Advice to the Married

You and your spouse may do the same simultaneously, dialogue on what you experienced as God's word to you (or both of you!), conclude with joint spontaneous prayer.

"A tiny whispering sound . . ."

ENVIRONMENTALISTS fight pollution of air and water. They want to keep the planet clean and as beautiful as possible. The human species owes this to itself. We will destroy ourselves if we don't fight pollution.

A pollution of a horrible kind is sound pollution, which is caused mainly by the abuse of electronic sound equipment. Many people feel uncomfortable, lonesome, and cannot fall asleep unless the television set, radio, or record player produces noise. They must be in company constantly. Talking is essential for their happiness. Constant sound, however, especially uncivilized noise, kills you as a person. You cannot be yourself. We need silence to reflect on the basics of life and most of all to encounter "The Ultimate Reality," "The Ground of our being," whom in faith we see as a person and call God.

The Bible reminds us of the necessity of silence in the following beautiful idyllic tradition on the prophet Elijah. Afraid of his life, Elijah had to fly to the desert. He went to a cave where he met the Lord—not in a mighty wind, an earthquake, or fire (traditional signs of God's awe-inspiring presence), but rather in a tiny whispering sound. A lesson for the prophet so fond of the spectacular!

Silence is a condition for encountering God in meditative prayer.

SCRIPTURE READING —

[Elijah] came to a cave, where he took shelter. But the word of the Lord came to him, "Why are you here, Elijah?" He answered: "I have been most zealous for the Lord, the God of hosts, but the Israelites have forsaken your covenant, torn down your altars, and put your prophets to the sword. I alone am left, and they seek to take my life."

Then the Lord said, "Go outside and stand on the mountain before the Lord; the Lord will be passing by." A strong and heavy wind was rending the mountains and crushing rocks before the Lord—but the Lord was not in the wind. After the wind there was an earthquake—but the Lord was not in the earthquake. After the earthquake there was fire —but the Lord was not in the fire. After the fire there was a tiny whispering sound. When he heard this, Elijah hid his face in his cloak and went and stood at the entrance o fthe cave. (1 Kings 19:9-12)

"Martha . . . , one thing only is required"

THE Church (you and I) is very much criticized nowadays because of her alleged lack of social concern. We read a great deal about "horizontal Christianity." It is Christianity practiced mainly or only in concern and love for the suffering fellowman. "As often as you did it for one of my least brothers . . ." (Matthew 25:40) makes headlines. It is said that "prayer of engagement" should have priority over "prayer of withdrawal."

Is time for withdrawal in silent meditative prayer a waste of time? One thing is sure: concern and love for fellowmen or just doing one's duty usually does not last, unless it is boosted regularly by reflection in prayer. A life of duty and concern for others is not always rewarding. It easily becomes narrowminded and limiting itself to the concern of relatives, friends and nice people only. But that is not Christianity. Jesus says: "And if you greet your brothers only, what is so praiseworthy about that? Do not pagans do as much?" (Matthew 5:47).

Genuine Christian concern needs more motivation than just vague emotions. A Christian finds it in periods of withdrawal. For a large part of your prayerful meditation should consist of reflection and listening, as Martha's sister did.

SCRIPTURE READING —

On their journey Jesus entered a village where a woman named Martha welcomed him to her home. She had a sister named Mary, who seated herself at the Lord's feet and listened to his words. Martha, who was busy with all the details of hospitality, came to him and said, "Lord, are you not concerned that my sister has left me to do the household tasks all alone? Tell her to help me."

The Lord in reply said to her: "Martha, Martha, you are anxious and upset about many things; one thing only is required. Mary has chosen the better portion and she shall not be deprived of it."

(Luke 10:38-42)

"Spending the night in communion with God"

"RUNNING off at the mouth"—talking too much—is one of the favorite pastimes of quite a few fellow human beings. Do these fast-talking busybodies really communicate? They do everything but listen! Yet communication consists of both speaking and listening. Nor must speaking necessarily be done by rattling many words. It can be carried on very effectively without verbal expression.

Apply this to your encounter with God, who is in you and around you. Before meditation, quiet down first! Have patience with yourself. Apply some of the techniques described in "How to Use This Book." In complete silence are you growing in awareness of God's presence to you?

Jesus went out to the mountain to pray, spending the night in communion with God. He prayed not just to bolster his morale, but because he found communication with his Father precious and rewarding in itself. And we can hardly visualize Jesus sitting under a tree reading a prayerbook by candlelight. Jesus was an Easterner. We do not know whether he sat in the lotus-position, nor whether he was acquainted with the meditation practices of India. In Jesus' time these techniques were already 3,000 years old, and there was cultural exchange. Whatever the case may have been, we can be sure that for the most part Jesus' prayer consisted of listening, pure awareness of his Father's presence.

Your meditation should grow in likeness of Jesus' meditative prayer.

SCRIPTURE READING —

Then he went out to the mountain to pray, spending the night in communion with God. At daybreak he called his disciples and selected twelve of them to be his apostles: Simon, to whom he gave the name Peter, and Andrew his brother, James and John, Philip and Bartholomew, Matthew and Thomas, James son of Alphaeus, and Simon called the Zealot, Judas son of James and Judas Iscariot, who turned traitor.

(Luke 6:12-16)

"If God has loved us so . . ."

IN THE wake of the Second Vatican Council, the Church practices a much more positive approach to other religions than she has done in the past. We try to see the good in all efforts to find meaning in life. What strikes theologians in dialogue with Zen masters and other great Buddhist meditators of the East is their awareness of the transcendent. And their concept of the transcendent (what goes beyond) is not even clearly a personal God.

The God-inspired contribution of the Hebrew-Christian tradition is that the Ground of my being, the Ultimate Reality, is not just some vague impersonal entity, but a person, an Absolute Thou, who relates to me in love. God is love. He loved me before I even was able to love him. And he dwells in me. Searching for a pure awareness of God in daily life is not something only priests and religious should. All Christians should try to achieve this by daily meditation.

The TM people (see Introduction) claim that 600,000 Americans meditate daily twice twenty minutes to achieve "pure awareness," peace of mind and mental discipline. Why can't we Christians do the same, but by tapping the riches of our Christian heritage as found in Scripture?

SCRIPTURE READING —

Beloved,
let us love one another
because love is of God;
everyone who loves is begotten of God
and has knowledge of God.
The man without love has known nothing of God,
for God is love.
God's love was revealed in our midst in this way:
he sent his only Son to the world
that we might have life through him.
Love, then, consists in this:
not that we have loved God
but that he has loved us
and has sent his Son as an offering for our sins.
Beloved,
if God has loved us so,
we must have the same love for one another.
No one has ever seen God.
Yet if we love one another
God dwells in us,
and his love is brought to perfection in us. (1 John 4:7-12)

"Before I formed you in the womb I knew you"

IN HIS book *I and Thou,* the learned and devout Jewish philosopher, Martin Buber, discusses human relations. I am related to a fellow human being as an I to a Thou. Respectfully I should participate in his personality, and never degrade this Thou to an It, which is done when I do not really love him but try to use him for my own purpose. By using him as such, I make him a tool, an It, to fit my pleasure.

In faith following Jesus of Nazareth, I know that the Ground of my being is a You, a person, whom I may address as Father. And I may enjoy an I-Thou relationship with him. Martin Buber states: "All real life is meeting." If it is true that meeting a good person enriches me, how much more must this be true when I apply it to my I-Thou relationship with God. Meeting him in prayerful meditation enriches my life and makes me live more really. Even the most powerful relationships, however, are doomed to fade when indifference enters the picture. That is why meditation is valuable in itself. Jeremiah had a wonderful experience of God relating to him as a real person who cares. He tells us about it by putting the words of this Bible passage into his mouth.

Pray that God may give you an awareness similar to that of Jeremiah.

SCRIPTURE READING —

The word of the Lord came to me thus:
Before I formed you in the womb I knew you,
before you were born I dedicated you,
a prophet to the nations I appointed you.
"Ah, Lord God!" I said,
"I know not how to speak; I am too young."
But the Lord answered me,
Say not, "I am too young."
To whomever I send you, you shall go;
whatever I command you, you shall speak.
Have no fear before them,
because I am with you to deliver you, says the Lord.
Then the Lord extended his hand and touched my mouth, saying,
See, I place my words in your mouth!
This day I set you
over nations and over kingdoms,
To root up and to tear down,
to destroy and to demolish,
to build and to plant.

(Jeremiah 1:4-10)

"They were overjoyed at seeing the star"

OFTEN people travel and pay $25 or $100 a plate to attend a dinner party where a famous politician makes an appearance. Many of the faithful travel miles to see the Pope.

In today's Liturgy we celebrate the appearance (manifestation—epiphany) of the Lord Jesus on the human scene. The Church brings out a prominent aspect of the Christian mystery, namely, the *universal* dominion of the newborn King, as dramatized in the Lord's manifestation to the magi (astrologers from the East, non-Jews). The symbolism of light is lavishly used.

The Balaam narrative (see Numbers 22; 23, esp. v.7; and 24, esp. v. 17) is part of the background of Matthew's story. Births and deaths of great men were marked by heavenly signs. A horoscope, telling about a Messiah (anointed king—freedom fighter) to come, may have been in the picture. Psalm 72:10-11 is reflected. The massacre in Bethlehem echoes the Egyptian Pharaoh's slaughter of the male children of the Hebrews. Thus Matthew makes Jesus, who is to save God's people, relive the Exodus, the great past event of salvation, in his own life. Read all of Matthew 2. His way of telling things is unusual to us, but his lesson is clear: God's epiphany (self-manifestation) in Jesus is for all! "It is no less than this: in Christ Jesus the Gentiles are now coheirs with the Jews" (Ephesians 3:6).

Expose yourself to the light of Christ in prayerful meditation and be overjoyed because of the direction it gives to your life! And share this light, which is for all, through word and example. "You can't be a beacon, if your light doesn't shine."

SCRIPTURE READING —

After Jesus' birth in Bethlehem of Judea during the reign of King Herod, astrologers from the east arrived one day in Jerusalem inquiring, "Where is the newborn king of the Jews? We observed his star at its rising and have come to pay him homage."

After their audience with the king, they set out. The star which they had observed at its rising went ahead of them until it came to a standstill over the place where the child was. They were overjoyed at seeing the star, and on entering the house, found the child with Mary, his mother. They prostrated themselves and did him homage. Then they opened their coffers and presented him with gifts of gold, frankincense, and myrrh.

They received a message in a dream not to return to Herod, so they went back to their own country by another route.

(Matthew 2:1-2, 9-12)

"He has given us of his Spirit"

THERE is no doubt that "how to pray" is a problem for many Christians. To begin with, one must get rid of the secret suspicion that prayer is nothing else but a good psychological means of comfort by talking persuasively to oneself, as it is for the man who cannot see God transcending creation as an Absolute Thou. Prayerful meditation does not make sense unless I grow evermore in that awareness that God as a person relates to me. **How to achieve this?**

Zen masters offer us their elaborate techniques. We mentioned some of them briefly in the Preface. They may be helpful to create a situation in which God can operate, but as such they cannot establish communion with God. After we have done whatever we can do, we must realize that we are in constant need of God's help. Ask for it!

"He who abides in love abides in God, and God in him" (1 John 4:16). This is not meant to be an abstract announcement, true but only to be experienced by a few favored mystics or in the hereafter. It is for you and me to be aware of now. We do whatever we can do, then humbly ask God to share his love and presence with us, and we know that he will grant us that favor, since he has given us his Spirit and sent the Son as a Savior of the world.

SCRIPTURE READING —

The way we know we remain in him
and he in us
is that he has given us of his Spirit.
We have seen for ourselves, and can testify,
that the Father has sent the Son as savior of the world.
When anyone acknowledges that Jesus is the Son of God,
God dwells in him
and he in God.
We have come to know and to believe
in the love God has for us.
God is love,
and he who abides in love
abides in God,
and God in him.
Our love is brought to perfection in this,
that we should have confidence on the day of judgment;
for our relation to this world is just like his. (1 John 4:13-17)

"For he who has become your husband is your Maker"

WE FEEL disappointed and angry when somebody "takes us for a ride." There is even more reason to feel so if this is done by a good friend whom we loved dearly and held in great esteem. Such an experience may be the instant end of a friendship. We should be careful ourselves, though, not to make similar mistakes. We should ever more cultivate our human relations. The more we open up and are loving on the human level, the more we are able to love God. If we don't believe in love in daily life, it does not make sense to meditate on love of God.

Does it happen that man takes God for a ride? Yes, when he degrades him to an "It" *(see January 5)*, approaching him only when he is in need. Man may drift away and even get very unfaithful. And this is the more deplorable since our relationship with God is so intimate that Scripture compares it with the beautiful relationship of husband and wife. It is God who wants it this way. Man himself would never have dared to dream of it. But suppose I have been seriously unfaithful. Can such a relationship be restored? Yes, it can. If you repent honestly, "with great tenderness God will take you back—his love shall never leave you."

SCRIPTURE READING —

For he who has become your husband is your Maker;
his name is the Lord of hosts;
Your redeemer is the Holy One of Israel,
called God of all the earth.
The Lord calls you back,
like a wife forsaken and grieved in spirit,
A wife married in youth and then cast off,
says your God.
For a brief moment I abandoned you,
but with great tenderness I will take you back.
In an outburst of warmth, for a moment
I hid my face from you;
But with enduring love I take pity on you,
says the Lord, your redeemer.
This is for me like the days of Noah,
when I swore that the waters of Noah
should never again deluge the earth;
So I have sworn not to be angry with you,
or to rebuke you.
Though the mountains leave their place
and the hills be shaken,
My love shall never leave you
nor my covenant of peace be shaken,
says the Lord, who has mercy on you. (Isaiah 54:5-10)

"In him we live and move and have our being"

RELATIONSHIPS are tested by physical separations. A husband in the armed forces overseas, a wife in the hospital, a salesman on the road for five days, a befriended family that is transferred far away—all of these create problems for relationships. Some form of presence is a necessity to maintain relationship with beloved ones. Physical presence is important, but not necessarily the most important one. Though physically present, partners can be miles apart as persons when they watch their soap operas or ball games one after another.

As for God, there is no problem with his presence as such. "In him we live and move and have our being" (Acts 17:18). The problem may be that he is unobservable to the human senses. The greater problem, however, is that man does not always open up to the Divine presence. Being present to one another is a two-way street. God is always available, but are we? And do we create the situation (silence, concentration) that makes an encounter possible?

A letter received in the mail can mean a great deal to someone in love. The Bible is such a letter. It is God's word for you. Do you open it regularly and read it with wonderment and care, being conscious of God present to you?

SCRIPTURE READING —

Then Paul stood up in the Areopagus and delivered this address: "Men of Athens, I note that in every respect you are scrupulously religious. As I walked around looking at your shrines, I even discovered an altar inscribed, 'To a God Unknown.' Now, what you are thus worshiping in ignorance I intend to make known to you. For the God who made the world and all that is in it, the Lord of heaven and earth, does not dwell in sanctuaries made by human hands; nor does he receive man's service as if he were in need of it. Rather, it is he who gives to all life and breath and everything else. From one stock he made every nation of mankind to dwell on the face of the earth. It is he who set limits to their epochs and fixed the boundaries of their regions. They were to seek God, yes to grope for him and perhaps eventually to find him—though he is not really far from any one of us. 'In him we live and move and have our being,' as some of your own poets have put it, 'for we too are his offspring.'" (Acts 17:22-28)

"I have come down to rescue them from the hands of the Egyptians"

WE ARE familiar with the Negro spiritual, *Let My People Go.*

"When Israel was in Egypt's land, let my people go.
Oppressed so hard they could not stand, let my people go.
Go down Moses, way down in Egypt's land.
Tell ole Pharaoh to let my people go.
O let my people go."

Oppressed, harassed, and enslaved for centuries, the black people of this country have turned to the Exodus saga of the Bible to express their yearning for freedom.

Whenever the Hebrews suffered from foreign oppression, this same Exodus theme appeared in their literature and in the songs they sang in temple and synagogue.

"When Israel came forth from Egypt,
the house of Jacob from a people of alien tongue,
Judah became his sanctuary,
Israel his domain" (Psalm 114:1-2).

But more pernicious than political slavery is the bondage which our inner self may suffer. Am I free, when jealousy, anger, lust, greed, hatred, avarice, or laziness directs my life? Left to myself, I am in a hopeless situation. Will I ever be the kind of person I would like to be or should be in the eyes of my Maker? Cry and God will rescue you! The Exodus saga is still a source of inspiration. Apply this passage from it to your own life situation and respond in prayer!

SCRIPTURE READING —

When the Lord saw him coming over to look at it more closely, God called out to him from the bush, "Moses! Moses!" He answered, "Here I am." God said, "Come no nearer! Remove the sandals from your feet, for the place where you stand is holy ground. I am the God of your father," he continued, "the God of Abraham, the God of Isaac, the God of Jacob." Moses hid his face, for he was afraid to look at God.

But the Lord said, "I have witnessed the affliction of my people in Egypt and have heard their cry of complaint against their slave drivers, so I know well what they are suffering. Come, now! I will send you to Pharaoh to lead my people, the Israelites, out of Egypt."

(Exodus 3:6, 7-10)

"God delivered them up to their own depraved sense"

ALL who work with dope addicts and alcoholics tell us that their patients are anything but free. The founder of Buddhism relates all enslavement and the restlessness that goes with it to "voluptuous desire," an unruly state of the mind, by which one attaches oneself to an object when it is perceived. It is a sickness of the mind. According to the Buddha, ascetical or penitential exercises are not necessary to heal this ailment of the mind. It can be achieved by detachment from the objects of the senses. The advice is: Train your mind to detachment by meditation.

To a certain extent the Christian diagnosis of the sick mind is the same. But the traditional word of the Christian to designate the cause of this state of "sin" is "concupiscence." And concupiscence is more than just attachment to the object of the senses. In the Christian tradition, we see concupiscence also as a revolt against the supreme reality behind life, which in faith we experience as a person whom we address as Father and call God. Moreover concupiscence is only one aspect of the cause. We suffer and are enslaved also because of pride, hatred of others, and refusal to accept humbly the realities of the universe.

The Apostle Paul is very pessimistic about humanity when thrown back on itself alone. We learn from this Scripture who we are and would be, if we drift away from God. Training of the mind by meditation is helpful, but it should result in a humble prayer for God's assistance. Only with God's help can we be really free persons.

SCRIPTURE READING —

They did not see fit to acknowledge God, so God delivered them up to their own depraved sense to do what is unseemly. They are filled with every kind of wickedness: maliciousness, greed, ill will, envy, murder, bickering, deceit, craftiness. They are gossips and slanderers, they hate God, are insolent, haughty, boastful, ingenious in their wrongdoing and rebellious toward their parents. One sees in them men without conscience, without loyalty, without affection, without pity. They know God's just decree that all who do such things deserve death; yet they not only do them but approve them in others. (Romans 1:28-32)

"If the Son frees you, you will really be free"

LIBERATION is a concept that in one form or another is spotlighted in every page of our daily papers, and is taken as the target of many secular organizations or institutes. Doctors offer liberation from sickness, teachers from ignorance, social workers from poverty, and revolutionaries from political oppression.

Liberation (salvation, redemption) is the aim of all religions. But the founders of religions have realized that every person is looking for a liberation from a deeper ill than just sickness, ignorance, poverty, or political oppression. Rich, educated, and healthy people, though living in a free country, are not always the happiest beings on earth. Perhaps one of the most ingrained ailments of the human species is "dissatisfaction" which causes restlessness. And as St. Augustine observed so well, the human heart will be restless until it rests in God. This is the Christian approach to the problem of human restlessness.

We turn to the philosophy of life of Jesus Christ, the Founder of Christianity. He offers freedom. You must be acquainted with his teaching and live by it. If you are his disciple, you will know the truth and the truth will set you free. In this Scripture, the Jews are right. Despite centuries of foreign occupation, they have never submitted. They have the true mind of God as revealed in the Bible. However, Jesus asks them to remember that blood descent as such does not give freedom. Freedom is a state of mind, which the person who submits to sin does not possess. Let yourself be set free by the Son; then you will really be free.

SCRIPTURE READING —

Jesus went on to say to those Jews who believed in him:
"If you live according to my teaching,
you are truly my disciples;
then you will know the truth,
and the truth will set you free."
"We are descendants of Abraham," was their answer. "Never have we been slaves to anyone. What do you mean by saying, 'You will be free?" Jesus answered them:
"I give you my assurance,
everyone who lives in sin
is the slave of sin.
(No slave has a permanent place in the family,
but the son has a place there forever.)
That is why, if the son frees you,
you will really be free."

(John 8:31-36)

"The blind recover their sight"

THE word "religion" causes a bad taste in the mouth of many people in our day. Numerous young people are drifting away and turning to other experiences: dope or religious imports from the Far East. Why? Could it be that preachers and teachers have presented religion too onesidely as a heap of laws and duties, which we have to obey and fulfill in order to gain the bliss of paradise?

Many reject religion only to the extent that it appears meaningless to them. By searching so hard in other directions, they are in effect telling those in charge of institutionalized religion: "What we expect of religion is a way of liberation from our deep-seated human problems." And if religion offers liberation (salvation, redemption), it should be presented as a therapy. Religion is in some sense akin, though not identical, to psychotherapy. A well-known Jewish psychotherapist, Frankl, practices "logotherapy" (*logos* standing for meaning). He wants the patient to reflect on his religion and find meaning in it. And this "meaning" should heal him.

Jesus characterizes his movement, originally called "The Way" (Acts 9:2), as a therapy or liberation from human problems. The prerequisite for being healed is, of course, that you admit that you need therapy. An alcoholic who does not admit his problem will not turn to "Alcoholics Anonymous," and consequently will not find liberation from his problem. Whenever depressed, do you turn to religion and try to find meaning?

SCRIPTURE READING —

John in prison heard about the works Christ was performing, and sent a message by his disciples to ask him, "Are you 'He who is to come' or do we look for another?" In reply, Jesus said to them: "Go back and report to John what you hear and see: the blind recover their sight, cripples walk, lepers are cured, the deaf hear, dead men are raised to life, and the poor have the good news preached to them. Blest is the man who finds no stumbling block in me." (Matthew 11:2-6)

January 14

"But [if I] have not love, I am nothing"

AFTER World War II, the colonies of the industrialized nations gained their freedom from foreign occupation. These developing countries often had excellent freedom fighters and a great determination to fight for freedom. They sacrificed blood, sweat, and tears to obtain the freedom they wanted. But the same skilled and courageous freedom fighters often failed once they were faced with the task of using their newly won freedom wisely, that is, building up an economically independent nation. *Freedom from* and *freedom for* are the two sides of one coin, but they are not the same.

We acknowledge the great mind-forming value of meditation and prayer. Mental culture, accompanied by prayer to God, may result in freedom from unruly inclinations to a great extent, and consequently in peace of mind and happiness. It is the good feeling of someone driving an expensive car and having it fully under control. But this "freedom from" is only negative. It causes a void, which must be filled with the great value of love.

According to the philosophy of life which Jesus of Nazareth offers, once free from slavery to sin and sinful (unruly) desires, we should use our "freedom for" love in the sense of being free for others. An empty canvas is not ugly, but neither is it a great work of art. It needs an artist and paint. "If [I have] not love, I am nothing" (1 Corinthians 13:2). A person growing toward the design the Maker has planned for him must be a loving person, who is concerned indeed about his fellow human beings. Paul brings this out beautifully in today's Scripture.

SCRIPTURE READING —

Now I will show you the way which surpasses all the others. If I speak with human tongues and angelic as well, but do not have love, I am a noisy gong, a clanging cymbal. If I have the gift of prophecy and, with full knowledge, comprehend all mysteries, if I have faith great enough to move mountains, but have not love, I am nothing. If I give everything I have to feed the poor and hand over my body to be burned, but have not love, I gain nothing. (1 Corinthians 13:2)

"Your grief will be turned into joy"

IN THE Louvre of Paris, France, there is a beautiful painting representing King David with his harp and dancing in front of the ark. Evidently, the painter was inspired by this Scripture: "Then David, girt with a linen apron, came dancing before the Lord with abandon as he and all the Israelites were bringing up the ark of the Lord with shouts of joy and to the sound of the horn" (2 Samuel 6:14-15). Religion and worship were a joyful occupation in those days. "All you people, clap your hands, shout to God with cries of gladness" (Psalm 47:2). And when Christ was born, the angel of the Lord came to bring good news. "You have nothing to fear! I proclaim to you tidings of great joy to be shared by the whole people. A savior [liberator] has been born." (See Luke 2: 9-11.) Jesus himself proclaimed his message as a Gospel, joyful tidings, a way of unprecedented joy and perennial peace.

But for some reason or other, joy and peace are concepts that many people hardly reconcile with religion. For many, religion is not a source of joy. It appears to them as a series of burdens or laws to be followed in order to earn access to heaven. Fear and boredom rather than joy fills their lives. Paul offers an allegory on freedom in Galatians 4:21-31. From a literary standpoint, it is rather artificial. But his point is clearly: Rejoice, you are free, and it was for liberty that Christ freed us (Galatians 5:1).

Are you a free person, free from fear and similar inhibitions and consequently free for love? If so, rejoice! We may have sad moments in life, but a constantly sad Christian is a bad Christian!

SCRIPTURE READING —

"I tell you truly:
you will weep and mourn
while the world rejoices;
you will grieve for a time,
but your grief will be turned into joy.
When a woman is in labor
she is sad that her time has come.
When she has borne her child,
she no longer remembers her pain
for joy that a man has been born into the world.
In the same way, you are sad for a time,
but I shall see you again;
then your hearts will rejoice
with a joy no one can take from you.
On that day you will have no questions to ask me.
I give you my assurance,
whatever you ask the Father,
he will give you in my name."

(John 17:20-23)

"If you had faith the size of a mustard seed . . ."

IN OUR time of progress and new insights into the human psyche, is there still room for the liberation (salvation) offered by Jesus of Nazareth? When man is depressed and ailing under the burden of subconscious problems, he goes to the psychiatrist. According to the ancients, all sickness was caused by evil spirits. Hence, sick people did not go to the doctor but to the holy man, who should expel the demons by prayer and exorcism.

Medical doctors, psychiatrists, counselors, and social workers have taken over tasks which Jesus of Nazareth fulfilled very efficiently in his time and culture. Allegedly, nowadays the mental health clinic takes away human alienation as effectively as Jesus did in the healing stories of the Gospels. To a certain extent this is true. The mental health clinic has a reason for existence.

The question is whether there is in us a deeper alienation, given with our finitude, which remains enigmatic to us and a real threat, and moreover whether there is an alienation caused by guilt and sin. Human self-liberation remains limited. And for this kind of deeper alienation we Christians turn to Jesus of Nazareth. He offers a freedom, which frees man really for a complete freedom, an autonomy, which is possible only in being bound to a transcendent, and hence liberating, living God (Galatians 5:1). Faith in Jesus of Nazareth is a necessity for achieving this freedom. There are still ailments which do not leave except by prayer and fasting. Lord, increase my faith!

SCRIPTURE READING —

A man came up to Jesus and knelt before him. "Lord," he said, "take pity on my son, who is demented and in a serious condition. For example, he often falls into the fire and frequently into the water. I have brought him to your disciples but they could not cure him." In reply Jesus said: "What an unbelieving and perverse lot you are! How long must I remain with you? How long can I endure you? Bring him here to me!" Then Jesus reprimanded him, and the demon came out of him. That very moment the boy was cured.

The disciples approached Jesus at that point and asked him privately, "Why could we not expel it?" "Because you have so little trust," he told them. "I assure you, if you had faith the size of a mustard seed, you would be able to say to this mountain, 'Move from here to there,' and it would move. Nothing would be impossible for you. [This kind does not leave but by prayer and fasting.]" (Matthew 17:14-21)

"My lover belongs to me and I to him"

JEAN-Paul Sartre, an atheistic philosopher who exerted tremendous influence on campus thinking and behavior during the sixties, does not believe in the value of love. His philosophy is negative and in last analysis a philosophy of non-being. The very existence of the family is profoundly suspect. Human communication is doomed to failure. Hence, the aim of love is to appropriate the will of the other. What we call love is another form of egotism.

A Christian French philosopher, Gabriel Marcel, himself an atheist till he was forty, replies to Sartre by observing that in his universe there is no room for the concept "participation." When I really love a person, I do not try to mold him/her into a blueprint of myself. This is often done, however, and that's why Sartre is seemingly right. No. When I love, respectfully I participate in the personality of the beloved. I accept the beloved as he/she is.

The Song of Songs is first of all a beautiful human love poem, and secondly it portrays the mutual love of the Lord and his people. The author follows the tradition of Israel and sees the covenant between the Lord and his people as a marriage. This is the way it should be. We are related to God in love. God loves me. But he does not use his infinite freedom to absorb me into himself to such a degree that it would annihilate me as a person. *Mirabile dictu* (wonderful to relate), he participates in my personality, takes me as I am, sinful and limited, and he invites me to do the same, to participate in his own infinite being. Isn't this something to appreciate?

SCRIPTURE READING —

Where has your lover gone,
O most beautiful among women?
Where has your lover gone
that we may seek him with you?
My lover has come down to his garden,
to the beds of spice,
To browse in the garden
and to gather lilies.
My lover belongs to me and I to him;
he browses among the lilies.
Set me as a seal on your heart,
as a seal on your arm;
For stern as death is love,
relentless as the nether world is devotion;
its flames are a blazing fire.
Deep waters cannot quench love,
nor floods sweep it away.
Were one to offer all he owns to purchase love,
he would be roundly mocked.
(Songs of Songs 6:1-3; 8:6-7)

"But now that you are freed from sin . . ."

THERE are as many definitions of freedom as there are philosophers. All want to shed some light on this most cherished of human values. What then is freedom? One of the best known philosophers of the last decades, Jean-Paul Sartre, who has recruited his disciples and so often his victims from the ranks of the misdirected and anarchical youth of our campuses, offers obscure definitions: Freedom is man's faculty to secrete his own non-being; or, it is man's capacity to be the foundation of himself; or, freedom is exile and I am condemned to freedom. If I am condemned to freedom, it must be a deprivation or defect. For Sartre, freedom is equivalent to choice, which is a fatal error.

Am I less free when fully aware I make a commitment? We think of any commitment: from the promise to visit a sick friend in the hospital tonight to my marital, religious, or baptismal commitment. After I have made this commitment, I cannot make another choice anymore. Does this mean that I am not a free person, since I work on my self-realization only in the framework of previous freely made commitments?

Paul seems to think along this line in today's Bible reading. He discusses freedom from self through union with Christ (Romans 6:1-23). Since we are free, and no longer under the Jewish law, are we free to sin? By no means! We who were baptized into Christ have died to sin. It is not I that live, but Christ that lives in me. Paradoxical as it may sound, the bond of love is the most valuable sign of freedom.

SCRIPTURE READING —

But now that you are freed from sin and have become slaves of God, your benefit is sanctification as you tend toward eternal life. The wages of sin is death, but the gift of God is eternal life in Christ Jesus our Lord. (Romans 6:22-23)

"Your faith has been your salvation"

THE more closed a society is, the more those closed up in it are prisoners and forced to comply with the unwritten rules of the group. The person who outgrows this narrowminded framework and dares to dress differently, socialize with persons the group frowns upon, or utter a few unconventional statements ostracizes himself/herself and becomes an outcast.

Jesus of Nazareth was such a freelancer. The Pharisee, doing the right thing for the wrong reason, as happens so often, is startled. Jesus, a holy man and prophet, letting himself be touched by a prostitute! Luke shows beautifully how the mere presence of Jesus creates a liberating situation. Petty prejudice is brushed aside. "Your faith has been your salvation" (Luke 7:50). The Pharisee, faithful to the letter of the law by keeping his distance from sinners but prejudiced and with little or no love in his heart, is on the losing end.

Jesus knew his secret pondering, and in the story the sinful but penitent woman is the clear winner. The sinner avows the reign of God in Jesus and that is exactly what the Pharisee does not do; therefore she is greater, because the least born into the kingdom of God is greater than even John the Baptizer (see Luke 7:28). What in this tradition could be God's word to you and me?

SCRIPTURE READING —

There was a certain Pharisee who invited Jesus to dine with him. Jesus went to the Pharisee's home and reclined to eat. A woman known in the town to be a sinner learned that he was dining in the Pharisee's home. She brought in a vase of perfumed oil and stood behind him at his feet, weeping so that her tears fell upon his feet. Then she wiped them with her hair, kissing them and perfuming them with the oil. When his host, the Pharisee, saw this, he said to himself, "If this man were a prophet, he would know who and what sort of woman this is that touches him—that she is a sinner." In answer to his thoughts, Jesus said to him, "You see this woman? I came to your home and you provided me with no water for my feet. She has washed my feet with her tears and wiped them with her hair. You gave me no kiss, but she has not ceased kissing my feet since I entered. You did not anoint my head with oil, but she has anointed my feet with perfume. I tell you, that is why her many sins are forgiven—because of her great love. Little is forgiven the one whose love is small." (Luke 7:36-40, 44-47)

"You shall love the Lord your God . . .[and] your neighbor as yourself"

ON AN island in the Indian Ocean, I became acquainted with a lady who had been born on a Portuguese ship in the harbor of Hongkong and was married to a rancher. Both were Eurasians and lived on their isolated ranch up in the mountains. It was an unwritten law always to stop by, exchange a few pleasant thoughts, and take mail or a package with you to be delivered in the nearest town. They were a very humanitarian couple but did not profess any religion. Once in a lively conversation the lady exclaimed: "Pastor, I can't believe in your God, an old man with glasses on."

Indeed, many Christians have warped ideas of God. Children see him portrayed as an old man with a white beard looking down from the clouds to the children of man on earth. Often the Old Man is portrayed as a nasty old judge, constantly checking on man's behavior. If not read intelligently, the Old Testament contributes to this mental picture of God. In Judaism of Jesus' time, the rabbis had added hundreds of laws to the Decalogue. And preachers, teachers, and parents of our own time have often taught a narrow legalism—many laws to be followed—as a condition for saving one's soul. The biblical "fear of the Lord," which means "filial respect" not fear, was predominant precisely as fear and fright in the lives of many Christians.

Jesus, however, experienced God as a father to be loved. He puts all laws in their proper perspective—namely, love—and by stressing love as the foundation on which any law must be based, he liberated man from an oppressive and burdensome image of God. How do you experience God?

SCRIPTURE READING —

A lawyer, in an attempt to trip [Jesus] up, asked him, "Teacher, which commandment of the law is the greatest?" Jesus said to him:

" 'You shall love the Lord your God
with your whole heart,
with your whole soul,
and with all your mind.'

This is the greatest and first commandment. The second is like it:

'You shall love your neighbor as yourself.'

On these two commandments the whole law is based, and the prophets as well."

(Matthew 22:35-40)

January 21

"Abba (O Father), you have the power to do all things"

THE French philosopher, Jean-Paul Sartre, for whom life is an absurdity, has written a play *Huis Clos (Closed Doors)*. There exists an English movie version, called *No Exit*. It is about people locked up in a room for always, just talking and asking questions, but there are no answers and there is no exit. Is life the way this doom-prophet depicts it, a senseless condition from which there is no escape and for which there is no explanation? A well-known playwright in this country seems to look at it the same way. Speaking about suicide, Tennessee Williams has said: "Sometimes one gets pretty tight and looks for a way out."[1]

The Lord Jesus was in a seemingly absurd situation in the garden of Gethsemani. Death in one's early thirties is, humanly speaking, senseless. And there was no exit. But Jesus' experience of God, present as Abba-Father, saved him from despair. His Abba-awareness shed light on his dark and seemingly senseless condition. His was an awareness of God as a liberating and loving power.

Through word and example Jesus of Nazareth calls you and me to faith precisely in this God, his God, who is powerful and loves you, also when seemingly there is no exit. "Brothers, over the world of the stars, a loving Father *must reside" (Ode to Joy*—Schiller). Are you aware of God, present as Father, in any situation of life?

[1]Tennessee Williams interviewed by Barbara Walters, *Today Show*, Nov. 6, 1975.

SCRIPTURE READING —

They went then to a place named Gethsemani. "Sit down here while I pray," he said to his disciples; at the same time he took along with him Peter, James, and John. Then he began to be filled with fear and distress. He said to them, "My heart is filled with sorrow to the point of death. Remain here and stay awake." He advanced a little and fell to the ground, praying that if it were possible this hour might pass him by. He kept saying, "Abba **(O Father), you have the power to do all things. Take this cup away from me. But let it be as you would have it, not as I."** (Mark 14:32-36)

"What [God] did for you in the desert . . ."

CAN religion be liberating? Trying to liberate the masses from the stranglehold of economic injustice, Marx compared religion with opium (dope), which allegedly keeps poor people numb, resigned to the status quo, and deprived of any desire to improve themselves. Occasionally, religion may have been abused for this purpose: "Submit yourself to your fate, work hard for your slavemasters, and in the hereafter God will reward you!" But if religion has been preached in this way, such preaching reflects anything but the biblical experience of God's people.

All through the Bible, we read about the saving (liberating) presence of God right now, though always with the aspect of "now, but not yet." The liberation of Israel from Egypt included political liberation but was not restricted to that. Time and again, it is stressed that this freedom had a transcendent dimension: freedom for service of God, and clearly in the New Testament, the eschatological (hereafter) freedom of God's children.

Christian liberation, be it a collective effort to free the poor from economic oppression, or a personal one to free man from psychological depression, must have that eschatological (hereafter) dimension, otherwise it becomes mere humanitarianism. It must keep the saving God in the picture, as the ancient Hebrews did. Religion should promote a total liberation of the person, and as such offer foretaste and anticipation of the total definitive liberation (salvation) promised by God. What did God fo for you, and how do you see your freedom in religious perspective? Read this Scripture existentially, i.e., apply it prayerfully to your own existence or life situation.

SCRIPTURE READING —

"Love the Lord, your God, therefore, and always heed his charge: his statutes, decrees and commandments. It is not your children who have not known it from experience, but you yourselves who must now understand the discipline of the Lord, your God; his majesty, his strong hand and outstretched arm; the signs and deeds he wrought among the Egyptians, on Pharaoh, king of Egypt, and on all his land; what he did to the Egyptian army and to their horses and chariots, engulfing them in the water of the Red Sea as they pursued you, and bringing ruin upon them even to this day; what he did for you in the desert until you arrived in this place." (Deuteronomy 11:1-5)

"Those who make use of the world [should conduct themselves] as though they were not using it"

THOMAS MORE, Lord Chancellor of England, wealthy, the successful author of *Utopia* (the most influential book on the State in the sixteenth century), happy family man, friend of the greatest European scholars of his time—by all standards he was a man of the world and simultaneously a Christian who seriously tried to live up to the ideals of Christ's Sermon on the Mount (Matthew 5:3-12). This sounds paradoxical. His was a life in the spirit of evangelical perfection without its "state."

The secret of More's life is that he had not given his heart to the goods of this world. He was wealthy, enjoyed his wealth, his family life, and political success, but was not subject to it. By inner detachment from "this world," he preserved a remarkable interior freedom for God. His biographies quote many examples to prove this. And More's interior freedom for God made it possible for him to say "no" to Henry VIII, the king of England, when he had to do so in good conscience, even at the cost of his life.

Is a life of evangelical perfection possible for the average Christian who does not choose "the state of perfection," as religious do? Though thinking that Christ would return during his own lifetime, Paul's statement that this world is passing away is timeless. In this passing world, it is a question of interior detachment! A poor person, and even a religious who has taken the three vows, *can* be attached to the little things he can grab, and a rich person *can* be detached from all his possessions and consequently be free for God. What about your interior freedom? The best gauge to check is your degree of willingness to share generously!

SCRIPTURE READING —

I tell you, brothers, the time is short. From now on those with wives should live as though they had none; those who weep should live as though they were not weeping, and those who rejoice as though they were not rejoicing; buyers should conduct themselves as though they owned nothing, and those who make use of the world as though they were not using it, for the world as we know it is passing away.

(1 Corinthians 7:29-31)

"You did not receive a spirit of slavery"

WITH the introduction of a friend of mine, a Jewish rabbi, I had the privilege of spending a whole day with his cousin on a kibbutz between Nazareth and Tiberias. I was impressed by the dedication of these people, many of them former victims of the Nazis in Germany. In the center of the kibbutz, they had built a beautiful functional synagogue. And in this peaceful hill country, with a magnificent view of Mount Tabor, a new future was built up, centered around their religious belief. We exchanged thoughts and experiences. Both of us had known the Nazis, they in the concentration camps, I in my home country, The Netherlands, during World War II. We exchanged religious thoughts too. And, of course, we differed in opinion, though very pleasantly: "Pastor, it was not Jesus who founded the Christian faith; it was Paul."

Indeed, Paul—though not the founder of the Christian faith—is one of the most eloquent promoters of Jesus' cause. He must have been very intelligent and a devout Jew, similar to the Jews on this kibbutz. That is why I love Paul. Better than any other author of the New Testament, Paul has grasped the spirit of Jesus' message, which was meant to be liberating, a message of salvation. Like the Jews on that kibbutz in Galilee, Paul appreciated freedom. Both knew what bondage was. The former had gone through the cruel and humiliating experience of the German concentration camps. Paul had been subjected to the legalistic outgrowth of the Judaism of his time, hence his abundant joy because of the freedom which he had found in Jesus and his Gospel.

And this joy should also be ours. If anything is alien to the Christian faith, it is a spirit of slavery and fear. Ours is the joy of God's children, even though we have to suffer sometimes to attain it.

SCRIPTURE READING —

All who are led by the Spirit of God are sons of God. You did not receive a spirit of slavery leading you back into fear, but a spirit of adoption through which we cry out, "Abba!" (that is, "Father"). The Spirit himself gives witness with our spirit that we are children of God. But if we are children, we are heirs as well: heirs of God, heirs with Christ, if only we suffer with him so as to be glorified with him.

(Romans 8:14-17)

"Be examples to the flock, not lording it over those assigned to you"

IN HIS master novel *The Brothers Karamazov,* Fyodor Dostoevski has Aloysha recite his poem, called "The Grand Inquisitor." The setting is Seville during the Spanish Inquisition. The grand inquisitor is an old cardinal, almost ninety, who condemns heretics to the stake. In front of the cathedral he meets Jesus Christ, who had come back once again to bring freedom to his people. The inquisitor does not agree and has him put in jail to be burned the next day. In that dark, gloomy, vaulted prison, the cardinal speaks to Jesus: "Why have you come back to hinder us? For fifteen centuries we have been wrestling with your freedom. It does not work. People have brought their freedom to us and laid humbly at our feet. And we shall give them the quiet humble happiness of weak creatures such as they are by nature. We have corrected your work."

Dostoevski has a point. The heirs of the Kingdom have not always honored Jesus' message of freedom. Church authority, which was designed to serve the brethren, has been abused, We know about the Spanish Inquisition, victims of religious fanaticism like Joan of Arc, Protestants killed by Catholics and vice versa.

Peter addresses the elders of the Church, i.e., the leaders. They were not perfect. There will never be perfect authority. There will be conservative and progressive shepherds (pastors), presbyters capable and less capable of leadership. Be patient and loyal, pray for those in authority, and be aware that it is sound Catholic doctrine that in regard to any law your informed conscience speaks the last word. This means that you should keep yourself informed and be tolerant of fellow human beings who follow their conscience, as you want to follow yours. Do you keep up-to-date on the faith by reading?

SCRIPTURE READING —

To the elders among you I, a fellow elder, a witness of Christ's sufferings and sharer in the glory that is to be revealed, make this appeal. God's flock is in your midst; give it a shepherd's care. Watch over it willingly as God would have you do, not under constraint; and not for shameful profit either, but generously. Be examples to the flock, not lording it over those assigned to you, so that when the chief Shepherd appears you will win for yourselves the unfading crown of glory. (1 Peter 5:1-4)

"In your relations with one another clothe yourselves with humility"

JOKINGLY, the lady who gave a group of priests a tour through a large penitentiary blamed the apostle of permissiveness, Doctor B. Spock (millions of young American mothers have been his docile disciples!) for so many inmates being there. Permissiveness and real freedom are strange bedfellows. We all agree that parents commit a crime when they grant their children more freedom than they are able to handle at a certain stage of life. Freedom may hurt the self and others, if not handled intelligently. As for minors in a family setting, it is obvious how the issue of freedom should be handled. There may be friction between parents and teenagers once in a while, but usually parents who have taught their children self-discipline from the beginning can work out things all right.

The real problem of freedom shows up in an open and free society as ours. How much freedom can an average citizen handle and who is going to decide this for whom? Lawlessness and crime are constantly on the rise and our prisons are crowded. There is far less crime in totalitarian countries, but we don't want to solve the issue the way the communists do.

Let us check ourselves! How do we handle our freedom in our relations with one another, in the family, the Church, and society at large? Are we aware of our responsibilities before we think of our rights? Only, if we possess inner freedom and self-discipline are we able to clothe ourselves with humility in our relations with one another!

SCRIPTURE READING —

In the same way, you younger men must be obedient to the elders. In your relations with one another, clothe yourselves with humility, because God "is stern with the arrogant but to the humble he shows kindness." Bow humbly under God's mighty hand, so that in due time he may lift you high. Cast all your cares on him because he cares for you. Stay sober and alert. Your opponent the devil is prowling like a roaring lion looking for someone to devour. Resist him, solid in your faith, realizing that the brotherhood of believers is undergoing the same sufferings throughout the world. (1 Peter 5:5-9)

"Live as free men, but do not use your freedom as a cloak for vice"

THE Grand Inquisitor of Dostoevski's novel *The Brothers Karamazov* does not believe that his fellow human beings can handle much freedom. He says to Jesus, whom he has jailed and will burn the next day: "Freedom, free thought and science will lead them into such straits that they will destroy themselves. And what did you do? Instead of taking men's freedom from them, you made it greater than ever.—Nothing is more seductive for man than his freedom of conscience, but nothing is a greater cause of suffering.—Hence, the most painful secrets of their conscience, all, all they will bring to us, and we shall have an answer for all. And our answer will save them from the great anxiety and terrible agony of making a free decision for themselves."

There is some truth in this statement. Sharing anxieties and even guilt has a saving impact. It is done in many prayer groups nowadays. In the Catholic tradition, we have for centuries firmly believed in this kind of mental therapy, but with a competent confessor, who besides being understanding, patient, and capable has the Lord's authority to forgive sins, and is bound to silence.

There are many Catholics who like this approach. "Father told me . . ." and that is what they go by. Others prefer to go by the adage: "What is the loving thing to do?" and figure out a few things for themselves. Though asking for professional advice never hurts, a well-informed Christian may act on his own. Christ gave us freedom of conscience. In today's Scripture, Peter gives us some valuable information on how to live as a free person.

SCRIPTURE READING —

Because of the Lord, be obedient to every human institution, whether to the emperor as sovereign or to the governors he commissions for the punishment of criminals and the recognition of the upright. Such obedience is the will of God. You must silence the ignorant talk of foolish men by your good behavior. Live as free men, but do not use your freedom as a cloak for vice. In a word, live as servants of God. You must esteem the person of every man. Foster love for the brothers, reverence for God, respect for the emperor. (1 Peter 2:13-17)

"What are you looking for?"

MATURE people are aware that only a meaningful life can impart lasting happiness. What gives meaning to my life? It is a task which I feel called to fulfill. Today's Bible reading relates a call in life explicitly to God. But in daily life it is not always simple to find out what one's call is. God works implicitly through our inclinations, natural abilities, friends, parents, educators, and church affiliation. These will guide us in deciding how we are going to make a living and, as a rule, in choosing our partner for life.

It is man's call to make life together with a beloved one meaningful. However, there is a special call in life, which we are used to terming a "vocation." It is the invitation to follow Christ as a religious or priest. The Christian who chooses this kind of life, celibacy for the sake of God's reign, chooses to relate his "openness to the other" not to one person but to the human community as a whole. He keeps himself free to dedicate himself entirely to the establishment of universal human relations, and as such he is a living sign that the reign of God (a reign of love, justice, fidelity, and peace) has been initiated already in our history. Young people should be open to God's call and challenge, and parents should generously cooperate if one of their children feels God's invitation to live a meaningful life of dedication in the ministerial priesthood or religious life. All of us should pray with the psalmist: "Here am I, Lord; I come to do your will" (Psalm 40:8-9).

Today's Scripture tells about our Lord's own call/task in life. John designates him as "the Lamb of God," a sacrificial lamb offered to God, in contemporary language, "the Man for Others," giving himself to God in his fellowmen. We also learn about the call of the first disciples. God's word to us asks us to question ourselves about our relationship with God. Is it a dynamic one of call and response? Is it an ongoing process?

SCRIPTURE READING —

John was . . . with two of his disciples. As he watched Jesus walk by he said, "Look! There is the Lamb of God!" The two disciples heard what he said, and followed Jesus. When Jesus turned around and noticed them following him, he asked them, "What are you looking for?" They said to him, "Rabbi (which means Teacher), where do you stay?" "Come and see," he answered. So they went to see where he was lodged, and stayed with him that day. (It was about four in the afternoon.)

(John 1:35-39)

"Those known as sinners joined him and his disciples at dinner"

ONE of the beautiful memories of my childhood in the old country is our family candlelight breakfast after the Midnight Mass of Christmas. The best hail-white tablecloth was spread. Over it red ribbons were neatly arranged, and specks of holly were all over. And those colored candles assured you that it was Christmas indeed! My proud father himself baked the traditional thick slices of blood sausage with apple. It smelled so good! But what I remember most was the annual presence of "Little Thomas" at our breakfast table.

In daily life, Thomas, a lonesome man in his early sixties, short of stature with no family, came with his pushcart through our street to sell kerosene for lamps and oil stoves. He smelled from his merchandise and never entered the house, but he was our steadfast guest at Christmas. Dressed in his best Sunday suit, little Thomas smoked then a big cigar, which my father had given him, and seriously discussed the topics of town. I think that my parents wanted to imitate Jesus in today's Scripture. Not that little Thomas was a sinner. He was a devout Christian, but poor and lonesome. And that is what he had in common with those sinners who joined Jesus and his disciples at dinner.

A sinner is a lonesome person, since he/she has cut off communication with God and fellow humans. Jesus came to call these people back to table fellowship with God and man. Find God's word in this tradition, and respond prayerfully!

SCRIPTURE READING —

Another time, while [Jesus] went walking along the lakeshore, people kept coming to him in crowds and he taught them. As he moved on he saw Levi the son of Alphaeus at his tax collector's post, and said to him, "Follow me." Levi got up and became his follower. While Jesus was reclining to eat in Levi's house, many tax collectors and those known as sinners joined him and his disciples at dinner. The number of those who followed him was large. When the scribes who belonged to the Pharisee party saw that he was eating with tax collectors and offenders against the law, they complained to his disciples, "Why does he eat with such as these?" Overhearing the remark, Jesus said to them, "People who are healthy do not need a doctor; sick people do. I have come to call sinners, not the self-righteous." (Mark 2:13-17)

"The Lord has done great things for us; we are glad indeed"

WHEN a communist army commander in the Far East interned me for a year and four months, I was humanly speaking in bad shape. I am not a hero and by no means material for martyrdom! Soldiers surrounded my rectory—"hands up"—with a soldier next to me on a plane, parishioners crying, and that was it, the end of my career as a foreign missionary. Such a time is nerve-wracking. But the Lord was good to me. I had books to study during my confinement and even wrote one myself.

But when finally I got my exit permit, I did not waste a minute. At 4:00 a.m. the Air France took me out. A delay in Saigon made me miss my connection in Paris, France. I had to stay there the night over, and will never forget that wonderful feeling of freedom when I walked leisurely on the Champs Elysée, just window shopping and watching the people. The human reality of liberation is a foretaste and the prophetic promise of definitive liberty and salvation *(see January 28)*. In my heart I thanked God.

A similar feeling must have overwhelmed the Hebrews, when after that long captivity in Babylon, they were permitted to go home. They had been doing menial jobs for their slavemasters. At night melancholically they had been singing their beautiful songs, longing for freedom. And now they saw their holy city Jerusalem. "We were like men dreaming." Did you ever have a liberating experience? How do you explain it? Apply this song to your own life situation and make your prayer!

SCRIPTURE READING —

When the Lord brought back the captives of Zion,
we were like men dreaming.
Then our mouth was filled with laughter,
and our tongue with rejoicing.
Then they said among the nations,
"The Lord has done great things for them."
The Lord has done great things for us;
we are glad indeed.

Restore our fortunes, O Lord,
like the torrents in the southern desert.
Those that sow in tears
shall reap rejoicing.
Although they go forth weeping,
carrying the seed to be sown,
They shall come back rejoicing,
carrying their sheaves.

(Psalm 126)

"In Jacob make your dwelling"

ONE of the most joyous books by the great Renaissance scholar Erasmus of Rotterdam is his *Praise of Folly*. Folly, as a goddess, declaims from a pulpit on her delights. With polished wit and pungent satire Desiderius Erasmus chastises both Church and society for abuses and vices so abundantly plaguing his time. Every so often it was fashionable in the realm of "belles lettres" to use personified Folly and Wisdom as literary devices to bring out a point. The Wisdom Books of the Bible are examples, e.g., see Proverbs 9.

In today's reading, the author has personified Wisdom come forth from the mouth of the Most High (as a word!) and making her dwelling place in Jacob (Israel—God's people). The Hebrews saw God's wisdom "made flesh" in the Torah, the Law. Although the author does not propose Wisdom as a real person, his thought prepared the way for later revelation, the doctrine of the Logos (God's wisdom—word) incarnated in Jesus *(see December 27)*.

In meditating, I thanked God that he is willing to share his wisdom with his people—in this case, me. His wisdom, as I find it in the Bible and in the guidance of my Church, enlightens me on my pilgrimage through the dark valley of the human condition.

SCRIPTURE READING —

Wisdom sings her own praises,
before her own people she proclaims her glory;
In the assembly of the Most High she opens her mouth,
in the presence of his hosts she declares her worth:
"From the mouth of the Most High I came forth
and mistlike covered the earth.
Then the Creator of all gave me his command,
and he who formed me chose the spot for my tent,
Saying, 'In Jacob make your dwelling, in Israel your inheritance.'
In the holy tent I ministered before him,
and in Zion I fixed my abode.
Thus in the chosen city he has given me rest,
in Jerusalem is my domain.
I have struck root among the glorious people,
in the portion of the Lord, his heritage.
He who obeys me will not be put to shame,
he who serves me will never fail."
All this is true of the book of the Most High's covenant,
the law which Moses commanded us
as an inheritance for the community of Jacob.

(Sirach 24:1-3, 8, 10-12, 21-22)

"Abram went as the Lord directed him"

IN SCHOOL, we learned about the founding fathers of our nation. From their struggle for freedom, their writings and speeches, we learned the philosophy which underlies our laws and way of life. As citizens of this country, we must be aware of who we are. But self-identity can be gained only by going back in our national history. All countries are proud of their national history and the great personages who contributed to the birth of the nation. The ancient Hebrews were no exception. Their literature has long traditions about their founding fathers: Abraham, Isaac, Jacob, Moses, David, and many more. The fascinating thing is that the Hebrews relate the great events of their national history constantly to the care and concern of Almighty God.

But why do we Christians still read these ancient traditions? We are not related to the great heroes of the Hebrews by racial descent, but we feel definite kinship with them in the spirit. Today's Scripture tells about God's promise to Abraham and his descendants. And Paul explains that those descendants are not only the Jews, but all who have Abraham's faith. "Yes, he is our father in the sight of God in whom he believed. . . . Hoping against hope, Abraham believed and so became the father of many nations" (Romans 4:17-18).

Abraham hoped against hope: God indeed promised to bestow the whole land of Canaan upon him and his offspring; yet he remained a foreigner in the Promised Land, and up until they were very old he and his wife did not have children. In this tradition, God's word to you and me could be: Go as the Lord directs you. Hope against hope, when you are depressed and hopeless, and God will take care of you.

SCRIPTURE READING —

The Lord said to Abram: "Go forth from the land of your kinsfolk and from your father's house to a land that I will show you.

"I will make of you a great nation,
and I will bless you;
I will bless those who bless you
and curse those who curse you.
All the communities of the earth
shall find blessing in you."

Abram went as the Lord directed him, and Lot went with him. Abram was seventy-five years old when he left Haran. (Genesis 12:1-4)

"Fear not, Abram! I am your shield"

THE poem *The Erl-king* (a goblin that haunts the Black Forest in Thuringia) and its composer, Johann Wolfgang Goethe, are world famous. Goethe has taken an old folk legend and retold it with the tremendous power of his own language. This is a translation, but it splendidly reflects the original beauty of the poem in German.

O, who rides by night and thro' woodland so wild?
It is the fond father embracing his child;
And close the boy nestles within his loved arm,
To hold himself fast, and to keep himself warm.
"O Father, see yonder! See yonder!" he says;

(Then a disaster follows.)

Sore trembled the father, he spurr'd thro' the wild,
Clasping close to his bosom his shuddering child;
He reached his dwelling in doubt and in dread,
But, clasp'd to his bosom, the infant was dead!

There is only so much a father can do! We Christians see a transcendent element in all fatherhood. The inspired author of the Bible points to Abraham, a simple Bedouin, and invites us to learn from him. Paul comments: "Abraham believed God, and it was credited to him as justice" (Romans 4:3). Have faith in God even if your case is seemingly hopeless. He is as fond a father as the father in Goethe's poem, but not finite and limited in power. Fear not.

SCRIPTURE READING —

This word of the Lord came to Abram in a vision:
"Fear not, Abram!
I am your shield;
I will make your reward very great."

But Abraham said, "O Lord God, what good will your gifts be, if I keep on being childless and have as my heir the steward of my house, Eliezer?" Abram continued, "See, you have given me no offspring, and so one of my servants will be my heir." Then the word of the Lord came to him: "No, that one shall not be your heir; your own issue shall be your heir." He took him outside and said, "Look up at the sky and count the stars, if you can. Just so," he added, "shall your descendants be." Abram put his faith in the Lord, who credited it to him as an act of righteousness. (Genesis 15:1-6)

"God himself will provide"

ONE of the wrong ideas many Christians harbor about Saints is that supposedly they are constantly living on the mountaintops, daily enjoying the bliss and loving presence of the Lord. A Saint like Teresa of Avila had overwhelmingly mystical (direct) experience of God. She describes the presence of the Beloved One in beautiful metaphors. She felt God. Yet she knew also the dark night of faith.

Teresa writes about her "spiritual marriage" with God, how in a vision the Lord handed her a symbolic nail saying: "It is a sign that from today onward you shall be my bride." For Saint Catherine of Siena it was done by Christ slipping a ring upon her finger. Paul had a similar experience, when he wrote: "But whoever is joined to the Lord becomes one spirit with him" (1 Corinthians 6:17). Yet the great mystics complain about periods in their lives when apparently God was absent.

Does God test our faith and fidelity to him? Today's Scripture indicates that this is so. Daily meditation will result in greater union with God. In his goodness, God will let you experience his presence, but don't despair when you too go through a darkness of faith. It should never result in giving up your daily prayer and meditation. If you don't know it anymore, "God himself will provide."

SCRIPTURE READING —

God put Abraham to the test. He called to him, "Abraham!" "Ready!" he replied. Then God said: "Take your son Isaac, your only one, whom you love, and go to the land of Moriah. There you shall offer him up as a holocaust on a height that I will point out to you." Early the next morning Abraham saddled his donkey, took with him his son Isaac, and two of his servants as well, and with the wood that he had cut for the holocaust, set out for the place of which God had told him.

On the third day Abraham got sight of the place from afar. Then he said to his servants: "Both of you stay here with the donkey, while the boy and I go on over yonder. We will worship and then come back to you." Thereupon Abraham took the wood for the holocaust and laid it on his son Isaac's shoulders, while he himself carried the fire and the knife. As the two walked on together, Isaac spoke to his father Abraham: "Father!" he said. "Yes, son," he replied. Isaac continued, "Here are the fire and the wood, but where is the sheep for the holocaust?" "Son," Abraham answered, "God himself will provide the sheep for the holocaust." Then the two continued going forward.

(Genesis 22:1-8)

"Who am I that I should go to Pharaoh?"

WE CANNOT agree with Dostoevski's Grand Inquisitor, where he explains his ideas on freedom *(see January 27).* Jesus Christ brought us freedom, and nobody should try to take it away. But the old inquisitor makes one good remark in his monologue to Jesus in jail, namely: "The secret of man's being is not only to live but to have something to live for." If we want to be happy and enjoy enduring peace of mind, we must bind ourselves to a task in life, and in the framework of that freely chosen task we must satisfy our hunger for self-realization. Failure to do so results in neurotic tensions, boredom, mental fatigue, and frequent visits to the psychiatrist. This does not mean that being faithful to freely chosen commitments is always easy. It may even require heroic fidelity.

The great Moses of the Hebrews had such a task, which in good conscience he had to fulfill. He was hesitant. He pondered the risks involved. Scripture describes his inner conflict as a dialogue with God. "Who am I . . .?" But God said: "I send you." And "I am who am," meaning: "I am not a far-away God, but your ever present God-Protector."

Conflicts, times of discouragement and depression should not make us give up our commitments. Quietly we should assess our options. Ask for competent advice and counsel, and most of all pray! God is with you. This is what we can learn as God's word to us in today's Scripture.

SCRIPTURE READING —

Moses said to God, "Who am I that I should go to Pharaoh and lead the Israelites out of Egypt?" He answered, "I will be with you; and this shall be your proof that it is I who have sent you: when you bring my people out of Egypt, you will worship God on this very mountain." "But," said Moses to God, "when I go to the Israelites and say to them, 'The God of your fathers has sent me to you,' if they ask me, 'What is his name?' what am I to tell them?" God replied, "I am who am." Then he added, "This is what you shall tell the Israelites: I AM sent me to you."

God spoke further to Moses, "Thus shall you say to the Israelites: The Lord, the God of your fathers, the God of Abraham, the God of Isaac, the God of Jacob, has sent me to you.

"This is my name forever;
this is my title for all generations." (Exodus 3:11-15)

"This is the blood of the covenant"

CONTEMPORARY psychology makes us aware that we are relational beings. The other day I tried to explain this to friends of mine who have two adopted children, a boy and a girl. They had followed the advice of the adoption agency and tried to prepare the children mentally for the "shock" to come: We are just your foster parents. They had not been too successful and were finally obliged to use the clear word "adoption." All cried. Questions, such as, "Who is my real mother and why didn't she want me?" added to the confusion.

However upon a deeper analysis of who I am and how much is physical and how much is relational in me as far as my parents are concerned, I arrive at the following certainty. Regardless of the genes that determined my gender, race, and other characteristics, I would be an entirely different person if I had been raised by other people instead of by my parents. Physicists point to the importance of the genes; process philosophy and experts in the behavioral sciences stress the relational. The person I am came into being to a very great extent through my relationship with those who crossed my path of life. Adopted children owe a great deal to dedicated foster parents, who rightly call them their children.

Among all my relationships, the direct one with God too has to do with me as a person. How am I related to God? Various concepts have been used to describe this relationship. The one used most in the Bible is the theme of "covenant" or "partnership." Today's Scripture describes it dramatically. Am I aware that I am God's adopted child, his partner in business? The more I foster the awareness of this beautiful relationship with God, the more I will grow into the person my Maker wants me to be.

SCRIPTURE READING —

Then, having sent certain young men of the Israelites to offer holocausts and sacrifice young bulls as peace offerings to the Lord, Moses took half of the blood and put it in large bowls; the other half he splashed on the altar. Taking the book of the covenant, he read it aloud to the people, who answered, "All that the Lord has said, we will heed and do." Then he took the blood and sprinkled it on the people, saying, "This is the blood of the covenant which the Lord has made with you in accordance with all these words of his."

(Exodus 24:5-8)

"Yet it was I [God] who taught Ephraim to walk"

A PAIN which causes parents sleepless nights is disappointment with children who frustrated their rightful expectations. Absalom rebelled against his father, King David. By our standards Absalom was a rascal who deserved the punishment he got. Yet, when he was killed, "the king covered his face and cried out in a loud voice, 'My son Absalom! Absalom! My son, my son!'" (2 Samuel 19:5). Israel [Jacob] loved Joseph best of all his sons, who broke his heart by their jealousy and strife (Exodus 37).

History repeats itself up to today. A friend of mine has a son who dropped out of high school and ended up as an inmate in the state penitentiary! Dope and crime have ruined his life and that of his parents. I have seen them during the visiting hours in our penal institutions together with other frustrated parents, all having their sad stories about children who should have done better.

Can God be frustrated? Hosea and with him contemporary process theology state that he can. Hosea has God tell his story about Israel, the people he has chosen as his own. "They have violated my covenant" (Hosea 8:1). And in Hosea, the covenant has clear overtones of love. God is a frustrated father! Israel, Ephraim (patriarchs) stand for God's people, you and me. What has God done for you? "Out of Egypt I called my son." Out of the bondage of evil and yourself, God called you. He drew you with bands of love. Do you live up to God's rightful expectations?

SCRIPTURE READING —

When Israel was a child I loved him,
out of Egypt I called my son.
The more I called them,
the farther they went from me,
Sacrificing to the Baals
and burning incense to idols.
Yet is was I who taught Ephraim to walk,
who took them in my arms;
I drew them with human cords,
with bands of love;
I fostered them like one
who raises an infant to his cheeks;
Yet, though I stooped to feed my child,
they did not know that I was their healer. (Hosea 11:1-4)

"I [God] will espouse you in fidelity"

WHAT is the secret of keeping a marital relationship exciting? Psychologists, marriage counselors, gynecologists—all in the supportive professions try to help in their own way. But they all agree that marriage is a two-way street. If one of the two partners does not cooperate, it does not work, regardless of how hard the other party tries. In case of failure, it is often difficult to find out who failed. Both partners in marriage are human beings. Both can make mistakes consciously or unconsciously.

We have mentioned *(February 5)* that the biblical writers often use the concept "covenant" (partnership) to describe how man is related to God. Actually, this is a political concept of biblical culture, where it is based on the so-called suzerainty treaty: a relationship between unequal partners in which the stronger (a mighty king) grants a covenant to the weaker (a petty king), who in turn, is obligated within definite boundaries. Inspired by God, the Hebrew writers use this concept to describe how Israel is related to the King of heaven and earth. In later literature, this covenant was seen more as a partnership based on love, more or less like a father taking his son into his business as a partner in our society *(February 6)*. Other writers like Hosea and Isaiah *(January 8)* give the covenant even marital overtones.

The author of today's Scripture sees Israel related to God as a spouse to her husband. The covenant becomes a marriage! Indeed, this is a beautiful metaphor, and note that it is suggested by God himself. Your relationship with God is a two-way street. When a marriage fails, one partner may blame the other. When there is something wrong between you and God, you cannot blame God. He is love and as such always available. If there is failure, it can only come from you! Is your love of God alive?

SCRIPTURE READING —

I will espouse you to me forever:
I will espouse you in right and in justice,
in love and in mercy;
I will espouse you in fidelity,
and you shall know the Lord.
I will say to Lo-ammi, "You are my people,"
and he shall say, "My God!" (Hosea 2:22, 25)

"A covenant not of a written law but of spirit"

CONSERVATIVE Americans are warning us that this country could become a police state. We are eager to protect our liberties, and yet we need laws which should be enforced strictly to maintain those very freedoms. History teaches that whenever balance is lost, a society is in trouble: either it becomes a police state that terrorizes its citizens, or it becomes a permissive society where everything goes and citizens cannot walk freely in the streets anymore.

Organized religious communities are no exception to this procedure. Late Judaism of Jesus' time had swung extremely to the right. God's covenant with Israel had become a covenant of the written law. Jesus had protested against this legalism (Matthew 15:3). In today's Scripture Paul reasons in accord with the mind of the Master. He does not denounce Moses as such but rather what men had made of Moses' covenant. The prophets had described the covenant as a relationship of love *(February 6, 7)*, but the rabbis had taken the spirit out of it. And it is precisely the spirit of the covenant which gives life.

Should we see the Church as a police state? Obeying Church law thoughtlessly, and feeling justified by "doing your duty" without being inspired by love means acting as the Pharisees did. We must keep the Lord Jesus in the picture all the time; and where the spirit of the Lord is, there is freedom (2 Corinthians 3:17). It is not easy to maintain a balance. Think of *Fiddler on the Roof*. Play your little tune in life, but don't fall off! Is this possible? Yes, if you keep on "gazing on the Lord's glory" (2 Corinthians 3:18), and ask him to guide you. The new covenant is a covenant of love, as Hosea *(February 1)* and Isaiah *(January 8)* have explained it. And the spirit of the Lord is a spirit of love!

SCRIPTURE READING —

This great confidence in God is ours, through Christ. It is not that we are entitled of ourselves to take credit for anything. Our sole credit is from God, who has made us qualified ministers of a new covenant, a covenant not of a written law but of spirit. The written law kills, but the Spirit gives life.

The Lord is the Spirit, and where the Spirit of the Lord is, there is freedom. All of us, gazing on the Lord's glory with unveiled faces, are transformed from glory to glory into his very image by the Lord who is the Spirit. (2 Corinthians 3:4-6, 17-18)

"With the dignity of a queen" February 9

IF YOU have had the fortune to witness a baptism close up, you have observed a variety of symbolisms: bathing with water, anointing with oil, clothing the child with a white robe. Where did the Church get these particular symbols? Christian baptism has its roots in Jewish baptism, which derived its symbols from customs that surrounded a wedding of biblical times and culture. Before the wedding ceremony the bride was bathed, anointed with oil and perfume, and dressed with an embroidered wedding gown, helped by mother and girlfriends. All cultures have similar ceremonies, and also in ours it takes quite some time before the bride is ready to march into the church on the arm of her father.

In today's Bible reading, Jerusalem (the capital) stands for God's chosen people, whom the writer considers as living in a covenant (sacred partnership) with Almighty God. In Ezekiel, this partnership has marital overtones. Hence, Jerusalem (God's people—you and I) is God's spouse. Figuratively, God says: "I chose you as my spouse! You are mine!"

Through faith and baptism, you are related to God in a bond of intimate love. You should keep that love alive. This requires constant concern just as in a marital situation. And of utmost importance is a living communication, which you must keep going in prayer and meditation. As Ezekiel mentions in verse 15, infidelity will occur if you drift apart by indifference. Be grateful that God has chosen you!

SCRIPTURE READING—

Then I [the Lord] bathed you [Jerusalem] with water, washed away your blood, and anointed you with oil. I clothed you with an embroidered gown, put sandals of fine leather on your feet; I gave you a fine linen sash and silk robes to wear. I adorned you with jewelry: I put bracelets on your arms, a necklace about your neck, a ring in your nose, pendants in your ears, and a glorious diadem upon your head. Thus you were adorned with gold and silver; your garments were of fine linen, silk, and embroidered cloth. Fine flour, honey, and oil were your food. You were exceedingly beautiful, with the dignity of a queen. You were renowned among the nations for your beauty, perfect as it was, because of my splendor which I had bestowed on you, says the Lord God.

But you were captivated by your own beauty, you used your renown to make yourself a harlot, and you lavished your harlotry on every passer-by, whose own you became. (Ezekiel 16:9-15)

"You have turned aside from your early love"

A FRIEND of mine, a successful planter, in speaking about all that is connected with cotton farming, once made the remark: "Getting older, you are not so enthusiastic anymore. Is that the same with your work as a priest?" His frank question made me think. Am I still the kind of priest I was a few decades ago? Have I reduced my interest to just doing my duty? Am I still as daring and full of new ideas for the future as I was those first years after my ordination?

If you are married, you might ask yourself a similar question. What about the dreams of your honeymoon? Your joy with that first child, fruit of your mutual love? Your plans for a life in mutual dedication together? If you are a religious, you could think of your first profession: a life of dedication and service to God and neighbor lying ahead, one rewarding experience after another! "Shout from the highest mountain tops praises of the Lord!"

In his *Ode to Joy*, the German poet Schiller sang: "Oh that the beautiful time of young and tender love would blossom for all eternity!" In our lives, is the stage of compromising inevitable? Figuratively, the author of Revelation has God say a few things to the churches of Asia Minor. The congregation at Ephesus is not doing too badly. They are patient and willing to endure hardship for God's sake. Yet . . . "you turned aside your first love." You are related to God in a sacred partnership (covenant of love). What about your first love? The church of Ephesus stands for you and me!

SCRIPTURE READING —

"To the presiding spirit of the church in Ephesus, write this:

" 'The One who holds the seven stars in his right hand and walks among the seven lampstands of gold has this to say: I know your deeds, your labors, and your patient endurance. I know you cannot tolerate wicked men; you have tested those self-styled apostles who are nothing of the sort, and discovered that they are impostors. You are patient and endure hardship for my cause. Moreover, you do not become discouraged. I hold this against you, though: you have turned aside from your early love. Keep firmly in mind the heights from which you have fallen. Repent, and return to your former deeds. If you do not repent I will come to you and remove your lampstand from its place."

(Revelation 2:1-5)

"Fill the earth and subdue it. Have dominion over . . ."

WHILE living in the Far East, I had occasion to observe primitive people coming home from their fields in the late evening. On a narrow footpath the man strode proudly in front and behind him came his wife, with a bamboo cane over her shoulder carrying two heavy loads of corn. He had paid the dowry to her parents, hence she should work! It often made me wonder as to whether it was a male or a female genius who invented the wheel. After all, the woman had all the reasons in the world to get fed up carrying heavy loads and to transfer them partly on a wheel!

In any case, whether humans are inventing the wheel in ancient times or building today's chemical plants, computers, and spacecrafts, they are God's coworkers. When you are repairing a car, giving birth to a child, cooking a meal for the family, or studying in school, you are creatively busy fashioning the chaos (unordered or less ordered matter) into a better world. Artists are especially conscious and proud of their creativity; but each of us can have these same sentiments, particularly when creatively occupied in education, molding and fashioning children into better men and women.

You have dominion over all the living things, but only as God's manager! How are you using the resources of the planet? Are you carelessly using more energy (light, fuel) than necessary and dumping material that could be recycled? Yours should be a responsible stewardship.

SCRIPTURE READING —

God created man in his image;
in the divine image he created him;
male and female he created them.

God blessed them, saying: "Be fertile and multiply; fill the earth and subdue it. Have dominion over the fish of the sea, the birds of the air, and all the living things that move on the earth." God also said: "See, I give you every seed-bearing plant all over the earth and every tree that has seed-bearing fruit on it to be your food; and to all the animals of the land, all the birds of the air, and all the living creatures that crawl on the ground, I give all the green plants for food." And so it happened. God looked at everything he had made, and he found it very good. Evening came, and morning followed—the sixth day.

(Genesis 1:27-31)

"Declare your sins to one another, and pray for one another, that you may find healing"

ON AN open field close to my rectory, a faith healer had set up his tent. The poor, the sick, the destitute, the problematics of the community came out begging for consolation. It was a midsummer night and hot. With a classmate of mine I took a stroll, and standing in the dark we could unobtrusively observe what was going on. It was an emotional event. The electric guitar, the shouting and clapping, the "Amens" and "Alleluias" heightened the feelings, and finally there was a laying on of hands. I must admit that in this setting it would not be my cup of tea. But in a Christian community should there not be a sharing, an opening up to one another, which may result in healing?

It is biblical whenever it is done. However, the exact manner in which Christians do this may differ! In prayer groups, some charismatic and quite emotional people open up, share their problems, confess their guilt, and pray. The new rite of penance offers the option of sharing guilt and problems with a professional priest, who may counsel, pray, and absolve from sin in Jesus' name.

It is good to share. Taxicab drivers and bartenders are often the confidants of desperate people. Do you know how to listen to a friend who is down in the dumps without burdening him/her with your own pain and soreness? Just listening may result in healing. James gives some advice. "A holy man" in this context is simply someone who preaches the word of God. Apply this to your situation and respond in prayer!

SCRIPTURE READING—

Declare your sins to one another, and pray for one another, that you may find healing.

The fervent petition of a holy man is powerful indeed. Elijah was only a man like us, yet he prayed earnestly that it would not rain and no rain fell on the land for three years and six months. When he prayed again, the sky burst forth with rain and the land produced its crop.

My brothers, the case may arise among you of someone straying from the truth, and of another bringing him back. Remember this: the person who brings a sinner back from his way will save his soul from death and cancel a multitude of sins. (James 5:16-20)

"The church of God which is in Corinth"

WHEN persons who are interested in some activity such as gardening decide to do it together, they need institution. They elect a chairperson, a secretary, a treasurer. Somebody must call the meetings, guide the discussions, and handle the money. If this is not done, the group cannot function and falls apart.

People who feel called to live their lives as outlined by Jesus of Nazareth have this same need for institution. Going back in history, we observe that the early Christian congregations had a strong leadership from the top. It is reflected in John's Gospel. "As the Father has sent me [Jesus], so I send you [the apostles]. Receive the Holy Spirit" (see John 20:21-22).

Authority from the top (not chosen by the people) is not very savory to those who believe in authority exercised "by the people and for the people." Hence, we observe strong tendencies to democratize Church authority nowadays. Councils on both the parish and diocesan level were established after Vatican II. Some Protestant bodies went all the American way. The congregations hire, authorize, and fire their preachers by a majority of votes. Can this be done? It depends of course on what the Founder willed expressly and what he has left up to the Church to decide for itself.

The outlook presented by Paul in today's Scripture may help keep our heads cool in this time of transition. He sends greetings to "the church of God which is *in* Corinth!" We are first of all "consecrated in Christ Jesus and called to be a holy people," and only secondly members of "St. Jude's"! Focus on the essentials and keep in mind that the institution, which will never be perfect, is secondary. In my Bible, I have marked "consecrated," "called," and "call on," and centered my meditation and reflective prayer around these concepts.

SCRIPTURE READING —

Paul, called by God's will to be an apostle of Christ Jesus, and Sosthenes our brother, send greetings to the church of God which is in Corinth; to you who have been consecrated in Christ Jesus and called to be a holy people, as to all those who, wherever they may be, call on the name of our Lord Jesus Christ, their Lord and ours. Grace and peace from God our Father and the Lord Jesus Christ. (1 Corinthians 1:1-3)

"Be united in mind and judgment"

ON FEDERAL buildings we see the American emblem with the motto: "*E pluribus unum*" ("One out of many"). This emblem is very appropriate for this country with its manifold ethnic groups that came from all over the globe in search for freedom and equal opportunities for all. "Many" stands for numerous and varied. We are different in culture, race, and religion, but we are one in our dedication to the ideals of the founding fathers of this country. And for two hundred years we have proven that we can be one and simultaneously different in an open society, i.e., without being forced by dictatorship.

However, the right to speak up for our convictions can easily result in "quarreling among ourselves," as was the case in the early congregation of Corinth, Greece. This scene can repeat itself in parish council meetings and after Mass in front of the church. A congregation that may be different in culture, race, formal education, and certainly age must nevertheless be "united in mind and judgment."

The uniting factor should be our common belonging to Christ. This oneness depends on our faith, love, and dedication. When this oneness is tested, how do you act? Wisdom is needed—not a wordy "wisdom" but the paradoxical wisdom of the cross which can be acquired only in patient prayer.

SCRIPTURE READING —

I beg you, brothers, in the name of our Lord Jesus Christ, to agree in what you say. Let there be no factions; rather, be united in mind and judgment. I have been informed, my brothers, by certain members of Chloe's household that you are quarreling among yourselves. This is what I mean: One of you will say, "I belong to Paul," another, "I belong to Apollos," still another, "Cephas has my allegiance," and the fourth, "I belong to Christ."

Has Christ, then, been divided into parts? Was it Paul who was crucified for you? Was it in Paul's name that you were baptized? For Christ did not send me to baptize, but to preach the gospel—not with wordy "wisdom," however, lest the cross of Christ be rendered void of its meaning! (1 Corinthians 1:10-13, 17)

"He has made him our wisdom"

PEOPLE may call me proud, egotistic, or even tag me with a few more unpleasant characteristics, and it would not ruffle me. But I would be really mad if they were to label me seriously as mentally disturbed, ready for a one-way trip to the state mental institution. One day, while discussing "depression" in high school and how to handle it, I purposely said slowly: "I was in Whitfield" (mental institution of Mississippi). And indeed, a teenager took the bait and snapped: "What were you there for?" "Sick in the head, of course," I answered jokingly.

I visited a member of the congregation there and later had a cup of coffee with her psychiatrist. He said: "At the first counseling session, all patients ask me to talk with . . . (the person who is allegedly the reason that the patient is here), in other words, to take their problems away. I can't The only thing I as a psychiatrist can do is help the patient to learn how to handle life's problems."

Handling life's problems requires wisdom, but not the kind that "men account wisdom." Jesus, the Man of Galilee, offers a wisdom which has helped millions to cope with the problems, pain, and frustrations of life. We find this wisdom in the stories and discussions of the New Testament. In today's Scripture, Paul exhorts us to take notice of that wisdom, which seemingly quite often is opposed to common sense, yet is in fact true. Whenever you are depressed, do you take your Bible, read till you find a word that applies to you, and respond in reflective prayer?

SCRIPTURE READING —

Brothers, you are among those called. Consider your situation. Not many of you are wise, as men account wisdom; not many are influential; and surely not many are well-born. God chose those whom the world considers absurd to shame the wise; he singled out the weak of this world to shame the strong. He chose the world's lowborn and despised, those who count for nothing, to reduce to nothing those who were something; so that mankind can do no boasting before God.

God it is who has given you life in Christ Jesus. He has made him our wisdom and also our justice, our sanctification, and our redemption. This is just as you find it written, "Let him who would boast, boast in the Lord." (1 Corinthians 1:26-31)

"The convincing power of the Spirit"

AS A YOUNG missionary in the Far East, I was appointed to a large territory where the Church was actually unknown. As the first Catholic priest, I had to prove myself. The people were good, but they simply did not trust me. They wanted to know what this foreigner without wife and children was after! To a certain extent, I had to face a similar situation when I was assigned to my first black parish in the South. A woman, who joined the Church later, told me that the people in the community had often discussed my presence in their neighborhood in terms of: "What is he hiding behind that smile?" They were confused by service that was offered without asking for payment or any favor in return.

Paul must have had similar problems when he first went to Corinth, Greece, to preach the good news of Jesus Christ and to found a Christian congregation. He came in weakness and fear, and with much trepidation. Yet he achieved his goal not with persuasive force of "wise" argumentation, but with the convincing power of the Spirit. Conversion is a gift of God, which nevertheless works mainly through the preacher. It all depends on whether or not he is able to convince people through his Christian life-style of care and self-effacing love.

Sharing in love is the convincing power of the Spirit! Apply this to your own life-style. Is it such that it can be a convincing power of the Holy Spirit? Sharing, especially of self, a sharing that hurts and can be a cross, is a "wisdom" which many do not accept. Yet it is that wisdom which is a convincing power.

SCRIPTURE READING —

As for myself, brothers, when I came to you I did not come proclaiming God's testimony with any particular eloquence or "wisdom." No, I determined that while I was with you I would speak of nothing but Jesus Christ and him crucified. When I came among you it was in weakness and fear, and with much trepidation. My message and my preaching had none of the persuasive force of "wise" argumentation, but the convincing power of the Spirit. As a consequence, your faith rests not on the wisdom of men but on the power of God.

(1 Corinthians 2:1-5)

"A mysterious, a hidden wisdom" February 17

I WAS bruised, wounded, and very angry, lying on a bed in a neighboring rectory. It was toward the end of World War II in The Netherlands, then occupied by the Germans. Allied bombers had destroyed the house where I was living with teaching brothers. It happened during the Sunday Mass in our chapel. A mother of eight died under my hands when I gave her the Anointing of the Sick. A brother was heavily wounded, and I collapsed after I had done my duty. Dutch marines of the underground, hidden in a chicken farm close by, had broadcast to the Allies that a German pontoon unit had occupied the lower floor of our house. Usually they warned people to get out when their property was going to be bombed, but they had not deemed it necessary to warn the brothers and that priest.

It was in this bad mood that an elderly priest found me. I told him that I was mad enough to inform the German commander about those marines. They would be shot on the spot. The wise old man said: "John, I can see your point. They should have warned you. What about waiting till Wednesday (i.e., three days later), and then making your decision?" Great wisdom! By Wednesday I had cooled off, and did not inform on those marines!

In today's Scripture, Paul discusses wisdom. As Aelred Graham *(Contemplative Christianity,* p. 4), observes, a philosophy of life should not be seen as a self-consistent intellectual system, the concern of academic specialists, but as a pursuit of wisdom and the path to the good and happy life. This wisdom, seen as a gift of the Spirit, is the great contribution of Christianity to mankind. We find it in the Bible and it becomes ours in reflective prayer.

SCRIPTURE READING —

There is, to be sure, a certain wisdom which we express among the spiritually mature. It is not a wisdom of this age, however, nor of the rulers of this age, who are men headed for destruction. No, what we utter is God's wisdom: a mysterious, a hidden wisdom. God planned it before all ages for our glory. None of the rulers of this age knew the mystery; if they had known it, they would never have crucified the Lord of glory. Of this wisdom it is written:

"Eye has not seen, ear has not heard,
nor has it so much as dawned on man
what God has prepared for those who love him."

Yet God has revealed this wisdom to us through the Spirit. The Spirit scrutinizes all matters, even the deep things of God.

(1 Corinthians 2:6-10)

"The wisdom of this world is absurdity with God"

SAINT Isidore, bishop of Seville in Spain (he died in 636) states in his book of maxims: "If a man wants to be always in God's company, he must pray regularly and read regularly. When we pray, we talk to God; when we read, God talks to us. *All spiritual growth comes from reading and reflection.* By reading we learn what we did not know, by reflection we retain what we have learned" (*Liturgy of the Hours,* April 4). Saint Isidore is talking about reading the Bible. The italics are my suggestion. I find this statement important.

In today's Bible reading, Paul draws a black-white picture about God's wisdom versus the wisdom of this world. Semites often do this to bring out their point. Paul has, of course, in mind a certain kind of worldly wisdom and is not denouncing the progress of science. Yet it is amazing that with all the progress man has made in science, sociology, politics, and education, he has not succeeded in coming up with an acceptable philosophy of life.

The ultimate conclusion of contemporary philosophers is that all is absurdity (Existentialism of Heidegger, Sartre, etc.) and Marxism with its faith in the class struggle has not brought the paradise it promised. Another philosophy of life, which is more in vogue in this country, is hedonism. Herod in *Jesus Christ Superstar,* patted all over by his women, is the classical specimen of the modern hedonist. His words: "Jesus, come walk over my swimming pool!" What a miserable creature, crying out finally: "Jesus, get out of my life!"

We should check our philosophy of life (our wisdom!) constantly and compare it with the wisdom of God. The temptation to deviate is always there.

SCRIPTURE READING —

Are you not aware that you are the temple of God, and that the Spirit of God dwells in you? If anyone destroys God's temple, God will destroy him. For the temple of God is holy, and you are that temple.

Let no one delude himself. If any one of you thinks he is wise in a worldly way, he had better become a fool. In that way he will really be wise, for the wisdom of this world is absurdity with God. Scripture says, "He catches the wise in their craftiness"; and again, "The Lord knows how empty are the thoughts of the wise." Let there be no boasting about men. All things are yours, whether it be Paul, or Apollos, or Cephas, or the world, or life, or death, or the present, or the future: all these are yours, and you are Christ's and Christ is God's.

(1 Corinthians 3:16-23)

February 19

"Mind you, I have nothing on my conscience"

AFTER the armed forces of Japan in Southeast Asia were defeated in 1945, suspected Japanese war criminals were detained in camps to wait for trial. At the request of a missionary German bishop, who was not interned during the war and had continued to work under extremely difficult circumstances, I visited such a camp in my parish and had several talks with a Japanese fleet admiral. He was a non-Christian but had done whatever he could during the war to help the few foreign missionaries who were allowed to take care of the thousands of Catholics on those islands.

The admiral was seemingly a very well educated and refined gentleman. He spoke his English well. We sat outside with a floodlight on us and a Dutch soldier watching from a wooden tower. Quite often our conversation was interrupted by Japanese soldiers who came running out of a barrack, saluted the guard on the tower, asked permission to go to the rest room, and ran off. I could hardly suppress a smile, but apparently it did not bother the admiral. The bishop disagreed with this man's internment, and recommended that I try to do something for him.

I remember one statement of the admiral verbatim: "*Tuan* (Sir—father), I don't understand why they keep me here. I am not a war criminal." Later, he was sent back to Japan. Impressed by what he had seen on the islands during the war, he became a Catholic and published a book about his experience.

This was a good man, who could state: "I have nothing on my conscience," yet he was judged and detained. Paul had a similar experience with the congregation in Corinth. How do you handle judgment passed on you unfairly? In my Bible I have underlined: "The Lord is the one to judge me."

SCRIPTURE READING—

Men should regard us as servants of Christ and administrators of the mysteries of God. The first requirement of an administrator is that he prove trustworthy. It matters little to me whether you or any human court pass judgment on me. I do not even pass judgment on myself. Mind you, I have nothing on my conscience. But that does not mean that I am declaring myself innocent. The Lord is the one to judge me, so stop passing judgment before the time of his return. He will bring to light what is hidden in darkness and manifest the intentions of hearts. At that time, everyone will receive his praise from God.

(1 Corinthians 4:1-5)

LENT

JUST guess how many hours it requires to prepare a wedding, which with the reception included lasts only a few hours! Nevertheless, the more carefully prepared, the more successful the wedding will be. Nothing and nobody may be overlooked. The wedding-bands and the punch, the pastor and the hairdresser, the invitation to Aunt Betty and the gowns of the flower girls—all must be taken into account.

The apostle Paul invites us to celebrate Easter with sincerity and truth (1 Corinthians 5:8). The feast lasts fifty days; hence the traditional preparation of forty days makes sense. Essentially, the preparation should consist in a more diligent cultivation of Christian life. If you deny yourself a good meal a week, donate the money you save to the U.S. Bishops Relief Fund in order to help feed the hungry of the world. Almsgiving and other works of charity have been part of Lent from the beginning. Denying yourself a few things, such as, meat, alcohol, and smoking, makes sense for various motives—e.g., to reinforce prayer (reflective Bible reading), or to do penance for your sins.

During Lent, Christians prepare to celebrate the paschal mystery "with mind and heart renewed." The more carefully prepared, the more meaningful the paschal festival will be for you.

Your Attitude must be Christ's

Philippians 2:6

"For we hold that man is justified by faith apart from observance of the law"

WHEN visiting a Buddhist temple, I listened to a beautiful elderly lady, Chinese with a blend of a few more races, as one sees so often in the Far East. With a gracious smile that showed her pride in her religion, this lady explained the meaning of the lotus flower which was used all over both for decoration and teaching. This lily white flower grows in ponds. It is rooted in mud and murky water, yet grows up into magnificent splendor.

And as such the lotus is a symbol of all who are justified by God's grace. All of us are rooted in the mud of the sinful human condition. "All men have sinned and are deprived of the glory of God" (Romans 3:23). But we are able to outgrow the condition and attain the original brilliant luster which our Maker has designed for us. When the Bible compares us to flowers, it is usually done to bring out our transiency. The land of the Bible has no ponds. Water is scarce. Yet the Song of Songs compares us to a lily. "I am a flower of Sharon [fertile plain between Mount Carmel and Jaffa], a lily of the valley. As a lily among thorns, so is my beloved among women" (Song 2:1-2).

We must be grateful for our justification, for the beauty (like the lotus and lily) which God bestows on us, not because of our own efforts but because of Jesus' meritorious death on the cross.

SCRIPTURE READING —

The justice of God has been manifested apart from the law, even though both law and prophets bear witness to it—that justice of God which works through faith in Jesus Christ for all who believe. All men have sinned and are deprived of the glory of God. All men are now undeservedly justified by the gift of God, through the redemption wrought in Christ Jesus. Through his blood, God made him the means of expiation for all who believe. He did so to manifest his own justice, for the sake of remitting sins committed in the past. For we hold that a man is justified by faith apart from observance of the law.

(Romans 3:21-25, 28)

"Yet he never questioned or doubted God's promise"

WHEN recuperating after a third major surgery in one year, my chest was hurting. Thrombosis was the first thing the sister-nurse thought of. Her face twitched. The surgeon was called in and X-rays taken. I was listening attentively and heard the roentgenologist say to the surgeon: "*Pleuritis duplex.*" I happen to know my Latin quite well and knew that with a double pleurisy I would be hospitalized for another long time, since penicillin was not available in that part of the world. The doctor was nice, thought that I had not understood his medical jargon, and assured me that there was nothing to worry about. But worry I did! In addition to this, the doctors suspected that I had tuberculosis. Their advice was to leave the tropics and go back to Europe.

I was down in the dumps. A young fellow in my early thirties, I loved my work: Riding on horseback through the mountains from one mission to another, free as a bird in the sky; rising to the challenge of being assigned as the first missionary in an entirely new territory *(February 16)*. Now all that would be gone—leaving only an ailing man in the sick ward of the seminary, well taken care of but as an object of charity. I was depressed and all but hoping against hope as Abraham of today's Scripture did. It was the sister-nurse, a beautiful person in her mid-forties, who squeezed me through with all the natural and supernatural means available. My own mother could not have done better! And things have worked out all right.

Hoping against hope is not easy. Paul tells us in today's reading that we should do so and that such a faith will be credited as justice. Think of your own life! When depressed, how do you handle your situation? These words were written for us too!

SCRIPTURE READING —

Hoping against hope, Abraham believed and so became the father of many nations, just as it was once told him, "Numerous as this shall your descendants be." Without growing weak in faith he thought of his own body, which was as good as dead (for he was nearly a hundred years old), and of the dead womb of Sarah. Yet he never questioned or doubted God's promise; rather, he was strengthened in faith and gave glory to God, fully persuaded that God could do whatever he had promised. Thus his faith was credited to him as justice.

(Romans 4:18-22)

"It is precisely in this that God proves his love for us"

THE *Hiding Place,* a motion picture dealing with a Dutch family hiding Jews to save them from Nazi extermination, brings out beautifully what Christian life is all about. It is a love that is willing to lay down one's (comfortable, secure) life to save a fellow human. (See John 10:11.) In today's Scripture, Paul remarks that Christ died for us while we were still sinners. Laying down your life for someone you love affectionately (a mother rescuing her baby from a burning house) is easier than doing the same for a stranger.

During the war, I lived as a young priest in The Netherlands occupied by the Germans just like the Ten Boom family of *The Hiding Place.* I knew families who were hiding Jews. They had problems like those of the Ten Booms. Jews were not always appreciative, not because they happened to be Jews but because they were people. Some had self-restraint and were beautiful, well-balanced persons; some were rotten and spoiled, hence demanding and ungrateful; others became nervous, restless, and irritable after many months of confinement in an attic. Loving them nevertheless was heroic. Many Dutch families were caught and went the way of the Ten Booms to the German concentration camps. Others held out and often experienced lack of gratitude as soon as everything was over.

Christ gave the example of how to handle this the Christian way. He says: "If you love those who love you, what merit is there in that? Do not tax collectors [matter of fact villains] do as much?" (Matthew 5:46). We are grateful for what Christ has done "for us godless men." And we should learn from him what we should do for others, who naturally speaking are not that sympathetic to us.

SCRIPTURE READING —

At the appointed time, when we were still powerless, Christ died for us godless men. It is rare that anyone should lay down his life for a just man, though it is barely possible that for a good man someone may have the courage to die. It is precisely in this that God proves his love for us: that while we were still sinners, Christ died for us.

(Romans 5:6-8)

"We believe that we are also to live with him"

THE real art of living includes the art of facing the end of life with dignity. The Swiss-born Dr. Elisabeth Kubler-Ross, who works long hours with terminally ill and dying patients, gives us valuable insights on death and dying in her well-known books.[1] She states that we should not shy away from the hopeless-ly" sick but get close to them. Those who can do this "will discover that this will be a mutually gratifying experience . . . and will emerge from it enriched and perhaps with fewer anxieties about their own finality." Dr. Kubler-Ross herself has! She says in her second book (p. 57): "Before I started working with dying patients, I did not believe in a life after death. I now do believe in a life after death, beyond a shadow of doubt."

We Christians share faith in a hereafter with the Lord Jesus. Does this mean that we don't have an eye for the beauty of life on this side of the grave? Since we have died with Christ in Baptism (best symbolized by baptism of immersion), we now live a new life with him, which will continue after we have gone through the metamorphosis of death. In a television interview referring to an unbelieving mother whose daughter of ten was dying of leukemia, Dr. Kubler-Ross explained how difficult it is to make death acceptable for a person without faith in an afterlife. Let us joyfully live our "life for God" now and hope prayerfully that we may face its change through death with dignity.

[1]*On Death and Dying* and *Questions and Answers on Death and Dying.*

SCRIPTURE READING —

Are you not aware that we who were baptized into Christ Jesus were baptized into his death? Through baptism into his death we were buried with him, so that, just as Christ was raised from the dead by the glory of the Father, we too might live a new life.

If we have died with Christ, we believe that we are also to live with him. We know that Christ, once raised from the dead, will never die again; death has no more power over him. His death was death to sin, once for all; his life is life for God. In the same way, you must consider yourselves dead to sin but alive for God in Christ Jesus.

(Romans 6:3-4, 8-11)

February 24

"Since the Spirit of God dwells in you"

THE controversial motion picture *The Exorcist* deals with the phenomenon of a person possessed by evil spirits. Instinctively, we experience a transcendent power in us, that may direct us into both bad and good directions. We call this power "spirit," hence speak of inspiration. Artists especially are in need of this inspiration, which makes them envision things that we common mortals don't see, and moves them to fashion their visionary experience into the form of their art: music, sculpture, painting, or poetry.

Not all artists are believers, but all believers need to have something of an artist in them. Believers have that visionary experience which we call faith, and which is brought about by divine inspiration, in other words, by the working of God's Spirit who dwells in us. We should take this indwelling of the Holy Spirit seriously. Without the Spirit we are infertile and unproductive like an artist without inspiration. Like artists, we are somehow different from those who don't have this inspiration.

Paul stresses this in today's Scripture. Note that "body" in the biblical sense does not mean body as opposed to soul (as in Greek thought), but the whole man, subject to sin and death yet open to redemption. "Flesh" in Paul's thinking stands for "unredeemed nature." The Spirit of God can only inspire you to the extent that you open up to him! What about your life as a Christian? In verse 13 (the last sentence) Paul mentions an alternative.

SCRIPTURE READING —

You are not in the flesh; you are in the spirit, since the Spirit of God dwells in you. If anyone does not have the Spirit of Christ, he does not belong to Christ. If the Spirit of him who raised Jesus from the dead dwells in you, then he who raised Christ from the dead will bring your mortal bodies to life also, through his Spirit dwelling in you.

We are debtors, then, my brothers—but not to the flesh, so that we should live according to the flesh. If you live according to the flesh, you will die; but if by the spirit you put to death the evil deeds of the body, you will live. (Romans 8:9, 11-13)

"Yet not without hope"

DURING the last few decades two outstanding philosophers have tried to shed some light on the mystery of hope. One of them is Ernst Bloch, a Marxist, who prefers to concentrate on the possibilities in this world and to link the power of hope to the role of the future, the not-yet. But when? Paradise on earth has been promised for about a century, but none of the socialistic countries has realized it.

We rather will concentrate on another philosopher, Gabriel Marcel, a Christian in the Catholic tradition, who delivered a lecture "Sketch of a Phenomenology and a Metaphysic of Hope," which I found in his collection *Homo Viator*. Marcel sees existence in general as a captivity (p. 32), more or less as Paul does in today's Bible reading, calling it "slavery to corruption" (yet not without hope!).

Marcel sees the act of hope as an interior creativity and links it to its source, the Absolute Thou (God). "I hope, I long for deliverance, which would bring my trial to an end. The 'I hope' aims at salvation, at coming out of the darkness in which I am presently plunged, be it illness, separation, exile, slavery, or the impossibility of rising to a certain fullness of life, which may be in the realms of sensation or even of thought in the strict sense of the word" (p. 30). Hope is intimately related to faith. "Faith in the Absolute Thou makes me look upon despair as a kind of betrayal" (pp. 46-47).

With these remarks in mind, apply Paul's words to your own life situation and respond in reflective prayer! Does this mean that we push Ernst Block aside? No. He reminds us Christians that we should be concerned for and give hope to the suffering by doing whatever is possible. But there are situations from which humanly speaking there is no escape. Then Marcel and especially Paul can help us.

SCRIPTURE READING —

I consider the sufferings of the present to be as nothing compared with the glory to be revealed in us. Indeed, the whole created world eagerly awaits the revelation of the sons of God. Creation was made subject to futility, not of its own accord but by him who once subjected it; yet not without hope, because the world itself will be freed from its slavery to corruption and share in the glorious freedom of the children of God.

(Romans 8:18-21)

"The Spirit too helps us in our weakness"

I ALWAYS enjoy reading about the idyllic riverside conversion near Philippi, a Roman colony in Macedonia, in Acts 16:13-15. A woman named Lydia believed, but Luke remarks significantly, "The Lord opened her heart to accept what Paul was saying" (Acts 16:14). Without the help of God's Spirit we are unable to do anything, even to pray as we ought. This is the reason why in the Introduction to this book, we suggest beginning daily meditation with a prayer for help. In the life of a Christian there is a constant tension between total dependence on God and the knowledge that we are God's partners, fully responsible for the world process.

Marxists *(see February 25)* often blame Christians for accepting situations like poverty, social injustice, and war too easily with the promise of a better life hereafter. Indeed, often Christians have overstressed the role of grace. There was a flare-up of social concern in the sixties: Catholics, sisters, and a few priests protesting in Selma, a bishop marching with Dr. King—but as a whole the Catholic Church in America was not in the vanguard. And now in the seventies, we observe even an opposite direction. There is a lively interest in charismatic and other prayer groups often at the cost of social concern. This book itself and the expectation that it will be used is part of this phenomenon.

I consider daily meditation of utmost importance, since in it we turn to the source of our energy, the Spirit, who must help us in our weakness. Perhaps the lack of personal reflective prayer is the very reason why so few Catholics are actively concerned about social issues. It requires a well-balanced judgment to accept the inevitable in faith and to do everything possible to improve a situation.

SCRIPTURE READING—

The Spirit too helps us in our weakness, for we do not know how to pray as we ought; but the Spirit himself makes intercession for us with groanings that cannot be expressed in speech. He who searches hearts knows what the Spirit means, for the Spirit intercedes for the saints as God himself wills. (Romans 8:26-27)

"We know that God makes all things work together for the good of those who love him"

A QUESTION that usually shocks teenagers is: "Do you think that your mother wanted you?" The answer is negative. Your mother wanted a baby, perhaps she had a preference for a boy or a girl, but she could not even want *you*, regardless of how much she loves you now. It is different with God. Paul states that he "foreknew" you, in other words, that you existed in God's mind from all eternity long before you actually came into being.

In today's Scripture, Paul enumerates four turning points in this life which bear evident traces of divine providence: (1) God foreknew us; (2) he predestined us; (3) he called us; (4) he justified (sanctified) us. In these four traces of divine providence in our lives, Paul sees a guarantee that ultimately God will also bestow upon us eternal salvation: he will glorify you.

This Bible reading deals again with hope *(see February 25)*. Hope, which deals with the "not-yet," is in constant need of encouragement in order to remain alive. Unless there is continual reassurance that the object of hope will someday materialize, it will die and we will become victims of despair or we will lose interest. Paul reasons: God's providence has started our Christian life on earth; his providence will also lead it to perfection in heaven. Keep this in mind whenever you are depresssed. An open eye for the traces of God's providence in our lives now will help keep hope for a bright future alive.

SCRIPTURE READING —

We know that God makes all things work together for the good of those who love him, who have been called according to his decree. Those whom he foreknew he predestined to share the image of his Son, that the Son might be the first-born of many brothers. Those he predestined he likewise called; those he called he also justified; and those he justified he in turn glorified. (Romans 8:28-30)

"Who will separate us from love of Christ?"

HAPPINESS on the human level is constantly exposed to the threat of the unexpected, which may terminate it at any time. Think of your own circle of friends or acquaintances: A happy marriage, financial security, lovely children—and then that car wreck which put an end to everything!

In chapter 8 of Romans, Paul has been dealing with God's love for us in Jesus Christ. Many Bible scholars see today's passage as a summary. Christ will not forsake us. It is not clear whether "the love of Christ" in verse 35 should be understood as "our love *for* Christ" or as "the love which Christ bears *for* us." In either case, as Paul states, nothing can come between us and Christ.

The threat which like a sword of Damocles hangs over all human happiness does not imperil our relationship of love with Christ Jesus. Paul lists a long series of possible dangers, even "angels and principalities" (good and bad spirits) and "powers, heights and depths" (mysterious cosmic forces, which to the mind of antiquity were hostile to mankind), but none of them can separate us from God's love that comes to us in Jesus Christ.

Some elderly friends of mine have gone through a great deal of pain and frustration, yet they are quite well balanced and never lose patience; they are kind, they are understanding, they radiate peace and happiness. What is their secret? Is it their awareness in faith that God is present to them with his loving care in Jesus Christ? I know that they read their Bible!

SCRIPTURE READING —

Who will separate us from the love of Christ? Trial, or distress, or persecution, or hunger, or nakedness, or danger, or the sword? Yet in all this we are more than conquerors because of him who has loved us. For I am certain that neither death nor life, neither angels nor principalities, neither the present nor the future, nor progress, neither height nor depth nor any other creature, will be able to separate us from the love of God that comes to us in Christ Jesus, our Lord.

(Romans 8:35, 37-39)

IN OBSERVING the animal world, we can be touched by the apparent affection a female is able to give to her puppies. But it shocks us, when we see how cruel that same animal can be to other animals which are not her offspring. Seemingly a woman has the same affectionate love for her baby. The instinctive emotional part of love is apparently the same. But there is a great difference. Human love is not merely emotional. It also contains an element of insight. Besides loving her own baby, a mother also loves other children.

This element of insight is even more decisive when love is elevated from the mere human level to the sacred, namely, Christian love, called charity. The insight which guides charity is faith. Today's Scripture deals with love of God and all others regardless of race, creed, or color. Paying attention to the insight of faith, which guides it, is important.

Being a good Samaritan requires faith, which tells me that all people, regardless of race, creed, or color, are brothers and sisters of one heavenly Father.

SCRIPTURE READING —

On one occasion a lawyer stood up to pose [to Jesus] this problem: "Teacher, what must I do to inherit everlasting life?" Jesus answered him: "What is written in the law? How do you read it?" He replied:

> **"You shall love the Lord your God with all your heart, with all your soul, with all your strength, and with all your mind; and your neighbor as yourself."**

Jesus said, "You have answered correctly. Do this and you shall live." But because he wished to justify himself he said to Jesus, "And who is my neighbor?" Jesus replied: "There was a man going down from Jerusalem to Jericho who fell prey to robbers. They stripped him, beat him, and then went off leaving him half-dead. A priest happened to be going down the same road; he saw him but continued on. Likewise there was a Levite who came the same way; he saw him and went on. But a Samaritan who was journeying alone came on him and was moved to pity at the sight. He approached him and dressed his wounds, pouring in oil and wine. He then hoisted him on his own beast and brought him to an inn, where he cared for him. The next day he took out two silver pieces and gave them to the innkeeper with the request: 'Look after him, and if there is any further expense I will repay you on my way back.'

"Which of these three, in your opinion, was neighbor to the man who fell in with the robbers?" The answer came, "The one who treated him with compassion." Jesus said to him, "Then go and do the same."

(Luke 10:25-37)

"How deep are the riches and the wisdom and the knowledge of God!"

ACCORDING to the little story that was circulating a few years ago, the first black female astronaut was asked whether she had seen God in outer space. The answer was: "Yes." "And what did he look like?" Answer: "*She* is *black*." We just cannot describe God as *he* is.

In attempting to approach the mystery of God, we do so necessarily in human terms, hence inadequately. If we sensitize ourselves in faith, we may experience him in daily life, in the love of a mother, spouse, child, friend. Most of all, we know about God through the experience of the Hebrews as reflected in the Bible and in the Christian tradition. Since the Bible came into being in a man's world, the biblical metaphors for God are usually masculine. When the lady-astronaut of the story states: "She [God] is black," she is as right as the authors of the Bible, who approach the Ultimate Reality as king, judge, or father. A Chinese or black God-the-Father picture is as appropriate as the traditional white grandfather of our grade school booklets!

In the faith that believes in Jesus of Nazareth, we see the Ultimate Reality as a person who cares, though we don't know whether God's personhood adequately covers our human concept of person. We should keep this in mind. A friend of mine, though highly educated, lost his faith and relates this to the fact that he has never loved his father. Possibly he has taken the biblical masculine metaphors for God too literally!

Paul has been trying to describe the bounteous love of God. In this Bible passage, we might say he gives up and exclaims in sudden emotion and gratitude: "How deep are the riches and the wisdom and the knowledge of God!" In our best moments, we should try to feel as Paul did, when prayerfully we meditate on the greatness, love, and wisdom of God.

SCRIPTURE READING —

How deep are the riches and the wisdom and the knowledge of God! How inscrutable his judgments, how unsearchable his ways! For "who has known the mind of the Lord? Or who has been his counselor? Who has given him anything so as to deserve return?" For from him and through him and for him all things are. To him be glory forever. Amen. (Romans 11:33-36)

"Do not conform yourselves to this age"

IN THE seventies, there is a complaint that our schools are no longer what they used to be. Employers complain that applicants for jobs can't read and write sufficiently, and colleges offer remedial reading classes. What is the reason why so many youngsters are not able to compose an intelligent paper after they have gone to school for twelve years? There is no reason to suppose that they are less capable than we were as high school students. Is it because the schools have lowered their standards, ever more complying with an easy-going society and perhaps with certain trends in contemporary psychology? Is it because they don't challenge our youngsters anymore to become the kind of persons they could be?

Paul states today: "Do not conform yourselves to this age, but be transformed by the renewal of your mind." We should constantly challenge ourselves and the youngsters in our care to grow into the design that God has in mind for each of us. We read the words: God's will—good—pleasing—perfect, and we should relate them to our growth as total persons. What is your value system? In the former chapters of Romans, Paul has been describing at length God's great love for man shown in sending his Son, Jesus Christ (Romans 1—11). Now he starts explaining Christian ethics as a response to that love. A life of love, a life of pleasing the beloved (God), is a challenge. Do you accept it? Have you lowered your ethical standards over the years? Taking the easy way out all the time will not obtain justification for you. Be constantly "transformed"!

SCRIPTURE READING —

And now, brothers, I beg you through the mercy of God to offer your bodies as a living sacrifice holy and acceptable to God, your spiritual worship. Do not conform yourselves to this age but be transformed by the renewal of your mind, so that you may judge what is God's will, what is good, pleasing and perfect. (Romans 12:1-2)

"Love is the fulfillment of the law"

AS CHILDREN we went by the rules laid down by our parents, and fear for punishment had much to do with our obedience. As grown-ups we should outgrow this childlike obedience to the laws of both country and Church and look at the reasons behind them. But I come across so many people who apparently have not not outgrown their childhood. Fear of punishment here or in the hereafter is their main reason for obeying the law. Perhaps Church leadership has something to do with this.

Jesus opposed the legalism of his religion. The awareness that love should be the guiding principle of a person's behavior was there (see Mark 12:28-34), but it was obscured by the many laws the rabbis had made and their insistence on following them meticulously. We saw a similar situation in the Catholic Church up to recent times. Perhaps as long as the majority of the faithful were not too well-educated we needed to be told in detail what to do and not do. Now we observe a growing awareness that the great law of love should be the starting point of our ethical thinking and not the many laws we have on the books.

"What is the loving thing to do in this situation?" That is what we must ask time and again. This kind of thinking does not make laws superfluous. We need laws that reflect the wisdom of our fellow human beings. They are helpful beacons in our dark and often confused situations. They may help us to find the way, and can be necessary to push us to do "the loving thing" in our situations whenever we are not as mature in our love as we should be.

Paul had to battle legalism, especially in his converts from Judaism who put such great emphasis on the observance of law. He puts the accent where it should be. Apply this to your own life situation!

SCRIPTURE READING —

Owe no debt to anyone except the debt that binds us to love one another. He who loves his neighbor has fulfilled the law. The commandments, "You shall not commit adultery; you shall not murder; you shall not steal; you shall not covet," and any other commandment there may be are all summed up in this, "You shall love your neighbor as yourself." Love never wrongs the neighbor, hence love is the fulfillment of the law. (Romans 13:8-10)

"While we live we are responsible to the Lord"

IN A WAY we are proud that in an open society like ours with a free press scandals can be brought into the open and criminals punished. On the other hand, it is disappointing to find out that high-ranking officials often abuse their power position by exercising irresponsible stewardship. Power seems to make the powerful dizzy. So easily they forget that power should be service and exercised responsibly.

We think here first of all of accountability on the human level. Just as it does not make sense to speak about love of God to a person who does not believe in love period, it is waste of time to speak of responsibility to God if a person is not ready to give account of the power he exercises even on the human level. Indeed, God gave us dominion over all living things (Genesis 1:28), but only as his partners in business. We must see management of this planet as "God & Children, Inc." As God's partners, we can and must develop our potentialities, but we remain responsible to the Lord.

All adults exercise power somehow, be it as parents, teachers, managers, priests, or religious superiors. Are you ready to render an account at any time, whether you practice power over fellow human beings (children, personnel, parishioners, fellow religious) or funds, both yours and whatever you handle for others?

Only when you are ready to open the books or explain your conduct at any time to somebody in charge are you practicing stewardship responsible to the Lord. As mentioned earlier *(March 2)*, Paul describes Christian ethics as a response to God's bounteous love for us. Is the power which you exercise a real service and always guided by love?

SCRIPTURE READING —

None of us lives as his own master and none of us dies as his own master. While we live we are responsible to the Lord, and when we die we die as his servants. Both in life and in death we are the Lord's. That is why Christ died and came to life again, that he might be Lord of both the dead and the living. (Romans 14:7-9)

"For me, 'life' means Christ"

IN PORT-AU-PRINCE, one of the poorest capitals of our northern hemisphere, I saw a huge banner in the center of town displaying a picture of the president-for-life Duvalier: *"L'idole du peuple Haitien"* ("The idol of the Haitian People"). I have my doubts about what most of the poorly clad and ill-fed Haitians think of it. Totalitarian countries seem to need idols to captivate the people around a hero and what he stands for. Think of the German people goiing wild over Hitler, the long lines of Russians in Moscow waiting to view the body of Lenin in his mausoleum, and the Chinese who are doing the same thing for Mao Tse-tung in Peking. I have more confidence in the thousands of Americans who visit the graveside of John F. Kennedy or who gather for a memorial march to honor Dr. Martin Luther King. At least their allegiance is freely chosen and not the result of threat or massive brainwashing.

Over the centuries millions of people have been captivated by the personality of Jesus of Nazareth and his ideas for a better world ("The Kingdom of God," as he called it). However, their image of him has been determined by time and culture. For the early Church, he was the Son of Man coming on the clouds of heaven; in the world of the Letter to the Hebrews, Jesus was the heavenly high priest; for Christians from Jewish background, he was the Messiah (Christ, king and freedom-bringer).

In Byzantium, we encounter the "Christ-Victor," Pantocrator and Sun-God, "Light of Light"; in the Middle Ages it was Jesus of the way of the cross and the Christmas cradle who captivated Christians. In France of the seventeenth century, "Christ, the Sacred Heart" became popular; in this century, it was first "Christ the King," and now after the experience of two world wars, we see Jesus as "the man for others" and recently as "The Liberator" (in some milieus even Jesus as Contestant and Revolutionary). Whatever the image of Jesus you cherish, are you captivated by it as Paul was?

SCRIPTURE READING —

For, to me, "life" means Christ; hence dying is so much gain. If, on the other hand, I am to go on living in the flesh, that means productive toil for me—and I do not know which to prefer. I am strongly attracted by both: I long to be freed from this life and to be with Christ, for that is the far better thing; yet it is more urgent that I remain alive for your sakes. (Philippians 1:21-24)

"United in spirit and ideals"

I HAD known him most of my life. John Smith had raised eight children. They had come one after another as God sent them. Respectfully obeying Holy Mother Church of those days, that's the way John and his wife had looked at it and though not without anxieties and problems, their common life had been a happy one. Now John's wife was dead, and all the children were married, raising children of their own—but none of them eight. The old man was not rich, but neither did he have financial problems. And all the children were doing fine as far as their monthly supply of greenbacks was concerned.

There was one thing, however, that ate John Smith up. He called it a nail in his coffin. His children were not getting along with one another as they should have been. True, they had their birthday parties, and John was always there. (Such things keep a family together.) But not all were present. Two of his children were not welcome. Somehow, somewhere, something had happened. I never found out whether it was the fault of in-laws or the big mouths of some of the children themselves. But they were not on speaking terms. And that hurt the old man's heart. Up in his eighties, he could cry about it. He used to say: "The only birthday present that pleases me is that all of you get along all right!"

Such things happen. The idealistic Paul of Tarsus, who had dedicated his entire life to preaching the Gospel, was at loggerheads with an equally great man, Barnabas (see Acts 15:36-41). It happens in the best of families, in convents, in rectories, and in congregations as well. But, definitely, it should *not* happen, since it is un-Christian. Check with yourself! And if things are all right, let God's word of today teach you how to keep it that way. Paul suffered as old John Smith did.

SCRIPTURE READING —

In the name of the encouragement you owe me in Christ, in the name of the solace that love can give, of fellowship in spirit, compassion, and pity, I beg you: make my joy complete by your unanimity, possessing the one love, united in spirit and ideals. Never act out of rivalry or conceit; rather, let all parties think humbly of others as superior to themselves, each of you looking to others' interests rather than his own. Your attitude must be that of Christ.

(Philippians 2:1-5)

"Dismiss all anxieties from your minds"

HE TOLD me that his mother was the Church. I got to know Pat when he was in his mid-sixties—a beautiful but to a certain extent also a sad person. Pat had never known his parents. His mother had brought him as a little boy of two to the orphanage. There was also a little girl, obviously his sister. But his mother had kept her. Time and again, Pat had tried to find out more about his origin, but was told by the chancery office and the sisters of the orphanage that it was better for him not to know. Finally, he had accepted.

Serving his country, Pat had gone through all the miseries of World War II. Working his way through the South Pacific, New Guinea, all the way up to the Philippines, he came out as one of the few survivors of his outfit. Never was he seriously wounded, but he had contracted an intestinal disease which had bothered him for many years. After his horrible experience in the Far East, Pat had wanted to dedicate his life to God as a religious brother, but no community wanted him. Maybe it was his obscure origin, or his health, or his independent way of thinking—I really don't know.

But Pat had worked all of his life in the home missions, mending, plumbing, painting, landscaping for pastors and sisters. He was appreciative of what the Church had done for him. He told me about the monsignor who had given him his own family name, and about the sisters in the orphanage where he stayed till he was eighteen and drafted into the army. But there was a lack. As a little fellow, Pat had never known affectionate love. Never had a sister taken him on her lap and hugged him. Nevertheless, he considered the Church as his mother, though not a very affectionate one.

I don't know whether Pat has ever read today's Bible passage. But he is a man of prayer, and by doing what Paul tells us to do he has been living a meaningful life. Certainly, God's own peace in Christ Jesus stands guard over his heart and mind. I am grateful for the parental love and affection which I experienced in my infancy. All of us should be! But when we are depressed, we should listen to Paul and do what Pat teaches by his example.

SCRIPTURE READING —

Dismiss all anxiety from your minds. Present your needs to God in every form of prayer and in petitions full of gratitude. Then God's own peace, which is beyond all understanding, will stand guard over your hearts and minds, in Christ Jesus. (Philippians 4:6-7)

"Nonetheless, it was kind of you"

FROM my history book in high school I remember a picture of a medieval friar with a crucifix in his hand and high up a man dangling on a rope, obviously sentenced to death by hanging. Assisting penitent criminals in their last moments was a lugubrious facet of the priestly profession which I thought of as past history. Never did it dawn on me then that I myself would have to exercise such a duty. Yet I have done it more than once, but I remember best Radja [King] Pius, who was sentenced to death for collaborating viciously with the Japanese occupation forces in the Dutch East Indies.

I visited Radja Pius quite often in jail, heard his confession, and gave him Holy Communion the morning before his death. At the place of execution, blindfolded, the Radja was ushered from the truck by soldiers and bound at a pole. An envelope was pinned on his shirt over his heart, while ten riflemen stood on duty. I said a few words about God's mercy, and we prayed an act of contrition. Then I stood behind the firing squad. The officer in charge gave a sign with his hand, a volley of rifle shots split the air, and all was over. The grave was already dug. No coffin was used. Japanese prisoners took care of the remains. Radja Pius, who was responsible for many murders, was ultimately able to accept death in the Christian perspective.

Paul states that he could do everything with the help of Christ but was simultaneously grateful for the supportive kindness of fellow human beings. In Radja Pius' case, God's supportive kindness was offered through the priest who happened to be his prison chaplain. In my Bible, I have underlined: "In him . . . I have strength for everything" and "it was kind of you to want to share in my hardships."

SCRIPTURE READING —

I am experienced in being brought low, yet I know what it is to have an abundance. I have learned how to cope with every circumstance —how to eat well or go hungry, to be well provided for or do without. In him who is the source of my strength I have strength for everything.

Nonetheless, it was kind of you to want to share in my hardships.

My God in turn will supply your needs fully, in a way worthy of his magnificent riches in Christ Jesus. All glory to our God and Father for unending ages! Amen. (Philippians 4:12-14, 19-20)

"Proving your faith . . . laboring in love . . . showing constancy in hope in our Lord"

IN THE puritanical society of Russia today the party member is expected to be the most puritanical of all. While others may occasionally get drunk, skip a day's work or even go to church, the party member is required to set an example of Soviet morality. If he fails to do so he can expect to lose his party card.

We Christians are supposed to be like yeast in dough, having an uplifting impact. The dough is the community. A Christian congregation is the yeast. Do we have an uplifting impact by word and example? And if we try, how do we do it? Only 5% of the Russian population belongs to the party. Membership is a highly prized privilege. Besides by giving a good example of Soviet morality, the party uses means like brainwashing and force.

Much to our shame we must confess that over centuries Christians have fallen for the worldly temptation to do the same. Wherever Christians establish a majority, the temptation to impose their outlook by force is there. And if not by force, as during the time of the Crusades and Inquisition, we have tried to impress others by what history calls "triumphalism." Expensive and impressive church buildings, school plants, organizations, and Catholic conventions were there to prove that we were right and they (the others!) were wrong.

And now we turn to today's Bible reading. What does Paul praise the congregation of Thessalonica for? It is for *proving* their faith, for *laboring* in love, for *showing constancy* in hope in our Lord! Are you like yeast in the dough, wherever you are, and do you try to do it the way Paul thought it should be done? We could learn a few things from the Soviet party members!

SCRIPTURE READING —

We [Paul and his associates] keep thanking God for all of you and we remember you in our prayers, for we constantly are mindful before our God and Father of the way you are proving your faith, and laboring in love, and showing constancy of hope in our Lord Jesus Christ. We know, too, brothers beloved of God, how you were chosen. Our preaching of the gospel proved not a mere matter of words for you but one of power; it was carried on in the Holy Spirit and out of complete conviction. You know as well as we do what we proved to be like when, while still among you, we acted on your behalf. (1 Thessalonians 1:2-5)

"The word of the Lord has echoed forth from you resoundingly"

THE other day, I was visiting friends of mine when the doorbell rang. The lady of the house peeped through the window and told us: "Those witnesses of Jehovah again"; then she told her teenage daughter: "Don't open!" The doorbell rang a second and a third time; then there was a persistent knocking for a few more seconds. Although I am not drawn to the way in which many bear witness to what they believe in, I still admire these people's dedication.

On a Sunday afternoon which happened to be Easter, Garry, a very artistic and creatively active friend of mine, had a talk with his neighbor on his patio. This neighbor was a certified accountant, hence not without formal education. But he did not know what Christians mean by Easter. Garry explained the mysterious transfiguration of death we go through to participate in the everlasting life of the risen Lord Jesus. The certified accountant answered laconically: "And you believe that?" "I certainly do!" Garry witnessed in his own spontaneous way. The accountant's children are now in the Catholic school, and Garry observes a change of thinking in his neighbor's household. Obviously, it is dawning upon them that computers and adding machines don't have all the answers!

Witnessing is part of your being a Christian. How you do it is part of your own psychic composition. Can Paul praise you as he did the Thessalonians?

SCRIPTURE READING —

You know as well as we do what we proved to be like when, while still among you, we acted on your behalf. You, in turn, became imitators of us and of the Lord, receiving the word despite great trials, with the joy that comes from the Holy Spirit. Thus you became a model for all the believers of Macedonia and Achaia. The word of the Lord has echoed forth from you resoundingly.

This is true not only in Macedonia and Achaia; throughout every region your faith in God is celebrated, which makes it needless for us to say anything more. The people of those parts are reporting what kind of reception we had from you, and how you turned to God from idols, to serve him who is the living and true God and to await from heaven the Son he raised from the dead—Jesus, who delivers us from the wrath to come. (1 Thessalonians 1:5-10)

"As gentle as any nursing mother"

ONE of the wrongs the Church is blamed for is male chauvinism. It happens that the Founder of the Christian movement has handed down his authority to males (see Matthew 28:16-20), and seemingly those males are not going to share their power with females in the near future. One of the most successful early preachers, Paul of Tarsus, followed the footsteps of the Master and is considered a male chauvinist as well (see 1 Corinthians 11: 1-16; 1:33-36). The founders of the Church were children of their time and culture, which was a man's world. We should keep in mind that the Holy Spirit who inspired Jesus of Nazareth and his early helpers did not give them an insight into how American women of the latter part of the twentieth century would look at male-female relations.

In today's Bible reading, Paul does not seem to be a diehard male chauvinist. He compares his love for the congregation, which he has founded in Thessalonica, with the love of a mother fondling her little ones. However, many Catholics in this country might qualify Paul's statement—if not "paternalistic" then "maternalistic." We still call our priests "father." Are we going to call our female priests of the future "mother"?

What we should learn from today's reading is that God's message in the Bible is necessarily wrapped in concepts and hence in a terminology which is conditioned by time and culture and as such not part of the message. Therefore, there should be a constant translation of the essentials. In the sixties we saw a push for civil rights for black citizens. The seventies will go down in history as the decade of women's liberation, which eventually will be realized also in the Church. Meanwhile, we should not damage the relationship of love between the faithful in the pews and those in the sanctuary, regardless of who happens to be in charge of proclaiming "the word of God."

SCRIPTURE READING —

While we were among you we were as gentle as any nursing mother fondling her little ones. So well disposed were we to you, in fact, that we wanted to share with you not only God's tidings but our very lives, so dear had you become to us. You must recall, brothers, our efforts and our toil: how we worked day and night all the time we preached God's good tidings to you in order not to impose on you in any way.

(1 Thessalonians 2:7-9)

"We shall be with the Lord unceasingly"

THE French philosopher Gabriel Marcel has given valuable insights into what friends can mean to one another. He states: "It can happen that a bond of feeling is created between me and the other person, if, for example, I discover an experience we have both shared (we have both been to a certain place, have run the same risks, have criticized a certain individual, or read and loved the same book); hence a unity is established in which the other person and myself become *we,* and this means that he ceases to be *him* and becomes *thou;* the words 'you too' in this context take on a primary value. Literally speaking, we communicate; the other person . . . has fused into the living unity he now forms with me. The path leading from dialectic to love has now been opened *(Creative Fidelity,* p. 33).

Though Paul had never seen the Lord bodily, he loved him dearly. He experienced him as present to him in faith and was convinced that this presence would flower into a face-to-face presence in the life to come. "We shall be with the Lord unceasingly" (1 Thessalonians 4:17). Notice that the way the message is worded is conditioned by Paul's time and culture *(see March 11):* (1) Paul is under the misconception that our Lord will return during his own lifetime. (2) He uses the traditional biblical imagery of clouds, angels, blasting trumpets, etc. to describe God's splendor and our sharing in it. (3) He describes the event against the background of the world vision of his time: heaven up—earth in the middle—netherworld (hell) down. Only the message: "We shall be with the Lord unceasingly" is God's word to you.

Apply Gabriel Marcel's analysis of how a friendship develops to your relationship with the Lord Jesus as you know him in faith. The more intimate (as a person to person) your relationship with Jesus grows now, the more beautiful it will be later.

SCRIPTURE READING —

We say to you, as if the Lord himself had said it, that we who live, who survive until his coming, will in no way have an advantage over those who have fallen asleep. No, the Lord himself will come down from heaven at the word of command, at the sound of the archangel's voice and God's trumpet; and those who have died in Christ will rise first. Then we, the living, the survivors, will be caught up with them in the clouds to meet the Lord in the air. Thenceforth we shall be with the Lord unceasingly. Console one another with this message.

(1 Thessalonians 4:15-18)

"Awake and sober"

WHEN I open our local newspaper on Monday, I always read the report on automobile accidents. Who has died or has been maimed for life this past weekend? Most of the victims are young people who had been drinking or in their youthful recklessness showing their dates how brave they were. Anyway, they were not awake, concentrating on what they were doing, and quite often not sober. Sometimes, they are known to me as alumni of our school. Brilliant young people with all of life ahead of them, they ruined it in one careless moment.

Although Paul obviously had reasons to praise the congregation of Thessalonica (see previous readings), he also has a serious warning for them. Do we need such a warning? If we read a passage like today's out of its context, forgetting that our relationship with God is one of love, it could make us see God as a law enforcement officer: Christ coming as a thief in the night, catching you off guard. The police are out with radar and catch you speeding!

When two married people love one another they will not put themselves in an embarrassing situation. They don't have to take precautions when the partner comes home. If love is alive, they don't even think of the possibility of being caught off guard. This would be the ideal situation between us and God! It is a relationship of love which we should foster and keep alive. But are we always that mature in love as far as our relationship with God is concerned? He is the great Lover, but invisible, and we as children of Adam and Eve are not always as mature as we should be. If God would call you right now, are you the kind of a person you want to be for all eternity? Bible readings like this are salutary so long as we walk in this valley of darkness.

SCRIPTURE READING —

As regards specific times and moments, brothers, we do not need to write you; you know very well that the day of the Lord is coming like a thief in the night. Just when people are saying, "Peace and security," ruin will fall on them with the suddenness of pains overtaking a woman in labor, and there will be no escape. You are not in the dark, brothers, that the day should catch you off guard, like a thief. No, all of you are children of light and of the day. We belong neither to darkness nor to night. (1 Thessalonians 5:1-5)

"So that God may be all in all"

FAMILY reunions are favored American happenings. It may be at Thanksgiving, July 4, or the grandparents' golden anniversary, but the children with their families come from all over the country to celebrate. The smell of barbecued chicken, ribs, and the like is all over the place. Grandchildren in all shapes and sizes play ball games in the backyard with dad or uncle Pat, who feels young for the occasion. Mothers wipe the little ones' noses, meanwhile preparing the salad. And the grandparents, who started all of this years ago, are the happy onlookers.

At the end of time, God will be "all in all." It will be a family reunion, indeed! Quite often the Bible uses the banquet or wedding-party model to describe the happy togetherness of all the elect with Almighty God (see Matthew 22:1-4; Revelation 19:7-8). But keep in mind that these are figures of speech. In the past, writers more pious than versed in sacred scholarship have ventured into all kinds of speculations concerning this happy future, but in reality we know very little about it other than the important point that our happiness will be "hundredfold" (see Matthew 19:23-30). Life is like the days before Christmas. The packages lie under the tree, but we must wait!

In today's reading, Paul sees all the elect as one in Christ. "The first fruits" refers to the offering of first fruits as a means of consecrating an entire harvest to God. Thus our resurrection is consecrated to God by that of Jesus.

SCRIPTURE READING —

But as it is, Christ is now raised from the dead, the first fruits of those who have fallen asleep. Death came through a man; hence the resurrection of the dead comes through a man also. Just as in Adam all die, so in Christ all will come to life again, but each one in proper order: Christ the first fruits and then, at his coming, all those who belong to him. After that will come the end, when, after having destroyed every sovereignity, authority, and power, he will hand over the kingdom to God the Father.

Christ must reign until God has put all enemies under his feet, and the last enemy to be destroyed is death. When, finally, all has been subjected to the Son, he will then subject himself to the One who made all things subject to him, so that God may be all in all.

(1 Corinthians 15:20-26, 28)

"Away with you, Satan!"

SINCE man is both God's masterpiece and a fallen creature, temptation and sin are daily realities which no psychology can talk away. It may be true that "temptation and sin" have been over-emphasized in the past. Theologians were wont to offer long lists of sins, listed for the most part under the tag of "mortal" and "venial," whereas the reality is not quite so simple. However, this does not mean that temptation and sin are all of a sudden non-existent either.

Pondering the words of Jesus in his heart, Matthew meditates on the meaning of three typical temptations which constantly threaten Christianity: (1) God may not be used for one's own gain or profit (turning stones into bread); (2) faith has nothing to do with the spectacular ("throw yourself down"); (3) and religion may not be mixed up with political power (kingdoms displayed in their magnificence). Jesus answers with three quotations from Scripture. We who are the Church of this age and prone to these same temptations should keep in mind our Lord's example.

SCRIPTURE READING —

Jesus was led into the desert by the Spirit to be tempted by the devil. He fasted forty days and forty nights, and afterward was hungry. The tempter approached and said to him, "If you are the Son of God, command these stones to turn into bread." Jesus replied, "Scripture has it:

'Not on bread alone is man to live
but on every utterance that comes from the mouth of God.'"

Next the devil took him to the holy city, set him on the parapet of the temple, and said, "If you are the Son of God, throw yourself down. Scripture has it:

'He will bid his angels take care of you;
with their hands they will support you
that you may never stumble on a stone.'"

Jesus answered him, "Scripture also has it:

'You shall not put the Lord your God to the test.'"

The devil then took him up a very high mountain and displayed before him all the kingdoms of the world in their magnificence, promising, "All these will I bestow on you if you prostrate yourself in homage before me." At this, Jesus said to him, "Away with you, Satan! Scripture has it:

'You shall do homage to the Lord your God;
him alone shall you adore.'"

At that the devil left him, and angels came and waited on him.

(Matthew 4:1-11)

March 16

"Did God really tell you not to eat?"

ONE of the great temptations which ruin beautiful relationships (marriage, friendship) is the routine of daily failures. It is a kind of indifference which renders a love-relationship stale and trite. Finally, it gets boring and the next step is a breakup.

Today's Scripture should make us take a realistic look at our relationship with our marriage partner, friends, children, and parents in whom God approaches us and our direct relationship with God in both private prayer and worship. Beware of the temptation of indifference!

Who am I? Who am I supposed to be? I am dust *(Ash Wednesday)* but also related to God. Inspired by God, the sacred writer uses a beautiful allegory to teach us about the reality of temptation and sin in our lives. Notice the woman (you and I) playing with temptation! The proposal is pleasing to her eyes! After some hesitation, the consent follows. Then the eyes of the man and woman are opened—too late of course! You and I could do the same!

SCRIPTURE READING —

Now the serpent was the most cunning of all the animals that the Lord God had made. The serpent asked the woman, "Did God really tell you not to eat from any of the trees in the garden?" The woman answered the serpent: "We may eat of the fruit of the trees in the garden; it is only about the fruit of the tree in the middle of the garden that God said, 'You shall not eat it or even touch it, lest you die.'" But the serpent said to the woman: "You certainly will not die! No, God knows well that the moment you eat of it you will be like the gods who know what is good and what is bad."

The woman saw that the tree was good for food, pleasing to the eyes, and desirable for gaining wisdom. So she took some of its fruit and ate it; and she also gave some to her husband, who was with her, and he ate it. Then the eyes of both of them were opened, and they realized that they were naked; so they sewed fig leaves together and made loincloths for themselves. (Genesis 3:1-7)

March 17

"God has saved us and has called us to a holy life"

IN THE Catholic tradition, the idea of vocation (calling) was very much restricted to priesthood and religious life. We should not forget that this special call rests upon the general call, which is basic to all Christians, namely, the call to a new existence.

Your call in life implies three elements. The first is *God's free choice*—"not because of any merit of ours, but according to his own design" (2 Timothy 1:9). The second is a *mission*, which could entail leaving the safe, the familiar, the known, and accepting the new and untried. "Bear your share of the hardship which the gospel entails" (2 Timothy 1:8). As a Christian, you do have a mission to your family, your parish, your community, co-workers on your job, fellow students in school, friends. The third is a *promise*, which in Abraham's case consisted of a posterity—children. "I will make of you a great nation" (Genesis 12:2). In the case of Christians it consists of life and immortality.

An appreciative fidelity to your calling requires faith. The promise of immortality is real but cannot be verified. Fidelity to your call may entail hardship, especially when you have to be among people who live more or less unholy lives. Do you have the courage to be different? Think of the promise and pray for faith!

SCRIPTURE READING —

Never be ashamed of your testimony to our Lord, nor of me, a prisoner for his sake; but with the strength which comes from God bear your share of the hardship which the gospel entails.

God has saved us and has called us to a holy life, not because of any merit of ours but according to his own design—the grace held out to us in Christ Jesus before the world began but now made manifest through the appearance of our Savior. He has robbed death of its power and has brought life and immortality into clear light through the gospel.

(2 Timothy 1:8-10)

"If only you recognized God's gift . . ."

PEOPLE will always be hungry and thirsty again. Besides a continued need for food and drink, man has many more wishes and desires, sometimes even conflicting ones. Man may yearn for truth, freedom, justice, love, which require more perfect fulfillment time and again. God-with-us in the Lord Jesus is ready to satisfy man's desires. The Bible uses a wealth of symbols to bring this out, among which are bread, wine, oil, and light.

Today's Bible reading uses the symbolism of water. Water is life-giving. God's people lived in a land surrounded by barren deserts, and water constituted a question of life and death. The symbol of water is used to describe God's life-giving presence. It is referred to as "God's gift." "living water," "the water which shall become a fountain within man, leaping up to . . . eternal life."

The Samaritan woman stands for all of us. We should cultivate our understanding of biblical symbols. You were baptized with water. It gave you life everlasting. Making the sign of the cross with holy water when you enter church for worship is a reminder of your baptism. Make this symbolism meaningful!

SCRIPTURE READING —

When a Samaritan woman came to draw water, Jesus said to her, "Give me a drink." (His disciples had gone off to the town to buy provisions.) The Samaritan woman said to him, "You are a Jew. How can you ask me, a Samaritan and a woman, for a drink?" (Recall that Jews have nothing to do with Samaritans.) Jesus replied:

"If only you recognized God's gift,
and who it is that is asking you for a drink,
you would have asked him instead,
and he would have given you living water."

"Sir," she challenged him, "you do not have a bucket and this well is deep. Where do you expect to get this flowing water? Surely you do not pretend to be greater than our ancestor Jacob, who gave us this well and drank from it with his sons and his flocks?" Jesus replied:

"Everyone who drinks this water
will be thirsty again.
But whoever drinks the water I give him
will never be thirsty;
no, the water I give
shall become a fountain within him,
leaping up to provide eternal life." (John 4:7-14)

March 19

"An upright man, unwilling to expose her to the law"

IN ORDER to have one's name on the "Who's Who" list, or to be mentioned in the obituary of the national maganizes, one must have accomplished something substantial by worldly standards. One must be at least a kind of hero, or in the negative a very controversial figure, if one wants to be remembered in an encyclopedia. St. Joseph, the husband of Mary, would never have qualified.

All we know about Joseph is that he was an upright man, unwilling to expose his fiancée in a very embarrassing situation; that, in faith, he was obedient to God; and that he searched for his lost child—something every parent would have done. Nevertheless, Joseph is remembered by a special solemnity. He had a very special call in life and was faithful to it. God's standard of greatness is different from ours.

Notice that in this tradition Joseph is central; it is he who receives the revelation from God. "Mary was engaged to Joseph": the marriage contract was drawn up between the parents of the couple. The marriage ceremony was accomplished when the groom took the bride into his house. Joseph shows great self-restraint in this situation.

Fidelity to your call in life and fairness in judgment of others, innocent till proven guilty, could be God's word to you today.

SCRIPTURE READING —

Jacob was the father of Joseph the husband of Mary.

It was of her that Jesus who is called the Messiah was born.

Now this is how the birth of Jesus Christ came about. When his mother Mary was engaged to Joseph, but before they lived together, she was found with child through the power of the Holy Spirit. Joseph her husband, an upright man unwilling to expose her to the law, decided to divorce her quietly. Such was his intention when suddenly the angel of the Lord appeared in a dream and said to him: "Joseph, son of David, have no fear about taking Mary as your wife. It is by the Holy Spirit that she has conceived this child. She is to have a son and you are to name him Jesus because he will save his people from their sins."

When Joseph awoke he did as the angel of the Lord had directed him and received her into his home as his wife.

(Matthew 1:16, 18-21, 24)

"I do believe, Lord"

WE ARE often asked to take a stand, be it concerning politics, the education of the children, or the way work should be done. Taking a stand, especially one concerning a controversial issue, may involve opposition.

The Scripture reading shows us the parents of the blind man (who do not want to be involved), the neighbors (who are indifferent), the Pharisees (who do not believe), the blind man himself (a believer). Where do you stand? Does the Lord Jesus and the philosophy of life he stands for have real impact on your life-style? Each of the four categories mentioned above is found in today's society. You must take a stand.

SCRIPTURE READING —

As [Jesus] walked along, he saw a man who had been blind from birth. Jesus spat on the ground, made mud with his saliva, and smeared the man's eyes with the mud. Then he told him, "Go, wash in the pool of Siloam." . . . So the man went off and washed, and came back able to see.

They took the man who had been born blind to the Pharisees. (Note that it was on a sabbath that Jesus had made the mud paste and opened his eyes.) The Pharisees, in turn, began to inquire how he had recovered his sight. He told them, "He put mud on my eyes. I washed it off, and now I can see." This prompted some of the Pharisees to assert, "This man cannot be from God because he does not keep the sabbath." Others objected, "If a man is a sinner, how can he perform signs like these?" They were sharply divided over him. Then they addressed the blind man again: "Since it was your eyes he opened, what do you have to say about him?" "He is a prophet," he replied.

The Jews refused to believe that he had really been born blind and had begun to see, until they summoned the parents of this man who now could see. "Is this your own son?" they asked, "and if so, do you attest that he was blind at birth? How do you account for the fact that now he can see?" The parents answered: "We know this is our son, and we know he was blind at birth. But how he can see now, or who opened his eyes, we have no idea. Ask him. He is old enough to speak for himself."

When Jesus heard of his expulsion, he sought him out and asked him, "Do you believe in the Son of Man?" He answered, "Who is he, sir, that I may believe in him?" "You have seen him," Jesus replied. "He is speaking to you now." "I do believe, Lord," he said, and bowed down to worship him. (John 9:1, 6-7, 13-21, 35-38)

"Lazarus, come out"

EVERYONE wants to make the best of his life. We love life, but we experience daily how brittle it is. There are people who try to live without restraints. They follow the epicurean philosophy of the pagan Romans: "Let us eat and drink, for tomorrow we may die." But we could also look at life in the following way: In order to transcend life, I must die to my old, immature, egotistic self. If I want to become a mature and grown-up person, I must leave my youth behind me. Does this make sense? Is it meaningful to be generous and dedicated to ideals, to "mature in Christ," as the Bible puts it, if everything collapses with death anyway?

John relates Jesus' miracles as "signs," earthly realities which indicate a full reality to come. Inspired by God, what does John wish to indicate by relating this miracle of Jesus? We notice that the evangelist places the Lazarus story just before the passion narrative. Significantly, he remarks: "From that day onward there was a plan afoot to kill Jesus!" (John 11:53). This passage teaches: Jesus, calling himself the resurrection and the life, will die to inaugurate the resurrection of man. "As the Father raises the dead and gives them life, so the Son gives life to anyone he chooses" (John 5:21). John suggests that you should put your faith in Jesus as many Jews did when they witnessed the raising of Lazarus.

SCRIPTURE READING —

Troubled in spirit, Jesus approached the tomb [of Lazarus].

It was a cave with a stone laid across it. "Take away the stone," Jesus directed. Martha, the dead man's sister, said to him, "Lord, it has been four days now; surely there will be a stench!" Jesus replied, "Did I not assure you that if you believed you would see the glory of God displayed?" They then took away the stone and Jesus looked upward and said:

"Father, I thank you for having heard me.
I know that you always hear me
but I have said this for the sake of the crowd,
that they may believe that you sent me."

Having said this he called loudly, "Lazarus, come out!" The dead man came out, bound hand and foot with linen strips, his face wrapped in a cloth. "Untie him," Jesus told them, "and let him go free."

(John 11:38-44)

"He stayed in the wasteland forty days"

SEEING New York from the Empire State Building gives a view which the man in the street cannot have. The astronauts saw the earth and life on it from a distance. This has changed them. Many of them have admitted that they experienced a new sense of God. We can only surmise their experience by looking at their pictures of that bluish ball silently circling around in an unfriendly universe. The POWs in Vietnam had a similar experience. That time of isolation has done something to them.

In the Catholic tradition, we have our retreat houses, parish missions, and annual Lenten observance. It is the idea of getting off "the merry-go-round" for a while and standing away from life in order to take a realistic look at ourselves. Through the mass media modern life is constantly imposing its neon-light values on all of us. These values are glittering and tempting.

In this passage, we read about the test (temptations), Satan (the devil), the wild beasts (every kind of threat and evil), and angels (God's protection). Nothing has changed. All of this is still in and around us! The temptation to fall for warped values is perhaps even more powerful than it has ever been. Jesus gives the example of going into solitude. Making a retreat occasionally is very beneficial. Observing Lent can be done by all. Jesus is victorious over the powers of evil. Angels will wait on us, if only we ask God for help. Have a realistic look at yourself and reform your life.

SCRIPTURE READING —

The Spirit sent [Jesus] out toward the desert. He stayed in the wasteland forty days, put to the test there by Satan. He was with the wild beasts, and angels waited on him.

After John's arrest, Jesus appeared in Galilee proclaiming the good news of God: "This is the time of fulfillment. The reign of God is at hand! Reform your lives and believe in the gospel!" (Mark 1:12-15)

"If God is for us, who can be against us?"

A TIME of obscurity in our lives can constitute a more severe mental pain than any physical suffering. It may be a time of doubt about values which we cherished as sacred in the past, fidelity in a stale marriage situation, commitment to religion in a parish setting which does not excite us, or dedication to a job under changed circumstances and with all other avenues closed. In each case, we do not know where to turn.

Young people have problems with their faith. In their process of maturation they question all values, religion included, till they find themselves. More serious is the obscure situation grown-ups may go through. We think of the professionals who work daily with test tubes, statistics, and computer results. They must know exactly what is going on. But this kind of one-sided pragmatism does not work in the field of interpersonal relations. How can we keep values like love and faith alive even when they are tempted by obscurity, confusion, and doubt?

"If God is for us, who can be against us?" This one line in today's Scripture states in a nutshell what the Bible teaches elsewhere time and again in story form. Abraham experienced it when he was faithful in the darkest moment of his life *(see February 3)*. The three apostles felt it when, in their doubt and embarrassment about the necessity of suffering in life, they enjoyed a moment of light and glory on the mountain (Mark 9:2-10). We, God's chosen ones, should find consolation and courage in these words when we pass through the valley of darkness, doubt, and mental suffering.

SCRIPTURE READING —

What shall we say after that? If God is for us, who can be against us? Is it possible that he who did not spare his own Son but handed him over for the sake of us all will not grant us all things besides? Who shall bring a charge against God's chosen ones? God, who justifies? Who shall condemn them? Christ Jesus, who died or rather was raised up, who is at the right hand of God and who intercedes for us?

(Romans 8:31-34)

"I, the Lord, am your God"

WE ARE proud to be a nation ruled by laws and not by whims of individuals. There is much wisdom invested in our Constitution and in most of our other laws as well. But when we permit things to get out of control and do not let the laws work as was intended by the founding fathers, the country is in trouble. However, when the insight that we are a nation under the laws prevails once again, and we let the system work, we recover from setbacks.

We must be careful, nevertheless, not to regard God's commandments as mere civil laws. In our relation to God, we Christians see ourselves in a family setting. The wish of a father who cares for his children is not a law, as we have civil laws on the books. We are related to God as children to a loving father. There is one absolute rule we go by and that is love for God and neighbor. Other commandments derive their reason for existence only from the law of love (Matthew 22:40).

Since civil and religious laws were so intimately intertwined in Hebrew culture, we must read the laws of the Old Testament with this in mind. Civil laws and laws clearly conditioned by time and culture (e.g., dietary laws) do not bind us any longer. The Ten Commandments, however, are timeless. There is not only human but also divine wisdom imbedded in them. But, in observing laws, we should be motivated by love: "You did not receive a spirit of slavery leading you back into fear, but a spirit of adoption through which we cry out, 'Abba!' (that is, 'Father')" (Romans 8:15).

SCRIPTURE READING —

God delivered all these commandments:

"I, the Lord, am your God, who brought you out of the land of Egypt, that place of slavery. You shall not have other gods besides me.

"You shall not take the name of the Lord, your God, in vain. For the Lord will not leave unpunished him who takes his name in vain.

"Remember to keep holy the sabbath day.

"Honor your father and your mother, that you may have a long life in the land which the Lord, your God, is giving you.

"You shall not kill.

"You shall not commit adultery.

"You shall not steal.

"You shall not bear false witness against your neighbor.

"You shall not covet your neighbor's house. You shall not covet your neighbor's wife, nor his male or female slave, nor his ox or ass, nor anything else that belongs to him." (Exodus 20:1-3, 7-8, 12-17)

"That all who believe may have eternal life in him"

TIME and again we see them pass by on our television screens, the refugees, driven away from their homes by floods, famine, wars. They live in miserable shacks or refugee camps. Clothed in rags, with starving babies on the hip, they stand in line with a plate, waiting for some meager food. What human misery! These people are homesick. They want desperately to go back to their homes, but often machine guns and barbed wire prevent their return.

The Jews carried away into exile in Babylon were exactly like the dislocated persons of our day. And since the Hebrew writers saw exile and suffering as a divine punishment for sin, the miserable situation, famine, want, and longing for home of these exiles point to the sinful human condition of all. The Bible invites us to be aware of how alienated sinful man is. Return is possible through Christ, who was lifted up on the cross, died, and rose again, "that all who believe may have eternal life in him" (John 3:15).

The Book of Numbers (21:4-9) relates a beautiful tradition. In the desert on their way to the promised land, some of the chosen people were bitten by serpents and many of them died. At God's command, Moses made a bronze serpent and mounted it on a pole. Whenever anyone who had been bitten by a serpent looked at the bronze serpent, he recovered. The serpent stands for the evil one (John 3:6). All who have been bitten must die, but looking to the Son of Man, lifted up on the cross, will save them. Looking to Christ means, of course, looking with faith and repentance! Do you have a crucifix in your home and do you ever look at it with faith and repentance?

SCRIPTURE READING —

[Jesus said to Nicodemus:]
Just as Moses lifted up the serpent in the desert,
so must the Son of Man be lifted up,
that all who believe
may have eternal life in him.
Yes, God so loved the world
that he gave his only Son,
that whoever believes in him may not die
but may have eternal life.
God did not send the Son into the world
to condemn the world,
but that the world might be saved through him.
Whoever believes in him avoids condemnation,
but whoever does not believe is already condemned
for not believing in the name of God's only Son.
(John 3:14-18)

EASTER

WHEN our country celebrates Independence Day and the Jews their Passover, both celebrate freedom gained at the cost of blood and tears. But what a difference between the two celebrations! Where ours is mainly a civic affair with cookouts and picnics, the Jews have kept God in the picture clearly. As Jewish tradition has it: "From generation to generation everyone must consider himself as having personally gone out of Egypt. Therefore we must thank him [God] and praise him who led our fathers and us through these wonderful things out of slavery to freedom" (Mishna 10, 5).

The early Church, emerging from Judaism, continued to celebrate the Jewish Passover, but with a new content. The Passover lamb offered to God in thanksgiving became "the Lamb of God who takes away the sins of the world." "Christ, our Passover, has been sacrificed. Let us celebrate!" (1 Corinthians 5:7-8). And the freedom gained in blood and tears is our redemption gained by the Lord's sufferings and consummated by his Resurrection.

Easter is the highlight of all Christian celebrations. With Pentecost as its completion it lasts fifty days. "Let us celebrate the feast not with the old yeast, that of corruption and wickedness, but with the unleavened bread of sincerity and truth" (1 Corinthians 5:8).

The Lord has been Raised.

Luke 24:34

Luke 24:34

"Unless the grain of wheat falls to the earth and dies . . ."

OBSERVING nature carefully makes us wonder about the mysterious cycle of life, death, and through death new life again. It is the mystery of the grain of wheat, which falls to the earth and dies in order to produce an abundance of new life, which transcends itself in both quality and quantity. From biology in high school, we remember "metamorphosis," the post-embryonic change in form of an animal, as when the larva of an insect becomes a pupa or a tadpole changes into a frog. Metamorphosis is a mysterious development of life.

In dealing with the mystery of human life and death, the Bible refers to these phenomena in nature in order to indicate that, for Christians, death is a metamorphosis (transfiguration: Mark 9:2) into a better life. Mark (9:2) says that on the mountain Jesus was "metamorphosed"—transformed. For a brief moment the disciples saw Jesus as he would be in the resurrection. And in today's Scripture the Lord Jesus uses the mystery of the dying grain of wheat to refer to his impending death and resurrection to a new life.

All of us will have to face death. But our lives are patterned after that of Jesus. As he did, we must go through the mystery of death, but in faith we know that death is a metamorphosis, and it will result in a glorious life with Christ.

SCRIPTURE READING—

Among those who had come up to worship at the feast were some Greeks. They approached Philip, who was from Bethsaida in Galilee, and put this request to him: "Sir, we should like to see Jesus." Philip went to tell Andrew; Philip and Andrew in turn came to inform Jesus. Jesus answered them:

"The hour has come
for the Son of Man to be glorified.
I solemnly assure you,
unless the grain of wheat falls to the earth and dies,
it remains just a grain of wheat.
But if it dies,
it produces much fruit.
The man who loves his life
loses it,
while the man who hates his life in this world
preserves it to life eternal." (John 12:20-25)

"You shall do homage to the Lord your God"

RELIGION as organized into groups has its "Confessions of Faith." They are brief formal statements of what the collective faithful believe in. These confessions determine the identity of the group or church. They are pronounced at meetings repeatedly and they strengthen mutual belonging, which is so important in religion. Think of our Profession of Faith during our weekly worship services!

Luke uses this tradition about our Lord to describe the temptations of the early Church. Notice the Confessions: "Not on bread alone shall man live. — You shall do homage to the Lord your God; him alone shall you adore. — You shall not put the Lord your God to the test." Jesus was tempted to give up his vocation; the Church is tempted time and again to be unfaithful to her original calling, and we as individuals are tempted as well. We should be a "confessing" Church. Others should know clearly what we stand for.

SCRIPTURE READING —

Jesus, full of the Holy Spirit, then returned from the Jordan and was conducted by the Spirit into the desert for forty days, where he was tempted by the devil. During that time he ate nothing, and at the end of it he was hungry. The devil said to him, "If you are the Son of God, command this stone to turn into bread." Jesus answered him, "Scripture has it, 'Not on bread alone shall man live.' "

Then the devil took him up higher and showed him all the kingdoms of the world in a single instant. He said to him, "I will give you all this power and the glory of these kingdoms; the power has been given to me and I give it to whomever I wish. Prostrate yourself in homage before me, and it shall all be yours." In reply, Jesus said to him, "Scripture has it,

'You shall do homage to the Lord your God;
him alone shall you adore.' "

Then the devil led him to Jerusalem, set him on the parapet of the temple, and said to him, "If you are the Son of God, throw yourself down from here, for Scripture has it,

'He will bid his angels watch over you';

and again,

'With their hands they will support you
that you may never stumble on a stone.' "

Jesus said to him in reply, "It also says, 'You shall not put the Lord your God to the test.' "

When the devil had finished all the tempting he left him, to await another opportunity. (Luke 4:1-12)

277-3

"Listen to him"

A FAMILY man exclaims to his wife: "Honey, please do not ask me anymore whether I love you. I told you so when we got married ten years ago. I provide for the family. Is that not enough?" The fact is that it is not. She wants to hear that he loves her over and over again, and he needs to say it.

Apply this to your relationship of love with God! Of course, God does not feel unhappy when you fail to say that you love him. But *you* need to say it in prayer. And if you do not, you will drift away from him, regardless of your charity to your neighbor.

In this highly symbolical narrative, Luke brings out an important lesson on prayer. Conversing with God in prayer changes us; it widens our vision, and with God's grace it often makes us experience the transcendent—in other words, it makes us feel that there must be something more than simply what we can observe with our senses. Jesus was a man of prayer. Luke compares him with Moses and Elijah who often conversed with God in prayer. He wants his disciples to do likewise. Peter said: "Master, how good it is for us to be here." Prayer-meditation is something you must learn and by doing it regularly you will find out it has meaning.

SCRIPTURE READING —

About eight days after saying this he took Peter, John and James, and went up onto a mountain to pray. While he was praying, his face changed in appearance and his clothes became dazzlingly white. Suddenly two men were talking with him—Moses and Elijah. They appeared in glory and spoke of his passage, which he was about to fulfill in Jerusalem. Peter and those with him had fallen into a deep sleep; but awakening, they saw his glory and likewise saw the two men who were standing with him.

When these were leaving, Peter said to Jesus, "Master, how good it is for us to be here. Let us set up three booths, one for you, one for Moses, and one for Elijah." (He did not really know what he was saying.) While he was speaking, a cloud came and overshadowed them, and the disciples grew fearful as the others entered it. Then from the cloud came a voice which said, "This is my Son, my Chosen One. Listen to him." (Luke 9:28-36)

"Unless you reform"

AS LONG as you are in the process of growing, you are alive. As far as our physical condition is concerned, at a certain moment we feel that the process of decay has set in. True, we can slow it down by keeping ourselves in good shape, and a whole industry is even helping us to do so. But we cannot stop the process of getting old. It is different, however, with our growth as persons. We are most aware of our personal growth during the years of formation: students in school, engaged partners getting to know and love one another, religious during the novitiate. The key to happy and meaningful life is to keep growing.

This Scripture reading refers to violent reprisals by the Romans who occupied Israel during Jesus' lifetime. There were constant uprisings on the part of the Jewish people which finally culminated in the wholesale destruction of Jerusalem in 70 A.D. According to popular thinking, disaster and suffering were caused by sin. Jesus corrects this way of thinking, but takes these incidents as a stepping-stone to teach about penance and reform using the parable of the fig tree to illustrate his lesson.

This lesson is God's word to you and me. Check your priority of values and ask yourself where God fits in! Stating that everything is all right means stating that you are "old" and not growing anymore as a person. We need constantly ongoing reform and growth into what God has designed us to be for all eternity.

SCRIPTURE READING —

At that time, some were present who told him about the Galileans whose blood Pilate had mixed with their sacrifices. He said in reply: "Do you think that these Galileans were the greatest sinners in Galilee just because they suffered this? By no means! But I tell you, you will all come to the same end unless you reform. Or take those eighteen who were killed by a falling tower in Siloam. Do you think they were more guilty than anyone else who lived in Jerusalem? Certainly not! But I tell you, you will all come to the same end unless you reform."

Jesus spoke this parable: "A man had a fig tree growing in his vineyard, and he came out looking for fruit on it but did not find any. He said to the vinedresser, 'Look here! For three years now I have come in search of fruit on this fig tree and found none. Cut it down. Why should it clutter up the ground?' In answer, the man said, 'Sir, leave it another year, while I hoe around it and manure it; then perhaps it will bear fruit. If not, it shall be cut down.' " (Luke 13:1-9)

"They celebrated the Passover"

A FRENCH king is said to have stated: "The crown of France is worth a Mass a week." In reality, he cared little about religion, but since all of France was Catholic, as king he had to go to church on Sunday. We could liken this to a modern teenager thinking: "The keys to the family car for my date are worth that Mass on Sunday." There are various reasons why the "faithful" observe religious obligations. Some do so out of fear. One never knows what will happen on the other side of the grave, so they want to play safe. Others calculate like the Pharisees of Jesus' time; they are "righteous" people, diligently observing the laws of their religion, and they expect God to give them salvation in return.

In the matter of leading a Christian life, it is the reason *why* one does so that counts. Love and gratitude should be the principal motivations, not calculation or fear, and certainly not commercial considerations!

In the promised land, the Hebrews celebrated the Passover. Their motivation was not to get something. They offered their lambs as a sign of gratitude to Almighty God. Our Passover Lamb is Jesus Christ, the Lamb of God, who takes away the sin of the world. Notice that the setting of our weekly Passover is the Eucharistic Prayer, a prayer of thanksgiving and praise, and these sentiments should be *your* main motivation for taking part in it.

In my Bible I have underlined: "They celebrated the Passover," and used it as the starting point for a meditation on my daily celebration of the Eucharist, my reasons for it, and the genuineness of my self-giving to God, as I symbolize it every so often.

SCRIPTURE READING —

The Lord said to Joshua, "Today I have removed the reproach of Egypt from you."

While the Israelites were encamped at Gilgal on the plains of Jericho, they celebrated the Passover on the evening of the fourteenth of the month. On the day after the Passover they ate of the produce of the land in the form of unleavened cakes and parched grain. On that same day after the Passover on which they ate of the produce of the land, the manna ceased. No longer was there manna for the Israelites, who that year ate of the yield of the land of Canaan. (Joshua 5:9, 10-12)

"But from now on, avoid this sin"

EVERY day we come into contact with optimists and pessimists, and traits of both are part of our own selves. The pessimist takes the gloomiest possible view of the human condition. He is a captive of the "good old days," of what is not anymore and never will be again. He is not creative because he regards all efforts as doomed to fail in the first place. This represents anything but the "spirit of '76." Imagine if the Founding Fathers had fostered this kind of thinking! The optimist looks to the bright side of things. He is creative and dynamic. He has confidence in life.

From the outset in this reading, it is clear that the Pharisees who bring the adulteress to Jesus are not honest. Jesus simply bends down and starts tracing on the ground with his finger, indicating that he is bored and not interested in their hypocritical nonsense, very much as we doodle when bored! Finally, they leave. And an unhappy woman who had faced death regains hope by meeting a good person. God's word to us through this tradition could be: With regard to the past, God is merciful. With faith in him work at a happy future. Be an optimist!

SCRIPTURE READING —

Jesus went out to the Mount of Olives. At daybreak he reappeared in the temple area; and when the people started coming to him, he sat down and began to teach them. The scribes and the Pharisees led a woman forward who had been caught in adultery. They made her stand there in front of everyone. "Teacher," they said to him, "this woman has been caught in the act of adultery. In the law, Moses ordered such women to be stoned. What do you have to say about the case?" (They were posing this question to trap him, so that they could have something to accuse him of.)

Jesus bent down and started tracing on the ground with his finger. When they persisted in their questioning, he straightened up and said to them, "Let the man among you who has no sin be the first to cast a stone at her." A second time he bent down and wrote on the ground. Then the audience drifted away one by one, beginning with the elders. This left him alone with the woman, who continued to stand there before him. Jesus finally straightened up and said to her, "Woman, where did they all disappear to? Has no one condemned you?" "No one, sir," she answered. Jesus said, "Nor do I condemn you. You may go. But from now on, avoid this sin." (John 8:1-11)

"Do not be afraid! Go and carry the news to my brothers"

IN PAUL'S first letter to the congregation of Corinth (56 or 57 A.D.) we have the oldest summary of Christian belief. "I [Paul] handed on to you first of all what I myself received, that Christ died for our sins in accordance with the Scriptures, that he was buried and, in accordance with the Scriptures, rose on the third day; that he was seen by Cephas, then by the Twelve. This is what we preach and this is what you believed" (1 Corinthians 15:3-5).

Some thirty to fifty years later, the evangelists preached the same message, but often drew on local traditions which extensively elaborate on the theme of our Lord's resurrection. There are legendary details in those traditions which have nothing to do with the faith in the resurrection.

The "angel of the Lord" in Matthew's version (28:2) the "young man" in Mark's version (16:5) and the "two young men" in Luke's version (24:4) are messenger-figures of the Old Testament. The authors want to bring out the message from God: "He [Christ] has been raised from the dead." The legendary details belong to the tradition as such. The evangelists took this tradition at face value and used it to proclaim the risen Lord and what he means to you and me: "Peace! Do not be afraid!"

SCRIPTURE READING —

After the sabbath, as the first day of the week was dawning, Mary Magdalene came with the other Mary to inspect the tomb. Suddenly there was a mighty earthquake, as the angel of the Lord descended from heaven. He came to the stone, rolled it back, and sat on it. In appearance he resembled a flash of lightning while his garments were as dazzling as snow. The guards grew paralyzed with fear of him and fell down like dead men. Then the angel spoke, addressing the women: "Do not be frightened. I know you are looking for Jesus the crucified, but he is not here. He has been raised, exactly as he promised. Come and see the place where he was laid. Then go quickly and tell his disciples: 'He has been raised from the dead and now goes ahead of you to Galilee, where you will see him.' That is the message I have for you."

They hurried away from the tomb half-overjoyed, half-fearful, and ran to carry the good news to his disciples. Suddenly, without warning, Jesus stood before them and said, "Peace!" The women came up and embraced his feet and did him homage. At this Jesus said to them, "Do not be afraid! Go and carry the news to my brothers that they are to go to Galilee, where they will see me." (Matthew 28:1-10)

"Christ our Passover has been sacrificed"

A PERSON who is privileged to visit the tombs of the Pharaohs in Egypt or reads about them in pictorial books is struck by those people's concern about the hereafter. The hieroglyphics for "life everlasting" appear on the murals time and again. Man wants to live. Easter is the feast of life. "The Lord has indeed risen, Alleluia" (Entrance Ant.). "Alleluia—Praise the Lord!" marks all prayers and songs of this festival season. It represents the joy of Christians: The Lord's death was not a defeat but a victory! And we share in the Lord's victory over suffering and death, knowing that life everlasting with Christ will be ours. "We look for the resurrection of the dead, and the life of the world to come" (Profession of Faith).

Jewish housewives used to bake their own bread. Yeast or leaven was a piece of the old (previous day's) dough which was exposed to decay and then mixed with the new batch. Hence, figuratively, yeast was seen as a principle of decay. It was part of the Passover preparation to do away with the old dough (yeast) and eat the Passover lamb with *unleavened* bread. The symbolism is obvious: Do away with the principle of moral decay and eat the Passover with a clean heart. Paul reinterprets this Jewish Passover. The Christian Passover lamb is the Lord himself, the Lamb of God, who takes away the sin of the world. "Christ our Passover has been sacrificed." Do away with moral decay. Celebrate the feast with the unleavened bread of sincerity and truth. Against this background, Christians see the Eucharist as a reinterpreted Jewish Passover!

SCRIPTURE READING —

This boasting of yours is an ugly thing. Do you not know that a little yeast has its effect all through the dough? Get rid of the old yeast to make of yourselves fresh dough, unleavened loaves, as it were; Christ our Passover has been sacrificed. Let us celebrate the feast not with the old yeast, that of corruption and wickedness, but with the unleavened bread of sincerity and truth. (1 Corinthians 5:6-8)

"What rises is incorruptible"

WE WANT to know: What is the manner of my existence after death? "How are the dead raised up? What kind of body will they have?" (1 Corinthians 15:35). Paul calls this a nonsensical question. And he adds: "The seed you sow does not germinate until it dies. When you sow, you do not sow the full-blown plant, but a kernel of wheat or some other grain. God gives body to it as he pleases—to each seed its fruition" (1 Corinthians 15:36-38).

This seems to indicate that our lives now are the kernels from which "earthly man" must grow into the person he will be for all eternity. "This corruptible body must be clothed with incorruptibility" (1 Corinthians 15:53). The words found in 1 Corinthians 15: 35-38 offer insight to the inquisitive reader, but ultimately we must leave the details up to God who promised that our reward will be a hundredfold.

I concentrated my meditation on the lines: "What rises is glorious. . . . Strength rises up." This helped me to cope with my present limitations.

SCRIPTURE READING—

Perhaps someone will say, "How are the dead to be raised up? What kind of body will they have?" A nonsensical question! The seed you sow does not germinate unless it dies. When you sow, you do not sow the full-blown plant, but a kernel of wheat or some other grain. God gives body to it as he pleases—to each seed its own fruition.

Not all bodily nature is the same. Men have one kind of body, animals another. Birds are of their kind, fish are of theirs. There are heavenly bodies and there are earthly bodies. The splendor of the heavenly bodies is one thing, that of the earthly another. The sun has a splendor of its own, so has the moon, and the stars have theirs. Even among the stars, one differs from another in brightness.

So is it with the resurrection of the dead. What is sown in the earth is subject to decay, what rises is incorruptible. What is sown is ignoble, what rises is glorious. Weakness is sown, strength rises up. A natural body is put down and a spiritual body comes up.

(1 Corinthians 15:35-44)

"A birth unto hope which draws its life from the resurrection of Jesus Christ"

"BIRDS of a feather flock together." With respect to certain instincts, we humans are no different from cows in a pasture flocking together when a thunderstorm is threatening. We need one another's company and inspiration to keep going. Marital love can survive only if the partners daily foster togetherness with all the means nature and religion suggest. The survival of faith is subject to the same conditions. A Christianity lived "alone," all by oneself, does not last.

This reading is taken from the First Epistle of Peter which is probably a homily (sermon) given on the occasion of a baptismal ceremony. Notice how the homilist relates our rebirth through baptism to the resurrection of Jesus Christ. Christian rebirth from water and Spirit is a birth to hope—to an imperishable inheritance.

A well-known Baptist preacher of Harlem used to say: "Keep the faith, baby!" This is a folksy way of saying it. But the underlying concern must be ours, and it should be done in fellowship with others!

SCRIPTURE READING —

Praised be the God and Father
of our Lord Jesus Christ,
he who in his great mercy
gave us new birth;
a birth unto hope which draws its life
from the resurrection of Jesus Christ from the dead;
a birth to an imperishable inheritance,
incapable of fading or defilement,
which is kept in heaven for you
who are guarded with God's power through faith;
a birth to a salvation which stands ready
to be revealed in the last days.

There is cause for rejoicing here. You may for a time have to suffer the distress of many trials; but this is so that your faith, which is more precious than the passing splendor of fire-tried gold, may by its genuineness lead to praise, glory, and honor when Jesus Christ appears. Although you have never seen him, you love him, and without seeing you now believe in him, and rejoice with inexpressible joy touched with glory because you are achieving faith's goal, your salvation.

(1 Peter 1:3-9)

"Do not persist in your unbelief, but believe"

READING this Scripture about the unbelieving Thomas brings to mind two friends of mine, one an agnostic and the other an atheist. Both of them are highly educated people, avid readers with extensive personal libraries (whose contents, however, are somewhat onesided—one buys the books one wants to read!), honest and lovable persons, with whom I am always welcome as a friend.

We speak about religion quite often. For some reason or another I can see the agnostic's point better than that of the atheist. The latter states categorically: "There is no God and with death it is all over!" How does he know? He is as dogmatic as the magisterium of the Catholic Church has ever been. The agnostic states: "I don't know. You don't convince me!" And that is true to a certain extent. Faith cannot be proved scientifically.

By relating the tradition concerning the unbelieving Thomas, the writer of John wants to shed further light on the point. He indicates that even seeing, as Thomas did, is no guarantee of faith. Faith comes by hearing the word of the risen Lord, who addresses Thomas personally. Christianity knows the golden rule: Faith comes from hearing. It is God personally addressing you in an "I-Thou" situation. This intangible situation can never be fully explained, just as we cannot explain what exactly happens when someone falls in love. Respond when the Lord says "Shalom—peace" to you in any situation of your life and keep that faith alive!

SCRIPTURE READING—

It happened that one of the Twelve, Thomas (the name means "Twin"), was absent when Jesus came. The other disciples kept telling him: "We have seen the Lord!" His answer was, "I will never believe it without probing the nailprints in his hands, without putting my finger in the nailmarks and my hand into his side."

A week later, the disciples were once more in the room, and this time Thomas was with them. Despite the locked doors, Jesus came and stood before them. "Peace be with you," he said; then, to Thomas: "Take your finger and examine my hands. Put your hand into my side. Do not persist in your unbelief, but believe!" Thomas said in response. "My Lord and my God!" Jesus then said to him:

"You became a believer because you saw me.
Blest are they who have not seen and have believed."

(John 20:24-29)

"Were not our hearts burning inside us?"

IN TODAY'S reading the disciples of Emmaus are "down in the dumps." We might compare them with the campaigners for Robert Kennedy, who had worked for him in the primaries. We remember their hope and joy in the hotel lobby in Los Angeles, and then their utter dismay, after witnessing the tragic assassination. "We had hoped that he would be the next president of the United States!" In a similar mood the two disciples are on their way back home. "We were hoping that he [Jesus] was the one [the Messiah—freedom fighter] who would set Israel free [from Roman occupation]."

The disciples respond both to God's word: "Were not our hearts burning inside us . . . as he explained the Scriptures?" and to God's sign (sacrament): "They had come to know him in the breaking of the bread." Our growth in faith is made through the ministry of God's word (first part of Mass: Bible readings and the explanation in the homily) and comes to its fulfillment in the celebration of the Eucharist—a sacramental (signifying) meal.

A Christian can know a great deal about our Lord without knowing him as a person! Make every Sunday worship service a personal encounter with the Lord Jesus in both Scripture and Sacrament (the Eucharist).

SCRIPTURE READING—

[Jesus] said to them: "What little sense you have! How slow you are to believe all that the prophets have announced! Did not the Messiah have to undergo all this so as to enter into his glory?" Beginning, then, with Moses and all the prophets, he interpreted for them every passage of Scripture which referred to him. By now they were near the village to which they were going, and he acted as if he were going farther. But they pressed him: "Stay with us. It is nearly evening—the day is practically over." So he went in to stay with them.

When he had seated himself with them to eat, he took bread, pronounced the blessing, then broke the bread and began to distribute it to them. With that they eyes were opened and they recognized him; whereupon he vanished from their sight. They said to one another, "Were not our hearts burning inside us as he talked to us on the road and explained the Scriptures to us?" They got up immediately and returned to Jerusalem, where they found the Eleven and the rest of the company assembled. They were greeted with, "The Lord has been raised! It is true! He has appeared to Simon." Then they recounted what had happened on the road and how they had come to know him in the breaking of bread.

(Luke 24:13-35)

"As he calls his own by name"

AT MANY moments of our lives, especially when we have to put up with suffering and unexpected problems, we feel that we are not self-sufficient. In such cases, the modern person goes to a psychiatrist, a marriage counselor, or a lawyer for guidance and advice. Where does God, visible in Jesus Christ, fit into your schedule? God's advice and wisdom is available in the words and example of the Lord Jesus.

The writers of the New Testament were concerned to bring out who the risen Lord is and how we are related to him. In today's Scripture we are invited to see the Lord as both the gate of a sheepfold, through which we should enter security, and as our Shepherd, whom we should follow. Though sheep and shepherds are not part of the contemporary American scene and we know them perhaps only from television, with a little goodwill we can understand what the inspired writer wants to say.

Prayerfully reading the Bible and diligently following the Lord Jesus who is "the shepherd, the guardian of your souls" (1 Peter 2:25), a modern Christian knows how to integrate the guidelines of his religion with whatever science offers him for the solutions of his problems!

SCRIPTURE READING —

[Jesus said:]
"Truly I assure you:
Whoever does not enter the sheepfold through the gate
but climbs in some other way
is a thief and a marauder.
The one who enters through the gate
is shepherd of the sheep;
the keeper opens the gate for him.
The sheep hear his voice
as he calls his own by name
and leads them out.
When he has brought out [all] those that are his,
he walks in front of them,
and the sheep follow him
because they recognize his voice.
They will not follow a stranger;
such a one they will flee,
because they do not recognize a stranger's voice." (John 10:1-5)

"Whoever has seen me has seen the Father"

EDUCATORS know that children have their particular sensitivity moments, which should be exploited for learning. Adults follow the same law of nature. There are times when we are more than usually sensitive to God's word. Sometimes these may be the result of a happy or sad event in life, such as a wedding, funeral, birth, success, failure, or even a deeply moving book, motion picture, or television program. At other times there is no apparent reason for them at all.

One speaks of "disclosure moments," i.e., times when we are more than usually open to some transcending reality. The New Testament word for one such moment or time is "kairos." The Greek language has two words for time: "chronos," time measurable in years, and "kairos," time of opportunity, time of grace.

Jesus said: "The *kairos* (time of favor or fulfillment) is at hand. Be converted and believe in the good news" (Mark 1:14-15). God is present to you in Christ, the Bible, the breaking of bread, any good person. The "kairos" (time of favor) for you is when you experience this mysterious presence. This "kairos" (time of favor) is a gift of God, which we should exploit.

SCRIPTURE READING —

Jesus told [Thomas:]
"I am the way, and the truth, and the life;
no one comes to the Father but through me.
If you really knew me, you would know my Father also.
From this point on you know him; you have seen him."

"Lord," Philip said to him, "show us the Father and that will be enough for us." "Philip," Jesus replied, "after I have been with you all this time, you still do not know me?

"Whoever has seen me has seen the Father.
How can you say, 'Show us the Father'?
Do you not believe that I am in the Father
and the Father is in me?
The words I speak are not spoken of myself;
it is the Father who lives in me accomplishing his works."

(John 14:6-10)

"Another Paraclete — the Spirit of truth"

A FOUNDER cannot expect his work to be lasting and to continue unless his disciples accept his message wholeheartedly. They must be faithful to the traditions he founded and have an open mind for his intuitive vision concerning the future of his work. Guided by the spirit of the founder, those who continue his work must operate creatively, constantly adapting themselves to new situations. This is what the early Church has tried to do as we see in the readings from the Acts of the Apostles.

We should accept this same situation in the Church of our time and culture. "There are different gifts but the same spirit" (1 Corinthians 12:4). There are charismatics, floating parishes, conservatives and liberals. We have young and old, emotionally involved and more cerebral members in one congregation. Let us bear with one another, as long as the same Spirit breathes upon all under the guidance of our bishops.

In my Bible, I have underlined "the Spirit of truth," and I have prayed that guided by the Spirit of the Founder I may forward his message in my life situation.

SCRIPTURE READING —

[Jesus said to his disciples:]
If you love me
and obey the commands I give you,
I will ask the Father
and he will give you another Paraclete—
to be with you always:
the Spirit of truth,
whom the world cannot accept,
since it neither sees him nor recognizes him;
but you can recognize him
because he remains with you
and will be within you." (John 14:15-17)

"May he enlighten your innermost vision"

NOT all members of our species have the same outlook on life. There are people for whom this life means everything and "heaven" nothing. Naturally good people, they may cherish love as a great value, but when one breathes his last, that is the end. There are others for whom "heaven" is all-important and this life almost completely unimportant. Save your soul! Many Christians have cherished this outlook, especially concerning others and as long as the self was not involved. Finally, we have those for whom "heaven" is realized already on earth in love!

If we understand Jesus' philosophy of life well, we could give it a try. We may live life, including marital sex and love, as an earthly reality. We may develop our potential as earthlings to its fullest. We may make use of the results of science (sociology, etc.) to achieve a better life on this planet. We may consult marriage counselors and psychiatrists and seek the best medical care available.

Yet in our best moments ("disclosure situations"), we know that there must be something more than all of this, a transcending reality. In faith, following Jesus of Nazareth, we see this "transcending reality" as a loving Father who is waiting for us. He (Jesus) is the beginning: "Where he, our head, has gone, we, his members, hope to follow him" (Preface of the Ascension). What could be your prayerful response?

SCRIPTURE READING —

May the God of our Lord Jesus Christ, the Father of glory, grant you a spirit of wisdom and insight to know him clearly. May he enlighten your innermost vision that you may know the great hope to which he has called you, the wealth of his glorious heritage to be distributed among the members of the church, and the immeasurable scope of his power in us who believe. It is like the strength he showed in raising Christ from the dead and seating him at his right hand in heaven, high above every principality, power, virtue, and dominion, and every name that can be given in this age or in the age to come.

(Ephesians 1:17-21)

"And know that I am with you always"

IN MATTHEW'S version of the ascension account, the final appearance takes place on a mountain. As the great appearance of God to Moses took place on Mount Sinai (Exodus 19), so Matthew has Jesus' great sermon delivered on a mountain (Matthew 5:1), and the transfiguration take place on a mountain as well (Matthew 17:1). This final appearance of Jesus on a mountain has theological significance for Matthew, who as a Jew writing for Christians of Jewish background constantly writes with concepts and allusions taken from the Hebrew Bible (Old Testament).

We should keep in mind that the primary significance of the Easter appearances is that they were revelations of the risen Lord Jesus. They could be doubted as well as believed. But once the disciples believed, they "fell down in homage," and with admirable dedication they heeded the Lord's mission and went out to all nations to preach the Gospel. "And know I am with you"—a great assurance to "the pilgrim Church" on its way to a great future!

You and I are this pilgrim Church. When depressed or frustrated, does that great assurance: "Know that I am with you," really help? Pray for faith!

SCRIPTURE READING —

The eleven disciples made their way to Galilee, to the mountain to which Jesus had summoned them. At the sight of him, those who had entertained doubts fell down in homage. Jesus came forward and addressed them in these words:

"Full authority has been given to me
both in heaven and on earth;
go, therefore, and make disciples of all the nations.
Baptize them in the name
'of the Father,
and of the Son,
and of the Holy Spirit.'
Teach them to carry out everything I have commanded you.
And know that I am with you always, until the end of the world!"

(Matthew 28:16-20)

"For these I pray"

MODERN man, young or old, constantly on the go, is not easily convinced that he needs some quiet time to have a look at himself and ask hard questions, such as: Am I consistent with my past? Have I changed values? How do I look at my future? Traditionally, a retreat or mission was the time to do this. Whatever our options are, we can do so right now in reflective prayer.

Today's Scripture is taken from Jesus' high priestly prayer, also called "prayer of consecration," because Jesus consecrates himself for his approaching redemptive death. Actually, this prayer reflects an elaborated meditation on the thoughts and aspirations of our Lord. Jesus begins his passion with prayer. Our Lord meditates on what he has to do. He recommends his disciples to his Father. He has made them know the Father. Now they must go out into the world and, filled with Jesus' Spirit, teach all nations. The task of a Christian in the world is not an easy one. As the Lord prayed in the difficult hours of his life, we should do the same.

SCRIPTURE READING —

Jesus looked up to heaven and said:
"Father, the hour has come!
Give glory to your Son
that your Son may give glory to you,
inasmuch as you have given him authority over all mankind,
that he may bestow eternal life on those you gave him.
I have given you glory on earth
by finishing the work you gave me to do.
Do you now, Father, give me glory at your side,
a glory I had with you before the world began.
I have made your name known
to those you gave me out of the world.
These men you gave me were yours;
they have kept your word.
Now they realize
that all that you gave me comes from you.
I entrusted to them
the message you entrusted to me,
and they received it.
They have known that in truth I came from you,
they have believed it was you who sent me.
For these I pray—
not for the world
but for these you have given me,
for they are really yours."

(John 17:1-2, 4-9)

"The Spirit too helps us in our weakness"

WE KNOW how difficult it would be to explain the intricacies of a computer or the complexity of ballistics used for space flights to a person wihout formal education. For such a person lacks the very concepts that would be needed for him to understand such things. We face somewhat the same problem when we apply our limited hearts and minds to the contemplation of the infinite God and the outpouring of his Spirit. We should therefore realize that all the Bible can do is attempt to say some meaningful things about the Spirit of God in limited human terminology. Human speech cannot possibly express adequately who God is.

In order to make us aware of what the Holy Spirit means to you and me, the biblical writers use metaphors such as breath, a strong driving wind, and fire. Paul states that without the animating Spirit "all creation groans and is in agony."

And even though we have the Spirit, we too groan, while we await full redemption in the hereafter. God, the Holy Spirit, is the animating principle of all life. Without the help of the Holy Spirit we cannot even pray as we ought. So many Christians nowadays complain about the difficulty they have in praying! They should turn to the Holy Spirit!

SCRIPTURE READING—

Yes, we know that all creation groans and is in agony even until now. Not only that, but we ourselves, although we have the Spirit as first fruits, groan inwardly while we await the redemption of our bodies. In hope we were saved. But hope is not hope if its object is seen; how is it possible for one to hope for what he sees? And hoping for what we cannot see means awaiting it with patient endurance.

The Spirit too helps us in our weakness, for we do not know how to pray as we ought; but the Spirit himself makes intercession for us with groanings that cannot be expressed in speech. He who searches hearts know what the Spirit means, for the Spirit intercedes for the saints as God himself wills. (Romans 8:22-27)

IN OUR confused and limited human condition, we are daily confronted with ignorance, knowledge, and understanding. Every human being starts out as a "tabula rasa" (a smoothed tablet, without impressions on it). Only by hard work can a youngster overcome ignorance, gather knowledge, and attain insight and understanding. We need knowledge in order to achieve insight. When a teenager states: "But I think . . .," and it turns out that he made his statement without first gathering information, most people will take this youthful blunder in stride. They know that a teacher will tell him what one is supposed to do before a statement is made. But when a grown-up does the same time and again, he gives himself away as a big talker!

Living in an isolated and closed society, Catholics could perhaps afford to leave knowledge and understanding up to the priest. But such a closed society for Catholics is a thing of the past. Through the mass media everybody enters our home today. We owe it to ourselves and others to be informed Christians. If not, the flood of information which overwhelms us daily will confuse us. However, even the grown-up can come to insight and understanding only by putting out effort. The adult Christian should read the Bible, the diocesan newspaper, and good books, and watch television programs that deal with his/her religion. Ignorance can be culpable and lead to disaster as today's Scripture reading clearly implies.

Judging others should be left up to God. But it is clear that ignorance on the part of those who should know is blameworthy and causes harm and disaster. The poorly informed Christian, though he may hold a doctorate in science, is a danger to himself and others. One cannot possibly cope with other visions of life, glittering and seemingly so much more appealing, if one knows one's own only poorly. Do you keep up to date on your religion?

SCRIPTURE READING —

[Peter said to the Jews:] "The God of Abraham, of Isaac, and of Jacob, the God of our fathers, has glorified his Servant Jesus, whom you handed over and disowned in Pilate's presence when Pilate was ready to release him. You disowned the Holy and Just One and preferred instead to be granted the release of a murderer. You put to death the Author of life. But God raised him from the dead, and we are his witnesses." (Acts 3:13-15)

"He opened their minds to the understanding of the Scriptures"

A RELIGIOUS sister wrote me: "You don't remember, I'm sure, the many sisters who come and go in the Mississippi area, but you were among the first people after Vatican II to open for me a few of 'Pope John's windows.' They will never close for me, I trust. I'm thriving on the fresh air and perhaps with the help of the Spirit I can help in even opening the front door of the Church. (I'm in pastoral ministries here in southern Kentucky.)"

It gave me a good feeling that I had been instrumental in opening the mind of this sister. It has made me feel even worse about a fellow pastor who is afraid of the breed of young associates that seminaries are turning out nowadays. They went through the post-Vatican II training, and he himself has not kept up to date. He reads the *Wall Street Journal,* is a capable manager, but is not acquainted with what he should know in the first place, his theology. His mind is closed to any renewal.

Luke states that our Lord opened the minds of the disciples to the understanding of the Scriptures. Experiencing God/Jesus Christ in meditative and prayerful Bible reading is the clue to Christian renewal. Understanding man's word in the Bible is a necessary condition for understanding God's word in Scripture. Hence, partaking in a study group is important. Doing things together under capable leadership makes study easier. But the real understanding of the Scriptures requires prayer and meditation, because the Lord must open your mind and give you insight.

SCRIPTURE READING —

[Jesus] said to [the disciples], "Recall those words I spoke to you when I was still with you: everything written about me in the law of Moses and the prophets and psalms had to be fulfilled." Then he opened their minds to the understanding of the Scriptures.

He said to them: "Thus it is written that the Messiah must suffer and rise from the dead on the third day. In his name, penance for the remission of sins is to be preached to all the nations, beginning at Jerusalem. You are witnesses of this. See, I send down upon you the promise of my Father. Remain here in the city until you are clothed with power from on high." (Luke 24:44-49)

"I know my sheep and my sheep know me"

THE collective representatives of the people of the United States are responsible for our safety. We have a National Safety Council and such agencies as the Federal Bureau of Investigation (FBI) and the Central Intelligence Agency (CIA)—all concerned with safety. The sooner a threat to our safety is detected, the better it is. Yet many are not aware that a dangerous threat to our personal safety is posed by a *meaningless existence.* Psychiatrists and mental institutions are reminders of it. Once someone has to be referred to them, harm to that person's safety has already been done.

Christianity, the movement started by Jesus of Nazareth, wants to save people from precisely such a meaningless existence which the Bible calls darkness. The word "salvation" is mentioned on almost every page of Scripture. A mental breakdown is a tragedy, resulting from the fact that a person cannot cope with life. Counseling and medication may help. Christianity, however, offers something which prevents it. Christians who faithfully live their faith will not break down easily. They have reserves unknown of elsewhere.

Today's Scripture deals with our safety. Hopefully, you will discover a few untapped reserves that could keep you going on your way to a great future. The Lord Jesus knows you and is concerned. He laid down his life for you. Turn to him in prayer and meditative encounter in your Bible and you will find peace of mind.

SCRIPTURE READING —

Jesus said:
"I am the good shepherd;
the good shepherd lays down his life for the sheep.
The hired hand—who is no shepherd
nor owner of the sheep—
catches sight of the wolf coming
to be snatched and scattered by the wolf.
That is because he works for pay;
he has no concern for the sheep.

"I am the good shepherd.
I know my sheep
and my sheep know me
in the same way that the Father knows me
and I know the Father;
for these sheep I will give my life."
(John 10:11-15)

"Live on in me, as I do in you"

AS A YOUNG missionary, when I started traveling alone in my jeep through the mountains and the jungles of Timor, an island in the Indian Ocean, I was taught a few rules of the game. Thus experienced colleagues told me that the physically very strong water buffaloes who roam the woods and savannas freely are harmless as long as they are together in herds. But whenever you meet one alone, an outcast from the herd, you are well-advised to be careful. He might be vicious and attack. Human beings follow a similar rule. A loner, an outcast, easily turns criminal. In order to develop harmoniously as human beings, we need the feeling of "belonging." Alone, the human person is insufficient.

Today's Scripture deals with this theme of "belonging." It tells us that Christians must live in Christ and let Christ live in them. There should be an "I-Thou," a person-to-person relationship between you and the living Lord Jesus. But this is only possible if we have first learned to relate to one another. A human openness to others is a condition for openness to the transcendent, God and Jesus Christ. Develop both! Encounter the Lord Jesus in prayerful Bible reading, listening and responding, but also in your fellow human beings!

SCRIPTURE READING —

[Jesus said to the disciples:]
"I am the true vine
and my Father is the vinegrower.
He prunes away
every barren branch,
but the fruitful ones
he trims clean
to increase their yield.
You are clean already,
thanks to the word I have spoken to you.
Live on in me, as I do in you.
No more than a branch can bear fruit of itself
apart from the vine,
can you bear fruit
apart from me.

"I am the vine, you are the branches.
He who lives in me and I in him,
will produce abundantly,
for apart from me you can do nothing.
A man who does not live in me
is like a withered, rejected branch,
picked up to be thrown in the fire and burnt." (John 15:1-6)

"Live on in my love"

DID you ever meet persons who told you bluntly that they did not believe in love? Social workers, prison chaplains, teachers in both ghetto and middle-class high schools meet them all the time. People who do not believe in love often have a sad history behind them. It may be a broken home, parents neglecting them, friends cheating and lovers double-crossing them. Where love was expected, rejection was received! The result is that entirely negative outlook of the lonesome and unhappy outcast.

Today's Scripture deals with love of God and neighbor. God loves you but it does not make sense even to mention this if the addressee does not believe in love at all. Love is something that must be learned and experienced from early infancy. It must be developed and fostered first on the human level; only then can it be given its religious dimension of God and (because of God) the neighbor. It is so important that all of us who must be witnesses of Christianity make outsiders first believe in our love on the human level. Only then can they believe in God's love.

John teaches us about love of God and neighbor, friendship and complete joy which result in a meaningful life, "bearing fruit." But why do so many fail in love even after starting out so beautifully? Over the years, did they try to listen to one another? Was there an emphasis on mutual understanding, forgiveness after failures, and fidelity to an initial "yes" when it was difficult? Love, like a plant, must be cared for daily; otherwise it withers. Check your own life, have an honest discussion if necessary, pray and pattern your love after Jesus' example: "Love one another as I have loved you."

SCRIPTURE READING —

[Jesus said to his disciples:]
"As the Father has loved me,
so I have loved you.
Live on in my love.
You will live in my love
if you keep my commandments,
even as I have kept my Father's
commandments,
and live in his love.
All this I tell you
that my joy may be yours
and your joy may be complete.
This is my commandment:
love one another
as I have loved you.
There is no greater love than this:
to lay down one's life for one's
friends." (John 15:9-13)

"That they may be one"

WHEREVER people are "one," in other words, establish a group, be it a garden club, a sorority, a fraternity, or the family, we may ask: "What motivates such people to come together and stay together?" Bypassing business concerns, we can pinpoint mutual interest and various levels of friendship and love. There is loyalty to the group and a body charged with the administrative and executive work.

The group charged by our Lord to establish God's reign on earth, and though marred by human deficiencies still together after 2,000 years, evokes the same question: "What motivates Christians to come together and stay together?" Today's Scripture dwells upon this question.

It is love that keeps the Christian community together and makes its mission in the world possible. Persevering in love, however, is not easy. As long as our Lord was with his little flock visibly, he could guard it more tangibly. But after his ascension into heaven, he is still with us through his prayers. The Lord prays that we may remain one.

Are you loyal to your Church as an institution? Do you contribute constructive criticism if things are not going your way? What about discussing issues with your elected parish board members? Defecting or undermining the group by bitter and destructive criticism has never done any good in history! Be with your Church by your creative fidelity!

SCRIPTURE READING —

[Jesus prayed:]
"O Father most holy,
protect them with your name which you have given me
[that they may be one, even as we are one].
As long as I was with them,
I guarded them with your name which you gave me.
I kept careful watch,
and not one of them was lost,
none but him who was destined to be lost—
in fulfillment of Scripture."

(John 17:11-12)

"The grace of the Lord Jesus Christ, and the love of God, and the fellowship of the Holy Spirit be with you all"

THE first thing our parents taught us about our religion was most probably the sign of the cross. The last thing a priest will do at our graveside is make the sign of the cross over our body. A Christian's life is marked "in the name of the Father, and of the Son, and of the Holy Spirit."

The revelation of God as Father, Son, and Holy Spirit tells us first of all what God is for us. But as to the mysterious unity of Father, Son, and Holy Spirit, we can only stammer with inadequate human concepts, which are not able to express the ineffable mystery of God in himself. We want to know. But we must realize the way two beloved know one another! An intimate person-to-person relationship gives a knowledge which cannot possibly be expressed in human terminology. It is that kind of knowledge of God which ultimately satisfies a human being. "How deep are the riches and the wisdom and the knowledge of God! How inscrutable his judgment, how unsearchable his ways" (Romans 11:33).

In this reading we have Paul's fervent wish for the congregation in Corinth, Greece. He mentions the Father, the Son, and the Holy Spirit—God related to us and our salvation. "The grace of the Lord Jesus Christ [which he acquired for us by his death and resurrection], and the love of God [the Father, the origin of our salvation], and the fellowship of the Holy Spirit [keeping us together] be with you all!"

SCRIPTURE READING—

And now, brothers, I must say good-bye. Mend your ways. Encourage one another. Live in harmony and peace, and the God of love and peace will be with you. Greet one another with a holy kiss. All the holy ones send greetings to you. The grace of the Lord Jesus Christ, and the love of God, and the fellowship of the Holy Spirit be with you all! (2 Corinthians 13:11-13)

April 21

"Do this in remembrance of me"

IN AN affluent society basic food such as bread and water is no problem. However, for many people in the world it still is. Thus, they can understand better than we do that it is a real sign of love and care when God intervenes to feed his people. For them, water and bread are a question of life and death. But we are often hungry and thirsty for other values than sustenance of physical life. In a depersonalized society we suffer from absence where there should be presence. We hunger and thirst for companionship, love, concern, mercy, and respect which are no problems in the great family of primitive people. Whose need is greater?

Where we suffer from absence, the Lord Jesus wants to be present to us with all the concern and love of a friend for a friend. In the signs of plain daily food for Orientals, water, bread, wine, Jesus indicates what he intends by being present to us. He wants to share life. He wants to strengthen. He wants to mean something to you and me.

The early Church celebrated the Eucharist as part of a communal meal, the "agape." Even today parish activities, picnics, and potluck-dinners keep the members together and impart that feeling of belonging which we all need to persevere in the Christian way of life. However, in Corinth it had gotten out of hand. The rich brought their own food and did not share it with those who had less or nothing. Hence, the meal, which should result in a closer oneness of Christians, became a means of division. Referring to this abuse, Paul invites the Christians of Corinth to meditate on the real meaning of the Eucharist. Are you aware that your partaking in the Eucharistic Banquet signifies not only your oneness with the Host, Jesus Christ, but also your oneness with the guests at that banquet, your fellow parishioners?

SCRIPTURE READING —

I received from the Lord what I handed on to you, namely, that the Lord Jesus on the night in which he was betrayed took bread, and after he had given thanks, broke it and said, "This is my body, which is for you. Do this in remembrance of me." In the same way, after the supper, he took the cup, saying, "This cup is the new covenant in my blood. Do this, whenever you drink it, in remembrance of me." Every time, then, you eat this bread and drink this cup, you proclaim the death of the Lord until he comes! (1 Corinthians 11:23-26)

"When Christ came as high priest . . ." April 22

THE more absurd the premature death of a beloved one seemingly is, the more those who admired and loved him will search for meaning in this mystery.

The beloved Founder of the Christian movement had died the death of a criminal, but was experienced as alive. The early theologians came up with three solutions:

1. Jesus died the death of a prophetical martyr. Like all prophets, Jesus had preached "metanoia"—conversion. Evil struck back. But God vindicated his faithful servant by raising him.

2. Another solution: "Did not the Messiah *have* to undergo all this so as to enter his glory?" (Luke 24:26). It was part of God's plan as to the eschatological (end-time) figure. Jewish dogma had it: Just people *have* to suffer, but God will vindicate them.

3. Finally, we have the soteriological schema. Jesus' death is seen as a vicarious sacrifice of atonement. The Lord's own interpretation of his oncoming death: "This is my blood—to be poured out *on behalf of many*" (Mark 14:24) could be the historical ground for this tradition.

Today's Scripture elaborates on this third interpretation: On the Day of Atonement the Jewish high priest would slaughter the victim outside the sanctuary, then take its blood and enter the Holy of Holies to sprinkle the mercy seat to bring about reconciliation between God and the people. The author applies this model to Jesus, whom he sees as both victim and high priest, in his ascension entering the heavenly sanctuary.

In my Bible, I have underlined: "the blood of Christ . . . cleanse our consciences . . . to worship the living God," and I have centered prayerful reflection around these thoughts.

SCRIPTURE READING—

But when Christ came as high priest of the good things which have come to be, he entered once for all into the sanctuary, passing through the greater and more perfect tabernacle not made by hands, that is, not belonging to this creation. He entered, not with the blood of goats and calves, but with his own blood, and achieved eternal redemption. For if the blood of goats and bulls and the sprinkling of a heifer's ashes can sanctify those who are defiled so that their flesh is cleansed, how much more will the blood of Christ, who through the eternal spirit offered himself up unblemished to God, cleanse our consciences from dead works to worship the living God! (Hebrews 9:11-14)

"Let us celebrate"

A BICENTENNIAL of freedom and self-determination is a reason for celebration. A nation does not want to forget this great event of the past. Likewise, we annually celebrate Thanksgiving Day, Independence Day, and Washington's and Lincoln's birthdays. These memorials foster our gratitude and our awareness as a nation under God.

The Jews celebrate their Exodus from bondage in Egypt, which is their Independence Day, with the annual Passover. The remarkable thing is that they attribute their redemption expressly to the intervention of Almighty God and celebrate it annually with a detailed ritual. Until the destruction of the Jewish temple in Jerusalem (70 A.D.) this ritual consisted of the Passover sacrifice (offering God a lamb as a symbol of appreciation) and a sacrificial repast (symbolizing both communion with God, to whom the victim was offered, and communion with fellow worshipers). Afterward the Jewish Passover became what it still is—only a memorial meal.

In meditating on our Lord's death on the cross, the early Church saw Jesus as a Jewish high priest offering sacrifice to God. This sacrifice, however, was not a lamb; it was his own body and blood, shed to set us free from the bondage of evil. *(See April 22.)*

Following this trend of thought, we understand Paul when he says: "Christ, our Passover, has been sacrificed" (1 Corinthians 5:7). Our Eucharistic celebration is a Jewish Passover with a new meaning. The Jews celebrate Passover as a memorial of their redemption from bondage in Egypt, brought about by God's mighty hand. We Christians celebrate the Eucharist as a memorial of our redemption from the slavery of evil, brought about by Christ's death on the cross. With these remarks in mind, reflect prayerfully on today's Scripture.

SCRIPTURE READING —

This boasting of yours is an ugly thing. Do you not know that a little yeast has its effect all though the dough? Get rid of the old yeast to make of yourselves fresh dough, unleavened loaves, as it were; Christ our Passover has been sacrificed. Let us celebrate the feast not with the old yeast, that of corruption and wickedness, but with the unleavened bread of sincerity and truth. (1 Corinthians 5:6-8)

"This is my blood . . . to be poured out on behalf of many"

AT A farewell party for a retiring employee most of the time is taken up by speaking words of thanks and appreciation for services rendered, and only at the end is a token of appreciation offered, a gift which signifies whatever has been said.

The Eucharistic Prayer should be considered in a similar setting. Most of it consists of words of praise and thanksgiving, and in that framework time and again we offer Almighty God a token of our gratitude, namely, the body and blood of Christ (Christ himself in the signs of bread and wine), offered in sacrifice on the altar of the cross "once for all" (Hebrews 10:10).

The Lord's Supper is a Christian Passover Sacrifice and Sacrificial Repast. It is an anticipated memorial of the Lord's sacrificial death on the cross, and we repeat it time and again "in memory." Our Lord's blood was shed in atonement, to ratify a new covenant between God and man: "This is my blood, the blood of the new covenant." When you partake in the memorial of Christ's death, make his body and blood present in the signs of bread and wine a token of your self-surrender to God.

As you partake of the Sacrificial Repast, Holy Communion, let it be a real encounter, a growing oneness of mind with our Lord. "In memory of his [Christ's] death and resurrection, we offer you, Father, this life-giving bread, this saving cup. Grant that we, who are nourished by his body and blood, may be filled with his Holy Spirit, and become one body, one spirit in Christ" (Eucharistic Prayer II and III).

SCRIPTURE READING —

During the meal he took bread, blessed and broke it, and gave it to them. "Take this," he said, "this is my body." He likewise took a cup, gave thanks and passed it to them, and they all drank from it. He said to them: "This is my blood, the blood of the covenant, to be poured out on behalf of many. I solemnly assure you, I will never again drink of the fruit of the vine until the day when I drink it new in the reign of God."

After singing songs of praise, they walked out to the Mount of Olives. (Mark 14:22-26)

"Do you love me?"

HOW do we remember a beloved person, father or mother, who has passed away? We console one another with our common faith that he/she is happy with God. As time heals the wound caused by death, the memory of this person lives on in our minds. We remember sayings: "Father used to say. . . ." Anecdotes that reflect him/her as a lovable person are told time and again: "Mother used to . . .," followed by a little flash which shows how concerned she could be. Something like this took place after the death of Jesus.

First, there was utter dismay and sadness. But then the disciples experienced the Master as alive. They told others about it. And long after the Lord's last apparition, they shared experiences with others, telling what he had meant to them. These narratives, related time and again in the congregation, reflect the personality of Jesus Christ, his forgiveness, his power, his care, his mercy. Only the most characteristic ones were used by the writers of the New Testament to teach us who the Lord Jesus is and what he means to Christians.

We have an example in today's Scripture. The tradition found in this reading brings out what the risen Lord meant to the disciples in the view of John who relates it, and at the same time what he means to you and me. Apply this prayerfully to your own situation.

SCRIPTURE READING—

When they had eaten their meal, Jesus said to Simon Peter, "Simon, son of John, do you love me more than these?" "Yes, Lord," he said, "you know that I love you." At which Jesus said, "Feed my lambs."

A second time he put his question, "Simon, son of John, do you love me?" "Yes, Lord," Peter said, "you know that I love you." Jesus replied, "Tend my sheep."

A third time Jesus asked him, "Simon, son of John, do you love me?" Peter was hurt because he had asked a third time, "Do you love me?" So he said to him: "Lord, you know everything. You know well that I love you." Jesus said to him, "Feed my sheep."

When Jesus had finished speaking he said to him, "Follow me."
(John 21:15-17, 19)

"A persecution started against Paul and Barnabas"

WE ARE told that day by day life can be a joyous experience. The commercials on television assure you that it will be if you buy what they try to sell you. This is also the message of not a few psychologists who assert that the learning process in school, home life, job, and religion/faith should all be one joyous experience! This is fine in theory but what happens if circumstances prevent our lives from being joyous all the time?

What if gradually a school becomes an anti-intellectual fun house? In this respect, teachers who do not dare to challenge their students are not their friends. As for the home, here too there are unpleasant chores to be done. And there are parents who spoil their children—doing them a great disservice for their later life. Even if we love our work, there is no job which does not entail unpleasant aspects as well. And as far as religion is concerned, worship services should be a mutual inspiration, and a Christian life of mutual love is a splendid thing; however, we cannot have that good warm feeling all the time, and neither is the church a theater where we go to enjoy "an exciting show"! Loyalty requires sacrifice.

Paul and Barnabas had the joyful experience of making many converts, but they also had to face the pain of rejection. Though persecuted, they could not but "be filled with joy and the Holy Spirit." Life is never a continuous success story. When things do not go your way, think of Paul and Barnabas and their disciples.

SCRIPTURE READING —

The following sabbath, almost the entire city gathered to hear the word of God. When the Jews saw the crowds, they became very jealous and countered whatever Paul said with violent abuse. Paul and Barnabas spoke out fearlessly, nonetheless: "The word of God has to be declared to you first of all; but since you reject it and thus convict yourselves as unworthy of everlasting life, we now turn to the Gentiles."

The Gentiles were delighted when they heard this and responded to the word of the Lord with praise.

But some of the Jews stirred up their influential women sympathizers and the leading men of the town, and in that way got a persecution started against Paul and Barnabas. The Jews finally expelled them from their territory. So the two shook the dust from their feet in protest and went on to Iconium. The disciples could not but be filled with joy and the Holy Spirit. (Acts 13:44-46, 48, 50-52)

April 27

"He shall wipe every tear from their eyes"

MAN cannot live without joy. If life consisted only of funerals without weddings, only of work without recreation (a party, a show, a vacation), the burden of human existence would be unbearable for most of us. However, expecting too much joy from life is also dangerous because it easily results in disappointment. Friends may tell us enthusiastically about a new movie in town: "You must see it!" We look forward with great anticipation to it and finally get to see it. In most cases, we come away sorely disappointed by it! Similarly, at every wedding, the mother of the bride sheds a tear of joy but it becomes a tear of sadness when the bride leaves home to follow her husband.

Christians have reasons for joy, but we should not forget that God's kingdom has only been initiated in us. The full realization will come later. On this side of the grave we will have to live with the tension between "already" and "not yet." Expecting too much from Church and religion may disillusion you, and it takes maturity and courage to cope with this situation.

Utilizing the language of vision in the following Scripture passage, the sacred writer consoles those "who must undergo many trials." According to the ancients, storms at sea were thought to be caused by evil monsters; hence, "sea" stood for threat and peril. Accordingly, the words "the sea was no more" meant that all peril had passed. The author also sees "a new Jerusalem, the holy city": God had been present in the sanctuary of the old Jerusalem temple; now there will be a new kind of divine presence, enjoyed by all the members of God's people. All these new things are initiated in their lives as Christians, but they will be fully realized only later. Meditation on God's saving presence may help us to persevere in the faith.

SCRIPTURE READING—

I saw new heavens and a new earth. The former heavens and the former earth had passed away, and the sea was no longer. I also saw a new Jerusalem, the holy city, coming down out of heaven from God, beautiful as a bride prepared to meet her husband. I heard a loud voice from the throne cry out: "This is God's dwelling among men. He shall dwell with them and they shall be his people and he shall be their God who is always with them. He shall wipe every tear from their eyes, and there shall be no more death or mourning, crying out or pain, for the former world has passed away." (Revelation 21:1-5)

"The Holy Spirit whom the Father will send in my name will instruct you in everything"

RENEWAL implies continuity, yet it outgrows the old. The founder of the Ford Motor Company, for example, would hardly recognize his own first assembly line if he could see the Ford plants now. Yet basically it is the same. His successors have renewed the process of producing constantly in the spirit of the founder. They would be unfaithful to his great vision if they were still working as he did so many years ago.

In reading today's Scripture we should keep in mind that Jesus did not outline all the institutional details of the Church he founded. He left this up to the apostles and their successors. However, Jesus specified that in organizing the Church they should be true to his words and Spirit, the Paraclete (Advocate, Helper): "The Holy Spirit, whom the Father will send in my name, will instruct you in everything." We should have confidence that Jesus keeps his promise.

An example of not having confidence in Jesus' promise is the rebellion of Archbishop Marcel Lefebvre, who does not agree with the renewal of the Church, as inaugurated by the Second Vatican Council. The archbishop defies the Pope by illicitly ordaining priests and staging Tridentine Latin Masses. Does this mean that we Catholics may not have a few thoughts of our own? Of course, we may. St. Catherine of Siena did not agree with the Pope having residence in Avignon, France. She told him clearly what he should do. But her criticism was constructive and loyal to the Church both as God's people and as institutionalized in the Roman tradition. Pray often to the Holy Spirit for guidance!

SCRIPTURE READING—

Jesus answered:
"Anyone who loves me
will be true to my word,
and my Father will love him;
we will come to him
and make our dwelling place with him.
He who does not love me does not keep my words.
Yet the word you hear is not mine;
it comes from the Father who sent me.
This much have I told you while I was still with you;
the Paraclete, the Holy Spirit
whom the Father will send in my name,
will instruct you in everything,
and remind you of all that I told you.
'Peace' is my farewell to you,
my peace is my gift to you;
I do not give it to you as the world gives peace.
Do not be distressed or fearful."

(John 14:23-27)

"I pray that they may be one in us"

CHILDREN of a family are one in the parents. It is the parent image which keeps them together. And when there is a strong and beautiful parent image, there is usually a harmonious oneness of the children. As grown-ups they love to come to see their parents, and to a certain extent continue their life-style in their own families. After the parents' deaths, they remember them at family reunions, repeat characteristic sayings, and tell anecdotes which bring out how beautiful, caring, humorous, and energetic they were.

Just as children are one in their parents, so Christians establish a similar oneness in the Lord Jesus Christ. His image keeps us together as a family, and his Spirit, the Holy Spirit, inspires us to go on establishing God's reign in ourselves and in all those entrusted to us.

We learn from this Scripture that the Lord Jesus wanted us to be one with him, and in him with one another. It is a oneness in love, founded on the oneness of Father and Son. Finally, Jesus prays that our oneness may be complete. Love must be fostered daily. It is like a plant. If you do not water it regularly, it withers. Friends who fail to keep in touch soon drift apart. Keep in touch with the Lord Jesus! The more Christians do this, the more they will establish a beautiful oneness with one another.

SCRIPTURE READING —

[Jesus prayed:]
"I do not pray for them alone.
I pray also for those who will believe in me through their word,
that all may be one
as you, Father, are in me, and I in you;
I pray that they may be [one] in us,
that the world may believe that you sent me.
I have given them the glory you gave me
that they may be one, as we are one—
I living in them, you living in me—
that their unity may be complete.
So shall the world know that you sent me,
and that you loved them as you loved me.
Father,
all those you gave me
I would have in my company
where I am,
to see this glory of mine
which is your gift to me,
because of the love you bore me before the world began."

(John 16:20-24)

"Come, Lord Jesus"

AS SOON as we enter the realm of love, we start expressing ourselves in a terminology of different shade. The language which lovers use sounds even slightly ridiculous to a tongue-in-cheek outsider. "Ah, you are beautiful, my beloved, ah, you are beautiful. Your eyes are doves behind your veil. Your hair is like a flock of goats streaming down the mountains of Gilead" (Song of Songs 4:1). It sounds good, but one must really love in order to use this language seriously.

Utilizing both the language of love and what Bible scholars call "the language of vision," the author of Revelation brings out how a Christian's life is wholly concentrated around the risen Lord Jesus. The words "the Alpha and the Omega" refer to the first and last letters of the Greek alphabet which are used to symbolize the fullness and eternity of God; the early Church fittingly applied them to Jesus, the Son of God. The expression "wash their robes" means to cleanse themselves from sin; and the phrase "access to the tree of life" refers to the tree of paradise in Genesis 3:3. "Come, Lord Jesus" is the ardent prayer of all genuine Christians.

"Coming" results in presence. The Lord Jesus is present to his people; hence, a repeated "coming" will result in an ever more intimate presence, a great oneness in love and mutual understanding of Jesus Christ. Come, Lord Jesus, and share your Spirit, the Holy Spirit, with us.

SCRIPTURE READING —

"Remember, I am coming soon! I bring with me the reward that will be given to each man as his conduct deserves. I am the Alpha and the Omega, the First and the Last, the Beginning and the End! Happy are they who wash their robes so as to have free access to the tree of life and enter the city through its gates!

"It is I, Jesus, who have sent my angel to give you this testimony about the churches. I am the Root and Offspring of David, the Morning Star shining bright."

The Spirit and the Bride say, "Come!" Let him who hears answer, "Come!" Let him who is thirsty come forward; let all who desire it accept the gift of life-giving water.

The One who gives this testimony says, "Yes, I am coming soon!" Amen! Come, Lord Jesus! (Revelation 22:12-14, 16-17, 20)

"Let us build ourselves a tower with its top in the sky"

MY FAVORITE sport is swimming and, when nobody bothers me, floating. Without moving a limb I love to look at the blue sky. There are a few clouds high up in the air. And I am part of all this. In this biosphere, a layer of two miles around the globe containing the exact percentage of oxygen that makes life possible, I breathe and move and have my being. And this globe turns around silently in a universe that is hostile to any life. Neither I nor the plants and animals which I need to sustain me can live there. And on the surface of the ocean of life, I popped up a few years ago and will disappear shortly hereafter, just a red blinker on a radio mast in a dark night, on and out!

God, Ultimate Reality, underlying the reality I am part of, who am I? There is so much I want to know. What is the key to that tantalizing mystery of being? Is this desire to know instilled by pride? Is it wanting to build a tower high enough to peep through the windows of your mansion up there, as the ancients tried to do? Their pride (making a name for themselves) resulted in confusion. But why, among all the living beings, did you endow me with an intellect that makes it possible to reflect on my condition? Or should I go home, turn on my record player and listen to Beethoven's ninth symphony: "Brothers, over the world of the stars, a loving Father *must* reside"?

St. Ignatius, a grandmaster in prayer and meditation, states that the best posture for prayerful meditation is the one that fits *you* best, even if it is lying on a couch! Hence, floating in a swimming pool and sitting up in the lotus position (*see* p. 8) are not really so outlandish as postures for meditation.

SCRIPTURE READING —

[The people] said, "Come, let us build ourselves a city and a tower with its top in the sky, and so make a name for ourselves; otherwise we shall be scattered all over the earth."

The Lord came down to see the city and the tower that the men had built. Then the Lord said: "If now, while they are one people, all speaking the same language, they have started to do this, nothing will later stop them from doing whatever they presume to do. Let us then go down and there confuse their language, so that one will not understand what another says." Thus the Lord scattered them from there all over the earth, and they stopped building the city. That is why it was called Babel, because there the Lord confused the speech of all the world. (Gn 11:4-9)

"The Spirit of the Lord . . . is all-embracing [i.e., holds all things together]"

IN THE Broadway musical *Fiddler on the Roof,* Tevye, the dairy man, tells about the peaceful life of the little Jewish community in Anatevka—till something happens. "He sold him a horse—no, it was a mule!" And then pandemonium breaks loose. All start screaming. It is good Jewish humor, of course, but it reflects the reality of life. There are many vices that cause division among human beings. It may be the result of alleged injustice, plain envy, lack of patience, pride. All of a sudden we don't speak one another's language anymore.

But it is not the Spirit of God which alienates people from one another through lack of understanding. The wise man of the Bible describes the Spirit of God as holding things together, as unifying (Wisdom 1:7). Luke points to that unifying force of God's spirit in his well-known narrative of Pentecost, a reversal of the story of Babel, where pride (making a name for oneself) caused confusion (Genesis 11:1-9). A strong, driving wind and tongues of fire are biblical symbolisms to signify the function of the Spirit.

God's Spirit of love, in whom we are baptized or immersed (see Matthew 3:11; Acts 1:5), should be a driving force in us and overcome alienation, misunderstanding, and division, as signified in the miracle of today's Scripture. "Come, Holy Spirit, and enkindle in us the fire of your love!"

SCRIPTURE READING —

When the day of Pentecost came it found them gathered in one place. Suddenly from up in the sky there came a noise like a strong, driving wind which was heard all through the house where they were seated. Tongues as of fire appeared, which parted and came to rest on each of them. All were filled with the Holy Spirit. They began to express themselves in foreign tongues and make bold proclamation as the Spirit prompted them.

Staying in Jerusalem at the time were devout Jews of every nation under heaven. These heard the sound, and assembled in a large crowd. They were much confused because each one heard these men speaking his own language. (Acts 2:1-6)

"He breathed on them and said: 'Receive the Holy Spirit' "

IN OUR age of advanced medical science, we are not certain anymore when a person can be declared dead. Is brain death the indication and does it entitle the physician to turn off a person's respirator? For the ancient Hebrews breath was the sign of life and lack of breath the indication of death. And we ourselves still practice mouth to mouth resuscitation in a case of emergency.

Jesus uses the symbolism of "breathing" when he communicates the Spirit to his disciples. This symbolism reminds us also of the first verse of the Bible, where the "ruah-Yahweh" (breath-spirit of the Creator-God) is mentioned as the life-giving and animating principle of all creation. Jesus was a Jew and as such deeply steeped in Hebrew literature and culture. Unlike Luke (Acts 2:1-11), John assigns the communication of the Spirit to Easter Day. The gift of the Spirit is one with the risen Lord Jesus.

We should be grateful that the Spirit has been given to us and pray that it may be "life-giving," animating, evermore. Lack of stamina leaves many things undone, and makes it necessary to "confess to Almighty God that I have sinned in what I have failed to do." A full-rigged ship under an unfurled sail makes a beautiful picture, but it does not move without wind. Am I such a full-rigged ship? God, send your Spirit into our lives with the power of a mighty wind!

SCRIPTURE READING —

On the evening of that first day of the week, even though the disciples had locked the doors of the place where they were for fear of the Jews, Jesus came and stood before them. "Peace be with you," he said. When he had said this, he showed them his hands and his side. At the sight of the Lord the disciples rejoiced. "Peace be with you," he said again.

"As the Father has sent me,
so I send you."

Then he breathed on them and said:

"Receive the Holy Spirit.
If you forgive men's sins,
they are forgiven them;
if you hold them bound,
they are held bound."

(John 20:19-23)

"You will receive power when the Holy Spirit comes down on you"

WE KNOW about the frightening power—dynamic, driving force—of money. What are people willing to do for money! With millions of dollars the multinational corporations manipulate politicians both at home and abroad. With the power of money, secret agencies have toppled foreign governments and, if feasible, kept them in being. And even a little tip can work miracles of goodwill on the everyday level. If wielded dishonestly, power is destructive of human dignity. It degrades the victim, a fellow human being, to the level of a tool used to facilitate certain operations.

That is why it is dangerous to invest too much power in one person for too long a time. Democracies understand this and replace their elected officers every so often. Religious men and women usually elect their superiors only for a certain time of office. In the Church at large, we still have vestiges of medieval power investment for life. There are strong voices nowadays to change this and follow the way modern religious societies operate.

Dynamic power, however, is needed in the Church. But it is not the power the apostles were thinking of that is needed (Acts 1:6). The power Jesus speaks of is the power of the Holy Spirit. It is not the power of money or brute enforcement, but rather the gentle power of persuasion and love. It is the power of witnessing, which persuades fellow human beings to commit themselves freely to what is true and beneficial to real happiness for all.

How do you exercise your power as a parent, a superior, a teacher, an employer, a friend? Besides the power of the Holy Spirit, we also need his prudence to use it wisely! In meditating on today's Scripture, I would underline the words "power," "Holy Spirit," and "witnesses." You should do it your way!

SCRIPTURE READING—

While they were with him they asked, "Lord, are you going to restore the rule to Israel now?" His answer was: "The exact time it is not yours to know. The Father has reserved that to himself. You will receive power when the Holy Spirit comes down on you; then you are to be my witnesses in Jerusalem, throughout Judea and Samaria, yes, even to the ends of the earth." (Acts 1:6-9)

"I will pour out a portion of my spirit on all mankind"

WE ALL know of situations in which we get on one another's nerves. "Don't get so excited!" may be the advice of a quiet person who irritates the other one precisely because he himself should be excited. It can be the case of a new dress for your wife or a favor you don't mention gratefully. Excitement is a beautiful characteristic most spontaneously brought out in children, but hopefully never consciously extinguished in adults! However, we are not all the same. Some are more easily excited than others, and show their excitement in different ways. We should accept one another as we are.

There are charismatic prayer groups in the Church. These people can get pretty ecstatic in their prayer sessions. More phlegmatic and not so easily aroused people should not condemn these fellow Christians as crazy (drunk: see Acts 2:15), nor should the charismatically inclined consider the quiet Christian as second class. One may hear the remark: "They are not as far yet as we are (our group)." In fact, they never will be, because they are different, which does not mean more or less advanced. Each experiences the Spirit as "a portion," i.e., the way he is. Paul handles this issue in the First Epistle to the Corinthians. He states: "There are different gifts but the same Spirit" (12:4). No one can experience the Spirit in his entirety. To do so one would have to be God! In today's Scripture, Peter quotes the prophet Joel to make his point.

Be ever more aware of the indwelling of God's Spirit by constant meditation and in your own way. Though unseen, it is a great and glorious event.

SCRIPTURE READING —

Peter stood up with the Eleven, raised his voice, and addressed them: "You who are Jews, indeed all of you staying in Jerusalem! Listen to what I have to say. You must realize that these men are not drunk, as you seem to think. It is only nine in the morning! No, it is what Joel the prophet spoke of:

'It shall come to pass in the last days, says God,
that I will pour out a portion of my spirit on all mankind:
Your sons and daughters shall prophesy,
your young men shall see visions
and your old men shall dream dreams." (Acts 2:14-17)

"You must reform and be baptized"

WHEREVER human beings lay hands on values, sooner or later they deform them. We are not much better than children playing with an expensive Christmas toy and demolishing it before the day is over. We are prone to overemphasize certain aspects of a value and neglect the other ones. The result is deformation. Christians, the custodians of the message which our Lord brought us from the Father, do the same thing time and again. That is the reason why the Church must be reformed constantly. If this is not done from inside, it will be done by certain elements that break away.

We know about the Reformation in the sixteenth century (Luther, Calvin, Zwingli) and the Counter-Reformation of Trent, which came too late. We know about Orthodox and Reformed Judaism and about Gautama Siddhartha, who broke with the Brahmin priesthood (Hinduism) and originated Buddhism. Whatever we think of certain reform movements, the originators are usually concerned people, who want to go back to the basics, though often by making the mistake of a onesided emphasis in their turn. The Second Vatican Council represented a genuine effort to reform the Church from within. We are part of this Church and must be willing to reform ourselves at all times. Young people who don't want to reform do it in a reformatory.

Reformation and baptism (immersion) in Christ is an ongoing process. Only when we are willing to reform from within and plunge as it were ever more in Christ, will we receive the gift of the Holy Spirit. The moment you are satisfied with yourself as an exemplary Christian, you are growing old and stale and certainly the driving power of the Spirit is not in you.

SCRIPTURE READING —

When they heard this, they were deeply shaken. They asked Peter and the other apostles, "What are we to do, brothers?"

Peter answered: "You must reform and be baptized, each one of you, in the name of Jesus Christ, that your sins may be forgiven; then you will receive the gift of the Holy Spirit. It was to you and your children that the promise was made, and to all those still far off whom the Lord our God calls." (Acts 2:37-39)

"With exultant and sincere hearts they took their meals in common"

THE ancient Romans had a saying: "*Vae Soli*—Woe the loner!" Our Maker has not designed us to be alone. We should communicate with others. The Other One we should communicate with is first of all God. He has revealed himself as love, and we are related to him in a partnership (covenant) of love. We should be aware of this "vertical" relationship and constantly foster that awareness through reflective prayer—though we cannot be explicitly aware of the transcendent God all the time. Secondly, we should not be loners on the "horizontal" level either. There should be communion with fellow human beings. Communication is a skill, in which we should qualify ourselves constantly. It is a precious skill, which easily fades away if not fostered. Indifference is the great enemy.

The early Christians were aware that in living the philosophy of life which our Lord left us we need one another's inspiration. They enjoyed table fellowship with those who were privileged table-fellows of our Lord. Paul's followers had the same "koinonia" (fellowship) with him (Acts 20:7). We cannot follow the early Jerusalem community in all details, but their idea of koinonia is of great importance also for us. If you are a religious, what do you contribute to "koinonia" in your community and, if living in a family, what to intimate family life? Check also what is possible on a broader level. Perhaps communication with fellow meditators, persons with the same religious interests as yours, is a feasible thing to seek. You could promote daily meditation!

SCRIPTURE READING —

[The Christians] devoted themselves to the apostles' instruction and the communal life, to the breaking of the bread and the prayers. A reverent fear overtook them all, for many wonders and signs were performed by the apostles.

Those who believed shared all things in common; they would sell their property and goods, dividing everything on the basis of each one's need. They went to the temple area together every day, while in their homes they broke bread. With exultant and sincere hearts they took their meals in common, praising God and winning the approval of all the people. Day by day the Lord added to their number those who were being saved. (Acts 2:42-47)

"It was done in the name of Jesus Christ"

WHAT is in a name? Indeed, not much in our culture most of the time. Whether your name is Jones or Johnson, it does not say a thing about you. Nicknames, though, can be very descriptive! In other cultures, e.g., Javanese and Chinese, namegiving is still a meaningful event. So it was in the culture of the Bible, in which the name reflects a person's function in the universe.

In the poem on creation of Genesis, God gives names to all his creatures and he instructs Adam to give names to all the animals in the garden of Eden (Genesis 2:20). Nahab was an appropriate name, because he was a fool (see 1 Samuel 25, especially verse 25). Rachel called her child Benoni (son of my right). The name signifies the person. That is why the name of the divinity is significant for all ancients. The Babylonians had fifty names for their chief God Marduk.

God himself has revealed his name to the Hebrews: "I Am" (Exodus 3:13-16). Later Jesus reveals God and calls him "Father" (John 17:6, 26). The name "Jesus" means "Yahweh is salvation." God, who became Emmanuel (God with us) in Jesus, fulfills his promise made to the first "Jesus" (Joshua) that he would be with him as a savior (Deuteronomy 31:7-8).

Christian faith cannot sever itself from the name Jesus. Hence it was in the name of Jesus that the early Church conveyed salvation to the people. You are saved in the name of Jesus. You were saved from yourself, from the crippling sickness of selfishness, pride, and the like! And no salvation should be expected from somewhere else. Though not everyone wants the bumper-sticker "Jesus saves" on his car, the idea is meaningful. Be grateful and remember that salvation in Jesus' name is an ongoing process.

SCRIPTURE READING —

Peter, filled with the Holy Spirit, spoke up: "Leaders of the people! Elders! If we must answer today for a good deed done to a cripple and explain how he was restored to health, then you and all the people of Israel must realize that it was done in the name of Jesus Christ the Nazorean whom you crucified and whom God raised from the dead. In the power of that name this man stands before you perfectly sound.

"This Jesus is 'the stone rejected by you the builders which has become the cornerstone.' There is no salvation in anyone else, for there is no other name in the whole world given to men by which we are to be saved." (Acts 4:8-12)

"They continued to speak God's word with confidence"

A SIGN of aging is the lack of stamina or dynamic power to achieve one's goals. This process cannot be stopped in the individual, but it is disastrous when the phenomenon of aging is going to be predominant in the Church at large. Every seven years, the World Council of Churches has its regular convention. It is a means to prevent aging. The Catholic Church is not yet a member of the W.C.C., but sends representatives to attend the meetings. At the convention in Nairobi, Kenya, December 1975, the observation was made: "I sometimes wonder if the greatest of all hindrances to evangelism today is not the poverty of our own spiritual experience" (Rev. John R. W. Stott).

Is the Christian experience something we know about in a detached way only, or is it a process we are actively involved in? Luke draws a picture of dynamic involvement of the early Church in the Christ event. There was enthusiastic sharing of the awareness of being saved in Christ. The opposition of the authorities only served to inspire greater confidence in God's power, the Holy Spirit, at work in all believers. Luke has the house shake when they were praying! We hear a resonance of the Pentecost event (Acts 2:1-4). It is Luke's favorite way of expressing the Christian message.

God's word in today's Scripture could be an invitation to check our own dynamics. Prayer is indispensable most of all when opposing forces threaten to discourage us.

SCRIPTURE READING —

After being released [from prison, Peter and John] went back to their own people and told them what the priests and elders had said. All raised their voices in prayer to God on hearing the story: "Sovereign Lord, who made heaven and earth and sea and all that is in them, you have said by the Holy Spirit through the lips of our father David your servant:

'Why did the Gentiles rage,
the peoples conspire in folly?
The kings of the earth were aligned,
the princes gathered together
against the Lord and against his anointed.' "

The place where they were gathered shook as they prayed. They were filled with the Holy Spirit and continued to speak God's word with confidence.

(Acts 4:23-26, 31)

"The community of believers were of one heart and one mind"

AS THE administrator of both a school and a church, I have to handle many checks every month. Many married people have their joint checking accounts. But every so often it happens that a couple gives it up and starts a separate checking account for each partner. I wonder why. Married people are supposed to be "of one heart and one mind." What happened, since apparently they don't trust one another any longer as far as the money is concerned?

Today's Scripture describes the ideal early congregation in Jerusalem, where "everything was held in common." These early Christians practiced "communism," but on the basis of free choice, as is still done in our convents and monasteries and ideally in many marriages. "Holding everything in common," however, was not a goal in itself. It was a means for achieving the Christian ideal of being "of one heart and one mind." If you are religious, do you see your vow of poverty in this perspective? Giving up property should result in inner detachment and the will to share. A similar detachment should be found in the Christian family. Can you share and trust one another? And that Christian detachment should be reflected in your willingness to share whatever you can in charity with those who need your help.

In the Western tradition, we do not believe in enforced communism. Our philosophy is that some form of private property is the best guarantee that all keep working responsibly and by doing so get a fair share of the goods of the earth. But inner detachment and willingness to share with those who are less fortunate is a Christian must!

SCRIPTURE READING —

The community of believers were of one heart and one mind. None of them ever claimed anything as his own; rather, everything was held in common. With power the apostles bore witness to the resurrection of the Lord Jesus, and great respect was paid to them all; nor was there anyone needy among them, for all who owned property or houses sold them and donated the proceeds. They used to lay them at the feet of the apostles to be distributed to everyone according to his need.

(Acts 4:32-35)

"We testify to this. So too does the Holy Spirit, whom God has given to those that obey him"

I HAVE a good friend, a medical doctor, with whom I do not always agree. When I meet him, we usually have quite lively conversations. He can get very excited, and more than once he has made the very determined statement: "But Louise [his wife] and I think. . . ." I often wonder. How come two people who love one another for many years ultimately think the same way to such a great extent? Does mutual love result in mutual way of thinking? Is love really a source of mutual enlightenment? Is it two lovers subconsciously pooling their brain force?

A mystic, intuitively contemplating God, who is love, seems to come to a similar oneness of thinking with him. It is the mysterious dynamics of love, "being of one heart and one mind" (Acts 4:32). Paul could exclaim: "Christ is living in me" (Galatians 2:20). In today's Scripture we deal with a similar phenomenon. Risking their lives, the apostles testify to the Christ event. No Sanhedrin (supreme court) could stop them from testifying. And we observe the same remarkable referral: "We testify to this. So too does the Holy Spirit." It is again that mysterious oneness of thinking and speaking, this time between men and God's Spirit of love, that has filled and permeated their minds.

How do you think and testify, especially where you have to take a stand and where your way of thinking is not in line with values cherished by society at large? Meditation helps you to penetrate into the mind of God ever deeper. With God's help you can reach the point that you state: "But I say: So too does the Holy Spirit, whom God has given me."

SCRIPTURE READING —

When they had led [the apostles] in and made them stand before the Sanhedrin, the high priest began the interrogation in this way: "We gave you strict orders not to teach about that name, yet you have filled Jerusalem with your teaching and are determined to make us responsible for that man's blood."

To this, Peter and the apostles replied: "Better for us to obey God than men! The God of our fathers has raised up Jesus whom you put to death, hanging him on a tree. He whom God has exalted at his right hand as ruler and savior is to bring repentance to Israel and forgiveness of sins. We testify to this. So too does the Holy Spirit, whom God has given to those that obey him." (Acts 5:27-32)

"Gamaliel, a teacher of the law highly regarded by all people"

I REMEMBER lively Brother Herman Joseph, my teacher in the first grade of elementary school. He was a remarkable educator and a master in imitating the sounds of animals. I can still hear him saying: "If you make a big statement but don't know what you are talking about, you are . . . ?" Answer: "A hee-haw." And the brother repeated that bray of an ass perfectly. I often think of my teachers, who gave me what I needed to make my dreams in life come true. They were all men, except my mother and sister Helen who taught me in kindergarten. I owe much to them, but I remember best Brother Herman Joseph.

Paul of Tarsus in Cilicia (Asia Minor) had a similar experience. He vividly remembered his teacher Gamaliel. After Paul had finished school in his hometown, being of the Jewish faith, he wanted to become a rabbi. His parents sent him to college in the capital of Judaism, Jerusalem. Paul must have mentioned Gamaliel quite often, since Luke remembered his name when he wrote his journal, The Acts of the Apostles (see Acts 22:3). Why Gamaliel? The answer may be in today's Scripture.

Gamaliel was highly regarded as a teacher of the law, and rightly so, be it only because of the very intelligent advice which he gave in the confused situation of his days. Let us not forget that the Pharisees of the first century were honest people and indeed upset about the movement started by the rabbi from Nazareth known as Jesus. Read Gamaliel's advice! Dedicated and intelligent teachers are gifts of God. Do you remember some who helped you shape your life? Be grateful and pray that God may reward them!

SCRIPTURE READING —

When the Sanhedrin heard this, they were stung to fury and wanted to kill [the apostles]. Then a member of the Sanhedrin stood up, a Pharisee named Gamaliel, a teacher of the law highly regarded by all the people. He had the accused ordered out of court for a few minutes, and then said to the assembly, "Fellow Israelites, think twice about what you are going to do with these men.

"My advice is that you have nothing to do with these men. Let them alone. If their purpose or activity is human in its origins, it will destroy itself. If, on the other hand, it comes from God, you will not be able to destroy them without fighting God himself." (Acts 5:33-35, 38-39)

"Full of joy that they had been judged worthy of ill-treatment for the sake of the Name"

WITH special joy I think of my visit to Israel, the land which our Lord blessed with his earthly presence for more than thirty years. I took a guided bus tour from Haifa on the Mediterranean through upper Galilee. We went up Mount Carmel and then down into the valley of Naphtalim, once again blossoming with fertility. The guide—I still remember his German-Jewish name Tannenbaum—was visibly proud, showing us Gentiles the reforested hills and irrigated farms all over the valley. And then he made a remark that impressed me: "You see, ladies and gentlemen, this is again our land. We have invested blood, tears, money, and hard labor. You understand that we will fight for it." And I observed a strange, almost fanatical glare in the eyes of this man who had survived Hitler's concentration camps.

What is this willingness and even joy to sacrifice and suffer for an ideal? Thousands have done it and are still risking life and comfort for great ideals. I think of our martyrs of all ages and even of the hero of Graham Greene's novel, *The Power and the Glory,* the simultaneously weak and great priest who answered the fateful sick call though he knew that he was trapped and would have to pay with his life.

What made the apostles endure ill-treatment with complete joy? One thing is sure: "The Name" had captivated their hearts and minds so that love-bound they took any risk in order to share what they had found in Jesus. What is my and your willingness to suffer for "The Name"? If one sees Christianity as only a number of duties to be fulfilled to gain the bliss of paradise, the willingness to take risks is nil. Only enthusiasm, being captivated by Jesus and his good news, makes it possible!

SCRIPTURE READING —

[Gamaliel's] speech persuaded [the Sanhedrin]. In spite of it, however, the Sanhedrin called in the apostles and had them whipped. They ordered them not to speak again about the name of Jesus, and afterward dismissed them. The apostles for their part left the Sanhedrin full of joy that they had been judged worthy of ill-treatment for the sake of the Name. Day after day, both in the temple and at home, they never stopped teaching and proclaiming the good news of Jesus the Messiah.

(Acts 5:39-42)

"Lord, do not hold this against them"

IF THERE has been an American citizen who had reasons to get embittered in this land of the free, it was Dr. Martin Luther King. He spoke up frankly for what he believed in: freedom and equal rights for all, as guaranteed in the Constitution. He delivered speeches as fiery as the one of deacon Stephen in Acts 7. But unlike Stephen, Dr. King lived in a free democracy, where freedom of speech is expressly guaranteed as a civil liberty. Nevertheless, he was jailed frequently in his own country because of his frankness, and only abroad was his greatness recognized. Sweden gave him the Nobel Prize for Peace in 1964.

But Dr. King never showed bitterness. As a Christian he knew how to forgive. I quote from one of his speeches: "Love is the most durable power in the world. When I say: 'Love those who oppose you,' I am not speaking of love in a sentimental or affectionate sense. It would be nonsense to urge men to love their oppressors in an affectionate sense. When I refer to love in this context, I mean understanding good will. . . . The Negro must love the white man, because the white man needs his love to remove his tensions, insecurities, and fears."

Great men have always been able to forgive. The Lord Jesus prayed for his persecutors: "Father, forgive them," and he taught us to do the same in the Lord's Prayer: "And forgive us . . . as we forgive those who trespass against us." Stephen is in line with his Master. And Luke relates this tradition to teach you and me as God's word that we should keep trying to forgive generously and always. Can you forgive and forget?

SCRIPTURE READING —

Those who listened to Stephen's words were stung to the heart: they ground their teeth in anger at him. Stephen meanwhile, filled with the Holy Spirit, looked to the sky above and saw the glory of God, and Jesus standing at God's right hand. "Look!" he exclaimed, "I see an opening in the sky, and the Son of Man standing at God's right hand."

The onlookers were shouting aloud, holding their hands over their ears as they did so. Then they rushed at him as one man, dragged him out of the city and began to stone him. The witnesses meanwhile were piling their cloaks at the feet of a young man named Saul. As Stephen was being stoned he could be heard praying, "Lord Jesus, receive my spirit." He fell to his knees and cried out in a loud voice, "Lord, do not hold this sin against them." And with that he died. (Acts 7:57-60)

277-4

"They received the Holy Spirit"

WORKING in what was formerly called The Dutch East Indies, and is presently known as Indonesia, I had regular business with colonial officials. Many of them were agnostic and not always favorably inclined to what the Church was doing. But agnostics, atheists, or just bon vivants, all were impressed and often puzzled when they observed so many highly educated men and women—priests, sisters, brothers—dedicating their lives on those primitive islands to a cause which was lying beyond their horizon. They saw the concrete church buildings, schools, rectories, convents, housing projects. What was the driving power behind it all?

Referring to the fact that a major seminary was graduating ever more native priests, an official stated: "You'd better be careful. You are digging your own grave." He could not understand that the foreign missionary's goal is exactly to make himself superfluous and let the native clergy take over. The Church at her best is a sign of contradiction and a puzzle for the outsider.

Simon in today's Scripture was such an outsider. He saw the apostles laying hands on the faithful and conveying the Spirit to them. And undoubtedly he observed also what God's Spirit worked in those people. He was impressed and as a good business man saw money in it. But Simon was far from understanding what was going on. The mystery of the Church can be approached only in faith. The driving force of the Church is and must be God's Spirit.

You and I have received the Holy Spirit. It is natural that other motivations (pride, appreciation of fellow human beings) will sneak into our actions, but none of them can and should replace the power of God's Spirit. Keep an eye on yourself: Is God's Spirit guiding and motivating you?

SCRIPTURE READING—

When the apostles in Jerusalem heard that Samaria had accepted the word of God, they went down to these people and prayed that they might receive the Holy Spirit. It had not as yet come down upon any of them since they had only been baptized in the name of the Lord Jesus. The pair upon arriving imposed hands on them and they received the Holy Spirit.

Simon observed that it was through the laying on of hands that the apostles conferred the Spirit, and he made them an offer of money with the request, "Give me that power too, so that if I place my hands on anyone he will receive the Holy Spirit." (Acts 8:14-19)

"Do you really grasp what you are reading?"

THE TM people state that the technique of transcendental meditation (see Preface) should usually be practiced at home. Complete silence is of paramount importance. But it may be done in any place where you can sit comfortably without being disturbed.

The same may be said about Christian meditation. The ideal is to meditate at home every day in a quiet place and during a time when nobody disturbs you. Quiet down first and then try to achieve that state of "being awake inside with nothing going on," gradually letting your thoughts go over the points of the Bible passage that cross your mind. But not all have the opportunity to do it this way all the time. Hence do it wherever you can, as the Ethiopian of today's Scripture did it.

We learn from this passage how the early theologians of the Church (all Jews) explained the good news of Jesus in the framework of their national expectations as reflected in their classical literature, the Hebrew Bible. Take the citation from Isaiah as a starting point for a prayerful meditation on what the Lord Jesus has done for you.

SCRIPTURE READING —

It happened that an Ethiopian eunuch, a court official in charge of the entire treasury of Candace (a name meaning queen) of the Ethiopians, had come on a pilgrimage to Jerusalem and was returning home. He was sitting in his carriage reading the prophet Isaiah. The Spirit said to Philip, "Go and catch up with that carriage." Philip ran ahead and heard the man reading the prophet Isaiah. He said to him, "Do you really grasp what you are reading?" "How can I," the man replied, "unless someone explains it to me?" With that, he invited Philip to get in and sit down beside him. This was the passage of Scripture he was reading:

"Like a sheep he was led to the slaughter,
like a lamb before its shearer he was silent
and opened not his mouth.
In his humiliation he was deprived of justice.
Who will ever speak of his posterity,
for he is deprived of his life on earth?"

The eunuch said to Philip, "Tell me, if you will, of whom the prophet says this—himself or someone else?" Philip launched out with this Scripture passage as his starting point, telling him the good news of Jesus. (Acts 8:27-35)

"I am Jesus, the one you are persecuting"

AN IDENTITY crisis is a crucial time in the life of anybody. Usually the problem is lack of identity not only with the self but also those with whom a person should identify himself. Mothers identify very strongly with their children most of the time. Spouses identify with one another *(see May 11)*, children with their parents, and friends do the same to various degrees. Christians identify themselves with the Church. It is painful for a mother to hear people slur her son and for a Christian likewise to hear his Church besmirched—presupposing, of course, that he identifies with her!

In a Church that is in the process of reforming herself *(see May 6)*, quite a few Christians—lay people, clergy, and religious—go through an identity crisis. This is at least a sign that they identify with the Church, which is an indication of love and dedication. Why this identity crisis? Is it perhaps that they identify too much with the institution and not enough with the heart of the matter, the Lord Jesus? The early Church with little or no institution as we know it now was intensively aware of Jesus' identity with his people and the other way around. Think of the beautiful metaphors of the shepherd and the sheep (John 10:11-15), the vine and the branches (John 15:4-7), the head and the body (Romans 12:4-5).

Very much aware of the mutual identity of Jesus and his people (see especially Acts 9:5), Luke describes the conversion of Paul. But a light of heaven (faith) is needed to experience this identity to such an intensity that a changing (self-reforming) institution does not affect it. What about your emphasis on identity? Is it primarily your living awareness that the Lord Jesus identifies with you and that you should identify with him?

SCRIPTURE READING—

Saul, still breathing murderous threats against the Lord's disciples, went to the high priest and asked him for letters to the synagogues in Damascus which would empower him to arrest and bring to Jerusalem anyone he might find, man or woman, living according to the new way. As he traveled along and was approaching Damascus, a light from the sky suddenly flashed about him. He fell to the ground and at the same time heard a voice saying, "Saul, Saul, why do you persecute me?" "Who are you, sir?" he asked. The voice answered, "I am Jesus, the one you are persecuting. Get up and go into the city, where you will be told what to do." (Acts 9:1-6)

"The Church was at peace . . . at the same time it enjoyed the increased consolation of the Holy Spirit"

BUDDHIST wisdom has it that the fullness of reality discloses itself to mental "emptiness." Though using different terminology Christian mystics state the same thing. Another word for mental emptiness, which can be achieved by meditation, is peace of mind. Can we achieve it? Yes, if we are determined to make "the journey homeward to the truest self" (Aelred Graham in *Contemplative Christianity*). Mental discipline is simultaneously goal and means for achieving this necessary condition to enjoy the increased consolation of the Holy Spirit.

Fluid poured into a bottle has of necessity its shape and size. The same is true of the Spirit poured into our hearts. Indeed, the Spirit of God is a precious gift, which God must give us. But it is our task to make room first. That is why daily meditation is so important. The journey homeward, where you find your true self and are at peace, is an ongoing process, a life-long job. But it is worthwhile to make that journey. During all the years I stayed in the Far East, I never saw a nervous breakdown. Why, apparently, can Orientals handle the problems of life so much better than we hyperactive Westerners are able to? Let us learn from them!

Bible scholars tell us that today's Scripture is a summary that provides a transition to Peter's missionary activity as described in the following verses. But meanwhile Luke's observation is very penetrating. We need peace to build up ourselves, make progress in fear (filial respect) of the Lord, and enjoy the increased consolation of his Spirit in us. Come, Holy Spirit, and enkindle in us the fire of your love!

SCRIPTURE READING —

Meanwhile throughout all Judea, Galilee, and Samaria the church was at peace. It was being built up and was making steady progress in the fear of the Lord; at the same time it enjoyed the increased consolation of the Holy Spirit. (Acts 9:31)

"No one should call any man unclean or impure"

JEWS of biblical times were forbidden to enter the house of a Gentile (non-Jew), lest they should be contaminated by ideas and practices not in line with the Jewish faith. That is why Peter, a Jew, had to explain a few things to Cornelius, his Gentile host (Acts 10:28). Catholics in this country have practiced a ghetto mentality for many years. As a Church of immigrants mainly in the big cities, it was perhaps the only way to maintain their identity.

This brings back to my mind a conversation I had with a Spanish Redemptorist priest who was my guest for a couple of days in the Far East. As was not unusual on those remote islands, he had to wait for a plane to fly to Timor Dili to preach a series of retreats for Portuguese missionaries working there. We discussed the situation of the Protestants in his home country, ruled by the dictator Franco. I asked: "Why do you restrict their freedom of religion?" And with a very self-assured smile on his lips, he answered in one short sentence: "We are right and they are wrong." This mentality may have sheltered many believers of various religions, but it has caused much uncharitable alienation as well.

The Second Vatican Council points in a different direction. There is truth and much good found in all religions. We should not shun people. The Bible tells us Christians to be like yeast in dough (Matthew 13:33). We should have an uplifting impact on those around us and never isolate ourselves. Temporary withdrawal for prayer and meditation is a necessity, but then we should return to our prayer of engagement. Luke brings this out by relating today's Scrpiture.

SCRIPTURE READING —

As Peter entered, Cornelius went to meet him, dropped to his knees before him and bowed low. Peter said as he helped him to his feet, "Get up! I am only a man myself." Peter then went in, talking with him all the while. He found many people assembled there, and he began speaking to them thus: "You know that it is not proper for a Jew to associate with a Gentile or to have dealings with him. But God has made it clear to me that no one should call any man unclean or impure. That is why I have come in response to your summons without raising any objection. I should, of course, like to know why you summoned me."

(Acts 10:25-29)

"Peter had not finished these words when the Holy Spirit descended upon all who were listening to his message"

AS A YOUNG lad, I made a bicycle tour along the Rhine in Germany with a first cousin of mine. We had the beautiful experience of seeing the vineyards on the slopes of the hills and the old castles on top of them. It was prewar Germany and the evil star of Hitler was rising. In Aachen, before crossing the border back to our native Netherlands, we ate a last dinner in a restaurant which turned out to be a party center of the Nazis. President von Hindenburg had died, and dressed in the brown uniforms men were listening to Hitler's eulogy on the radio. His speech was very emotional and grew louder and louder like a strong driving wind.

At a certain moment he screamed frantically at the top of his voice: "Reichspresident General Fieldmarshal Paul von Hindenburg is not dead; he lives." That was it. We could not suppress our chuckling any longer as we watched those deadly serious Nazis captivated by the empty rhetoric of their "Fuehrer." But not so with the uniformed men around the radio set. They looked with threatening eyes in our direction, and finally one of them came over to our table: "Where are you from?" "From Holland." "Dumb Dutchmen, get out." And we got out as fast as we could, pumped on our bikes and pedalled back to Holland. These men, as insiders having faith in Hitler, were spellbound by his speech, and we Dutch boys, outsiders, laughed—which we should not have done, of course.

Today's Scripture describes a similar phenomenon, the power of the inspired word. Listening to God's word in a good sermon or Bible reading should be done as an insider, faithfully involved in the event!

SCRIPTURE READING —

Peter had not finished [his] words when the Holy Spirit descended upon all who were listening to Peter's message. The circumcised believers who had accompanied Peter were surprised that the gift of the Holy Spirit should have been poured out on the Gentiles also, whom they could hear speaking in tongues and glorifying God.

Peter put the question at that point, "What can stop these people who have received the Holy Spirit, even as we have, from being baptized with water?" So he gave orders that they be baptized in the name of Jesus Christ. After this was done, they asked him to stay with them for a few days. (Acts 10:44-48)

"God has granted life-giving repentance even to the Gentiles"

WHEN the Eastern Orthodox Metropolitan of Chalcedon celebrated an ecumenical service in the Vatican's Sistine Chapel with Pope Paul in December 1975, the Pope made a quite unusual gesture of humility and penance in the name of all believers in the Roman Catholic tradition both past and present. He knelt down and kissed the feet of the Patriarch, who as dean of the Orthodox synod announced the decision to establish a joint commission to prepare for unification talks with the Roman Catholic Church.

The schism which has existed between the two traditions for more than seven centuries is a scandal, and both sides must be blamed for it. If the high-ranking prelates who represented their churches at the time of the split would have exercised more humility and willingness to listen to one another, this separation could have been avoided. Pope Paul made a clear gesture to indicate that mistakes had been made also by those who represented the Catholic Church. And such a gesture is life-giving. Only great personages can afford to say: "I am sorry." And this willingness to say: "I am sorry" on the human level is a necessary condition for arriving at repentance toward our Maker.

Today's Bible reading sees the Christian faith as a gift of the Holy Spirit, who is a Spirit of life-giving repentance. And mind well, repentance is not seen as downgrading the ego, but as life-giving and liberating. Psychologists point to this fact. Whether we are enslaved by pride, egotism, dope, or nicotine, we are slaves, hence less human. Alcoholics Anonymous cannot help a victim unless that person admits being an alcoholic. Do we exercise repentance on the human level, admitting failures toward both self and others, and in them toward God? It should be an ongoing thing under the guidance of God's Spirit, and certainly liberating and life-giving.

SCRIPTURE READING —

[Peter said to the circumcised Christians:] "I remembered what the Lord had said: 'John baptized with water but you will be baptized with the Holy Spirit.' If God was giving [the Gentiles] the same gift he gave us when we first believed in the Lord Jesus Christ, who was I to interfere with him?" When they heard this they stopped objecting, and instead began to glorify God in these words: "If this be so, then God has granted life-giving repentance even to the Gentiles." (Acts 11:16-18)

"The disciples were called Christians for the first time"

GROUPS require commitment from their members and expect to demonstrate it. A car may carry the name of a university by which the driver demonstrates his love for his alma mater. A uniform, whether that of the armed forces or an RN, a Roman collar, or the veil of a religious sister, is a gracious sign of commitment, presupposing that it is real. However, the sign of brand name on a truckdriver's shirt gives me a bad taste in a mouth. The man must wear it since the corporation feeds him and his family. Each name tag must be evaluated on what it really stands for.

It was in Antioch that the disciples of the Lord Jesus were called Christians for the first time. This name tag has served ever since to qualify the disciples of Jesus Christ.

In this Scripture, it strikes me that discipleship is clearly related to commitment to the Lord, and hence not commitment to a set of values, a certain philosophy of life, but to a person. That is why discipleship of Jesus claims not just intellectual assent but the attachment of the whole person—mind, heart, and body. Dietrich Bonhoeffer wrote: "When Christ calls a man, he bids him come and die." And describing discipleship elsewhere, he says: "We are summoned to an exclusive attachment to the person of Christ."

Bonhoeffer accepted all the consequences of Christ's discipleship by defying Nazism in his native Germany, and dying for his stand. Can it be done? Barnabas was a dedicated disciple. What is the explanation? "He was a good man filled with the Holy Spirit and faith." That was his secret and the secret of Bonhoeffer as well. You have opted for Christ's discipleship and call yourself a Christian. How do you evaluate your name tag? If you get discouraged, think of Barnabas' secret and pray!

SCRIPTURE READING—

News of [a great number of conversions in Antioch] reached the ears of the church in Jerusalem, resulting in Barnabas' being sent to Antioch. On his arrival he rejoiced to see the evidence of God's favor. He encouraged them all to remain firm in their commitment to the Lord, since he himself was a good man filled with the Holy Spirit and faith. Thereby large numbers were added to the Lord.

Then Barnabas went off to Tarsus to look for Saul; once he had found him, he brought him back to Antioch. For a whole year they met with the church and instructed great numbers. It was in Antioch that the disciples were called Christians for the first time. (Acts 11:22-26)

"We must undergo many trials if we are to enter the reign of God"

NO COUNSELOR will suggest to a young couple that their honeymoon will never end. It would be a crime to do so. Married life has its beautiful moments of intimacy and excitement but also its trials. Wise people prepare mentally for moments of trial to come in order to be able to handle them and retain their equilibrium in time of pressure and distress.

By faith and Baptism we are related to God in a sacred partnership (covenant), which has marital overtones. In the Acts of the Apostles, Luke tells about the excitement of the early Christians, aware of their newfound intimacy with God. They spoke in tongues (Acts 2:4). The Gentiles shared that same excitment when they were filled with the Holy Spirit (Acts 10:45-46). We observe the same emotional reactions in the early congregations founded by Paul (1 Corinthians 14). Similar phenomena are reported as happening in charismatic prayer-groups all over the country in our own time. It seems that these Christians are going through a new honeymoon with God to whom we are espoused (Hosea 2:2-22).

However, Paul and Barnabas knew very well that honeymoons don't last, and neither does our honeymoon with God. They told their disciples: "We must undergo many trials if we are to enter into the reign of God; . . . persevere in the faith!" Trials in the faith are not the same for all Christians of all times and cultures. Possibly, you must be prepared mentally for times of tediousness and ennui. Should we give up in such a situation?

Married people who go through a period of tediousness and threatening alienation should sit down and talk things over. Similarly, if you experience ennui, a feeling of weariness with daily meditation, let alienation be your topic of reflective prayer and ask God for perseverance in the faith.

SCRIPTURE READING —

After [Paul and Barnabas] had proclaimed the good news in [Derbe] and made numerous disciples, they retraced their steps to Lystra and Iconium first, then to Antioch. They gave their disciples reassurances, and encouraged them to persevere in the faith with this instruction: "We must undergo many trials if we are to enter into the reign of God."

(Acts 14:21-22)

"Praying . . . as their fellow prisoners listened"

A FRIEND of mine, a naval officer who found his way to the Church in later life, told me that his conversion was greatly influenced by a chaplain, who used to pray his rosary every night walking up and down the deck of the man-of-war they were on. He never talked about faith with this priest. He made his decision much later. But the image of this genial man saying his prayers never left him. God, who does not undo his own handiwork, operates through the simple means of daily life.

Luke describes the conversion of a jailer and his family. To underline the impact of Paul and Silas, their feet chained to a stake but nevertheless praying and singing hymns to God, Luke uses visionary language. Clouds, smoke, fire and earthquakes are biblical images often used to describe the awe-inspiring presence of God. What the author wants to bring out is clear. The jailer found his way as did my friend the naval officer, namely, through the prayerful example of fellow human beings.

Does this mean that we should make a display of our prayer life? By no means! But being persons of prayer—as all Christians should be, laypeople, religious, and priests alike—we cannot remain unobserved and will have a salvific impact on fellow wayfarers. Where do you stand?

SCRIPTURE READING —

About midnight, while Paul and Silas were praying and singing hymns to God as their fellow prisoners listened, a severe earthquake suddenly shook the place, rocking the prison to its foundations. Immediately all the doors flew open and everyone's chains were pulled loose. The jailer woke up to see the prison gates wide open. Thinking that the prisoners had escaped, he drew his sword to kill himself; but Paul shouted to him, "Do not harm yourself! We are all still here." The jailer called for a light, then rushed in and fell trembling at the feet of Paul and Silas.

After a brief interval he led them out and said, "Men, what must I do to be saved?" Their answer was, "Believe in the Lord Jesus and you will be saved, and all your household." They proceeded to announce the word of God to him and to everyone in his house. At that late hour of the night he took them in and bathed their wounds; then he and his whole household were baptized. He led them up into his house, spread a table before them, and joyfully celebrated with his whole family his newfound faith in God. (Acts 16:25-34)

"Each day they studied the Scriptures"

A PHENOMENON of renewal in the Church since Vatican Council II is that ever more Catholics are joining Bible study groups. It is a very promising upswing of biblical piety as well. Since Hebrew literature, as we possess it in the Bible, reflects a time and culture so alien from ours, it needs to be studied under competent guidance and with a good handbook in order to be understood. Moreover studying together is inspirational.

The Bible is God's word, but man's word as well. We cannot possibly understand God's word, if we don't understand man's word first. We must find out what literary form a writer is using, what Oriental ways of saying things are employed, in order to find God's word in this human way of expression. Indeed, we believe that the whole Bible is inspired (guided) by God, but not all passages are equally inspiring to a prayerful response. Hence, we read selectively. The author of this book has selected a number of inspirational portions, and there are other ones.

Today's Scripture states that the members of the Jewish synagogue in Beroea (modern Verria in Greece) studied the Bible to see (find out) the truth and as a result many of them came to believe in Jesus Christ. And they studied with great enthusiasm under the leadership of Paul and Silas! In my Bible I have underlined: "with great enthusiasm"—"studied"—"to see"—"came to believe." All of this is important for prayerful Bible reading.

After I have studied and found out (seen) what the author wants to bring out as God's word to the readers of his time, I apply the message to my own situation: What does this mean to *me?* And I do so with enthusiasm, as an involved reader *(see May 20).* It is not enough to learn in a detached way that Christ is the savior of the world. I come to believe that he saves *me* from *my* bondage of evil (pride, selfishness, short temper, and all that dehumanizes *me),* and gratefully I respond in prayer. How do you read your Bible?

SCRIPTURE READING—

As soon as it was night, the brothers sent Paul and Silas off to Beroea. On their arrival, they went to the Jewish synagogue. Its members were better disposed than those in Thessalonica, and welcomed the message with great enthusiasm. Each day they studied the Scriptures to see whether these things were so. Many of them came to believe, as did numerous influential Greek women and men. (Acts 17:10-12)

PENTECOST

WHEN farmers have worked hard, invested much money, and taken their risks by submitting seed and labor to the unpredictable elements, they have reason to celebrate once a good crop is safely stored up in their barns. When the harvest consists of grapes, the joy is even greater. The produce itself is giving spirit and vigor! Harvest celebrations are part and parcel of country life. "Thanksgiving" originated in this setting, and the ancient Hebrews had a harvest festival (Pentecost) on the fiftieth day after Passover.

The early Christians went on celebrating this Jewish festival but with a new content. The harvest is God's people, born again from water and Spirit. "Through our rebirth in the Holy Spirit we became a harvest collected in the Churches of the Catholics as on a huge threshing floor" (Eusebius of Caesarea).

The fiftieth day, Pentecost, marks the completion of the Easter season, foundation and core of the liturgical year. The animating presence of God's Spirit in all of us is a reason to celebrate. An ever more "coming" of the Spirit should result in an ever more intimate presence! Hence, Christians pray in the spirit of the Pentecost liturgy: Come, Holy Spirit! Keep within us your vigor and protect the gifts you have given to your Church

Come, Holy Spirit.

"I put no value on my life, if only . . ."

PERSONS with a prophetic call in life know that they run risks. The prophets of the Hebrews knew this (Matthew 23:34-39), and our contemporary prophets were aware of the same. Inspired by God, these men must point their finger at the wounds of society, and then evil as a wounded animal strikes back. Dr Martin Luther King, the prophet of freedom for the downtrodden, had a feeling that sooner or later something would happen. Two weeks before he was killed I met him.

He had come to speak in one of the Baptist churches of a little Southern plantation town. There were black and white spectators and heavy police protection. I had compassion on this courageous man. Getting out of his car nervously and with frightened eyes, he looked left and right and then walked quickly to the entrance of the church. Life was a duty for him and in his successful moments he experienced it as joy that comes with fulfillment.

The apostle Paul had a prophetic call in life. In today's Scripture, Luke depicts him as having that same warning as mentioned by Dr. King. Paul felt that something was going to happen in Jerusalem. In Miletus, he spoke about it to the presbyters of the region. Since life was a duty for him, Paul went to Jerusalem nevertheless. "I put no value on my life." But deeply underneath his anxiety, Paul experienced the joy of fulfillment. "Despite my many afflictions my joy knows no bounds" (2 Corinthians 7:4). Applied to your call in life, what is inspirational in this Scripture for you? It may be God's word to you for today.

SCRIPTURE READING —

Paul sent word from Miletus to Ephesus, summoning the presbyters of that church. When they came to him he delivered this address: "You know how I lived among you from the first day I set foot in the province of Asia.

"But now, as you see, I am on my way to Jerusalem, compelled by the Spirit and not knowing what will happen to me there—except that the Holy Spirit has been warning me from city to city that chains and hardships await me. I put no value on my life if only I can finish my raee and complete the service to which I have been assigned by the Lord Jesus, bearing witness to the gospel of God's grace. I know as I speak these words that none of you among whom I went about preaching the kingdom will ever see my face again." (Acts 20:17-18, 22-25)

"There is more happiness in giving than receiving"

IT DOES not happen very often that a religious sister makes the cover of *Time* magazine. Mother Teresa was accorded that honor in the 1975 Christmas issue. Born of Albanian parents in Yugoslavia, she dedicates her life to the homeless and destitute, who live and sleep in the streets of Calcutta, India. Meanwhile, many idealistic women have joined her and do the same kind of work in cities all over the world. Why is it that the established communities of sisters are dwindling, and Mother Teresa's group is growing with such vigor? Puzzled superiors of established religious societies have visited Mother Teresa's community in Calcutta. What is her secret? It is the same as Paul's who states that it is unselfish giving that makes us happy and gives fulfillment in life. And the secret behind that secret is the love of Christ.

Mother Teresa knows that the poor are not always appreciative and grateful. That is why she emphasizes a living love for Christ so much. A priest who visited her in Calcutta told me that after the sisters have been in the hot streets all day long dressing the abominable wounds of the sick and dying people, they spend a full hour together in prayer. My friend asked Mother Teresa: "Why do you add this additional burden to the sisters' load of daily work?" Her answer was: "How can we love Christ in his poor, if we don't know what he looks like?" Theirs is the contemplative and the active life blended in a splendid fashion. Mother Teresa follows Paul's example and both follow the Lord, who states that there is happiness in giving. In relating Paul's sermon, what do you think Luke wants to teach as God's word to you and to me?

SCRIPTURE READING —

Never did I set my heart on anyone's silver or gold or envy the way he dressed. You yourselves know that these hands of mine have served both my needs and those of my companions. I have always pointed out to you that it is by such hard work that you must help the weak. You need to recall the words of the Lord Jesus himself, who said, 'There is more happiness in giving than receiving.' "

After this discourse, Paul knelt down with them all and prayed. They began to weep without restraint, throwing their arms around him and kissing him, for they were deeply distressed to hear that they would never see his face again. Then they escorted him to the ship.

(Acts 20:33-38)

May 28

"I wear these chains solely because I share the hope of Israel"

WILLY-NILLY a person discloses his real self when he is under pressure and things don't go his way. Dietrich Bonhoeffer, a minister of the Confessional Church in his native Germany, was such a man.

G. Leibholz writes in his *Memoirs:* "In prison and concentration camps, Bonhoeffer greatly inspired by his indomitable courage, his unselfishness and his goodness, all who came in contact with him. He even inspired his guards with respect, some of whom became so attached to him that they smuggled out of prison his papers and poems written there, and apologized to him for having to lock his door after the round in the courtyard." Indeed, he was a man showing his real self while under pressure!

Bonhoeffer, though, was not the first who preached the Gospel while in jail. Thousands of Christian martyrs (witnesses) have done it, the Lord Jesus did so from his cross, and Paul of today's Scripture preached the Gospel as an inmate with a soldier to keep guard over him. We should never blame those fellow humans who break down under pressure. It is God who judges. But we may admire those who seemingly still have something to give where most others are only recipients.

How do you behave under pressure? Do you build up moral strength and gain insight from reflective prayer on the Scriptures, so that when the time of adversity comes at a moment you least expect, you can stand it, of course with the help of God?

SCRIPTURE READING—

Upon our entry into Rome Paul was allowed to take a lodging of his own, although a soldier was assigned to keep guard over him.

Three days later Paul invited the prominent men of the Jewish community to visit him. When they had gathered he said: "My brothers, I have done nothing against our people or our ancestral customs; yet in Jerusalem I was handed over to the Romans as a prisoner.

"This is the reason, then, why I have asked to see you and speak with you. I wear these chains solely because I share the hope of Israel."

With that, they arranged a day with him and came to his lodgings in great numbers. From morning to evening he laid the case before them, bearing witness to the reign of God among men. He sought to convince them about Jesus by appealing to the laws of Moses and the prophets. Some, indeed, were convinced by what he said; others would not believe. (Acts 28:16-17, 20, 23-24)

"The spirit of the Lord shall rest upon him"

THE Watergate scandal has occupied the American mind for quite a while, and the history books of this country will mention it from now on. The corruption and evil revealed were shocking but not new in the history of mankind. In the prophet Isaiah's time and country it was not much better. The leaders of a nation were not presidents but kings. Jesse of today's Scripture is the father of the great king David, the founder of the Judean dynasty. Kings were seen as sons of God, adopted by the Almighty when they were anointed and enthroned.

But these kings did not live up to the rightful expectations of God and the people. Isaiah saw the Judean dynasty (royal family tree) chopped down by slow disintegration to such a degree that he compares it with a stump—the stump of Jesse. But God will not abandon his people for always. There is hope. A shoot, a new and efficient king, shall sprout from that apparently dead stump. And the spirit (life-giving breath) of the Lord shall rest upon him.

The theologians of the early Church have applied this classical poem of their national literature to Jesus Christ and his universal mission. He is that sprout from the stump of Jesse, God's Son, anointed as king of God's universal kingdom on earth. And God's Spirit rests upon him. The list of gifts of the Spirit, to which piety was added later, has become the traditional seven gifts of the Holy Spirit, given to all, who establish one body with Christ through faith and Baptism.

Isaiah sees a king as an efficient ruler and son of God only if he is filled with the spirit of the Lord. Jesus was filled with the Holy Spirit. And we are Christians worth our salt only to the degree that God's Spirit fills us and directs our thoughts and actions. Meditate on each of these gifts and ask God to bestow them on you ever more. ("Fear of the Lord" stands for "filial respect for the Lord.")

SCRIPTURE READING —

But a shoot shall sprout from the stump of Jesse,
and from his roots a bud shall blossom.
The spirit of the Lord shall rest upon him:
a spirit of wisdom and of understanding,
A spirit of counsel and of strength,
a spirit of knowledge and of fear of the Lord,
and his delight shall be the fear of the Lord. (Isaiah 11:1-3)

"Who can conceive what the Lord intends?"

WE ALL have had our time in life when we thought we knew it all, or at least much more than our adult educators! We had ready-made answers for all problems and could not understand why adults did not see things as we did. This presumptuous attitude is part of the maturation process a young person goes through. We accept it in our youngsters, but find it loathsome in an adult who has not outgrown it.

Wisdom, insight, or sound judgment is a precious possession. During all ages of human history, tribes and nations have had their sages, philosophers, friends of wisdom. But human wisdom, and also the wisdom of adults, is not always adequately the same as truth. Often sages have narrowed their observations by working with their intellect alone. This resulted in all forms of rationalism which had no eye for the transcendent.

In the Bible we find a type of wisdom which originates from both heart and intellect. It is an often intuitive wisdom of the total person. Moreover, biblical wisdom is a special gift of God. That is why we pay attention to it. In today's Scripture the wise man observes how complicated the problems of life can be and how difficult to find an answer; therefore we pray for guidance and ask for advice, since God can give wisdom through fellow human beings.

What is your priority of values? Wise and mature Christians have a sound judgment about what is more or less important in life, since they blend human insight with God-inspired wisdom. God, send your Holy Spirit from on high, your Spirit of wisdom!

SCRIPTURE READING—

For what man knows God's counsel,
or who can conceive what the Lord intends?
For the deliberations of mortals are timid,
and unsure are our plans.
For the corruptible body burdens the soul
and the earthen shelter weighs down the mind that has many concerns.
And scarce do we guess the things on earth,
and what is within our grasp we find with difficulty;
but when things are in heaven, who can search them out?
Or who ever knew your counsel, except you had given Wisdom
and sent your holy spirit from on high? (Wisdom 9:13-17)

"There are different gifts but the same Spirit"

IN A CLOSED society one has to comply with what is accepted as decent, or one is in for trouble. Whether such a society is an isolated rural community or a ghetto in the big city, the outsider is looked upon with suspicion and the non-complying insider is punished with ostracism or even violence. The Southland of the sixties was such a closed society. The Blacks wanted their equal rights as guaranteed by the Constitution, and most Whites did not want a change.

As pastor of a little town, I had opened the parish hall for dialogues between Blacks and Whites. My philosophy was: "As long as the two groups talk, they don't shoot. Hopefully we can straighten out things in a peaceful way." All went relatively well for a while, and even the mayor was scheduled to attend one of the meetings. Then one night the parish hall was on fire and a telltale smell of gasoline filled the air. I must give credit to the fire department that came out right away and saved the church, which was already starting to burn. The arsonists have never been found. The closed society had reacted with violence.

Can we accept one another as different? Paul has a few observations for his congregation in Corinth. We must accept one another as different and not try to mold the other into a blueprint of ourselves. If we just keep in mind that God's Spirit manifests himself to each as he wills, usually frictions can be handled without hurting one another. Apply Paul's remarks to your own situation and pray for the Spirit of counsel and strength *(see May 29)*.

SCRIPTURE READING—

There are different gifts but the same Spirit; there are different ministries but the same Lord; there are different works but the same God who accomplishes all of them in everyone. To each person the manifestation of the Spirit is given for the common good. To one the Spirit gives wisdom in discourse, to another the power to express knowledge. Through the Spirit one receives faith; by the same Spirit another is given the gift of healing, and still another miraculous powers. Prophecy is given to one; to another power to distinguish one spirit from another. One receives the gift of tongues, another that of interpreting the tongues. But it is one and the same Spirit who produces all these gifts, distributing them to each as he wills. (1 Corinthians 12:4-11)

"I confess that I did not recognize him"

WE MAY be acquainted with persons for a long time, have social or business contacts, and yet not know them as they really are, for our contacts are superficial. I may even love someone because of that person's beautiful qualities of character which I experience daily. Yet all of this very pleasant relationship remains on the level of the verifiable. To a certain extent, I can explain it to others. Then at a certain moment there is a real encounter. Behind that casual smile, I discover an entirely different person. I experience a new dimension that I did not recognize earlier. In contemporary language, we speak of a disclosure-experience. It is not just loving this person any longer; I am *in* love. I experience this disclosure as very real, but it is beyond the level of the verifiable. I cannot explain to an outsider why I am in love.

John the Baptizer knew Jesus, but for a long time he did not recognize him. In today's Scripture, John attributes his disclosure (faith)-experience to the working of the Holy Spirit.

We learn from this Scripture the way we should act. How do you regard Jesus Christ? You have heard about him your whole life. You believe that he is alive, that he knows you, that he invites you to a person-to-person relationship. Yet you may know him only superficially. Reflective prayer and meditation on the Lord Jesus may give you a disclosure (faith)-experience similar to that of Jesus' early disciples.

SCRIPTURE READING —

When John caught sight of Jesus coming toward him, he exclaimed:
"Look! There is the Lamb of God
who takes away the sin of the world!
I confess I did not recognize him, though the very reason I came baptizing with water was that he might be revealed to Israel."
John gave this testimony also:
"I saw the Spirit descend
like a dove from the sky,
and it came to rest on him.
But I did not recognize him. The one who sent me to baptize with water told me, 'When you see the Spirit descend and rest on someone, it is he who is to baptize with the Holy Spirit.' Now I have seen for myself and have testified, 'This is God's chosen One.'" (John 1:31-34)

"Come after me"

DISCIPLESHIP and ministry are part and parcel of the Christian scene. All Christians are called to discipleship and service. The Lord continues his mission of service to mankind through the Church. And the Church is not just the ordained ministers! It is all of us.

The very beginning of Jesus' ministry is marked by the calling of co-workers. Jesus said to the Galilean fishermen Simon and Andrew: "Come after me and I will make you fishers of men." The co-workers of our Lord must forward this message, and hand on the torch of faith! One may ask: "How strong is that light of Christ shining in the darkness of the human condition?" If Christians leave it up to the ordained ministers to continue Christ's mission, then Christian impact on society is negligible. If all would be dedicated to Christian discipleship and ministry, a tremendous untapped source of energy would be activated for the benefit of "the people who walk in darkness." What about your discipleship and ministry?

In my Bible, I have underlined: "A people living in darkness has seen a great light," and "Come after me," and taken these words as a starting point for my meditation.

SCRIPTURE READING —

When Jesus heard that John had been arrested, he withdrew to Galilee. He left Nazareth and went down to live in Capernaum by the sea near the territory of Zebulun and Naphtali, to fulfill what had been said through Isaiah the prophet:

"A people living in darkness
has seen a great light.
On those who inhabit a land overshadowed by death,
light has arisen."

From that time on Jesus began to proclaim this theme: "Reform your lives! The kingdom of heaven is at hand."

As he was walking along the Sea of Galilee he watched two brothers, Simon now known as Peter, and his brother Andrew, casting a net into the sea. They were fishermen. He said to them, "Come after me and I will make you fishers of men." They immediately abandoned their nets and became his followers. He walked along farther and caught sight of two other brothers, James, Zebedee's son, and his brother John. They too were in their boat, getting their nets in order with their father, Zebedee. He called them, and immediately they abandoned boat and father to follow him.

(Matthew 4:12-14, 16-22)

"How blest are the poor in spirit"

IT IS not easy to find a market nowadays for the value called humility. Human ingenuity and technology have achieved so much during the last few decades! Perhaps humility is misunderstood. A person with an identity crisis and unsure of self is not necessarily humble in the Christian sense. Christians should develop themselves to their full potentiality, but always seeing themselves as God's partners. Covenant-partnership with God the Creator of the universe is an ancient biblical concept. It is Hebrew wisdom, which Christians inherited from their Jewish brethren. With them they see it as divine wisdom.

Matthew was a Jew, writing for Christians of Jewish background. He compares Jesus often with the great lawmaker of Israel, Moses, with whom all Jews were familiar. In this Bible passage, Matthew states indirectly: Moses announced the laws (figuratively) from Mount Sinai. Jesus, greater than Moses, does (figuratively) the same "on the mountainside." Notice that Luke has the Lord preach this sermon on the *plain*. Actually, Matthew combines various sayings of Jesus and has the Lord proclaim them in what is known now as the Sermon on the Mount. The beatitudes are ideals which we should pursue constantly, though humbly admitting that it is not easy to do so!

SCRIPTURE READING —

When [Jesus] saw the crowds he went up on the moutainside. After he had sat down his disciples gathered around him, and he began to teach them:

"How blest are the poor in spirit:
the reign of God is theirs.
Blest too are the sorrowing;
they shall be consoled.
[Blest are the lowly; they shall inherit the land.]
Blest are they who hunger and thirst for holiness;
they shall have their fill.
Blest are they who show mercy; mercy shall be theirs.
Blest are the single-hearted for they shall see God.
Blest too the peacemakers; they shall be called sons of God.
Blest are those persecuted for holiness' sake; the reign of God is theirs.
Blest are you when they insult you and persecute you and utter every kind of slander against you because of me.
Be glad and rejoice, for your reward is great in heaven;
they persecuted the prophets before you in the very same way." (Matthew 5:1-12)

"But what if salt goes flat?"

IN DAILY life, we must be concerned about priorities. If your sorority is meeting at the same time as the parish council on which you serve you are faced with a conflict of duties. Your priority of values decides where to go. Prayer in the family and worship even in an expensive and luxurious church building are wonderful but not enough. We must be socially concerned; otherwise we are not like salt in the community, not a city seen by all, not a light to those in town who walk in darkness. What is your priority of values as to prayer and action?

On June 2, we focused our attention on discipleship and ministry by all. Today's reading suggests the same idea, but now by using metaphors: salt, a city set on a hill, and light. "*You* are the salt of the earth." Only by being dissolved in food does salt give its taste. "*You* are the light of the world." Only by diffusing itself in the darkness does light enlighten. Only by losing ourselves (sharing of self!) can we give "taste" to the life of the underprivileged and enlighten the path of others when they falter. What do *you* do for the old and lonely? Sharing time and self can be as important in our depersonalized society as sharing bread. It is the mark of Christians "worth their salt," and their "generosity shall endure forever" (Psalm 112:3). Blend the contemplative and the active harmoniously in your life!

SCRIPTURE READING —

[Jesus said:] "You are the salt of the earth. But what if salt goes flat? How can you restore its flavor? Then it is good for nothing but to be thrown out and trampled underfoot.

"You are the light of the world. A city set on a hill cannot be hidden. Men do not light a lamp and then put it under a bushel basket. They set it on a stand where it gives light to all in the house. In the same way, your light must shine before men so that they may see goodness in your acts and give praise to your heavenly Father." (Matthew 5:13-16)

"Unless your holiness surpasses that of the scribes and Pharisees . . ."

HUMAN beings are free but they encounter laws as well. It seems to be ever more difficult for the modern person to accept rules and regulations, which often are considered as handicaps for full self-realization. Freedom is of paramount importance in the "land of the free and the home of the brave." Paul states that "it was for liberty that Christ freed us" (Galatians 5:1). Comparing various sayings of Scripture may help us. Paul says also: "God sent his Son to deliver us from the law, so that we may receive our status as adopted sons" (Galatians 4:4-5). This gives us a clue. Paul sees freedom not just as "free from" but more as "free for," i.e., free to love God as his adopted children.

Love of God and neighbor is the great law from which there is never an exception. Other laws should be tested on that great law of love, of which they are supposed to be applications. Laws tell us how other reasonable persons have applied the law of love to situations which may be very similar to ours. Do not discard such wisdom too easily: Laws may be beacons in our often confused human condition.

Jesus did not come to do away with the law, but to reinterpret it and raise it to a different level. Jesus stresses that we should pay attention not just to what is actually done, but also to the inner motive, which is known only to ourselves and to God. It is principally this inner motive which constitutes aversion from or conversion to God, and for which we will have to account. In strong Semitic language, Jesus draws a black-versus-white picture. The idea is clear. God claims our whole being in the entirety of love.

SCRIPTURE READING —

[Jesus said:] "I tell you, unless your holiness surpasses that of the scribes and Pharisees you shall not enter the kingdom of God.

"You have heard the commandment imposed on your forefathers, 'You shall not commit murder; every murderer shall be liable to judgment.' What I say to you is: everyone who grows angry with his brother shall be liable to judgment.

"You have heard the commandment, 'You shall not commit adultery.' What I say to you is: anyone who looks lustfully at a woman has already committed adultery with her in his thoughts."

(Matthew 5:20-22, 27-28)

"You must be made perfect as your heavenly Father is perfect"

IT IS the Hebrew genius, under divine guidance, that has related morality expressly to God and religion. Why should man be holy? Because God is holy (Leviticus 19:2). "You must be perfect as your heavenly Father is perfect" (Matthew 5:48). "You are the temple of God—the Spirit dwells in you—the temple of God is holy" (1 Corinthians 3:16-17). Of course, the nations surrounding Israel had morality too. But it was more related to an efficient understanding of what was good to keep society going than to their gods, who were often anything but holy!

Christians see their moral lives related to God. Hence, it is important to know what God thinks of morality. God's ideas on morality are best reflected in Jesus Christ and what he stands for. "He is the image of the invisible God" (Colossians 1:15). Imitation of Christ is the best guide for a morally good life!

"Love your enemies!" A civil rights leader who strove to follow this command till he was ultimately killed comments: "I am not speaking of love in a sentimental or affectionate sense. It would be nonsense to urge men to love their oppressors in an affectionate sense. When I refer to love in this context, I mean understanding goodwill—we must in strength and humility meet hate with love." Respond to God's word in reflective prayer!

SCRIPTURE READING —

[Jesus said:] "You have heard the commandment, 'An eye for an eye, a tooth for a tooth.' But what I say to you is: offer no resistance to injury. When a person strikes you on the right cheek, turn and offer him the other. If anyone wants to go to law over your shirt, hand him your coat as well. Should anyone press you into service for one mile, go with him two miles. Give to the man who begs from you. Do not turn your back on the borrower.

"You have heard the commandment, 'You shall love your countryman but hate your enemy.' My command to you is: love your enemies, pray for your persecutors. This will prove that you are sons of your heavenly Father, for his sun rises on the bad and the good, he rains on the just and the unjust. If you love those who love you, what merit is there in that? Do not tax collectors do as much? And if you greet your brothers only, what is so praiseworthy about that? Do not pagans do as much? In a word, you must be made perfect as your heavenly Father is perfect." (Matthew 5:38-48)

"Which of you by worrying can add a moment to his life span?"

CHRISTIAN life requires a decision. "No man can serve two masters." Today's Scripture speaks in hyperbolic language: either-or. There is one thing we can learn from it, namely, that we Christians should be familiar with the whole Bible. We should be like birds in the sky and wild flowers in the field: carefree. But the grocery bill and the car payments must be taken care of as well.

The Bible speaks about man's handiwork as often as it urges us to have trust in the providence of God. The secret of the Christian life-style is to make the best of it without incurring the nervous breakdown and high blood pressure which afflict so many! After we have done what we reasonably can and must do, we can kneel down and pray with the psalmist: "He [God] only is my rock and my salvation, my stronghold; I shall not be disturbed at all" (Psalm 62:3).

Over-zealous pursuit of all the niceties of life is ultimately harmful. Too much work, "moonlighting" or urging one's partner to do so in order to keep up with one's neighbors is damaging to family life and inevitably leads to misery and trouble. Do we need all the gadgets possessed by the people next door in order to be happy? Where do you let your heavenly Father step in? (An effective way to arrive at reflective prayer as response to a Bible reading is to write down the prayer once in a while.)

SCRIPTURE READING —

[Jesus said:] "No man can serve two masters. He will either hate one and love the other or be attentive to one and despise the other. You cannot give yourself to God and money. I warn you, then: do not worry about your livelihood, what you are to eat or drink or use for clothing. Is not life more than food? Is not the body more valuable than clothes?

"Look at the birds in the sky. They do not sow or reap, they gather nothing into barns; yet your heavenly Father feeds them. Are not you more important than they? Which of you by worrying can add a moment to his life-span? As for clothes, why be concerned? Learn a lesson from the way the wild flowers grow. They do not work; they do not spin. Yet I assure you, not even Solomon in all his splendor was arrayed like one of these. If God can clothe in such splendor the grass of the field, which blooms today and is thrown on the fire tomorrow, will he not provide much more for you, O weak in faith!" (Matthew 6:24-30)

"Anyone who hears my words and puts them into practice . . ."

ALL of us know people who seem to be experts on the theory of life. They can explain beautifully what an ideal society, family, or work situation should be all about. High-ranking politicians, for example, may urge the people to practice frugality, but they are not credible in their own life-styles, which deviate widely from what they preach. The Lord Jesus fought such hypocrisy in his lifetime: "Woe to you Pharisees! You pay tithes while neglecting justice and the love of God" (Luke 11:42).

Parents who tell their children one thing while acting differently in their private lives are like those Pharisees. So are politicians, teachers, or employers who talk smoothly but are involved in shady practices. Young people resent this. They want honesty, though often they themselves may be deficient in this regard. Can we be honest with ourselves and others?

This Scripture marks the conclusion of the Sermon on the Mount with a warning against hypocrisy. We find it everywhere and not least in religion. This does not mean that we can do without religion and even organized religion. Since we need one another's inspiration and guidance, we must live religion in groups, keeping in mind, however, that in requesting a perfect group we are pursuing a utopia. Those who practice religion should constantly check whether they themselves are being honest.

SCRIPTURE READING —

[Jesus said:] "Anyone who hears my words and puts them into practice is like the wise man who built his house on rock. When the rainy season set in, the torrents came and the winds blew and buffeted his house. It did not collapse; it had been solidly set on rock. Anyone who hears my words but does not put them into practice is like the foolish man who built his house on sandy ground. The rains fell, the torrents came, the winds blew and lashed against his house. It collapsed under all this and was completely ruined."

Jesus finished this discourse and left the crowds spellbound at his teaching. The reason was that he taught with authority and not like their scribes.

(Matthew 7:24-29)

"It is mercy I desire and not sacrifice"

AS A prisoner of a communist army commander, I had to spend two months on the fabulous island of Bali. My house arrest, however, was not very strict. With the promise that I would not leave the island, I could freely move around. During that time, I had the opportunity to visit dozens of Hindu temples, attend cremations, and witness colorful and dazzling processions and worship services, which often lasted all night. With the moon shining over a balmy temple yard, the gamelan music[1] going on and on, and women in sacred dance offering their gift baskets to the divinity, one could not but get into an eerie sacred mood.

I often wondered what made these strikingly handsome people spend so much money, time, and energy on these very elaborate ceremonies. Experts state that anxiety has a great deal to do with it. The gods may hurt us, and so we must placate them. To what extent these worship services were just routine is hard to say. The problem of more or less void and meaningless religious ceremonies exists in all religions.

The Pharisees of Jesus' time stressed the external observance of many man-made religious precepts as a means for justification. Jesus refutes them. God desires mercy and not sacrifices (i.e., sacrifices of lambs and bulls offered in the temple of Jerusalem). God is interested more in fine lives than in fine liturgy. Does this mean that we should not worship any longer? Of course not! What God does not want is *meaningless* worship. And worship is only meaningful if it symbolizes reality.

Jesus practiced "mercy-love" by eating with social outcasts, tax collectors, and those regarded as sinners. What do we practice in order to make our worship services authentic?

1 Gamelan gong kebyar, Balinese orchestra.

SCRIPTURE READING —

While Jesus was at table in Matthew's home, many tax collectors and those known as sinners came to join Jesus and his disciples at dinner. The Pharisees saw this and complained to his disciples, "What reason can the Teacher have for eating with tax collectors and those who disregard the law?" Overhearing the remark, he said: "People who are in good health do not need a doctor; sick people do. Go and learn the meaning of the words, 'It is mercy I desire and not sacrifice.' I have come to call, not the self-righteous, but sinners." (Matthew 9:10-13)

"His heart was moved with pity"

WHEN human beings try to describe God, they are bound to do so with human concepts and limited terminology. We cannot adequately describe God, the "wholly Other." We simply do not have either the concepts or the words to do so. The biblical writers were limited by the same human condition, though we view their message as inspired (guided) by God. Hence, in reading the Bible, we should first find out what the *human* word means (by analyzing its historical setting and literary form: history, poem, allegory, etc.); then through it we will discover what *God* has to say to us.

Today's Bible reading portrays God as kind, good, loving, compassionate, even moved with pity. Can God be emotionally moved with compassion? We do not know. But he can be so in and through the heart of the Lord Jesus.

Notice that in the mind of the ancients disease was caused by evil spirits or demons. Hence, a sick person did not go first of all to a doctor but to the holy man to ask him to pray and cast out the demon. The healing activity of Jesus and his co-workers, seen as expelling the evil one, is a beautiful sign of the coming of God's reign in this world. "The reign of God is at hand! Cure the sick—expel demons!" All of this is another sign of God's kindness and compassionate love for ailing man.

I should be appreciative of and grateful for God's tender love, shown to me in the heart of Jesus, who was moved with pity whenever he came across human misery.

SCRIPTURE READING —

At the sight of the crowds, [Jesus'] heart was moved with pity. They were lying prostrate from exhaustion, like sheep without a shepherd. He said to his disciples: "The harvest is good but laborers are scarce. Beg the harvest master to send out laborers to gather his harvest."

Then he summoned his twelve disciples and gave them authority to expel unclean spirits and to cure sickness and disease of every kind.

Jesus sent these men on mission as the Twelve, after giving them the following instructions:

"Do not visit pagan territory and do not enter a Samaritan town. Go instead after the lost sheep of the house of Israel. As you go, make this announcement: 'The reign of God is at hand!' "

(Matthew 9:36-37; 10:1, 5-7)

"What you hear in darkness speak in the light"

THE mystery of God's kingdom on earth, a reign of justice, love, and truth, can only be known by the witness of those who are committed to a better society, as God envisions it. Witnessing for God's reign implies denouncing evil. But witnessing for God's values can be risky when the Lord's disciple encounters that ominous power of evil and must oppose it. Like a wild and wounded animal evil can strike back. We know the evil that overtook great men. Think of Blessed Maximilian Kolbe who offered his life in exchange for that of a family man condemned to death in a Nazi concentration camp, and of many unsung heroes!

In the Bible reading, the question is not fear in general; it is the particular fear which a Christian feels at the moment he must witness to his faith in God, the Lord Jesus, and that mysterious reign of justice and love to be established in society. The temptation is to keep silent, not to rock the boat. But may we?

Christianty has its long history of glorious martyrs. When we have to witness and must oppose injustice, we too may fear. Then we should pray: "[God] for your sake I bear insult, and shame covers my face. I pray to you, O Lord, for the time of your favor, O God!" (Psalm 69:8, 14).

SCRIPTURE READING —

[Jesus told his disciples:] "Do not let them intimidate you. Nothing is concealed that will not be revealed, and nothing hidden that will not become known. What I tell you in darkness, speak in the light. What you hear in private, proclaim from the housetops.

"Do not fear those who deprive the body of life but cannot destroy the soul. Rather, fear him who can destroy both body and soul in Gehenna. Are not two sparrows sold for next to nothing? Yet not a single sparrow falls to the ground without your Father's consent. As for you, every hair of your head has been counted; so do not be afraid of anything. You are worth more than an entire flock of sparrows. Whoever acknowledges me before men I will acknowledge before my Father in heaven. Whoever disowns me before men I will disown before my Father in heaven." (Matthew 10:26-33)

"He who welcomes you welcomes me"

A SIDE-effect of daily reflective prayer on Scripture is that one may get bored with the Sunday homily. You are a captive in that audience when the priest delivers his talk. Through your daily meditation you may be ahead of most of the other people in church, who don't read and study the Bible. Yet the preacher must gear his address to all in the audience. What should you do? Stay away? No, the congregation needs the witness of your presence.

If the homily is extremely poor, you have the Bible readings in your Missal. Well, meditate on one or another thought which you find there. But most of the time in any talk you will hear some thought that strikes you. Take it as a starting point for meditation! Of course, Christians have a right to expect that the minister of God's word is trained in biblical exegesis (explanation of Scripture), so that he will not air just his own opinions from the pulpit but will declare God's word enshrined in Scripture.

The Bible reading for today mentions receiving a holy man. "A holy man" in the Bible does not signalize a man's mystical experiences with God, but simply refers to a bearer of God's word, in other words, a preacher. As such we should receive the preacher of the Sunday homily. We should not expect primarily an eloquent speech, but an honest explanation of the Bible. Neither should we wish the preacher always to be "the nice guy" who practices some gentle shoulder patting. The priest has the serious duty of applying the biblical message to the life situation of the congregation (see 2 Timothy 4:2). What is the reason that you accept your "holy man"? Do you listen as one who is involved? *(See May 20).*

SCRIPTURE READING —

[Jesus said:] "Whoever loves father or mother, son or daughter, more than me is not worthy of me. He who will not take up his cross and come after me is not worthy of me. He who seeks only himself brings himself to ruin, whereas he who brings himself to nought for me discovers who he is.

"He who welcomes you welcomes me, and he who welcomes me welcomes him who sent me. He who welcomes a prophet because he bears the name of prophet receives a prophet's reward; he who welcomes a holy man because he is known to be holy receives a holy man's reward. And I promise you that whoever gives a cup of cold water to one of these lowly ones because he is a disciple will not want for his reward."

(Matthew 10:37-42)

"What you have hidden from the learned and the clever you have revealed to the merest children"

EARTHLY kingdoms and nations came into being through violence (war, revolution). Even necessary improvements in society (social justice and civil rights for all) are often carried out only after violent killing. The divine Master was sent to initiate God's kingdom (reign) of love and justice on our planet. But our Lord wants it to be done in his own way. Jesus, too, is a king, ruling a kingdom. But how different he is from the leaders of this world!

Today's Bible reading is a summary of sayings of Jesus, uttered at various occasions. "The learned and the clever" are obviously the wise according to this world, self-sufficient and unwilling to listen; "the merest children" are the humble and simple of heart who feel the need for a transcendent message, and hence listen. The second part of this Scripture characterizes Jesus and his rule over all who choose to live under his dominion. If you are weary, submit to our Lord's dominion and you will find rest.

The Church, all of us, must continue our Lord's work of establishing God's kingdom on earth. The latest techniques of public relations, television, radio, pictorial books, and magazines should be used to forward the message. But the most simple way to establish God's reign, which all of us can use, is that of gentle persuasion, especially the persuasion of a good example. The existentialist philosopher, Gabriel Marcel, an agnostic till the age of forty, writes (in a way, about himself): "An unbeliever can begin by believing in the faith of others, until this openness to belief leads to his own call and his own response." Is your faith such a beacon?

SCRIPTURE READING —

On one occasion Jesus spoke thus: "Father, Lord of heaven and earth, to you I offer praise; for what you have hidden from the learned and the clever you have revealed to the merest children. Father, it is true. You have graciously willed it so. Everything has been given over to me by my Father. No one knows the Son but the Father, and no one knows the Father but the Son—and anyone to whom the Son wishes to reveal him.

"Come to me, all you who are weary and find life burdensome, and I will refresh you. Take my yoke upon your shoulders and learn from me, for I am gentle and humble of heart. Your souls will find rest, for my yoke is easy and my burden light." (Matthew 11:25-30)

"Part of it [the seed] yielded grain a hundred- or sixty- or thirtyfold"

I LOVE to walk on a cement sidewalk close to my house in the shadow of a line of beautiful ancient oak trees. I often wonder. The roots of those trees must have tremendous power. They burst and lift up the cement of that sidewalk. What a mysterious force there is in those seemingly dead trunks! What is the living power of seed and plants that breaks through the soil after the lull of winter every spring again?

Walking through the countryside of Galilee, the Lord Jesus must have observed that same mysterious process. In today's parable he compares the power of God's word with the germinal force of the seed, which makes us hope for fruit and harvest. Jesus lived during an age of prescientific farming, which is still found among primitive tribes on this planet. Crop dusting is something only done during the last two decades. In the Far East, I have seen farmers, ten or more men in a row, turning over the soil with a sharp stick while singing their tribal tunes. Rocks are avoided. Chapping is done occasionally, but often also neglected. The yield is in proportion. Adapting himself to his audience, Jesus refers to this kind of farming in today's parable.

A word, be it spoken or written, always has something to do with the person who speaks or writes. There is power and inspiration in a human word and through it we feel contact with a living person. The same can be said of the word of God. As the great Hebrew poet Isaiah says, it never returns void but is always fertile. The power of God's word is like the germinal force of the seed, which makes us hope for fruit and harvest. (See Isaiah 55:10-11.)

Various kinds of people hear God's word, but the harvest (the results of that living contact through his word) are not the same in all people. Where do you classify yourself?

SCRIPTURE READING —

[Jesus said:] "One day a farmer went out sowing. Part of what he sowed landed on a footpath, where birds came and ate it up. Part of it fell on rocky ground, where it had little soil. It sprouted at once since the soil had no depth, but when the sun rose and scorched it, it began to wither for lack of roots. Again, part of the seed fell among thorns, which grew up and choked it. Part of it, finally, landed on good soil and yielded grain a hundred- or sixty- or thirtyfold. Let everyone heed what he hears!" (Matthew 13:4-9)

"Let them grow together until harvest"

IN OBSERVING others, we should be careful not to think in just two categories: good and evil. No person is entirely good, neither is anyone entirely evil. Some people look harshly upon all who are not in perfect consonance with their opinions about what good people should be and do. They speak of "law and order" (which must be!) without considering the whole situation, i.e., the person in the total environment, which determines character to a very great extent.

Advocating and pleading for law and order without eliminating poverty and slum conditions, without promoting equal education and job opportunities (so that the poor can help themselves), without furthering constructive family life programs and facilities, and without efficient rehabilitation programs for prisoners to be paroled is shameless hypocrisy. Better than any physician, social worker, or psychologist, God knows the case history of a person who has failed, and he is patient! What can a Christian do as an individual and what can a congregation do as a group to give persons who are considered a failure a chance to prove themselves?

Moreover, check the people you are associated with: children, students in school, co-workers, employers, and employees. We should try to cultivate something of that broadmindedness which we admire so much in God and, while praying "Forgive us our trespasses, as we forgive those who trespass against us," leave final judgment up to him.

SCRIPTURE READING —

[Jesus] proposed to [the crowd] another parable: "The reign of God may be likened to a man who sowed good seed in his field. While everyone was asleep, his enemy came and sowed weeds through his wheat, and then made off. When the crop began to mature and yield grain, the weeds made their appearance as well.

"The owner's slaves came to him and said, 'Sir, did you not sow good seed in your field? Where are the weeds coming from?' He answered, 'I see an enemy's hand in this.' His slaves said to him, 'Do you want us to go out and pull them up?' 'No,' he replied, 'pull up the weeds and you might take the wheat along with them. Let them grow together until harvest; then at harvest time I will order the harvesters, First collect the weeds and bundle them up to burn, then gather the wheat into my barn.' "

(Matthew 13:24-30)

Eventually, the whole mass of dough began to rise"

REFLECTING on my past, I must state humbly that I have done some good with the help of God, and even that my good influence has snowballed. Through my impact others have done and are still doing some good in their turn. But who cannot state this, mixture of good and evil as we are? On the other hand, there are many persons who had an uplifting impact on me. I think of my parents, a brother-teacher who encouraged my decision to become a priest, and many wise and dedicated counselors. The Creator does not undo his own work. He works through fellow creatures. It is all a very mysterious but seemingly effective way of doing things.

I admire the wisdom of my Maker; as Mother Teresa of Calcutta *(see May 27)* puts it: "We are nothing. The greatness of God is that he has used this nothing to do something." Augustine, the great bishop of Hippo (North Africa), lived a rough and tumble life till his early thirties. He attributes his conversion to the influence of his mother, St. Monica, and the bishop of Milan, St. Ambrose. We see again a mysterious chain reaction. St. Augustine wrote his *Confessions,* which has greatly influenced the thinking and conversion of many. Would this book exist if St. Monica and St. Ambrose had not played their role in Augustine's life?

In today's Scripture, Jesus brings out the same idea by using a metaphor: "The reign of God is like yeast." We collectively as a family, a religious community, a parish, as well as individuals must have an uplifting impact on our environment by word, work, and example. The faith factor in this process should be kept in mind. We should not be discouraged if we don't see immediate and visible results. Jesus never promised that the whole world will become yeast. Our environment is the dough in which Christians must have a constantly uplifting impact, which, however, cannot be computed statistically. "Lord, increase my faith!"

SCRIPTURE READING —

He offered them still another image: "The reign of God is like yeast which a woman took and kneaded into three measures of flour. Eventually the whole mass of dough began to rise." All these lessons Jesus taught the crowds in the form of parables. (Matthew 13:33-34)

"All those present ate their fill"

IMPORTANT diplomatic activity is usually sealed with a banquet. A festive meal together or a joyous picnic is a symbol of human togetherness in love and happiness. What a salesman does when he stops on the road to eat his lunch is entirely different from participating in a Thanksgiving banquet. Parties, eating and drinking together, play an important role in our society and signify beautiful values. In biblical times it was the same. Hence the Bible repeatedly evokes the banquet symbol to describe God's love and our relationship of love with him.

Matthew sees the episodes in today's reading as taking place in a crucial time in Jesus' life. John the Baptizer was thrown into prison. Is it possible that Jesus felt called upon to take John's place to proclaim the Good News of the kingdom at hand? He initiated his ministry with the same message as John's, "Reform your lives! The kingdom of God is at hand'" (Matthew 4:11, 17). Ultimately, John the Baptizer was put to death. "When Jesus heard this, he withdrew by boat to a deserted place." Did Jesus see his own impending death in the beheading of John? To continue his mission was to risk death. Yet Jesus took this risk!

The event of this passage (feeding the people) is a messianic sign that will find its fulfillment in the true messianic banquet, the Eucharist, which contains the promise of everlasting life in God's kingdom. When we are depressed, hope for a better future should keep us going.

SCRIPTURE READING —

When Jesus heard [about John's death], he withdrew by boat to a deserted place by himself. The crowds heard of it and followed him on foot from the towns. When he disembarked and saw the vast throng, his heart was moved with pity, and he cured their sick. As evening drew on, his disciples came to him with the suggestion: "This is a deserted place and it is already late. Dismiss the crowds so that they may go to the villages and buy some food for themselves." Jesus said to them: "There is no need for them to disperse. Give them something to eat yourselves." "We have nothing here," they replied, "but five loaves and a couple of fish." "Bring them here," he said.

Then he ordered the crowds to sit down on the grass. He took the five loaves and two fish, looked up to heaven, blessed and broke them and gave the loaves to the disciples, who in turn gave them to the people. All those present ate their fill. (Matthew 14:13-20)

"How little faith you have"

HUMAN life is a remarkable mixture of that famous "smile and a tear." We all have our ups and downs. We attend both weddings and funerals. Parents witness graduations and often the failures of their children as well. Married life can be like the smell of roses and turn into a nightmare. Young people are successful today and can be turned down tomorrow. Friends may disappoint us and we may witness infidelity not only in our government but even in our Church. All this may leave us confused and downcast. What are we to do? Are we to give up our faith in God?

Jesus' best friend, John the Baptizer, was beheaded in jail (Matthew 14:1-12), and "he went up on the mountain by himself to pray, remaining there alone as evening drew on." That night, Jesus' disciples were in serious trouble, their boat being tossed about in the waves. Lack of faith made them desperate and perhaps Peter, becoming frightened, would have drowned if he had not cried out: "Lord, save me!" Matthew has molded this tradition in such a way that it is clearly a lesson for the harassed Church of his day and God's people of all times! The Church, the traditional bark of Peter, is tossed on the waves of affliction. It needs encouragement. It should have faith in Jesus, for he saves us if we have faith and pray with confidence.

You may think of the Lord's anxiety (his friend beheaded) and his reaction (prayer alone!), or you may apply Peter's trouble to yourself and to our troubled Church of today. This would determine your prayerful answer to God's word in this Scripture.

SCRIPTURE READING —

While dismissing the crowds, Jesus insisted that his disciples get into the boat and precede him to the other side. When he had sent them away, he went up on the mountain by himself to pray, remaining there alone as evening drew on. Meanwhile the boat, already several hundred yards out from shore, was being tossed about in the waves raised by strong headwinds. At about three in the morning, he came walking toward them on the lake.

Peter spoke up and said, "Lord, if it is really you, tell me to come to you across the water." "Come!" he said. So Peter got out of the boat and began to walk on the water, moving toward Jesus. But when he perceived how strong the wind was, becoming frightened, he began to sink and cried out, "Lord, save me!" Jesus at once stretched out his hand and caught him. "How little faith you have!" he exclaimed. "Why did you falter?" (Matthew 14:22-25, 28-31)

"Woman, you have great faith"

THE "I am better than you" syndrome is part of the human condition. The evil of triumphalism has stained the Church for many centuries. Let us humbly admit it. If a certain kind of triumphalism would have been confined to "Jesus Christ and his abundant love for us is unsurpassed," it would have been all right. But often the beauty, truth, and riches of the Catholic Faith were identified with its proud sharers, and resulted in that ominous "we are right and you are wrong" complex which has caused so much damaging alienation.

Matthew took the basic story of today's Scripture from Mark. But he molded it to bring out a message for the Church of his day, which was beset with constant friction between Christians from Jewish background and pagan converts. We see therein classic Jewish exclusionism as opposed to God's universal will of salvation for all. Matthew wants to stress the fact that faith breaks down the barrier between Jews and Gentiles. "Jesus then said in reply, "Woman, you have great faith! Your wish will come to pass.'" God's word to the Church of today is clear: Do not condemn people! Have an open-minded respect for all who seriously follow their religious convictions, provided of course that they fulfill their obligation to find the truth. "He [God] wants all men to be saved and come to know the truth" (1 Timothy 2:4).

What could be God's word to you, and your prayerful response?

SCRIPTURE READING —

Jesus withdrew to the district of Tyre and Sidon. It happened that a Canaanite woman living in that locality presented herself, crying out to him, "Lord, Son of David, have pity on me! My daughter is terribly troubled by a demon." He gave her no word of response. His disciples came up and began to entreat him, "Get rid of her. She keeps shouting after us." "My mission is only to the lost sheep of the house of Israel," Jesus replied. She came forward then and did him homage with the plea, "Help me, Lord!" But he answered, "It is not right to take the food of sons and daughters and throw it to the dogs." "Please, Lord," she insisted, "even the dogs eat the leavings that fall from their masters' tables." Jesus then said in reply, "Woman, you have great faith! Your wish will come to pass." That very moment her daughter got better.

(Matthew 15:21-28)

"And the fever left her"

THE German poet Goethe writes: "Whoever wants to understand the poet must go to the poet's country." We must apply this saying also to the literature of the Bible. One cannot possibly understand the parable of the seed (Matthew 13:4-9), if mentally one does not go to Jesus' country of prescientific farming *(see June 14)*. I had the privilege of getting to know precritical people over a long time. When one understands their primitive way of thinking, one finds that those people are not as ignorant as they seem to be.

Their areas of interest are different. Their culture is prescientific, and so is their way of relating history. We expect our historians to find out exactly what has happened in the past, relate the facts, and, if they wish, offer their comments—but as clearly distinct from those facts. In a precritical culture, however, the narrator integrates his comment (interpretation) in the way he tells the story. He molds it freely to bring out a point, which may be the challenge to a certain philosophy of life. His vision of certain characters is not added after he has described them objectively; rather it is incorporated in the way he presents his characters: heroes are idealized, cowards are made even more cowardly. The authors of the Gospels wrote "history" as it was done in their time and culture.

We apply this way of writing to the miracle stories. A few miracles can be considered as events that happened; others are probably just reconstructions after Old Testament models. Since the sacred writer was not interested in finding out what exactly had happened, neither should we be. We should heed the point he wants to bring out. And since the author is inspired by God, his point is God's word to us. Apply today's miracle story to your own life situation and respond in reflective prayer. What prevents you from *waiting* on the Lord Jesus?

SCRIPTURE READING —

Jesus entered Peter's house and found Peter's mother-in-law in bed with a fever. He took her by the hand and the fever left her. She got up at once and began to wait on him. (Matthew 8:14-15)

"I will entrust to you the keys of the kingdom of heaven"

IT IS CLEAR that perseveringly living up to what Jesus Christ stands for cannot be done alone. We need one another's inspiration and encouragement. In accord with the will of our Lord himself and the oldest traditions, we live Christianity in groups or congregations. Consequently, wherever one establishes a group one needs organization, rules and regulations as an alternative to chaos. Hence, authority (one or another form of government) becomes a necessity.

As it is, authority in the Catholic tradition, exercised in Jesus' name and seen as brotherly service, is invested in our bishops and their head the bishop of Rome who holds "the office of Peter." Indeed, bishops receive their mission and authority in the name of God's people and as such they stand before God like any other "receiving" faithful. On the other hand, authority is not given to the bishops as in a democracy. Christ gave authority to God's people by putting it into the hands of his apostles and their successors, the bishops: "I send you. . . ." Our bishops are human beings. Some are conservative, some progressive, and others just careful. We should responsibly think with our bishops and support them with our "creative fidelity" and constant prayer!

This Gospel tradition puts things in their right perspective. Jesus is the Son of the living God. All authority has been given to him; hence he can delegate it. No longer visibly with his people, our Lord gives authority to the Church (Matthew 18:18), by putting it into the hands of Peter, who rules over God's people together with his fellow apostles. "Peace be with you," he said again. "As the Father has sent me, so I send you." Then he breathed upon them, and said: "Receive the Holy Spirit" (John 20:21-22).

SCRIPTURE READING —

"And you," [Jesus] said to [the disciples], "who do you say that I am?" "You are the Messiah," Simon Peter answered, "the Son of the living God!" Jesus replied, "Blest are you, Simon son of Jonah! No mere man has revealed this to you, but my heavenly Father. I for my part declare to you, you are 'Rock,' and on this rock I will build my church, and the jaws of death shall not prevail against it. I will entrust to you the keys of the kingdom of heaven. Whatever you declare bound on earth shall be bound in heaven; whatever you declare loosed on earth shall be loosed in heaven." (Matthew 16:15-19)

ORDINARY TIME

FOR years in the Fiddler on the Roof on Broadway, Teyve has been singing the melancholic lyric "Sunrise, Sunset — One season following another." Birth, maturation, procreation, decline and death determine the human condition. In the American tradition we celebrate Independence Day, mark the end of the summer with Labor Day, eat turkey on Thanksgiving, and exchange gifts at Christmas. One season following another!

Being part of this continually repeated cycle of events is seemingly a meaningless circling around as some of the Greek philosophers thought it was—"one season following another" till man goes down into the pit!

Christians see this constant flow of life in the perspective of the Christ event, celebrated in the Liturgy of both Word and Sacrament. Both the Christmas and the Easter cycle of festivals are not just circles of events but rather spirals, which lead me up higher and higher till I reach my destiny, the person I am called to be with God for all eternity. The liturgies in your Missal remind you of this time and again. Christ, the King of all creation, is our food for everlasting life! We pray: "Help us to live by this gospel, and bring us to the joy of his Kingdom" (Feast of Christ the King).

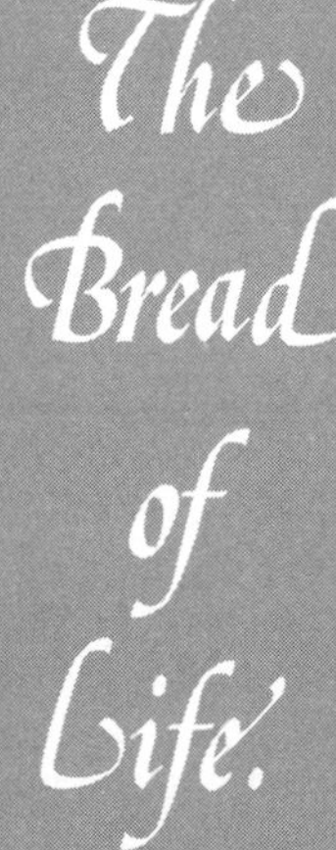

"If a man wishes to come after me, he must deny his very self"

THOSE who are dedicated to a once given commitment know that their dedication implies sacrifice. Married people may think of their mutual commitment in love; religious sisters, brothers, and priests may think of their vows; children and parents, if committed to mutual happiness in the family, may think of their daily living under one roof. Love means giving of self. This self-giving is a source of happiness but it entails sacrifice as well. For Jeremiah, duped by the Lord into loving, it was "derision and reproach all the day" (Jeremiah 20:7). After Paul has described God's redemptive work in Christ (Romans 1—11), he explains man's response in love: "Offer your bodies [selves] as a living sacrifice . . . to God" (Romans 12:1).

Christian life, though seen as a response to God's love for man, implies carrying a cross, as the Lord himself has done. Is Christian life then a miserable life, a life of those trapped in a situation from which there is no escape? Not as long as "sacrifice" is seen in the perspective of love. The secret of a happy Christian life is not to avoid "the cross," but to keep love alive!

What is your prayerful response to this challenge?

SCRIPTURE READING —

Jesus then said to his disciples: "If a man wishes to come after me, he must deny his very self, take up his cross, and begin to follow in my footsteps. Whoever would save his life will lose it, but whoever loses his life for my sake will find it. What profit would a man show if he were to gain the whole world and destroy himself in the process? What can a man offer in exchange for his very self?" (Matthew 16:24-26)

"Go and point out his fault"

IT SEEMS that the set of values ("do's and don'ts") by which an adult is guided becomes fixed in early infancy. Hence, from the very beginning, sound education is important—emphasizing its positive function (encouragement to do good) but not neglecting its negative function (correction of evil).

If parents would be more concerned about correcting their children from early infancy on, if marriage partners and friends would be honest in their love and friendship, which demands fraternal correction once in a while, perhaps the government would not have to do it so frequently in its penal institutions. Children who are either spoiled or neglected are on their way to becoming the criminals of tomorrow. Always being patted on the back or feared, hence flattered constantly and never corrected, makes one blind to his own faults till it is too late.

Many a fellow human being would be less narrow and not so peculiar if he had friends who were honest with him. This applies as well to little children, who need playmates to correct them, as to grown-ups: laypeople, priests, and religious for whom a sound community life or fellowship with peers is a must for the same reason.

Check your own relations with fellow human beings and respond in reflective prayer.

SCRIPTURE READING —

[Jesus said:] "If your brother should commit some wrong against you, go and point out his fault, but keep it between the two of you. If he listens to you, you have won your brother over. If he does not listen, summon another, so that every case may stand on the word of two or three witnesses. If he ignores them, refer it to the church. If he ignores even the church, then treat him as you would a Gentile or a tax collector. I assure you, whatever you declare bound on earth shall be held bound in heaven, and whatever you declare loosed on earth shall be held loosed in heaven." (Matthew 18:15-18)

"No, not seven times; I say seventy times seven times"

THE lesson of today may run counter to certain opinions on what it means to be "a man," "a strong person," a person who stands for principles which are not for sale. Where do the values of the Lord Jesus fit into this traditional picture of strong and unyielding personhood? One thing is certain: our Lord did not come to destroy human nature; he came to elevate it, to preserve the best in us, to ennoble us to what a Christian man or woman should be.

All Christians have today's reading in their Bible, and all pray: "Our Father . . . forgive us our trespasses, as we forgive those who trespass against us." Yet some favor violence and hatred to solve both social and personal issues. Can a real Christian be selective, ignore God's word whenever it is inconvenient, and practice what most do? Christian commitment is total and not selective! Jesus states: "He who is not with me is against me" (Matthew 12:30), and during Mass we pray: "May he [Christ] make us an everlasting gift to you [God]."

SCRIPTURE READING —

Peter came up and asked [Jesus], "Lord, when my brother wrongs me, how often must I forgive him? Seven times?" "No," Jesus replied, "not seven times; I say, seventy times seven times. That is why the reign of God may be said to be like a king who decided to settle accounts with his officials. When he began his auditing, one was brought in who owed him a huge amount. As he had no way of paying it, his master ordered him to be sold, along with his wife, his children, and all his property, in payment of the debt. At that the official prostrated himself in homage and said, 'My lord, be patient with me and I will pay you back in full.' Moved with pity, the master let the official go and wrote off the debt.

"But when that same official went out he met a fellow servant who owed him a mere fraction of what he himself owed. He seized him and throttled him: 'Pay back what you owe," he demanded. His fellow servant dropped to his knees and began to plead with him, 'Just give me time and I will pay you back in full.' But he would hear none of it. Instead, he had him put in jail until he paid back what he owed. When his fellow servants saw what had happened they were badly shaken, and went to their master to report the whole incident." (Matthew 18:21-31)

"Or are you envious because I am generous?"

THE dollar is a much cherished value in our culture. The person who makes an honest dollar in abundant numbers is thought to have succeeded in life. Students learn in school whatever can be cashed in dollars tomorrow. Doing something or not doing it depends largely on the amount of dollars that go with it. More effort, more recompense!

Indeed, the Bible speaks of reward, but focusing all attention on this aspect alone may result in the immature attitude of the child who thinks his father "owes" him money for every little job he does. Then questions come up like: "Are you envious because God is generous?"

The main reason for serving God should be love and gratitude, not merely reward, and certainly not a reward God owes us! Today's Scripture challenges this "recompense-only" attitude.

SCRIPTURE READING —

[Jesus told this parable:] "The reign of God is like the case of the owner of an estate who went out at dawn to hire workmen for his vineyard. After reaching an agreement with them for the usual daily wage, he sent them out to his vineyard. He came out about midmorning and saw other men standing around the marketplace without work, so he said to them, 'You too go along to my vineyard and I will pay you whatever is fair.' At that they went away. He came out again around noon and midafternoon and did the same. Finally, going out in late afternoon he found still others standing around. To these he said, 'Why have you been standing here idle all day?' 'No one has hired us,' they told him. He said, 'You go to the vineyard too.'

"When evening came the owner of the vineyard said to his foreman, 'Call the workmen and give them their pay, but begin with the last group and end with the first.' When those hired late in the afternoon came up they received a full day's pay, and when the first group appeared they supposed they would get more; yet they received the same daily wage. Thereupon they complained to the owner, 'This last group did only an hour's work, but you have put them on the same basis as us who have worked a full day in the scorching heat.' 'My friend,' he said to one in reply, 'I do you no injustice. You agreed on the usual wage, did you not? Take your pay and go home. I intend to give this man who was hired last the same pay as you. I am free to do as I please with my money, am I not? Or are you envious because I am generous?' Thus the last shall be the first and the first shall be the last." (Matthew 20:1-16)

"Tax collectors and prostitutes are entering the kingdom of God before you"

PROJECTION ("Not I, but he did it; he is responsible, not I") is as old as the story of Adam and Eve. With great psychological insight the author of Genesis has Adam reply: "The woman . . . gave me fruit from the tree, and so I ate it." And the woman answers: "The serpent tricked me into it, so I ate it" (Genesis 3:12-13). Every teacher hears the same thing daily: "Not me! He did it!"

No one who goes to jail can be said to bear the total guilt for his crime. Past family upbringing and society also contribute to making a person what he is, but only to a certain extent. In point of fact, a free grown-up person is responsible for what he does. Judges, lawyers, and psychologists wrangle daily with the tension between individual responsibility and the collective guilt of the environment.

Today's Bible reading discusses this problem of man, the sinner, related to God, his judge. We should be careful in judging others since we do not know how much a failing brother is determined by his past; but knowing ourselves we should be realistic and accept full responsibility for what we do and should do!

SCRIPTURE READING —

[Jesus spoke this parable:] "What do you think of this case? There was a man who had two sons. He approached the elder and said, 'Son, go out and work in the vineyard today.' The son replied, 'I am on my way, sir'; but he never went. Then the man came to his second son and said the same thing. This son said in reply, 'No, I will not'; but afterward he regretted it and went.

"Which of the two did what the father wanted?" They said, "The second." Jesus said to them, "Let me make it clear that tax collectors and prostitutes are entering the kingdom of God before you. When John came preaching a way of holiness, you put no faith in him; but the tax collectors and the prostitutes did believe in him. Yet even when you saw that, you did not repent and believe in him."

(Matthew 21:28-32)

"My friend had a vineyard"

PARENTS and teachers may sacrifice time and talents to give children the best they have to offer. Nevertheless, their task is not always rewarding. They love their children and students, but they are frequently disappointed by them. Lack of response can hurt badly. Following Jesus of Nazareth, we call God "Father." In his infinite love and wisdom, he has bestowed his riches upon us. Hence, as all parents and educators do, God has his expectations.

Today's reading is Isaiah's beautiful "song of the vineyard," written in the form of a ballad, a love song. Isaiah, calling God his friend, sees him in an affectionate relationship with his vineyard, the house of Israel, the chosen people, you and me. God has done whatever he could do. And see what happened! Notice God's painful disappointment when people do not live up to what he expects them to be.

God may ask you and me: "What more was there to do to my vineyard that I had not done?"

SCRIPTURE READING —

Let me now sing of my friend,
my friend's song concerning his vineyard.
My friend had a vineyard
on a fertile hillside;
He spaded it, cleared it of stones,
and planted the choicest vines;
Within it he built a watchtower,
and hewed out a wine press.
Then he looked for the crop of grapes,
but what it yielded was wild grapes.

Now, inhabitants of Jerusalem and men of Judah,
judge between me and my vineyard:
What more was there to do for my vineyard
that I had not done?
Why, when I looked for the crop of grapes,
did it bring forth wild grapes?

Now, I will let you know
what I mean to do to my vineyard:
Take away its hedge, give it to grazing,
break through its wall, let it be trampled!
Yes, I will make it a ruin:
it shall not be pruned or hoed,
but overgrown with thorns and briers;
I will command the clouds
not to send rain upon it.
The vineyard of the Lord of hosts
is the house of Israel,
and the men of Judah are his cherished plant;
He looked for judgment, but see, bloodshed!
for justice, but hark, the outcry!

(Isaiah 5:1-7)

"A king who gave a wedding banquet . . ."

FOOD and drink are important at parties, but more important than food and drink are the host, the hostess, and the guests we hope to meet there. People to be met can even be the deciding factor as to whether or not we go to a certain party in the first place.

Parties/banquets can be the beginnings of beautiful friendships or seal and deepen existing human relations since such parties enrich us as human beings.

In the Bible, the invitation to a banquet is one of the favorite images of messianic times. Today's Bible reading uses it to describe the bliss of God's kingdom, once it has been established on earth. God rules through his vicegerent, the Messiah—Anointed King on earth. The people (you and I) are related to God in a sacred partnership called a covenant. Inspired by God, prophets give this covenant marital overtones. The banquet becomes a wedding in which God is the husband and his people the bride. And in the inspired awareness of the New Testament, this bridal relationship of people with God has a transcendent dimension, its full blossoming and realization in a life hereafter.

In virtue of your baptism, you have a standing invitation to God's eschatological (end-time) banquet. How do you respond?

SCRIPTURE READING —

Jesus began to address them, once more using parables. "The reign of God may be likened to a king who gave a wedding banquet for his son. He dispatched his servants to summon the invited guests to the wedding, but they refused to come. A second time he sent other servants, saying: 'Tell those who were invited, See, I have my dinner prepared! My bullocks and cornfed cattle are killed; everything is ready. Come to the feast.'

"Some ignored the invitation and went their way, one to his farm, another to his business. The rest laid hold of his servants, insulted them, and killed them.

"At this the king grew furious and sent his army to destroy those murderers and burn their city. Then he said to his servants: 'The banquet is ready, but those who were invited were unfit to come. That is why you must go out into the byroads and invite to the wedding anyone you come upon.' The servants then went out into the byroads and rounded up everyone they met, bad as well as good. This filled the wedding hall with banqueters." (Matthew 22:1-10)

"Then give to Caesar what is Caesar's"

THE theme of *Fiddler on the Roof* is: "Play your little tune in life, but keep your balance and do not break your neck!" This is not always easy for Christians who are citizens of two cities: the earthly one (for example, the United States) and the heavenly one (the Church). We favor separation of the two, but there are areas which overlap.

A Christian is supposed to be a good citizen, pay his taxes, and exercise his voting right. He must love his country, though in certain periods of national history politicians and leaders may turn out to be corrupt. As in all institutions, not even excluding the Church, the human element will always be there. A Christian should be concerned about the cultural and social well-being of his community.

The Pharisees of Jesus' time were against paying taxes to the Romans but the Herodians (supporters of Herod, puppet king of the Romans) collaborated and paid taxes. Jesus goes beyond the question they asked him: Legitimate government has its rights, but God has his rights too. "Give to God what is God's." In case of conflict, we should obey God rather than man! Pray for guidance to keep your balance.

SCRIPTURE READING —

The Pharisees went off and began to plot how they might trap Jesus in speech. They sent their disciples to him, accompanied by Herodian sympathizers, who said: "Teacher, we know you are a truthful man and teach God's way sincerely. You court no one's favor and do not act out of human respect. Give us your opinion, then, in this case. Is it lawful to pay tax to the emperor or not?" Jesus recognized their bad faith and said to them, "Why are you trying to trip me up, you hypocrites? Show me the coin used for the tax." When they handed him a small Roman coin he asked them, "Whose head is this, and whose inscription?" "Caesar's," they replied. At that he said to them, "Then give to Caesar what is Caesar's, but give to God what is God's." (Matthew 22:15-21)

"Which commandment of the law is the greatest?"

UNTIL a few years ago, outsiders regarded Catholics as people who had to go to church on Sunday, did not eat meat on Friday, fasted during Lent and did not believe in divorce. With a grain of salt, that was the ordinary idea of a Catholic. And, indeed, a good Catholic was seen as a law-abiding citizen in the City of God. Judaism of our Lord's time suffered from legalism (i.e., strict adherence to a code of actions and observances as a means of justification). It was said that there were 613 precepts in the Law of Moses, and many interpretations on priority concerning them.

Our Lord reacts against legalism by putting all laws in their proper framework: love. Laws have reason to exist only insofar as they are explanations and adaptations of the great law of love of God and neighbor. Christians should not see a law-abiding life as a tool for obtaining eternal salvation. It is love that makes the observance of laws compatible with human dignity.

This statement of Jesus is actually a combination of Deuteronomy 6:5 (love of God) and Leviticus 19:18 (love of neighbor). What is new is Jesus' interlocking of these two commandments, namely, that one cannot be thought of without the other. Without love of neighbor the love of God remains a sterile figment of the mind, and without love of God love of neighbor may end up in a vague humanitarianism which usually does not last, especially when faced with disappointments. The vertical and horizontal must go together in sound Christian religion.

SCRIPTURE READING —

When the Pharisees heard that he had silenced the Sadducees, they assembled in a body; and one of them, a lawyer, in an attempt to trip him up, asked him, "Teacher, which commandment of the law is the greatest?" Jesus said to him:

" 'You shall love the Lord your God
with your whole heart,
with your whole soul,
and with all your mind.'

This is the greatest and first commandment. The second is like it:

'You shall love your neighbor as yourself.'

On these two commandments the whole law is based, and the prophets as well." (Matthew 22:34-40)

"Keep your eyes open!"

IT IS wonderful if over the years a person acquires wisdom which results in a meaningful life. It is even greater if by the evening of his life a person acquires the wisdom which helps him to die a meaningful death. Physicians, nurses, priests, and ministers take special courses which train them to accompany terminal patients in their last difficult days and hours. But one thing is certain: if the counselor of a terminal patient has to depend on human wisdom alone, he has a very difficult task in making the apparent absurdity of death meaningful.

We Christians possess a God-given wisdom which tells us that death is not only a sad and inevitable necessity, but that it has a positive meaning. Christians see death as the optimum opportunity for accepting God and full realization of one's self. Dying with Christ, a Christian believes that he will arise with him. All Christians, not just nurses, physicians, and priests, should feel responsible for the suffering members of God's people. We should be able to share our wisdom of faith with a friend who knows that his sickness is terminal.

Matthew's parable deals with two classes of people: the foolish ones who were not ready, and those who had wisdom and were ready when the groom (Jesus) arrived. Be prepared!

SCRIPTURE READING —

[Jesus told this parable:] "The reign of God can be likened to ten bridesmaids who took their torches and went out to welcome the groom. Five of them were foolish, while the other five were sensible. The foolish ones, in taking their torches, brought no oil along, but the sensible ones took flasks of oil as well as their torches. The groom delayed his coming, so they all began to nod, then to fall asleep. At midnight someone shouted, 'The groom is here! Come out and greet him!' At the outcry all the virgins woke up and got their torches ready.

"The foolish ones said to the sensible, 'Give us some of your oil. Our torches are going out.' But the sensible ones replied, 'No, there may not be enough for you and us. You had better go to the dealers and buy yourselves some.' While they went off to buy it the groom arrived, and the ones who were ready went in to the wedding with him. Then the door was barred. Later the other bridesmaids came back. 'Master, master!' they cried. 'Open the door for us.' But he answered, 'I tell you, I do not know you.' The moral is: keep your eyes open, for you know not the day or the hour."

(Matthew 25:1-13)

"He handed his funds over to them according to each man's abilities"

FIDELITY to a commitment requires constancy, courage, dedication, perseverance, and sometimes even heroism. "The fact is that when I commit myself, I grant in principle that the commitment will not again be put in question. . . . It at once bars a certain number of possibilities, it bids me invent a certain *modus vivendi* which I would otherwise be precluded from envisaging. Here there appears in a rudimentary form what I call *creative fidelity*. My behavior will be completely colored by this act embodying the decision that the commitment will not again be questioned" (Gabriel Marcel, French philosopher).

We may apply this to any commitment: baptismal, marital, religious, the promise to do a certain job.

The parable, as Matthew relates it, refers to Jesus Christ who will come back to judge the Church. All members have made their baptismal commitment and renew it every year at Easter or whenever they are godparents at a baptism. Today, God's question to us is: Do we practice "creative fidelity"? Passivity is culpable, as in the case of "the worthless, lazy lout." Is creative fidelity to an active Christian life possible? Yes, but there must be love for our Lord, which "the lazy lout" did not have. ("I knew you were a hard man.") Check yourself on "what I have failed to do" (Pen. Rite of Mass).

SCRIPTURE READING —

[Jesus told this parable:] "The case of a man who was going on a journey is similar. He called in his servants and handed his funds over to them according to each man's abilities. To one he disbursed five thousand silver pieces, to a second two thousand, and to a third a thousand. Then he went away.

"After a long absence, the master of those servants came home and settled accounts with them. The man who had received the five thousand came forward bringing the additional five. 'My lord, he said, 'you let me have five thousand. See, I have made five thousand more.'

"Finally the man who had received the thousand stepped forward. 'My lord,' he said, 'I knew you were a hard man. You reap where you did not sow and gather where you did not scatter, so out of fear I went off and buried your thousand silver pieces in the ground. Here is your money back.' His master exclaimed: 'You worthless, lazy lout!' "

(Matthew 25:14-15, 19-20, 24-26)

"When the Son of Man comes in his glory"

IN OUR democratic culture, we know about kings and emperors only from television and picture magazines. But we believe in leaders who derive "the just powers from the consent of the governed" (Declaration of Independence). Enlightened and reliable leadership is a great benefit to any society. We expect our leaders to be conscientious people, responsible to God, since we are "one nation under God." Our leaders must be equally concerned about all, since "all men are created equal."

If we had to describe what Jesus Christ means to Christians, we would most probably do so with this familiar terminology of the founding fathers. Hence, we should not be amazed that the Bible describes Jesus as a king, since leader and king were identical in Biblical culture. The Hebrews knew about the splendor of King Solomon, the heroic dedication and courage of their "founding father," King David, the might and power of the kings of Egypt and Babylon; hence, they used these familiar images to describe Jesus' relationship to the people "he sanctified by his own blood" (Hebrews 13:12).

In today's Scripture, a beautiful imaginative scene which depicts the parousia, the second coming of Jesus, Matthew sees the core of Jesus' moral teaching. Notice that Jesus, introduced as king and judge, identifies himself with the deprived and the downtrodden of society, and that the supreme law of love will be the measure in judgment.

SCRIPTURE READING —

[Jesus said:] "When the Son of Man comes in his glory, escorted by all the angels of heaven, he will sit upon his royal throne, and all the nations will be assembled before him. Then he will separate them into two groups, as a shepherd separates sheep and goats. The sheep he will place on his right hand, the goats on his left. The king will say to those on his right: 'Come. You have my Father's blessing! Inherit the kingdom prepared for you from the creation of the world. For I was hungry and you gave me food, I was thirsty and you gave me drink. I was a stranger and you welcomed me, naked and you clothed me. I was ill and you comforted me, in prison and you came to visit me.'

"Then the just will ask him: 'Lord, when did we see you hungry and feed you or see you thirsty and give you drink? When did we welcome you away from home or clothe you in your nakedness? When did we visit you when you were ill or in prison?' The king will answer them: 'I assure you, as often as you did it for one of my least brothers, you did it for me.'"

(Matthew 25:31-40)

"It was with a strong hand that the Lord brought you away"

ALL nations have their freedom days. We celebrate July 4, and all the young nations that gained their independence since World War II celebrate the day the colonizers quit their countries.

It accords with biblical revelation to view salvation and liberation as equivalent terms. Time and again, the Exodus saga provides the key to the inner meaning of salvation. The human experience of winning freedom from bondage realizes and makes manifest a salvation found in God himself. Reading history with the eyes of faith, we see God in it. We understand the historical Exodus as a paradigm for all Jewish and Christian religious experience. In the New Testament this paradigm of the Exodus finds its perfect fulfillment in the death and resurrection of our Lord, which was a definite exit (Passover) from bondage to complete freedom and salvation.

Christian salvation is incarnate in the human reality of liberation. It is the prophetic promise of definitive liberty. Independence Day and Thanksgiving Day should be celebrated with this eschatological (end-time) perspective in mind. They are American "Passovers."

SCRIPTURE READING —

Moses said to the people, "Remember this day on which you came out of Egypt, that place of slavery. It was with a strong hand that the Lord brought you away. Nothing made with leaven must be eaten. This day of your departure is in the month Abib. Therefore, it is in this month that you must celebrate this rite, after the Lord, your God, has brought you into the land of the Canaanites, Hittites, Amorites, Hivites and Jebusites, which he swore to your fathers he would give you, a land flowing with milk and honey.

"For seven days you shall eat unleavened bread, and the seventh day shall also be a festival to the Lord. Only unleavened bread may be eaten during the seven days; no leaven and nothing leavened may be found in all your territory. On this day you shall explain to your son, 'This is because of what the Lord did for me when I came out of Egypt.' It shall be as a sign on your hand and as a reminder on your forehead; thus the law of the Lord will ever be on your lips, because with a strong hand the Lord brought you out of Egypt. Therefore, you shall keep this prescribed rite at its appointed time from year to year."

(Exodus 13:3-10)

"Come after me"

WITH reference to our call/task in life, we may go through periods of reluctance when we just do not feel up to our previously made commitment. Such reluctance is part of human nature. However, our first reaction to do something about it should not be a visit to the lawyer. As mature people we should have an honest discussion, seek counseling, and pray to God.

Mark deals with two calls. He first sets forth the call for repentance to all of us: "Reform your lives and believe in the good news." Conversion, time and again averting yourself from evil in all its forms and converting yourself in even more perfect love to God, is a lifetime job which requires perseverance!

Secondly, Mark relates another call of the disciples. Yesterday (July 4), we meditated on "call-vocation," in particular as total dedication to Christ, including one's sexuality, as an ongoing process. The disciples have just spent the day with our Lord. In today's reading we see a definitive decision. "They abandoned their nets [their father] and became his followers." The first call to repentance is addressed to all Christians; the second one to those whom God calls to a life of service in the ministerial priesthood and/or religious life. It requires generosity to respond. Pray that it always may be found among God's people!

SCRIPTURE READING —

After John's arrest, Jesus appeared in Galilee proclaiming the good news of God: "This is the time of fulfillment. The reign of God is at hand! Reform your lives and believe in the gospel!"

As he made his way along the sea of Galilee, he observed Simon and his brother Andrew casting their nets into the sea; they were fishermen. Jesus said to them, "Come after me; I will make you fishers of men." They immediately abandoned their nets and became his followers. Proceeding a little farther along, he caught sight of James, Zebedee's son, and his brother John. They too were in their boat putting their nets in order. He summoned them on the spot. They abandoned their father Zebedee, who was in the boat with the hired men, and went off in his company.

(Mark 1:14-20)

"The people were spellbound by [Jesus'] teaching"

MEETING people for the first time, hearing them in a public address, may prompt various reactions. We might state: "He/she did not impress me too much," that is, as a person, he/she does not have much to offer. Our reaction could also be: "I was very much impressed," that is, we see a person who stands for something, who is a real "somebody." This first impression, though perhaps mainly intuitive, is often decisive for our final opinion about a person. Only for very good reasons do we revise it.

The Lord Jesus must have impressed people as a real "Somebody." He was so impressive that he has prompted people to agree with him, to give up everything and follow him, not just in his own time and country, but all over the globe and already for some 2,000 years. What is that mysterious authority which people felt during his lifetime, and which they still feel when they read the faith experience of his early followers in Scripture? Today's reading describes such an initial reaction and it should provide much food for thought for us.

"The people were spellbound by his teaching—a new teaching in a spirit of authority." The prophets, including the great Moses, used to say: "Thus says the Lord." Jesus says: "I tell you . . ." The exorcism accompanying Jesus' teaching in Mark's account underlines this authority. Where God's word breaks through in human history, announcing the coming of his kingdom of justice, love, and peace, there evil must cease! Listen often and with faith to the Lord Jesus and his teaching with authority, as we have it in Scripture. "Spellbound" by his words, you will keep balance in a society where so much other "wisdom" is for sale.

SCRIPTURE READING —

The people were spellbound by [Jesus'] teaching because he taught with authority, and not like the scribes.

There appeared in their synagogue a man with an unclean spirit that shrieked: "What do you want of us, Jesus of Nazareth? Have you come to destroy us? I know who you are—the holy One of God!" Jesus rebuked him sharply: "Be quiet! Come out of the man!" At that the unclean spirit convulsed the man violently and with a loud shriek came out of him. All who looked on were amazed. They began to ask one another: "What does this mean? A completely new teaching in a spirit of authority! He gives orders to unclean spirits and they obey!" From that point on his reputation spread throughout the surrounding region of Galilee. (Mark 1:21-28)

"Those whom he cured were variously afflicted"

OUR community hospitals and mental clinics are hopeful havens for suffering mankind. But they also constitute the signs that pain and misery form an integral part of the human condition. We would hail the genius who could make it possible for our species to have no more need of physicians and hospitals. It would be wonderful, but it will never be realized. Pain and suffering, both physical and mental, and ultimately death, are going to remain with us. Hence, how do we handle this facet of our human existence?

The Bible discusses the problem of pain and suffering quite often. It does not offer a final solution, but under God's guidance the sacred writers attain some very consoling insights which help us Christians to cope with pain when it strikes us. Scripture should be the constant companion of each suffering person. The Gideons put Bibles in motel rooms. They should be found in all hospital rooms and be available for patients whose health permits them to read.

In reading about the healing ministry of the Lord Jesus, we should keep in mind that the ancient Hebrews did not see a scientific relation between medication and healing, as we do. Their understanding of medication was mainly a magical one. Sickness was caused by evil spirits. Hence, a sick person turned first of all to the priest or a holy man for help. Healing was identical with expelling demons. Hence, the ministry of healing is one of the signs of the messianic era, the time of salvation from the power of Satan and of God's reign on earth. Proclaiming the good news and healing went hand in hand. According to Mark, these healings foreshadowed the ultimate healing of all the brokenhearted by Jesus' death on the Cross. When we are depressed and suffering, we should meditate on our Lord's death and resurrection, and see pain as our passage to eternal life with him.

SCRIPTURE READING —

After sunset, as evening drew on, they brought [Jesus] all who were ill, and those possessed by demons. Before long the whole town was gathered outside the door. Those whom he cured, who were variously afflicted, were many, and so were the demons he expelled. But he would not permit the demons to speak, because they knew him.

(Mark 1:32-36)

"The one who bears the sore of leprosy . . . shall cry out, 'Unclean, unclean!' "

SINCE Hansen's disease or leprosy is actually unknown in this country, one must go to Third World countries in order to get first hand acquaintance with this terrible malady. I have visited leper colonies and remember the stench of decaying flesh in my nostrils. But whenever I read in the Bible about leprosy, I think of Regina, one of the teachers in my school. She was a beautiful Indonesian young woman and about to marry. One day I was called to the hospital. Regina had attempted suicide. I asked the nurse what had happened. "*Tuan, dia berkusta*—Father, she has leprosy."

Regina had discovered the first signs, gray spots on her arm. Her father had died of the disease, and she knew what her fate would be: a gradual decay of years, boils and sores on her skin, limbs rotting and falling off, a distorted face with openings where the nose had been and finally death. On her bed, turned to the wall, Regina did not want to talk. I could have cried! Fortunately, however, a new medicine to cure leprosy had just been put on the market at that time. It was not available on the island and the whole cure was very expensive. After talking with the doctor, I found two benefactors willing to help—and the young lady fully recovered is now a happy wife and mother.

In biblical times, people were not so fortunate. The disease was considered dangerous and detestable. It was thought to be caused by sin. Avoided by fellow citizens, these outcasts lived in miserable, poor, and squalid quarters. The Bible reading deals with leprosy and uncleanness, but transferred to another plane—the uncleanness of heart through sin. A sinner is an unhappy outcast, alienated from God and his religious community. Sinners, all of us who fail, should turn to the Lord for help.

SCRIPTURE READING —

The Lord said to Moses and Aaron, "If someone has on his skin a scab or pustule or blotch which appears to be the sore of leprosy, he shall be brought to Aaron, the priest, or to one of the priests among his descendants.

"The one who bears the sore of leprosy shall keep his garments rent and his head bare, and shall muffle his beard; he shall cry out, 'Unclean, unclean!' As long as the sore is on him he shall declare himself unclean, since he is in fact unclean. He shall dwell apart, making his abode outside the camp." (Leviticus 13:1-2. 45-46)

"If you will to do so, you can cure me"

FOR one reason or another society expels members from its midst. Reasons may be crime, disease, inability to live up to community standards or simply discrimination based on prejudice. Society confines outcasts to prison, isolates them in quarantine, or just ignores them. In any case, outcasts are unhappy persons. They feel unwanted and often turn to bitterness and hatred. Over the centuries, leprosy, for which no cure existed until recently, was a reason to ostracize one's fellowmen. Mostly in the developing countries, there are still thousands of lepers considered as unclean, contagious, and dangerous, who live in leper colonies, often in utter misery and filth.

This healing of a leper and sending him to the priest *(see July 8)* should not be seen as just a proof of Jesus' power. St. John calls Jesus' miracles "signs." They are signs that indicate the breakthrough of God's reign of love, justice, concern, peace and happiness into human history. Jesus shows why he has come, namely, to share our helpless and miserable human condition and to redeem us from evil.

Healing is possible if we turn to him. Do you take part in any of your parish penitential services? Confession of guilt is part of Christian life!

SCRIPTURE READING —

A leper approached [Jesus] with a request, kneeling down as he addressed him: "If you will to do so, you can cure me." Moved with pity, Jesus stretched out his hand, touched him, and said: "I do will it. Be cured." The leprosy left him then and there, and he was cured. Jesus gave him a stern warning and sent him on his way. "Not a word to anyone, now," he said. "Go off and present yourself to the priest and offer for your cure what Moses prescribed. That should be a proof for them."

The man went off and began to proclaim the whole matter freely, making the story public. As a result of this, it was no longer possible for Jesus to enter a town openly. He stayed in desert places; yet people kept coming to him from all sides. (Mark 1:40-45)

"My son, your sins are forgiven"

THE beautiful song *Miracle of Miracles* in the Broadway musical *Fiddler on the Roof*, of some years back, brings out how Jewish tradition regards miracles. It refers to the traditional Bible miracles of Daniel in the lions' den, the parting of the waters of the Red Sea, and the manna in the wilderness. But it is a miracle too that God made people and "has given you [my wife] to me." The Biblical miracles are not just unexplainable interferences of God with his laws of nature. In the Bible, any event, whether natural or supernatural, in which one sees an act or a revelation of God, is considered a miracle.

Mark tells the healing story of the paralytic as tradition had couched it to bring out a point, namely, the mysterious reality that the Church has the authority to forgive sins in God's name. Over the centuries the Church, God's people, has been aware that this authority has been entrusted to her. It has been exercised in various ways and even in our time we see some changes. But the authority is there and we should call upon it. *(See July 9.)*

Do you make the penitential rite before the Eucharistic Celebration meaningful, as far as you are concerned? "I confess to Almighty God and *to you, my brothers and sisters.*"

SCRIPTURE READING —

When [Jesus] was delivering God's word to them, some people arrived bringing a paralyzed man to him. The four who carried him were unable to bring him to Jesus because of the crowd, so they began to open up the roof over the spot where Jesus was. When they had made a hole, they let down the mat on which the paralytic was lying. When Jesus saw their faith, he said to the paralyzed man, "My son, your sins are forgiven." Now some of the scribes were sitting there asking themselves: "Why does the man talk in that way? He commits blasphemy! Who can forgive sins except God alone."

Jesus was immediately aware of their reasoning, though they kept it to themselves, and he said to them: "Why do you harbor these thoughts? Which is easier, to say to the paralytic, 'Your sins are forgiven,' or to say, 'Stand up, pick up your mat, and walk again'? That you may know that the Son of Man has authority on earth to forgive sins" (he said to the paralyzed man), "I command you: Stand up! Pick up your mat and go home." The man stood and picked up his mat and went outside in the sight of everyone. They were awestruck; all gave praise to God, saying, "We have never seen anything like this!" (Mark 2:3-12)

"So long as the groom stays with them . . ."

A PERSON'S "do's and don'ts" are greatly determined by how he/she is related to others. A young lady at home may not be very happy when mother asks her to do the ironing of the week's family clothes. But ironing her boyfriend's shirt on Friday night is different! Love casts a very particular kind of light on our habits and way of life. This becomes even more evident when, by contrast, love has gone. Things people in love did so happily for one another become a burden once love is absent.

Apply this to your "do's and don'ts" as far as God is concerned. Are they boring and burdensome where once they were pleasant events? Love of God can get stale if it is not kept alive. When married love loses its tang, usually both partners are to be blamed. In our love relationship with God, it is only we ourselves who drift away. God is faithful. If we have failed by indifference, we should return to him who "is slow to anger and abounding in kindness" (Psalm 103:8).

The early Church was in constant conflict with Judaism. The Jews often fasted twice a week, though a wedding was a legal reason to make an exception. The Christians did not follow that rule. Mark uses a tradition concerning Jesus in conflict with the Pharisees to explain why Christians do not follow the Jewish laws on fasting. He states: "One doesn't fast at weddings."

The Bible compares our covenant with God to the intimate love-partnership of husband and wife. (See Hosea 2:16-17, 21-22.) In today's Scripture, Mark does the same. God, visible in Jesus, is the groom; the disciples and all of us Christians are the bride. Do you see yourself as related to God in a partnership of love? Then love should be guiding your "do's and don'ts." And reflective prayer should foster that awareness of being related to him who is love.

SCRIPTURE READING —

John's disciples and the Pharisees were accustomed to fast. People came to Jesus with the objection, "Why do John's disciples and those of the Pharisees fast while yours do not?" Jesus replied: "How can the guests at a wedding fast as long as the groom is still among them? So long as the groom stays with them, they cannot fast. The day will come, however, when the groom will be taken away from them; on that day they will fast." (Mark 2:18-20)

"Remember that you too were once slaves in Egypt"

ON THE weekends we "take off." We take off *from* the work we do to make a living. All agree on that. But not all will agree on the question, "What do you take off *for*?" Freedom from and freedom for are two sides of one coin, but they are not the same. On weekends we should be glad to be free for more time with those we love, not excluding God. However, this entails a love which is very much alive and makes togetherness a happy event.

If love is stale, we will escape togetherness by means of the various excuses available: an extra job, meeting a business friend, just walking out "for a while" (how long?) or endless hours before the television. Furthermore, excuses for not being together with God [Sunday worship] are very simple since God does not ask questions. It is love which determines our "do's and don'ts," including those of our weekends. What do you take off *for* this weekend?

Notice that the author of Deuteronomy mentions two elements concerning the Sabbath (meaning roughly, "to leave off"): abstinence from work and "remembrance." Abstinence from work should give ample opportunity for "remembrance." The Sabbath was seen as a grateful response to the exodus from bondage in Egypt. Initially, Christians from Jewish background continued to observe the Sabbath and celebrated the Eucharist on the Lord's Day (Day of his resurrection). Later, when even more Gentiles joined the Church, the Lord's Day (Sunday) became the Christian day of worship.

Freedom from work should give opportunity for "remembrance," for the memorial of our exodus from evil through Christ's death and resurrection, celebrated in the signs of bread and wine. Partaking of this "memorial of our redemption" (Mass) is an integral part of a Christian's Sunday.

SCRIPTURE READING —

[Moses spoke to the people in the Lord's name:] "Take care to keep holy the sabbath day as the Lord, your God, commanded you. Six days you may labor and do all your work; but the seventh day is the sabbath of the Lord, your God. For remember that you too were once slaves in Egypt, and the Lord, your God, brought you from there with his strong hand and outstretched arm. That is why the Lord, your God, has commanded you to observe the sabbath day." (Deuteronomy 5: 12-13, 15)

"If a household is divided according to loyalties . . ."

IN ANY contest it is of the utmost importance that those involved have the firm determination to win. Those who are not sure of themselves lose out. Coaches know this, hence their pep talk to the team with the assurance that they are going to win. Civil rights demonstrators in the sixties often started their marches in church, where they listened to a talk and prayed for strength and determination.

Evil exists and has tremendous power. We feel its strength in us and experience its sinister threat around us. We encounter corruption and pursuit of self-interests where we would expect dedication and fidelity to an oath of office. There is the evil of social injustice, juvenile delinquency, and an ever-rising crime rate. Values such as right to life and fidelity to the marital commitment are openly questioned. And we see rich nations abusing the poor ones shamelessly.

Today's Bible reading calls this total phenomenon of evil: Satan—Beelzebul—the serpent. Can we overcome it? Christians should never give up. The reign of God, a reign of justice, love, fidelity, and peace, was initiated in this world when its Redeemer died on a cross but rose from the dead. Determination is the key to overcoming evil. In improving the world, start with yourself, your family, your direct environment. Your word and example do oppose evil! Then, collectively, see what your parish community can do to oppose evil in your community: "We shall overcome, one day," completely, though only in the world to come.

SCRIPTURE READING —

[Jesus] returned to the house with [the apostles] and again the crowd assembled, making it impossible for them to get any food whatever. When his family heard of this they came to take charge of him, saying, "He is out of his mind"; while the scribes who arrived from Jerusalem asserted, "He is possessed by Beelzebul," and "He expels demons with the help of the prince of demons." Summoning them, he then began to speak to them by way of examples: "How can Satan expel Satan? If a kingdom is torn by civil strife, that kingdom cannot last. If a household is divided according to loyalties, that household will not survive." (Mark 3:20-25)

"The reign of God . . . is like a mustard seed"

ALL of us have our expectations in life and, related to our hope for fulfillment, our disappointments. Hope implies an element of uncertainty. A student works hard and hopes for a beautiful future. Young people fall in love, discuss their future, and hope to do better than most grown-ups have ever done. Parents rear children and hope to be proud of them. A dedicated social worker hopes to improve society drastically. Christians also have expectations as far as their Church is concerned.

It is important for our hope to be realistic. Hoping too much leads necessarily to disappointment and even despair. Today, we apply this to the reign of God and the Church. We should realize that these two are not the same. The reign of God, a reign of justice, love, and peace, is found in the Church. The Church itself, a community of human beings, is not necessarily God's reign on earth. Keeping this in mind, our expectations (hope) for the Church will be realistic.

Christian hope implies uncertainty and requires patience. God's word is like a seed in us. Through Jesus Christ he scattered it on the ground. We want this seed (God's word) to bear bountiful fruit in the Church right now. There are members who leave the Church if things do not go their way. They have in mind an ideal Church with the reign of God already realized in it. But it does not work that way. The reign of God—justice, love, fidelity, peace—is submitted to the slow process of growing (a mustard seed!). Its fully realized splendor will appear only in the world to come. Meanwhile, have hope and patience. If you want to improve the Church, start with yourself.

SCRIPTURE READING —

[Jesus] also said: "This is how it is with the reign of God. A man scatters seed on the ground. He goes to bed and gets up day after day. Through it all the seed sprouts and grows without his knowing how it happens. The soil produces of itself first the blade, then the ear, finally the ripe wheat in the ear. When the crop is ready he 'wields the sickle, for the time is ripe for harvest.' "

He went on to say: "What comparison shall we use for the reign of God? What image will help to present it? It is like a mustard seed which, when planted in the soil, is the smallest of all the earth's seeds, yet once it is sown, springs up to become the largest of shrubs, with branches big enough for the birds of the sky to build nests in its shade."

(Mark 4:26-32)

"Who can this be?"

July 15

MANY of us have experienced the awesome power of a hurricane or tornado. All of us have seen on television what their devastating force can do. Small wonder that in prescientific times people saw God's anger and threat in storms and bad weather. "They cried to the Lord in their distress; he hushed the storm to a gentle breeze, and the billows of the sea were stilled" (Psalm 107). Today, there are still Christians who light a blessed candle and pray to God when thunder and lightning threaten. Nor is this such a bad thing! Prayer in faith is meaningful in any anxiety because it gives strength. God is with us!

In biblical times the threatening forces of nature were so automatically related to God that they became the customary imagery used to describe a theophany (manifestation of God). See the great theophany of Mount Sinai (Exodus 19:16-19). Quite often the Bible has God speak out of a storm. This same imagery is still applicable. Life can be like a storm. We can lose hope and be on the brink of giving up. The sight of the Church, the bark of Peter, being so frighteningly rocked nowadays, may confuse us. But, while we are doing whatever is humanly possible to solve our own problems, we should never forget to pray with faith. "When I called, you [God] answered me; you built up strength within me" (Psalm 138).

"Who can this be that the wind and the sea obey him?" Jesus has a power similar to the one God claimed for himself. He is "God with us," and we should turn to him in faithful prayer whenever difficulties overwhelm us.

SCRIPTURE READING —

As evening drew on [Jesus] said to [the disciples], "Let us cross over to the farther shore." Leaving the crowd, they took him away in the boat in which he was sitting, while the other boats accompanied him. It happened that a bad squall blew up. The waves were breaking over the boat and it began to ship water badly. Jesus was in the stern through it all, sound asleep on a cushion.

They finally woke him and said to him, "Teacher, does it not matter to you that we are going to drown?" He awoke and rebuked the wind and said to the sea: "Quiet! Be still!" The wind fell off and everything grew calm. Then he said to them, "Why are you so terrified? Why are you lacking in faith?" A great awe overcame them at this. They kept saying to one another, "Who can this be that the wind and the sea obey him?"

(Mark 4:35-41)

"'Talitha koum,' which means, 'Little girl, get up'"

ALL of us treasure life as the highest good. We cherish our physical lives. We try to keep ourselves in good shape. Many make regular trips to the doctor and the beautician. We care for the health of our children. We also care for the quality of the life we are living. Mental health clinics are filled to capacity. We do not want to destroy life, yet we do not want a miserable life.

The quality of human life is measured by the quality of its relations with others. Improving life means actually improving relations, first our relations on the human level (with our marriage-partner, children, parents, friends, co-religious, co-workers) and then our relationship with God, which is called grace. Being in "the state of grace" means being in good standing with God. This good standing, close relationship of love with God, is also called "life."

By overcoming death in this little girl, Jesus prefigures his victory over the death of alienation from God. Mark brings out that Jesus is the prophet of the end-time who has come to bring life, in other words, to restore our relationship of love with God.

SCRIPTURE READING —

When Jesus had crossed back to the other side again in the boat, a large crowd gathered around him and he stayed close to the lake. One of the officials of the synagogue, a man named Jairus, came near. Seeing Jesus, he fell at his feet and made this earnest appeal: "My little daughter is critically ill. Please come and lay your hands on her so that she may get well and live." The two went off together and a large crowd followed, pushing against Jesus.

People from the official's house arrived saying, "Your daughter is dead. Why bother the Teacher further?" Jesus disregarded the report that had been brought and said to the official: "Fear is useless. What is needed is trust." He would not permit anyone to follow him except Peter, James, and James' brother John. As they approached the house of the synagogue leader, Jesus was struck by the noise of people wailing and crying loudly on all sides. He entered and said to them: "Why do you make this din with your wailing? The child is not dead. She is asleep." At this they began to ridicule him. Then he put them all out.

Jesus took the child's father and mother and his own companions and entered the room where the child lay. Taking her hand he said to her, "Talitha, koum," **which means, "Little girl, get up." The girl, a child of twelve, stood up immediately and began to walk around. At this the family's astonishment knew no bounds.** (Mark 5:21-24, 35-42)

"They found him too much for them"

"WHO does he think he is?" This remark is often made when a person of well-known humble stock has become a success and issued a statement of some kind. Is it reasonable to act in this way? We know that children do not learn well with a teacher they dislike. Children go by their instinctive likes and dislikes and let these influence their behavior. Adults, on the contrary, should have outgrown them and be able to distinguish between what is said, how it is said, and who says it. However, it is not an easy thing to do.

Listening time and again to the sermons of a priest whom we do not like humanly speaking can be a problem, but one that can and should be overcome. No bishop can guarantee to have pastors available who are liked by all the members of every congregation in a diocese. The priest represents Christ and his ministerial priesthood in our midst. However, no priest is such a saint or genius that he can reflect all the beautiful characteristics of our Lord and be "good" in all the facets of his ministry.

In today's Scripture, Jesus is shown as being unable to accomplish much in his hometown because of the people's lack of faith. Why does Mark recount this tradition? He has no intention of entertaining us. Guided by God, he wants to teach his word. It may be as follows: Without faith it is impossible to be aware of the truth and the sacred in our midst. A child, a hobo, a neighbor, a co-worker, any person even without formal education can teach us the truth. Do we accept it?

SCRIPTURE READING —

[Jesus] returned to his own part of the country followed by his disciples. When the sabbath came he began to teach in the synagogue in a way that kept his large audience amazed. They said: "Where did he get all this? What kind of wisdom is he endowed with? How is it that such miraculous deeds are accomplished by his hands? Is this not the carpenter, the son of Mary, a brother of James and Joses and Judas and Simeon? Are not his sisters our neighbors here?" They found him too much for them. Jesus' response to all this was: "No prophet is without honor except in his native place, among his own kindred, and in his own house." He could work no miracle there, apart from curing a few who were sick by laying hands on them, so much did their lack of faith distress him. He made the rounds of the neighboring villages instead, and spent his time teaching. (Mark 6:1-6)

"They went off, preaching the need of repentance"

WHAT do you expect from the Church, which is not only the hierarchy (the leaders) but all of God's people, you and I included? What is its mission? There are conflicting ideas. Many are in favor of a kind of civil religion ("ole time religion"?) which stands for the *status quo* and stern patriotism. We think of political prayer breakfasts, of worship services in the White House, and of how civil religion would approach draft evasion versus how it should be done in the light of the Gospel.

After the Second Vatican Council, there is a clear change of course. The Church is stripping itself of the many man-made burdensome matters that had accumulated over the centuries and designedly going back to a more original evangelical pattern. Change causes friction. This is necessary and even good. Both "progressives" and "conservatives" in the Church need one another's corrective attitude. The bond of love and mutual respect should keep us together.

The mission of the Twelve consists in preaching the need for repentance, which necessarily implies confrontation with evil. In addition to preaching, mention is made of exorcism (expelling demons), and healing, including anointing. The possibility of not being accepted should be considered. What is the mission of the Church, your own mission of Christian witness included? It is similar to that of the Twelve, and we should consider whether or not a "civil religion" fits this mold.

SCRIPTURE READING —

Jesus summoned the Twelve and began to send them out two by two, giving them authority over unclean spirits. He instructed them to take nothing on the journey but a walking stick—no food, no traveling bag, not a coin in the purses in their belts. They were, however, to wear sandals. "Do not bring a second tunic," he said, and added: "Whatever house you find yourself in, stay there until you leave the locality. If any place will not receive you or hear you, shake its dust from your feet in testimony against them as you leave." With that they went off, preaching the need of repentance. They expelled many demons, anointed the sick with oil, and worked many cures. (Mark 6:7-13)

"He pitied them, for they were like sheep without a shepherd"

A HIGH school teacher, discussing the importance of mutual care in the family, mentioned the nightly television flash: "Do you know where your children are?", at which a senior snapped: "They better ask: 'Do you know where your parents are?'" So many youngsters drop out of our impersonal and anonymous society to join communes! Broken families and homes where parents have no time for their children are not without guilt concerning this phenomenon. Nobody can live in the vacuum of loneliness. We need care. Parents should provide it. Wherever possible, we should try to personalize situations in which we are together as human beings: schools, offices, jobs, church. Using the familiar image of shepherd and flock, the Bible readings emphasize the necessity of a real person-to-person care, which all of us need.

The image of shepherd entails first of all the idea of ruling, but it also implies the notion of feeding and providing. In the Sunday liturgy, the Lord Jesus shepherds by teaching his word during the Liturgy of the Word, and by "spreading the table before us" (Psalm 23) during the Liturgy of the Eucharist. Jesus still has compassion for any vast crowd which is like sheep without a shepherd, but he has only us to show this.

Do you make everyone, especially visiting strangers, feel at home in your congregation? Does your congregation have a committee of members to welcome strangers? What about your handshake of peace? What is done to give young members a feeling of belonging?

SCRIPTURE READING —

The apostles returned to Jesus and reported to him all that they had done and what they had taught. He said to them, "Come by yourselves to an out-of-the-way place and rest a little." People were coming and going in great numbers, making it impossible for them to so much as eat. So Jesus and the apostles went off in the boat by themselves to a deserted place. People saw them leaving, and many got to know about it. People from all the towns hastened on foot to the place, arriving ahead of them.

Upon disembarking Jesus saw a vast crowd. He pitied them, for they were like sheep without a shepherd; and he began to teach them at great length. (Mark 6:30-34)

"Jesus took the loaves of bread, gave thanks, and passed them around"

EATING together not only signifies togetherness but also sustains and promotes it. It constitutes a beautiful means of communication. One must have been exposed to a warm and animating table fellowship time and again to savor it as an inspiring symbolism of person-to-person relationship. Happy the family that still insists on at least one meal together every day! It should be a meal begun with a blessing and, if possible, concluded with a short Bible reading and spontaneous meditative prayer. The family that prays (eats) together stays together!

A well-understood table fellowship at the family level is a prerequisite for appreciating the table fellowship of the Eucharist and the biblical banquet symbolism which describes the end-time (Matthew 22:1-10). Today's reading utilizes the symbolism of eating to bring out a message.

Just as Moses fed the people in the desert by giving them the miraculous manna, our Lord, the new Moses, re-creates that ancient desert wonder and feeds the crowds in the wilderness. Like Elisha (2 Kings 4:42-44), Jesus does not have enough, but he organizes the meal anyway. He presides, as he does at our Eucharistic Celebration, when we break bread together. Does our participation in the Eucharistic Banquet really promote togetherness with fellow Christians?

SCRIPTURE READING —

Jesus . . . went up the mountain and sat down there with his disciples. The Jewish feast of Passover was near; when Jesus looked up and caught sight of a vast crowd coming toward him, he said to Philip, "Where shall we buy bread for these people to eat?" (He knew well what he intended to do but he asked this to test Philip's response.) Philip replied, "Not even with two hundred days' wages could we buy loaves enough to give each of them a mouthful!"

One of Jesus' disciples, Andrew, Simon Peter's brother, remarked to him, "There is a lad here who has five barley loaves and a couple of dried fish, but what good is that for so many?" Jesus said, "Get the people to recline." Even though the men numbered about five thousand, there was plenty of grass for them to find a place on the ground. Jesus then took the loaves of bread, gave thanks, and passed them around to those reclining there; he did the same with the dried fish, as much as they wanted. (John 6:3-11)

" . . . but for food that remains unto life eternal"

WE CAN look at flowers in various ways. For example, I can see them from the viewpoint of a florist, a painter, or an artist who loves to arrange them. When I see flowers in church, I take them as symbols of life. When I glimpse flowers around a casket, I regard them as symbols of sympathy and signs of the resurrection. If flowers are sent to me as a present, they become for me a symbol of attention, love, and friendship; accordingly, I will love these flowers and think of the person who did me this honor.

We are familiar with contemporary symbolism: the burning of a man's effigy, hunger strike, peace signs, et al. We should develop a feeling for natural symbols and signs, since they play such an important role in religion. Water, bread, wine, salt, yeast, fire, light, rain, dew, thunder, lightning—time and again these are used to impart a message and when properly understood they do so more efficiently than theoretical concepts can do. Symbolism contains an intuitive (suggestive) power which appeals not only to the intellect but to the total person, heart and mind. Today's reading utilizes the symbolism of bread to bring out the message that God wants to feed us, to take care of us on all levels of human existence.

Jesus states that he is the bread from heaven which man needs on his way through life. Feeding the crowd was a sign which those who had eaten did not understand. Patiently, our Lord explains: "You should not be working for perishable food but for food that remains unto life eternal. . . . I myself am the bread of life." We should be aware of this whenever we encounter our Lord in the signs of bread and wine.

SCRIPTURE READING —

Once the crowd saw that neither Jesus nor his disciples were there, they too embarked in the boats and went to Capernaum looking for Jesus.

When they found him on the other side of the lake, they said to him, "Rabbi, when did you come here?" Jesus answered them:
"I assure you,
you are not looking for me because you have seen signs
but because you have eaten your fill of the loaves.
You should not be working for perishable food
but for food that remains unto life eternal,
food which the Son of Man will give you;
it is on him that God the Father has set his seal." (John 6:24-27)

"I am the bread of life"

LOOKING back to our past, we remember people we have met. Some of them hold a prominent place in our memory. They are people who have meant something to us: our parents, a parish priest, a school teacher, an aunt or uncle, a close friend, or someone who helped us make a difficult decision, one perhaps that determined the course in life we have chosen. The latter may have been a friend who stood by us in dark moments of life or a teacher who with patience and understanding convinced us to finish our education. We are grateful to these people, and we realize that we would be different persons if we would not have met them.

Suppose you would not have met Christ? What would be your outlook on life? It is difficult to visualize this since we are part of a culture that is so deeply rooted in the Judeo-Christian tradition. Even without knowing it, many live by the Christian values. But without Christ in our lives we would be entirely different.

Using the symbolism of bread, Jesus indicates that we need him on our journey through life. "I [Jesus] am the bread of life. . . . If anyone eats this bread he shall live forever." In other words, a person closely related to Jesus Christ will not die the death of alienation from God. *(See July 16.)* The essential condition for this is faith (trust) in the Lord Jesus: "He who believes has eternal life." Christians see the Eucharistic bread and wine, signs of Christ's mysterious presence to us, as a viaticum, "food for our journey" to the mountain where we hope to meet God. Gratefully, we should "take and eat it" as the Lord has told us to do.

SCRIPTURE READING —

[Jesus told the people:]
"Let me firmly assure you,
he who believes has eternal life.
I am the bread of life.
Your ancestors ate manna in the desert, but they died.
This is the bread that comes down from heaven
for a man to eat and never die.
I myself am the living bread
come down from heaven.
If anyone eats this bread
he shall live forever;
the bread I will give
is my flesh, for the life of the world." (John 6:47-51)

"He who feeds on my flesh and drinks my blood has life eternal"

ABSENCE, alienation, loneliness, communication gaps, are the ailments of modern life. We yearn for presence and the loving care of a person who is close by. The great consolation which Christianity offers to mankind, haunted by the threat of alienation, is that God is close by, Emmanuel, in Jesus Christ. "The Lord Jesus is always present in his Church, especially in the liturgical celebrations. He is present in the sacrifice of Mass, not only in the person of the minister, but especially under the Eucharistic species. By his power he is present in the Sacraments, so that when man baptizes it is really Christ himself who baptizes. He is present in his word, since it is he himself who speaks when the holy Scriptures are read in the Church. He is present, finally, when the Church prays and sings, for he promised: 'Where two or three are gathered together for my sake, there am I in the midst of them' " (Matthew 18:20) (Vatican II, *Constitution on the Sacred Liturgy, 7).*

Like the Scripture of the last two days, today's reading is also taken from the "Discourse on the Bread of Life" as we have it in the sixth chapter of John's Gospel. The previous two portions of this discourse were primarily figurative references to our Lord's teaching and referred secondarily to the Holy Eucharist. In this reading we have reference to how the early Church and the Lord Jesus himself saw the Eucharistic Banquet. "The man who feeds on my flesh and drinks my blood remains in me, and I in him." By his mysterious presence our Lord heals the wounds caused by absence and alienation. By your participation in the Eucharistic Banquet time and again, Jesus' presence to you should become ever more intimate, a closer sharing of life together.

Note that the words "flesh, body, blood" stand for the person!

SCRIPTURE READING —

[Jesus told the people:]
"Let me solemnly assure you,
if you do not eat the flesh of the Son of Man
and drink his blood,
you have no life in you.
He who feeds on my flesh
and drinks my blood
has life eternal,
and I will raise him up on the last day.
For my flesh is real food
and my blood real drink.
The man who feeds on my flesh
and drinks my blood
remains in me, and I in him."

(John 6:54-56)

"Lord, to whom shall we go?"

ENGAGEMENT, betrothal, and marriage imply the faith which two young people have in one another. Though there are and should be reasons for this mutual faith, it cannot possibly be thought out logically. Attempting to do so would destroy the intuitive element of love in it. Dissecting a rose results in insight but kills the beautiful flower in the process.

Applying this remark to our faith-relationship with God, we observe that faith is not understanding but taking the risk of the engagement. We have reasons for faith. In our best moments intuitively we feel there must be a transcendent element in reality —an ultimate reality. But the ultimate reason for faith escapes analytical thinking.

Like love, faith also knows its dark moments in which man thinks that God is absent, maybe even "dead." Great mystics have gone through this and in their writings refer to it as "the night of faith." It is not God who causes doubts and uncertainty, but our own frail human condition which blurs our vision so often. Today's Bible reading deals with the faith-love commitment. Keep it exciting and alive as long as you live.

SCRIPTURE READING—

After hearing [Jesus'] words, many of his disciples remarked, "This sort of talk is hard to endure! How can anyone take it seriously?" Jesus was fully aware that his disciples were murmuring in protest at what he had said: "Does it shake your faith?" he asked them.

"What, then, if you were to see the Son of Man
ascend to where he was before . . . ?
It is the spirit that gives life;
the flesh is useless.
The words I spoke to you
are spirit and life.
Yet among you there are some who do not believe."
He went on to say:
"This is why I have told you
that no one can come to me
unless it is granted him by the Father."

From this time on, many of his disciples broke away and would not remain in his company any longer. Jesus then said to the Twelve, "Do you want to leave me too?" Simon Peter answered him, "Lord, to whom shall we go? You have the words of eternal life. We have come to believe; we are convinced that you are God's holy one." (John 6:60-69)

"You disregard God's commandment and cling to what is human tradition"

ON LEAVING the safe family setting and going to college, many young intellectuals begin to have doubts about their religion. An agnostic professor may make a sneering remark about "The Good Book"; fellow students, though ostensibly Catholics, may show by their behavior that they could not care less about religion. Though there are many reasons for such confusion in young minds, one may be that many do not make a distinction between what is God-made and what is man-made in religion, especially as we used to live it in the Catholic tradition.

Basic Christianity is a beautiful way of life, but many may object to the way it has been institutionalized over the centuries. Many man-made details were added and some of them are/were undoubtedly outdated. The renewal movement begun by the Second Vatican Council aims at divesting the Church of human baggage picked up along its path through history. Naturally, this requires sound and informed leadership in order not to "dump the child with the bathwater," in other words, in the process of cleaning not to do away with divine elements. As the saying goes: "Pope John wanted to open the windows to let in fresh air, not to throw out the furniture!" Young and old should update themselves.

Jesus castigates the experts of the law for the countless man-made traditions they want the faithful to follow. "You disregard God's commandment [love for God and neighbor!] and cling to what is human tradition."

What is your attitude toward Church renewal? Pray for guidance.

SCRIPTURE READING —

The Pharisees and the scribes questioned [Jesus]: "Why do your disciples not follow the tradition of our ancestors, but instead take food without purifying their hands?" He said to them: "How accurately Isaiah prophesied about you hypocrites when he wrote,

'This people pays me lip service
but their heart is far from me.
Empty is the reverence they do me
because they teach as dogmas mere human precepts.'

You disregard God's commandment and cling to what is human tradition."

(Mark 7:5-8)

"At once the man's ears were opened"

A HEALTHY person, who seldom or never needs a physician, finds difficulty in understanding the anguish, frustration, and never-to-be-fulfilled desires of the physically handicapped. In primitive societies and prescientific times, the condition of the handicapped was even worse than it is today. There were no rehabilitation programs for them, no wheel chairs or any equipment that gave them at least some relief. Since religious beliefs regarded their misery as related to sin and moral guilt, they were often outcasts for whom nobody cared.

We find it altogether natural, therefore, that the writers of the Bible used the wretched situation of the lame, the blind, the deaf, the epileptics, and the lepers (all of whom they believed to be in the power of demons) as a figure to describe man's alienation from God, and the healing of these people as the sign of God's powerful and caring presence. Ethically speaking, we could be like some of those handicapped. Pray that the Lord may open your ears to listen to his message.

We must be careful to note that Mark wants us to see the miracles of Jesus as signs of a hidden reality to come. Jesus is not like the traditional miracle-workers circulating in his day; his miracles are not ends in themselves. Mark brings this out by having Jesus order silence time and again after each miracle. Hence, we must meditate on what Mark wants to teach by relating this tradition.

SCRIPTURE READING —

[Jesus] left Tyrian territory and returned by way of Sidon to the Sea of Galilee, into the district of the Ten Cities. Some people brought him a deaf man who had a speech impediment and begged him to lay his hand on him. Jesus took him off by himself away from the crowd. He put his fingers into the man's ears and, spitting, touched his tongue; then he looked up to heaven and emitted a groan. He said to him, "Ephphatha!" **(that is, "Be opened!") At once the man's ears were opened; he was freed from the impediment, and began to speak plainly. Then he enjoined them strictly not to tell anyone; but the more he ordered them not to, the more they proclaimed it. Their amazement went beyond all bounds: "He has done everything well! He makes the deaf hear and the mute speak!"** (Mark 7:31-37)

"If a man wishes to come after me, he must deny his very self"

OUR affluent society does all it can to do away with the reality of suffering. In the eyes of those who are blind to the transcendent, suffering and pain are incompatible with happiness. Funeral homes make it their profession to blur suffering. Medical science alleviates pain, the drug commercials on television advertise their pain killers and sleeping pills, and dope peddlers make it possible to escape a harsh reality. Not all of this is bad. It is a service to alleviate pain, to arrange a worthy funeral, and to pray to God for help when we suffer.

However, we should regard as un-Christian an attitude which desires at any cost or with dubious means (dope abuse) to do away with both mental and physical suffering that is unavoidable! Since our lives are patterned after the life, death, and resurrection of our Lord, we should in faith be willing to die with him (die to our egotistic selves, which is a painful process, and accept unavoidable suffering) in order to live with him forever. Today's Bible reading deals with the theme of taking up our cross and following in our Lord's footsteps.

In this tradition as Mark relates it, Peter cannot correlate the idea of suffering with that of Messiahship. Jesus corrects him in clear language and teaches all Christians about taking up their cross and following in his steps. We should think of this when things do not go our way and pray for strength.

SCRIPTURE READING —

[Jesus] began to teach [his disciples] that the Son of Man had to suffer much, be rejected by the elders, the chief priests, and the scribes, be put to death, and rise three days later. He said these things quite openly. Peter then took him aside and began to remonstrate with him. At this he turned around and, eyeing the disciples, reprimanded Peter: "Get out of my sight, you satan! You are not judging by God's standards but by man's!"

He summoned the crowd with his disciples and said to them: "If a man wishes to come after me, he must deny his very self, take up his cross, and follow in my steps." (Mark 8:31-34)

"If anyone wishes to rank first, he must remain . . . the servant of all"

WHEREVER people establish a group, the necessity of management arises. No enterprise can do without it and the executives of any group are human beings, hence subject to human failings, such as jealousy and strife. Furthermore, they will "manage" according to a pattern which they are used to in their own time and culture. The Christian movement came into being in the Roman empire, hence institutionalized itself according to the pattern of which it was a part—Roman law and order. In the feudalistic Middle Ages with its pompous and splendiferous kings, Church management shaped itself automatically after that system. And the Church in the United States is today inclined to manage dioceses and parishes as General Motors manages its enterprise.

From the very beginning, the Founder of the Church, the Lord Jesus, had to remind his human co-workers that his movement to establish the reign of God on earth should not be managed by human standards alone. Today's Scripture tells us that the twelve apostles had been arguing about who was the most important! Jesus' words to them on this occasion give us an idea of how he envisioned the management of the Church—from the parish council level to the diocesan and as far as the top or Vatican level. The key characteristic of his type of Church management is service.

The ministry [i.e., service] of the Church must imply humility, more or less the simplicity of a child. The Church as institution, the committee on finances included, is not General Motors! In Church enterprises we must go by rules the Lord Jesus has given us. Whenever we take part in Church activities, we should keep this service idea well in mind.

SCRIPTURE READING —

They returned to Capernaum and Jesus, once inside the house, began to ask [the disciples], "What were you discussing on the way home?" At this they fell silent, for on the way they had been arguing about who was the most important. So he sat down and called the Twelve around him and said, "If anyone wishes to rank first, he must remain the last one of all and the servant of all." Then he took a little child, stood him in their midst, and putting his arms around him, said to them, "Whoever welcomes a child such as this for my sake welcomes me. And whoever welcomes me welcomes, not me, but him who sent me."

(Mark 9:33-37)

"Anyone who is not against us is with us"

IT SEEMS to be an inborn instinct to mistreat and disqualify people who are different from us. Let a bearded and long-haired youngster or a lady whose dress code is not ours appear and immediately eyebrows are raised! The more isolated life is, be it geographically in rural areas or socially by self-imposed isolation (the railroad dividing black and white sections of little towns in the South or the inner city versus the suburbs of the North), the more narrow-minded and biased people are, even to the extent of expelling the "outside agitator" violently or ostracizing him socially.

This very thing happened to our Lord, who came to his own "yet his own did not accept him" (John 1:12). He was *different.* In his hometown of Nazareth the people even became hostile. "They found him too much for them" (Mark 6:3). Being a Jew, our Lord would be refused membership today in many a country club! Over the centuries, Christian denominations have isolated themselves socially. Small wonder then that they mistrust one another. Today's Bible reading deals with this topic.

The spirit (charism) to expel demons was given to Jesus and his disciples first, but also to others. John did not like it and tried to stop one who had it from using it. Jesus said in reply: "Do not try to stop him." We should learn to see God's Spirit at work wherever we meet good people. "For or against Jesus" does not necessarily follow Church-denomination lines, but means acting honestly according to one's conscience. "Anyone who is not against us is with us," be it often anonymously! This does not blur the truth as we see it in the Catholic tradition; it simply recognizes that a ray of truth and much goodness are found everywhere. We should respect and love other conscientious persons—no matter how different they may be!

SCRIPTURE READING —

John said to [Jesus], "Teacher, we saw a man using your name to expel demons and we tried to stop him because he is not of our company." Jesus said in reply: "Do not try to stop him. No man who performs a miracle using my name can at the same time speak ill of me. Anyone who is not against us is with us. Any man who gives you a drink of water because you belong to Christ will not, I assure you, go without his reward." (Mark 9:38-41)

"Let no man separate what God has joined"

IN A rapidly changing world, many values are questioned. One of them is the lasting marriage commitment. There is no doubt that the outlook on marriage has changed in a changing culture. The patriarchal marriage pattern of the Bible is no longer our own. The point is: what can be changed in marriage and what constitutes its core which cannot be called into question? Our Lord's statement in today's reading: "Let no man separate what God has joined," is the rule Christians follow.

The New Testament gives the Church the authority to make a few concessions that are pastorally necessary. Rather than going into the matter of complicated exceptions (ask any priest for literature!), let us meditate on the beauty of commitment, in other words, the reason why the law was made. Much depends on how one looks at the cherished value of freedom. For some, freedom claims unshakable fidelity; for others, freedom is incompatible with a definitive commitment. We should check which opinion is most in line with the dignity of the human person and assures the happiness of all involved, wife, husband, and children. Even more depends on what role love plays in one's life and on the art of keeping it exciting!

By living the earthly reality of their marriage as it should be done, Christians should be a beacon for so many who waver in their commitments. (If you are a bachelor or a religious, you can apply this to your own commitments.)

SCRIPTURE READING —

Some Pharisees came up and as a test began to ask [Jesus] whether it was permissible for a husband to divorce his wife. In reply he said, "What command did Moses give you?" They answered, "Moses permitted divorce and the writing of a decree of divorce." But Jesus told them: "He wrote that commandment for you because of your stubbornness. At the beginning of creation God made them male and female; for this reason a man shall leave his father and mother and the two shall become as one. They are no longer two but one flesh. Therefore let no man separate what God has joined." Back in the house again, the disciples began to question him about this. He told them, "Whoever divorces his wife and marries another commits adultery against her; and the woman who divorces her husband and marries another commits adultery."

(Mark 10:2-12)

"There is one thing more you must do"

A SONG from the musical *Godspell* has these lines concerning Jesus of Nazareth: "See [know] him more clearly, love him more dearly, follow him more nearly." Millions have done so over the centuries and countless others are still doing so today; and all have found the key to a meaningful life. In the Catholic tradition we know of two life-styles in which Christians search for meaning and happiness.

One of them is marriage, which is the life-style of most people. Facing life together, they try to see the Lord Jesus more clearly, love him more dearly, and follow him more nearly through the good stewardship of all the beauty and goodness of life that God has bestowed upon them. The other life-style, for those who are called to it, is "celibacy for the sake of the kingdom." It is a life of renunciation not as an end in itself but for a life of discipleship. If they are well-understood, both life-styles should witness to the same Christian mystery, namely, God's reign of justice, love, and peace as already initiated in human history. Today's reading deals with the issue of life-style.

SCRIPTURE READING —

As [Jesus] was setting out on a journey a man came running up, knelt down before him and asked, "Good Teacher, what must I do to share in everlasting life?" Jesus answered, "Why do you call me good? No one is good but God alone. You know the commandments:

'You shall not kill;
You shall not commit adultery;
You shall not steal;
You shall not bear false witness;
You shall not defraud;
Honor your father and your mother.' "

He replied, "Teacher, I have kept all these since my childhood." Then Jesus looked at him with love and told him, "There is one thing more you must do. Go and sell what you have and give to the poor; you will then have treasure in heaven. After that, come and follow me." At these words the man's face fell. He went away sad, for he had many possessions.

Peter was moved to say to him, "We have put aside everything to follow you!" Jesus answered: "I give you my word, there is no one who has given up home, brothers or sisters, mother or father, children or property, for me and for the gospel who will not receive in this present age a hundred times as many homes, brothers and sisters, mothers, children and property—and persecution besides—and in the age to come, everlasting life." (Mark 10:17-22, 28-30)

"You must serve the needs of all"

"OUR business is to serve you"—we see this advertised in enterprises of various kinds. From the local gas station up to the congress, service is offered. Those who serve us in government are called "public servants." The Prime Minister of Great Britain is the "First Servant" (ministry means service) of his nation. Professional service is offered by physicians and psychiatrists with a few days later a substantial bill in the mail.

The business of the Church is also to serve. Time and again our Lord emphasizes this aspect. What is the difference between service as mentioned above and the ministry (service) of the Church? It should be the quality of service and the personal touch in it, though many public servants, doctors, nurses, salesladies, waitresses, and bank tellers "serve" as true Christians should—with dedication and a personal touch. If so, they are the "Church of Christ" and carry out what our Lord says in today's Gospel: "You must serve the needs of all." Our service is more clearly Christian when no bill follows. We do such a free service for a poor or suffering neighbor whenever possible; children should do it for parents. Church workers, religious, and priests offer free service wherever service is needed.

What makes a person really great? Society lays down rules for greatness: success in business, a charming personality, physical beauty, excellence in the performing arts. One must have done something spectacular! Our Lord has a few ideas of his own: "Anyone among you who aspires to greatness must *serve the rest.*" We may admire those who are great in unselfish service to others. But do we realize that Jesus' statement is also directed to us, and that service which makes us great in the eyes of God does not have to be spectacular?

SCRIPTURE READING —

Jesus called the disciples together and said to them: "You know how among the Gentiles those who seem to exercise authority lord it over them; their great ones make their importance felt. It cannot be like that with you. Anyone among you who aspires to greatness must serve the rest; whoever wants to rank first among you must serve the needs of all. The Son of Man has not come to be served but to serve—to give his life in ransom for the many." (Mark 10:42-45)

"I want to see." . . . "Your faith has healed you"

"I HAVE never seen it that way," we might exclaim when a friend opens our eyes. "I did not know him/her that well," we might murmur when circumstances have shown us some beautiful facets of an individual's personality which we had overlooked during years of social contact. Meeting a good person may change our lives. This person may open our eyes to values we have overlooked, broaden our way of looking at things, encourage us when we are "down in the dumps," and show us danger where we do not see it.

Mark wrote his Gospel to heal a certain "Christological blindness" in the Church of his day. Spectacular preachers, themselves a type of miracle-workers and faith healers, had come along. They preached Jesus as a divine miracle-man and themselves as his successors. Mark did not find this picture of Jesus compatible with Jesus as he really was: the one who redeemed us by his suffering, death, and resurrection. Hence, Mark describes Jesus' miracles as signs that indicate a spiritual reality. In the healing of the blind man the reality is the healing of a "Christological blindness," a blindness of mind which kept Mark's congregation from seeing Jesus as he really is.

The miracle narratives of the Gospel tell us about deprived and unhappy people who started a new life once they had met our Lord. Have you "met" our Lord to such an extent that he fascinates you, that you are convinced that doing things his way will brighten your life? Pray that your eyes may be opened to see such a meeting! Blindness of mind may deserve blame—if it is caused by indifference and lack of care.

SCRIPTURE READING —

As he was leaving [Jericho] with his disciples and a sizable crowd, there was a blind beggar Bartimaeus ("son of Timaeus") sitting by the roadside. On hearing that it was Jesus of Nazareth, he began to call out, "Jesus, Son of David, have pity on me!" Many people were scolding him to make him keep quiet, but he shouted all the louder, "Son of David, have pity on me!" Then Jesus stopped and said, "Call him over." So they called the blind man over, telling him as they did so, "You have nothing to fear from him! Get up! He is calling you!"

He threw aside his cloak, jumped up and came to Jesus. Jesus asked him, "What do you want me to do for you?" "Rabboni," the blind man said, "I want to see." Jesus said in reply, "Be on your way! Your faith has healed you." Immediately he received his sight and started to follow him up the road.

(Mark 10:46-52)

"Yes, 'to love him with all our heart' "

NO VALUE in human life has been sung about so much as love. Poems, songs, and novels of all literatures of the globe deal with it endlessly. Almost no motion picture leaves it unmentioned. Jokes caricature it, wise sayings try to define what love really is, and suicide/murder quite often follow upon the failure of love. Hebrew literature, that is, the Bible, is no exception. It deals often with love, but relates it constantly to its deepest root, love of God.

Especially in the awareness of the New Testament writers, love of God and neighbor cannot be separated. "Whoever loves God must also love his brother" (1 John 4:21). Any attempt to separate these two loves is bound to fail in Christian experience. "If anyone says, 'My love is fixed on God,' yet hates his brother, he is a liar" (1 John 4:20). And the other way around, loving the brother, but not paying enough attention to God in prayer and worship, results in failure as well.

Many a social worker has tried to love God mainly or only "horizontally" (i.e., in "the brother"). Usually this does not last long. When frustrations undo our best efforts to love "the brother," love of God is needed to keep going.

SCRIPTURE READING —

One of the scribes came up, and when he heard them arguing he realized how skillfully Jesus answered them. He decided to ask him, "Which is the first of all the commandments?" Jesus replied: "This is the first:

'Hear, O Israel! The Lord our God is Lord alone!
Therefore you shall love the Lord your God
with all your heart,
with all your soul,
with all your mind,
and with all your strength.'

This is the second,

'You shall love your neighbor as yourself.'

There is no other commandment greater than these." The scribe said to him: "Excellent, Teacher! You are right in saying, 'He is the One, there is no other than he.' Yes, 'to love him with all our heart, with all our thoughts and with all our strength, and to love our neighbor as ourselves' is worth more than any burnt offering or sacrifice." Jesus approved the insight of this answer and told him, "You are not far from the reign of God." And no one had the courage to ask him any more questions. (Mark 12:28-34)

"This poor widow contributed more than all the others"

IN THE early sixties I was asked by one of my parishioners: "Father, how much should I spend on my wife's Christmas present?" In plain language the answer was: "If you love her, you know. And if you do not love her, give nothing!" Around Christmas, Mother's Day, and Father's Day millions are made on our desire to express our affections for loved ones by giving presents. ("Say it with flowers!") Giving is a beautiful symbolical way of saying: "I love you—I am grateful—I'm sorry, forget what has happened!", expressing meanwhile a whole gamut of feelings in between.

The tradition in today's reading deals with two kinds of people as they were found in the Jewish synagogues and perhaps still are found in our churches—the scribes, desiring front seats in the synagogues, and the poor widow, "contributing more than all the others who donated to the treasury." Jesus offers his idea on giving!

Most important is not what you give but why you give. All giving should symbolize self-giving. The giving of the poor widow is precious in God's eyes because it stands for a generous giving of self. Make your giving to God (your partaking in the Eucharistic sacrifice), and your sharing with fellow human beings a meaningful symbol of self-giving. Contemplate the widow's attitude. Find God's word to you, and respond in prayer.

SCRIPTURE READING—

In the course of his teaching [Jesus] said: "Be on guard against the scribes, who like to parade around in their robes and accept marks of respect in public, front seats in the synagogues, and places of honor at banquets. These men devour the savings of widows and recite long prayers for appearance' sake; it is they who will receive the severest sentence."

Taking a seat opposite the treasury, he observed the crowd putting money into the collection box. Many of the wealthy put in sizable amounts; but one poor widow came and put in two small copper coins worth a few cents. He called his disciples over and told them: "I want you to observe that this poor widow contributed more than all the others who donated to the treasury. They gave from their surplus wealth, but she gave from her want, all that she had to live on." (Mark 12:38-44)

"The reason why I came into the world is to testify to the truth"

ARE you satisfied with the achievement of your Church? First, we should make a distinction between Jesus' movement to establish God's reign of justice, love, and peace on earth, and the Church as institutionalized over the centuries. Let us confine our question to the Christian movement as such and ask again: Has it achieved its goal of establishing God's reign on earth during the 2,000 years of its existence? The answer is obviously: We may speak only of a partial success! Seeing so much evil around us, we cannot state that God's reign of love, justice, and peace has been fully realized on planet earth. But was the Christian movement designed to be a one-hundred-percent success?

In today's reading, Christ, stating that he is king, says also: "The reason why I came into the world is to testify to the truth." Earlier our Lord had said that the Church would be like yeast in dough (Matthew 13:33). The dough is the world. Jesus never promised that the whole world would become yeast! The Church (God's people), as yeast in the dough, should have a constant uplifting impact in the community in which it is situated, and testify to the truth!

If you have an uplifting impact, wherever you are, and testify to the truth by word and example, you are establishing God's reign of which Jesus Christ is the Messiah, the anointed king. What is your prayerful response?

SCRIPTURE READING —

Pilate went back into the praetorium and summoned Jesus. "Are you the King of the Jews?" he asked him. Jesus answered:

"My kingdom does not belong to this world.
If my kingdom were of this world,
my subjects would be fighting
to save me from being handed over to the Jews.
As it is, my kingdom is not here."

At this Pilate said to him, "So, then, you are a king?" Jesus replied:

"It is you who say I am a king.
The reason I was born,
the reason why I came into the world,
is to testify to the truth.
Anyone committed to the truth hears my voice."

(John 18:33, 36-37)

"For the Lord delights in you"

WHEN in a marriage two people have grown into a mature love for one another, one of them can be heard to say in the course of a lively conversation: "But my wife and I think. . . ." Such partners have grown into the conjugal oneness mentioned by the Bible: "The two of them become one body" (Genesis 2:24; Matthew 19:6: note that in Biblical language "body-flesh" stands for the whole person!). It can also happen that the marital oneness is overly stressed by one of the partners. The man, who once loved that charming little woman so much because of certain beautiful qualities of character, may become a tyrant and seek to mold his wife into a blueprint of himself. This is love turned into egotism.

Real love is participation in one another's personality with great respect, never destroying it! In the awareness of the Bible, man is related to God in a sacred partnership (covenant), which has conjugal overtones. But in his great love, God does not destroy us as persons. We are and should be different, though the same Spirit of love has been given to all of us. Christians should live in the joy of the wedding (partnership-covenant) between God and man.

In today's reading it is one of Isaiah's disciples who takes up this theme to console the people of his day. He assures them that although past infidelity was punished with defeat and exile to Babylon, God forgives and takes his people back as his spouse. God's word to you in this passage could be a question: How do you see yourself in relation to God? Is the promised reward or love the main incitement of your Christian life-style? God loves you.

SCRIPTURE READING —

You shall be called by a new name
pronounced by the mouth of the Lord.
You shall be a glorious crown in the hand of the Lord,
a royal diadem held by your God.
No more shall men call you "Forsaken,"
or your land "Desolate,"
But you shall be called "My Delight,"
and your land "Espoused."
For the Lord delights in you,
and makes your land his spouse.
As a young man marries a virgin,
your Builder shall marry you;
And as a bridegroom rejoices in his bride
so shall your God rejoice in you.

(Isaiah 62:2-5)

August 7

"He stood up to do the reading"

THE word has a formidable impact. Campaigning politicians, lawyers in court, and preachers of revivals are aware of its magic power and work miracles with it. The word is conveyed both in its written and spoken form. A book like Hitler's *Mein Kampf* led millions into the calamity of World War II, while the sermons of Bishop Sheen on television have showed the path of righteousness to a multitude of listeners.

The bestseller par excellence, which remains unsurpassed by any book, is the Bible. What does the "Good Book" mean to you? Do you read/listen with faith? Bible reading just for information's sake becomes boring, since many passages are already known to us. Bible reading should be done always prayerfully and meditatively, applying God's word to our own situation.

We should make note of a few points in this narrative. Jesus entered the synagogue on the sabbath "as he was in the habit of doing." Hence, besides healing and expelling demons, Jesus took time for regular worship. Moreover, Jesus *read* Scripture, sat down to *explain* it, and *applied* it to a situation, i.e., to himself: "Today this Scripture passage is fulfilled in your hearing."

Bible reading should always result in reflective prayer. It is your "Amen" (or assent) to God's word to you.

SCRIPTURE READING —

[Jesus] came to Nazareth where he had been reared, and entering the synagogue on the sabbath as he was in the habit of doing, he stood up to do the reading. When the book of the prophet Isaiah was handed him, he unrolled the scroll and found the passage where it was written:

"The spirit of the Lord is upon me;
therefore he has anointed me.
He has sent me to bring glad tidings to the poor,
to proclaim liberty to captives,
Recovery of sight to the blind
and release to prisoners,
To announce a year of favor from the Lord."

Rolling up the scroll he gave it back to the assistant and sat down. All in the synagogue had their eyes fixed on him. Then he began by saying to them, "Today this Scripture passage is fulfilled in your hearing." (Luke 4:16-21)

"They rose up and expelled him"

CHRISTIANITY as a beautiful philosophy of life is preached all over the globe. Some accept it and find a meaningful life which leads to satisfaction and happiness. Others reject it, possibly because they see it as a threat to their own set of values. Still others really do not care, and among these are those seeking a short-term meaning in life. Not all who fail to accept the message of Christ are bad people. Accepting Christ and his outlook on life requires faith, and faith is a free gift of God. It is risky to accuse non-believers of guilt and ill-will. We do much better to leave judgment up to God, and by word and example to give witness of a Christian life-style which we believe leads to lasting happiness.

This passage is intelligible only if you read what comes before in the passage of yesterday *(August 7)*. Notice: "They marveled." Others asked: "Is not this Joseph's son?" Who does he think he is? Why does he not work a few miracles here also? And finally they reject him. Since Judaism as a whole rejected Jesus, the message was directed to the Gentiles.

God's word to all who suffer because of Christian witness is: "But he [Jesus] went straight through their midst and walked away." Suffering is part of Christian witness. Final victory belongs to Christ and all who are willing to suffer with him.

SCRIPTURE READING —

[The people of Nazareth] marveled at the appealing discourse which came from [Jesus'] lips. They also asked, "Is not this Joseph's son?"

He said to them, "You will doubtless quote me the proverb, 'Physician, heal yourself,' and say, 'Do here in your own country the things we have heard you have done in Capernaum.' But in fact," he went on, "no prophet gains acceptance in his native place. Indeed, let me remind you, there were many widows in Israel in the days of Elijah when the heavens remained closed for three and a half years and a great famine spread over the land. It was to none of these that Elijah was sent, but to a widow of Zarephath near Sidon. Recall, too, the many lepers in Israel in the time of Elisha the prophet; yet not one was cured except Naaman the Syrian."

At these words the whole audience in the synagogue was filled with indignation. They rose up and expelled him from the town, leading him to the brow of the hill on which it was built and intending to hurl him over the edge. But he went straight through their midst and walked away.

(Luke 4:21-30)

"Amazement seized him and all his shipmates"

IN THE awareness of a person who forms part of a technological society it is better to keep the sacred and the secular in life separated. Phenomena that were considered mysterious in the past can now be explained by science. When we are sick, we do not go to the priest to have him expel a demon; we go to the doctor for our antibiotics. Counselors delve into the psychological structure of a youngster and advise him as to what direction in life he should choose. It seems that the intuitive awe for the sacred and the mysterious presence of God in all of life is disappearing to the degree that psychology steps in.

Can only artists, painters, and poets still have the intuitive awareness of the sacred in the reality of life? All believers have it in their best moments. We should keep it alive.

"Leave me, Lord. I am a sinful man." These words indicate Peter's awareness when our Lord showed a glimpse of his real being by working a miracle. "Amazement seized him." Amazement could be the beginning of faith! Peter and his mates left everything and became Jesus' followers. What was there so extraordinary about the call of these men? We know that God is present to you and me just as he was to Peter and his companions. Hence, we can say that the "extraordinary" element lay simply in an "awareness in faith" on their part. The signals of all television stations of your area are in your room. But you must "tune in" in order receive the sound and images emitted by them, that is, in order to be "aware" of them. In faith, we should keep "tuned in" to God. Then we will hear his daily call, and with his help our answer will be: "Here I am."

SCRIPTURE READING—

Upon doing [as Jesus said the fishermen] caught such a great number of fish that their nets were at the breaking point. They signaled to their mates in the other boat to come and help them. These came, and together they filled the two boats until they nearly sank.

At the sight of this, Simon Peter fell at the knees of Jesus saying, "Leave me, Lord. I am a sinful man." For indeed, amazement at the catch they had made seized him and all his shipmates, as well as James and John, Zebedee's sons, who were partners with Simon. Jesus said to Simon, "Do not be afraid. From now on you will be catching men." With that they brought their boats to land, left everything, and became his followers.

(Luke 5:6-11)

"Blest are you poor. . . . But woe to you rich"

THERE is no human being in the world who does not want to be happy. There is only a difference of opinion about what happiness is and how to attain it. Happiness implies that certain desires are being satisfied; and since man's desires are never fully satisfied, a happy person trusts, has hope, for more to come. Happiness that is present is beautiful, but it always prompts the question: What about tomorrow?

There are people who want instant happiness. "I am only young once; hence let me live it up!" Others search for happiness in an affluent life. But what about getting old and finally facing the end? Many want happiness—if necessary at the cost of destroying the well-being of others. It requires a sound philosophy of life to obtain a happiness that fully satisfies the human heart, which goes on searching restlessly. Christianity is such a philosophy (wisdom) of life.

We should see the beatitudes in today's reading as a challenge to perfection directed to all who seriously search for happiness. "Blest are you poor. . . . Woe to you rich." It is true that the poor feel the insufficiency of the human condition, hence the need for God, more keenly than the rich do. Matthew's version speaks of "poor in spirit," which refers to responsible stewardship. If the have's are constantly aware that they do not own anything, but that they are just God's stewards, and that having more means more responsibility (social justice, charity by sharing), then they too will receive their reward in heaven. Applied to your situation, do you accept the challenge to perfection?

SCRIPTURE READING —

Raising his eyes to his disciples, [Jesus] said:
"Blest are you poor; the reign of God is yours.
Blest are you who hunger; you shall be filled.
Blest are you who are weeping; you shall laugh.

Blest shall you be when men hate you, when they ostracize you and insult you and proscribe your name as evil because of the Son of Man. On the day they do so, rejoice and exult, for your reward shall be great in heaven. Thus it was that their fathers treated the prophets.

But woe to you rich, for your consolation is now.
Woe to you who laugh now; you shall weep in your grief.

Woe to you when all speak well of you. Their fathers treated the false prophets in just this way." (Luke 6:20-26)

"Be compassionate, as your Father is compassionate"

CAREFUL observance of our own instinctive drives and the behavior of fellow human beings especially at moments when they do not control themselves (anger, frustration, fear) teaches how much we have in common with animals, not only in our physical make-up but in our instinctive and subconscious life as well. The motion pictures of Walt Disney show how selfish and cruel animals in the jungle can be. And which of us has not experienced how horribly little children can behave toward one another! It takes a lifetime of constant maturation to outgrow the animal in us. And some hardly make it. Even as old people, their minds are not yet in control of their passions and selfish desires.

Christianity, that beautiful philosophy of life, offers guidelines on how to grow into maturity, but it also gives motivations and reasons for doing so. Christian growth into maturity is growth into maturity in Christ and a challenge to be the kind of person our heavenly Father is.

The exhortation to "lend without expecting repayment" should cause us no wonder if we remember that in biblical times money did not yet have the commercial function it has now. Moreover, there is a vast difference between a bank granting a business loan and an individual helping a friend as well as possible under the circumstances. Finally, we must keep in mind that the words "Give, and it shall be given to you" provide just *one* motive for generosity. It does not have to be our only one. The Gospels offer many reasons for us to be generous. Select whatever applies to you and respond in reflective prayer!

SCRIPTURE READING —

[Jesus said:] "If you love those who love you, what credit is that to you? Even sinners love those who love them. If you do good to those who do good to you, how can you claim credit? Sinners do as much. If you lend to those from whom you expect repayment, what merit is there in it for you? Even sinners lend to sinners, expecting to be repaid in full.

"Be compassionate, as your Father is compassionate. Do not judge, and you will not be judged. Do not condemn, and you will not be condemned. Pardon, and you shall be pardoned. Give, and it shall be given to you. Good measure pressed down, shaken together, running over, will they pour into the fold of your garment. For the measure you measure with will be measured back to you." (Luke 6:27-38)

August 12

"Each tree is known by its yield"

WHETHER we like it or not, our language shows whether we are educated or not. It usually indicates which country we are from and, within the country, even which part. It tells something about our age and sex, our temperament, our profession, our honesty, our moral values, and our outlook on life.

However, not all language is honest and reflects the real person. We are constantly exposed, for example, to the multi-faceted language of diplomacy and the deceptive language of the slick commercial. Our language, though, should be the language of the heart, honestly reflecting our best selves. Only by being honest with one another can human beings communicate and overcome the ailment of alienation.

In their language of preaching, the disciples must check whether their words are genuinely inspired by the standards of the Lord Jesus. His light should shine through their rhetoric. If such is not the case with preachers, they are like the blind guiding the blind. The same should be true when preachers are correcting sinners. Their language is credible only if they are honest with themselves. Finally, since not only priests but all Christians should bear witness, we should be honest with one another. Only if people feel that I am a good person who produces goodness from the good of my heart will my words be accepted by them.

SCRIPTURE READING —

[Jesus] also used images in speaking to [the people]: "Can a blind man act as guide to a blind man? Will they not both fall into a ditch? A student is not above his teacher; but every student when he has finished his studies will be on a par with his teacher.

"Why look at the speck in your brother's eye when you miss the plank in your own? How can you say to your brother, 'Brother, let me remove the speck from your eye,' yet fail yourself to see the plank lodged in your own? Hypocrite, remove the plank from your own eye first; then you will see clearly enough to remove the speck from your brother's eye.

"A good tree does not produce decayed fruit any more than a decayed tree produces good fruit. Each tree is known by its yield. Figs are not taken from thornbushes, nor grapes picked from brambles. A good man produces goodness from the good in his heart; an evil man produces evil out of his store of evil. Each man speaks from his heart's abundance."

(Luke 6:39-45)

"I tell you, I have never found so much faith among the Israelites"

TWO extremes which have hurt the Church over the 2,000 years of its existence are indifferentism and fanaticism. Let us look at fanaticism and intolerance. It has done much harm to the establishment of God's reign of love and justice on earth, which is the primary task the Divine Founder has given us. We think immediately of the inquisition and one of its best known victims Joan of Arc. We think too of the fierce wars in which Catholics and Protestants have senselessly shed one another's blood.

Fanaticism caused many devout Christians to leave their home countries and come to the "land of the free," often to continue their intolerance, though in a milder form, on these shores. Only in the wake of the Second Vatican Council are we outgrowing a "ghetto" Catholicism and trying to see positive values in other Churches.

Luke brings out that Jesus sees the good in a Gentile centurion, admires his great faith, and heals his servant. Luke intended this message for his congregation, which had to contend with a certain "ghetto" mentality in the Judaism of its day. We learn that we should be open-minded. Acknowledging the positive good in other religions in no way endangers our own faith! God works wherever he wishes, as Jesus did. Pray for open-mindedness!

SCRIPTURE READING —

A centurion had a servant he held in high regard, who was at that moment sick to the point of death. When he heard about Jesus he sent some Jewish elders to him, asking him to come and save the life of his servant. Upon approaching Jesus they petitioned him earnestly. "He deserves this favor from you," they said, "because he loves our people, and even built our synagogue for us." Jesus set out with them. When he was only a short distance from the house, the centurion sent friends to tell him: "Sir, do not trouble yourself, for I am not worthy to have you enter my house. That is why I did not presume to come to you myself. Just give the order and my servant will be cured. I too am a man who knows the meaning of an order, having soldiers under my command. I say to one, 'On your way,' and off he goes; to another, 'Come here,' and he comes; to my slave, 'Do this,' and he does it." Jesus showed amazement on hearing this and turned to the crowd which was following him to say, "I tell you, I have never found so much faith among the Israelites." When the deputation returned to the house, they found the servant in perfect health. (Luke 7:2-10)

"Young man, I bid you get up"

THE well-known writer Stewart Alsop made headlines some time ago because he was able to speak so frankly and quietly on television about his death which he knew was impending. Physicians had told him, and newsmen were anxious to know how he felt about it. How one looks at death has much to do with one's religious faith. The Jews before Christ had no clear idea about a hereafter; hence their outlook was somber. "We must indeed die; we are then like water that is poured out on the ground" (2 Samuel 14:14). But there was also a growing awareness that death could not have a part in God's original plan of creation (Genesis 2:17). Hence, death appears as an evil power in opposition to God. It is the envy of the devil which causes it (Wisdom 2:24).

We find in the Old Testament momentary glimpses of a possible overcoming of death (Proverbs 14:32), but full assurance of survival after death came only with the Easter-event. Christ's victory over death is the Good News of the Gospel (2 Timothy 1:10). Since that time, death, though still a sad separation from beloved ones, has lost its sting (1 Corinthians 15:55). We Christians possess a living hope (1 Peter 1:3). There will be no more death in the consummated kingdom of God (Revelation 21:4).

The reaction of the people was amazement. "A great prophet has risen among us." This is precisely the way we should see these miracle narratives. They indicate the hidden reality of God's kingdom which is victory over death. Life everlasting was initiated in us when with Christ we died to sin in baptism. It will be fully realized in "the resurrection of the dead, and the life of the world to come" (*Profession of Faith* during Mass).

SCRIPTURE READING —

[Jesus] went to a town called Naim, and his disciples and a large crowd accompanied him. As he approached the gate of the town a dead man was being carried out, the only son of a widowed mother. A considerable crowd of townsfolk were with her. The Lord was moved with pity upon seeing her and said to her, "Do not cry." Then he stepped forward and touched the litter; at this, the bearers halted. He said, "Young man, I bid you get up." The dead man sat up and began to speak. Then Jesus gave him back to his mother. Fear seized them all and they began to praise God. "A great prophet has risen among us," they said; and, "God has visited his people." This was the report that spread about him throughout Judea and the surrounding country. (Luke 7:11-17)

"God who is mighty has done great things for me"

EVERY one of us feels a sense of satisfaction after having done a good job whether it be a mother who has given birth to a healthy baby, a man who has pleased his wife with the gift she had secretly desired for a long time, or a teenager who has mowed the lawn and feels his father's hand on his shoulder: "Son, you have done a good job." We all have a job to do in life. We must make it meaningful for ourselves and those around us. In order to do so, we need images to go by, and we have a beautiful image in Mary—simply because she did nothing spectacular and nevertheless had a very meaningful life.

In this passage, Luke describes Mary as a pious Jewish woman. Mary is great not primarily in what she does (helping out a pregnant kinswoman is done daily!) but in why she does it, namely, out of great love and gratitude toward God, as Luke illustrates by figuratively putting a series of psalm verses (a Jewish song?) into Mary's mouth. "His servant" is God's people, of which Mary is the most outstanding member. United with Mary in spirit, we too may pray this hymn since we are also God's people, servants, on whose lowliness God looks.

SCRIPTURE READING —

Mary set out, proceeding in haste into the hill country to a town of Judah, where she entered Zechariah's house and greeted Elizabeth. When Elizabeth heard Mary's greeting, the baby leapt in her womb.

Then Mary said:
"My being proclaims the greatness of the Lord,
my spirit finds joy in God my savior,
For he has looked upon his servant in her lowliness;
all ages to come shall call me blessed.
God who is mighty has done great things for me,
holy is his name;
His mercy is from age to age
on those who fear him.
He has shown might with his arm;
he has confused the proud in their inmost thoughts.
He has deposed the mighty from their thrones
and raised the lowly to high places.
The hungry he has given every good thing,
while the rich he has sent empty away.
He has upheld Israel his servant,
ever mindful of his mercy;
Even as he promised our fathers,
promised Abraham and his descendants forever."

(Luke 1:39-41, 46-55)

"But you—who do you say that I am?"

WHEN two young people pronounce their marriage vows and promise one another to go on together for the rest of their lives, they have already gotten to know one another previously, and they have mutual faith and love. Both will admit, however, that their mutual knowledge is only an understanding "to a certain extent." Knowing one another is an ongoing process, and it should be such in our lives in order to remain exciting. Seeing new aspects of one another's character time and again implies the element of surprise and overwhelming wonder which underlies happiness.

If we read the Gospels carefully, we see that the disciples came to understand and know Jesus only gradually. Their initial attitude toward him was one of curiosity: " 'Teacher, where do you stay?' 'Come and see,' he answered. So they went to see where he was lodged, and stayed with him that day" (John 1:38-39). Then they received his call and became his disciples: "They became his followers" (Luke 5:11). As such, they held discussions with him, asked questions, and received answers. Slowly, the disciples became aware of something special about this Teacher. Today's passage reflects the growth in awareness: "You are the Messiah of God." Yet when Jesus brought up the necessity of suffering, they could not comprehend him (Mark 8:32-33; Luke 9:46). Only after the resurrection did their knowledge and understanding grow clearer.

We should apply this to our own faith-commitment to the Lord Jesus. Our knowledge and understanding of his mysterious personality should grow all the time!

SCRIPTURE READING —

One day when Jesus was praying in seclusion and his disciples were with him, he put the question to them, "Who do the crowds say that I am?" "John the Baptizer," they replied, "and some say Elijah, while others claim that one of the prophets of old has returned from the dead." "But you—who do you say that I am?" he asked them. Peter said in reply, "The Messiah of God." He strictly forbade them to tell this to anyone. "The Son of Man," he said, "must first endure many sufferings, be rejected by the elders, the high priests and the scribes, and be put to death, and then be raised up on the third day."

Jesus said to all: "Whoever wishes to be my follower must deny his very self, take up his cross each day, and follow in my steps. Whoever would save his life will lose it, and whoever loses his life for my sake will save it." (Luke 9:18-24)

"Whoever puts his hand to the plow . . ."

IN HIS book *The Cost of Discipleship,* Dietrich Bonhoeffer, a minister of the Confessional Church in Germany during the Hitler regime, wrote: "When Christ calls a man, he bids him come and die." He knew by experience the truth of his statement. Arrested by the Gestapo, he inspired his guards in prison and concentration camps. He obtained permission to minister to his fellow prisoners and his ability to comfort the anxious and depressed was amazing. A few days before the liberation of his concentration camp, he was executed. *The Cost of Discipleship* is a powerful attack on an "easy Christianity."

From this passage we learn that Jesus resolutely accepted the consequences of his preaching of God's reign. Renewing society and cleansing it from evil provokes resistance and even violence when the preacher of righteousness attacks an evil power structure. And Jesus requires that same resoluteness from his followers.

Like Jesus himself, the disciple must be a homeless wanderer. The *dead* (those insensible to the call of Jesus) will take care of his father. And Jesus is even more demanding than the prophet Elijah, who, indeed, permitted Elisha first to kiss his father and mother goodbye and then to follow him as a disciple. (See 1 Kings 19:19-21.)

These are strong Semitic hyperboles. But the idea is clear. Putting one's hand to the plow but looking back makes one unfit for the reign of God. How strong is your commitment to Christ, and where are you inclined to take the easy way?

SCRIPTURE READING —

Someone said to [Jesus], "I will be your follower wherever you go." Jesus said to him, "The foxes have lairs, the birds of the sky have nests, but the Son of Man has nowhere to lay his head." To another he said, "Come after me." The man replied, "Let me bury my father first." Jesus said to him, "Let the dead bury their dead; come away and proclaim the kingdom of God."

Yet another said to him, "I will be your follower, Lord, but first let me take leave of my people at home." Jesus answered him, "Whoever puts his hand to the plow but keeps looking back is unfit for the reign of God."

(Luke 9:57-62)

"The reign of God is at hand"

THE decades after World War II have seen many nations emerging from the mixed blessings of colonialism to self-determination. In such nations the urge for freedom was great. Many of their people risked their lives to oust the colonizers. And jubilant celebrations took place when finally the flag of dominance went down and their own national flag was raised. However, these nations quickly discovered that gaining freedom is one thing while building up an economically strong nation with a reasonable level of well-being for all is another one. The Jews who returned from exile in Babylon had a similar experience. Reconstruction entailed much frustration. Where were the blessings (Shalom—peace—prosperity) promised them by God's holy men, the prophets?

Those who take a life of Christian witness seriously may also be frustrated. Time and again they read in their Bible that the reign of God (justice, love, peace) has been initiated in this world. But they look in vain for an abundance of it in their children! For their part, young people are critical of what the Church has failed to do and turn away from it. Even religious are afflicted with the same problem: after years of work in the inner city, a dedicated Sister may feel disappointed!

This is the "already" and "not yet" of God's reign in each individual and in the world at large. Shalom—peace—spiritual prosperity is with us. We should be grateful for what God has given us in baptism. But we should realize that God's reign is only *initiated* in this world. Full realization and perfect bliss will come later. A Christian can be an optimist always, as long as he does good to the best of his ability.

SCRIPTURE READING—

The Lord appointed a further seventy-two and sent them in pairs before him to every town and place he intended to visit. He said to them: "The harvest is rich but the workers are few; therefore ask the harvest-master to send workers to his harvest. Be on your way, and remember: I am sending you as lambs in the midst of wolves. On entering any house, first say, 'Peace to this house.' If there is a peaceable man there, your peace will rest on him; if not, it will come back to you.

"Into whatever city you go, after they welcome you, eat what they set before you, and cure the sick there. Say to them. 'The reign of God is at hand.' "

(Luke 10:1-3, 5-6, 8-9)

August 19

"A woman named Martha welcomed him"

THE concept of hospitality has had various connotations over the centuries. In the 6th century St. Benedict wrote in his rule that his monks should receive the stranger as Christ himself. The abbeys were havens for the lonesome traveler. For centuries, men and women have dedicated their lives as religious Brothers and Sisters to welcoming the stranger and the suffering in their hospitals, which were centers of charity, real "guest houses." Now it is different. Though there are still a few sporadic "hospices" run by Sisters, and Christian denominations still operate hospitals which bear their names, as a rule the stranger checks in at a motel and the sick person is taken care of in the community hospital, both paying for the service they receive.

However, hospitality is still a Christian form of charity. Think of the family. How do we receive our guests? A visit of friends can still be an enriching experience for both the guests and the host and the hostess, provided that there is mutual openness, real hospitality. Many Christians make their living by welcoming the strangers and the sick: receptionists, waitresses, physicians, nurses. In doing so they can practice service with a smile. That smile could make their service Christian!

Martha and Mary were hospitable toward our Lord—each in her own way. Martha was "busy with all the details of hospitality" and doing "the household tasks." Mary listened to Jesus' words. Both aspects of hospitality are important. But the openness to the guest as a person, in this case to our Lord's message of salvation, is more important. When we receive Christ in our fellow human beings, we should have an open eye for this mystery.

SCRIPTURE READING —

Jesus entered a village where a woman named Martha welcomed him to her home. She had a sister named Mary, who seated herself at the Lord's feet and listened to his words. Martha, who was busy with all the details of hospitality, came to him and said, "Lord, are you not concerned that my sister has left me to do the household tasks all alone? Tell her to help me."

The Lord in reply said to her: "Martha, Martha, you are anxious and upset about many things; one thing only is required. Mary has chosen the better portion and she shall not be deprived of it."

(Luke 10:39-42)

"How much more will the heavenly Father give the Holy Spirit to those who ask him"

PARENTS often display a remarkable patience in smilingly listening to the talk of their little children. And the little ones not only ask questions, they also ask for favors. Parents listen, but do they always grant what the little ones ask? Of course not! The horizon of a child is limited. Often he asks for favors which would hurt him. Prudent parents show their real love by never giving a child more freedom or favors than he is able to handle at a particular moment in life.

However, whether one is a teenager or an adult, it takes humility to admit that one's horizon is limited. Yet when we think of both the infinite wisdom and love of the heavenly Father, in faith we should be able to admit that he knows better whatever is best for us. It is in this context that we should see our prayer of petition. Does it make sense to pray for a beloved one who has terminal cancer? Should we pray in a seemingly hopeless marriage situation? Today's Scripture offers some insights on this point.

Jesus taught us how to pray. We should address God as Father. We should pray with perseverance. But will we obtain exactly what we ask? Comparing God with our father here on earth, Jesus says: "How much more will the heavenly Father *give the Holy Spirit* to those who ask him." Remember Psalm 138 says: "You answered me; you built up *strength within me.*" God knows best what we really need! Perhaps we need "his Spirit of wisdom and understanding, his spirit of counsel and of strength, his spirit of knowledge and of fear [filial respect] of the Lord" (Isaiah 11:2). If we become filled with God's Spirit and can cope effectively with some difficult situation or obtain the insight to solve a problem, then God has answered our prayer!

SCRIPTURE READING —

"So I say to you, 'Ask and you shall receive; seek and you shall find; knock and it shall be opened to you.'

"For whoever asks, receives; whoever seeks, finds; whoever knocks, is admitted. What father among you will give his son a snake if he asks for a fish, or hand him a scorpion if he asks for an egg? If you, with all your sins, know how to give your children good things, how much more will the heavenly Father give the Holy Spirit to those who ask him."

(Luke 11:9-13)

August 21

"The man who grows rich for himself"

LIFE only makes sense if we can relate it to lasting values. If a man seeks only values that perish, he will never be satisfied. Money and all that it can buy cannot impart lasting happiness. Think of the high suicide rate among the wealthy! Life is meaningful so far as it is related to others: fellow human beings and ultimately God in Christ Jesus. Think of people who have meant something to you in the past. These people—parents, teachers, sisters, brothers, friends, partner in marriage and finally Jesus Christ himself—have all contributed to whatever you are now as a person! Remove one person from this list and you would be different, perhaps less fortunate.

The rich fool of this passage lived his life without reference to God. And, indeed, a life without reference to God is an absurdity. Where does God fit into your money-making process? Concern for the future is good stewardship. But if concern becomes greed, egotism, keeping up with the neighbors, inspired by the philosophy that "we live only once," you are in trouble. You are only God's steward of all that you possess! Do you feel responsible for those less fortunate?

Money is not a lasting value, but relationships with others are. Go on building communication with others. In love, friendship, and dedication relate to others, and do not overlook your direct relationship with God—Jesus Christ through prayerful Bible reading and regular worship with fellow Christians.

SCRIPTURE READING —

Someone in the crowd said to [Jesus], "Teacher, tell my brother to give me my share of our inheritance." He replied, "Friend, who has set me up as your judge or arbiter?" Then he said to the crowd, "Avoid greed in all its forms. A man may be wealthy, but his possessions do not guarantee him life."

He told them a parable in these words: "There was a rich man who had a good harvest. 'What shall I do?' he asked himself. 'I have no place to store my harvest. I know!' he said. 'I will pull down my grain bins and build larger ones. All my grain and my goods will go there. Then I will say to myself: You have blessings in reserve for years to come. Relax! Eat heartily, drink well. Enjoy yourself.' But God said to him, 'You fool! This very night your life shall be required of you. To whom will all this piled-up wealth of yours go?' That is the way it works with the man who grows rich for himself instead of growing rich in the sight of God."

(Luke 12:13-21)

"Be like men awaiting their master's return"

"LISTEN here, Joe.
Don't you know
That tomorrow
You got to go
Out yonder where
The steel winds blow?
. . . Don't ask me why.
Just go ahead and die."

These lines are from Langston Hughes' poem *Without Benefit of Declaration.* Apparently, life is just such a journey "without benefit of declaration." Simply live it and die! The ancient Hebrew sages searched for "declaration" and, guided by God, they came up not with all the answers but certainly with some remarkable insights. They reasoned that if God is good, he *must* have a plan of salvation. Life cannot be a journey without destiny!

This outlook on life requires faith in God, and though it does not offer all the answers it gives enough of them to enable man to see meaning in his life. It is like the faith in his father that makes a child feel safe even when the child does not know where they are going. To a certain extent, limited as our human horizon is, we are like children. Trust in a loving God takes away absurdity and gives hope for a destiny to come.

But be prepared! "Let your belts be fastened around your waists," like the Jews about to leave Egypt! The moment you least expect it, you could be summoned to make "that loath journey," from which there is no return *(Everyman).*

SCRIPTURE READING —

[Jesus said to the disciples:] "Let your belts be fastened around your waists and your lambs be burning ready. Be like men awaiting their master's return from a wedding, so that when he arrives and knocks, you will open for him without delay. It will go well with those servants whom the master finds wide-awake on his return. I tell you, he will put on an apron, seat them at table, and proceed to wait on them.

"Should he happen to come at midnight or before sunrise and find them prepared, it will go well with them. You know as well as I that if the head of the house knew when the thief was coming he would not let him break into his house. Be on guard, therefore. The Son of Man will come when you least expect him." (Luke 12:35-40)

"I [Jesus] have come to light a fire on the earth"

"LEAVE me alone! Mind your own business!" is the usual reaction when others interfere with our way of life. We want to be happy in our own little world, with our good and perhaps also bad habits! Children do not like to be corrected by parents or teachers. Grown-ups unduly resent their employers' attempts to enhance their working methods. Parishioners may concede that priests should preach on sin, but they do not want them to go into details in which the audience may be involved! And in the "closed society" of the South in the sixties, people who came in to encourage blacks to stand up for their rights were termed "outside agitators." They were told: "Go home and leave us alone!"

Can we stand honest correction? The Bible reading tells us about Jesus of Nazareth, who did not leave people alone. In the name of God, he had to speak. His sermons were corrective and aimed at restoring life as it should be!

The fire which Jesus desires to be enkindled seems to be the fire that will purify those who are meant for the kingdom. In declaring: "I have a baptism to receive," Jesus refers to baptism by immersion." In other words, he says: "I will be immersed in pain and death." And he shows that he is human by feeling anguish! Jesus could not conceive of himself as running a popularity contest. The description of family dissension is an emphatic presentation of the divisions he brings. Those who follow him must be willing to make even painful decisions. "Avoiding the occasion of sin" could be such a decision!

SCRIPTURE READING —

[Jesus said:] "I have come to light a fire on the earth. How I wish the blaze were ignited! I have a baptism to receive. What anguish I feel till it is over! Do you think I have come to establish peace on the earth? I assure you, the contrary is true; I have come for division. From now on, a household of five will be divided three against two and two against three; father will be split against son and son against father, mother against daughter and daughter against mother, mother-in-law against daughter-in-law, daughter-in-law against mother-in-law."

(Luke 12:49-53)

"Lord, are they few in number who are to be saved?"

"SAFETY first." "Better safe than sorry." Nowadays, safety is almost an obsession. We have our savings. We pay our social security. We insure our cars, our homes, our lives, and we buckle our safety belts faithfully. But what about our ultimate safety, our eternal salvation? It gives you an unpleasant feeling if you miss the bus, train, or airplane. Your feeling is even more miserable if you know that it was your own fault because you wasted time doing unnecessary things which could have been done later.

Should we not then seriously consider the possibility that we might come too late for the kingdom of God? Could it happen that though we have been paying our church dues and taking part in the Eucharistic Banquet, we will not be saved?

Luke puts a question into the mouth of "someone": "Are they few in number who are to be saved?" He answers by placing three parables of our Lord in a row. The first parable is the one about the narrow door. There are a few conditions if we want to be saved. We know them! "Oh, when the saints go marchin' in. . . ." The second parable is directed to those who are late. They have not repented in time and miss the boat by their own fault: "Away from me, you evildoers!" The third parable warns Israel not to have pretensions as God's chosen people. Only those who repent, both Jews and Gentiles, will be saved. Constant conversion is part of a Christian life-style!

SCRIPTURE READING —

Someone asked [Jesus], "Lord, are they few in number who are to be saved?" He replied: "Try to come in through the narrow door. Many, I tell you, will try to enter and be unable. When once the master of the house has risen to lock the door and you stand outside knocking and saying, 'Sir, open for us,' he will say in reply, 'I do not know where you come from.' Then you will begin to say, 'We ate and drank in your company. You taught in our streets.' But he will answer, 'I tell you, I do not know where you come from. Away from me, you evildoers!"

"There will be wailing and grinding of teeth when you see Abraham, Isaac, Jacob, and all the prophets safe in the kingdom of God, and you yourselves rejected. People will come from the east and the west, from the north and the south, and will take their place at the feast in the kingdom of God. Some who are last will be first and some who are first will be last." (Luke 13:23-30)

"He who humbles himself shall be exalted"

ONLY those who are really great can afford to be humble. Humility stands actually for truth. There is a story about an actor who wanted a famous photographer-friend to shoot him and instinctively assumed the pose of a character in one of his movies. The photographer had to remind him: "I want a picture of *you!*" That actor had trouble being himself in front of a camera. He was always acting. It is well-adjusted persons who can honestly be themselves always and everywhere. Such persons do not need status symbols, neither do they have any desire to keep up with their neighbors. They have no need to prove themselves, for "good wine needs no bush."

Humble parents have no pretensions. They know that they are loved and respected by their children for what they are. They can afford to apologize for mistakes, since it is human to make them. A humble person gives in easily when the other proves to be right. One cannot be an expert in all fields. As a Christian virtue, humility is rooted in God. Christians know that all they are and have is a gift of God. Hence they are in constant need of God.

Jesus is the sublime example of humility and that is why he can speak about it, as he does in today's Scripture. Apply this to yourself and respond in reflective prayer!

SCRIPTURE READING —

[Jesus] went on to address a parable to the guests, noticing how they were trying to get the places of honor at the table: "When you are invited by someone to a wedding party, do not sit in the place of honor in case some greater dignitary has been invited. Then the host might come and say to you, 'Make room for this man,' and you would have to proceed shamefacedly to the lowest place. What you should do when you have been invited is go and sit in the lowest place, so that when your host approaches you he will say, 'My friend, come up higher.' This will win you the esteem of your fellow guests. For everyone who exalts himself shall be humbled and he who humbles himself shall be exalted."

(Luke 14:7-11)

"If anyone comes to me . . ."

IN A computerized society we stress the value of planning and calculation. The computer helps the human mind to make quick and prudent decisions. Does calculation have a place in interhuman relationships, or, on a higher level, in the way people decide to style their lives as related to God and religion?

Biblical peoples did not know the computer, but they did know about wisdom and prudence. Even if we speak of love, dedication, and faith, the element of prudence must be there! Intuitive and emotional decisions are sometimes feasible and even heroic. But, as a rule, we must sit down, apply wisdom and prudence, and even calculate our resources. The Scripture reading deals with prudence and even calculation.

The first part of this passage consists of Jesus' statement on the demands of discipleship. It is followed by a parable which relates to those demands. "Turning his back on his father and mother" (in other translations, "hate") is a Semitic way of saying "giving his father and mother second place in his affection"; Matthew's version has: "He who loves father or mother *more than me* . . ." Jesus requires detachment from family ties and the willingness to carry a cross. If our Lord suggests giving up marriage and possessions, he does so for the reason of following him.

The Church has always known young men and women who have accepted Jesus' challenge. Let us pray that we may always have them. And when you are young, calculate your resources, and pray for wisdom.

SCRIPTURE READING —

On one occasion when a great crowd was with him, [Jesus] turned to them and said, "If anyone comes to me without turning his back on his father and mother, his wife and his children, his brothers and sisters, indeed his very self, he cannot be my follower. Anyone who does not take up his cross and follow me cannot be my disciple. If one of you decides to build a tower, will he not first sit down and calculate the outlay to see if he has enough money to complete the project? He will do that for fear of laying the foundation and then not being able to complete the work; for all who saw it would jeer at him, saying, 'That man began to build what he could not finish.' In the same way, none of you can be my disciple if he does not renounce all his possessions."

(Luke 14:25-30, 33)

"There will be likewise more joy in heaven over one repentant sinner"

PARENTS of teenagers know about mistakes being made and the need for understanding and forgiveness. It is part of the process of growing up for children to make mistakes. The real problem arises when teenagers do not feel sorry for their mistakes and want to do things their way, right or wrong. We can easily envision youngsters dropping out of school, being on dope, running away from home. Though parents suffer, they are always ready to forgive; but what can they do as long as a child is recalcitrant and unwilling?

Relating this to our relationship with the heavenly Father, we often have the same situation. If we determine what is sinful, and do not go by what God thinks, we are in trouble. Sin has not disappeared! Have I given up the diligent search for perfection? Am I failing to be the kind of person I should be in God's eyes? Am I just indifferent?

Today's Bible reading deals with God's clemency. In my Bible, I have marked the words: "This man welcomes sinners" and "There will likewise be more joy in heaven over one repentant sinner." A prayer of thanksgiving could be your response.

SCRIPTURE READING—

The tax collectors and sinners were all gathering around to hear [Jesus], at which the Pharisees and the scribes murmured, "This man welcomes sinners and eats with them." Then he addressed this parable to them: "Who among you, if he has a hundred sheep and loses one of them, does not leave the ninety-nine in the wasteland and follow the lost one until he finds it? And when he finds it, he puts it on his shoulders in jubilation. Once arrived home, he invites friends and neighbors in and says to them, 'Rejoice with me because I have found my lost sheep.' I tell you, there will likewise be more joy in heaven over one repentant sinner than over ninety-nine righteous people who have no need to repent.

"What woman, if she has ten silver pieces and loses one, does not light a lamp and sweep the house in a diligent search until she has retrieved what she lost? And when she finds it, she calls in her friends and neighbors to say, 'Rejoice with me! I have found the silver piece I lost.' I tell you, there will be the same kind of joy before the angels of God over one repentant sinner." (Luke 15:1-10)

"A man had two sons . . ."

CHAPTER fifteen of Luke's Gospel is a perfect example of the fact that the writer did not intend to provide a biography of Jesus. What he intended to do was write a catechism, a digest of what Christians ought to know. However, Luke did not write a question-and-answer type of catechism which was used for the last few centuries in the Church and with which most of the older Catholics were taught their religion. He did it his way.

In this chapter, he makes a thought-provoking statement which he puts into the mouth of the Pharisees: "This man welcomes sinners and eats with them." Then he responds to it with three parables of Jesus: "the lost sheep" and "the lost silver piece" (both concerning God's care for the sinner) *(see August 27),* and the "prodigal son" (concerning the condition for forgiveness: "I will . . . return to my father," and God's willingness to forgive the penitent sinner).

There are two sons in this parable: the prodigal son (tax collectors and sinners) and the elder son who did the right thing but often for the wrong reason, i.e., with little or no love (the Pharisees and scribes). With which of the two do you identify yourself in reflective prayer?

SCRIPTURE READING —

Jesus said to them: "A man had two sons. The younger of them said to his father, 'Father, give me the share of the estate that is coming to me.' So the father divided up the property. Some days later this younger son collected all his belongings and went off to a distant land, where he squandered his money on dissolute living. [Returning home,] the son said to [his father], 'Father, I have sinned against God and against you; I no longer deserve to be called your son.' The father said to his servants: 'Quick! bring out the finest robe and put it on him; put a ring on his finger and shoes on his feet. Take the fatted calf and kill it.'

"Meanwhile the elder son was out on the land. As he neared the house on his way home, he heard the sound of music and dancing. The son grew angry at this and would not go in; but his father came out and began to plead with him.

"He said to his father in reply: 'For years now I have slaved for you. I never disobeyed one of your orders, yet you never gave me so much as a kid goat to celebrate with my friends. Then, when this son of yours returns after having gone through your property with loose women, you kill the fatted calf for him.'

" 'My son,' replied the father, 'you are with me always, and everything I have is yours. But we had to celebrate and rejoice!' "

(Luke 15:11-13, 21-25, 28-32)

"No servant can serve two masters"

SUCCESS in business can easily lead to a presumptuous feeling of absolute ownership and the desire for more, often regardless of the rights and needs of others. The Bible reminds us that there is no such a thing as absolute ownership. Man is God's partner and with God is responsible for a better world. In partnership with God, man has the right to use the resources of the planet. Therefore, everyone must be guaranteed a fair share in their ownership. Historical and sociological considerations indicate that the most practical means of insuring everyone's access to the goods of the earth is some system of private property.

The gift of private property is derived from the collective right of the human race to use the goods of the earth. "To each his own" is the golden rule of justice. Workers are entitled to earn a just wage and to receive human treatment, and they must do a good job. We have our unions to protect these rights. Both employers and employees must be careful that their unions do not commit collective injustice!

"You cannot give yourself to God and money"; the meaning is obvious. If you sever the management of your possessions from your religious faith, you will soon be going by a double standard. The motto "To each his own" should be our guide whenever we handle money and do business. Only then can God trust us!

If you are a religious, you could apply this to your commitment to live a life of evangelical poverty. Your willingness to share whatever you don't need really could be the gauge of your self-giving to God, which is incompatible with giving of self to money.

SCRIPTURE READING—

[Jesus said:] "If you can trust a man in little things, you can also trust him in greater; while anyone unjust in a slight matter is also unjust in greater. If you cannot be trusted with elusive wealth, who will trust you with lasting? And if you have not been trustworthy with someone else's money, who will give you what is your own?

"No servant can serve two masters. Either he will hate the one and love the other or be attentive to the one and despise the other. You cannot give yourself to God and money." (Luke 16:10-13)

August 30

"They have Moses and the prophets. Let them hear them"

SHOULD bishops and priests speak up for social justice? Should priests and nuns be involved in the civil rights movements of our deprived minorities, blacks, Chicanos, Indians, poor whites in Appalachia? Isn't it enough that we contribute whenever a special collection is taken up for them?

The Bible today warns against luxury-loving and not being concerned about our unfortunate fellow human beings. A well-to-do friend of mine once had occasion to drive the nuns of her parish to the slum area of town to deliver Christmas baskets. Her eyes were opened: "I did not know that such a poverty existed right here!" In the Gospel, we read, the rich man's eyes were opened too late! Abraham tells all who live luxuriously: "You have Moses and the prophets," i.e., your Bible. Why do you not read it, and apply its message honestly to your own life situation?

SCRIPTURE READING —

[Jesus spoke this parable:] "Once there was a rich man who dressed in purple and linen and feasted spendidly every day. At his gate lay a beggar named Lazarus who was covered with sores. Lazarus longed to eat the scraps that fell from the rich man's table. The dogs even came and licked his sores. Eventually the beggar died. He was carried by angels to the bosom of Abraham. The rich man likewise died and was buried. From the abode of the dead where he was in torment, he raised his eyes and saw Abraham afar off, and Lazarus resting in his bosom.

"He called out, 'Father Abraham, have pity on me. Send Lazarus to dip the tip of his finger in water to refresh my tongue, for I am tortured in these flames.' 'My child,' replied Abraham, 'remember that you were well off in your lifetime, while Lazarus was in misery. Now he has found consolation here, but you have found torment. And that is not all. Between you and us there is fixed a great abyss, so that those who might wish to cross from here to you cannot do so, nor can anyone cross from your side to us.'

" 'Father, I ask you, then,' the rich man said, 'send him to my father's house where I have five brothers. Let him be a warning to them so that they may not end in this place of torment.' Abraham answered, 'They have Moses and the prophets. Let them hear them.' 'No, Father Abraham,' replied the rich man. 'But if someone would only go to them from the dead, then they would repent.' Abraham said to him, 'If they do not listen to Moses and the prophets, they will not be convinced even if one should rise from the dead.' " (Luke 16:19-31)

"If you had faith the size of a mustard seed . . ."

WHEN we are in real distress, we find out who are our real friends. They are the ones who stay with us even at the cost of sacrifice. They have time for us. They have the patience to listen and the nobility to keep secrets. They are the people we can trust and have confidence in. Unfortunately, there are not many friends who can stand the test. Patients who have to stay in the hospital for a long time know this.

However, Christians who maintain a living relationship with God are fortunate. They know by experience that God never disappoints those who have faith in him. Such a faith is a gift of God, which must grow with us when we mature. Like love, faith knows its doubts. There are dark periods, but never despair or desolation. Loneliness must be overcome by friendship and confidence in "the other." If this "other" can be God as well, that person is happy!

Like the apostles, all Christians must pray often that God may increase their faith. Either your faith in God grows or it withers! Since children are baptized into the faith of their parents, father and mother must help them grow in the faith. This is a serious duty. But we are warned to keep commercialism out of faith, just as we must keep it out of love. Faith and the service of God that it entails cannot *earn* the reward of heaven. God does not owe us anything. When gratefully we have done our duty, we are still useless servants who hope for God's graciousness.

SCRIPTURE READING —

The apostles said to the Lord, "Increase our faith," and he answered: "If you had faith the size of a mustard seed, you could say to this sycamore, 'Be uprooted and transplanted into the sea,' and it would obey you.

"If one of you had a servant plowing or herding sheep and he came in from the fields, would you say to him, 'Come and sit down at table'? Would you not rather say, 'Prepare my supper. Put on your apron and wait on me while I eat and drink. You can eat and drink afterward'? Would he be grateful to the servant who was only carrying out his orders? It is quite the same with you who hear me. When you have done all you have been commanded to do, say, 'We are useless servants. We have done no more than our duty.' " (Luke 17:5-10)

"Was there no one to return and give thanks to God except this foreigner"

THOUGH medical science has advanced tremendously, there are still cases where physicians "do not know." This is frightening for patients and relatives involved. Eventually one can adjust to the inevitable. But when there is no certainty as to the diagnosis, the treatment, and final result, one hopes, one prays, one worries.

From these cases we can understand how in prescientific times people worried when they had to face diseases. They regarded sickness, epilepsy, leprosy, fever as caused by demons and evil spirits. Hence, they turned to the holy man, the prophet, for help. They were asked to pray and expel the demons. God had to intervene and show his mighty strength. Actually, these people did right away what we do after the doctors have exhausted all their means —they directed themselves to God.

Notice that the only one who came back to thank our Lord was a Samaritan. "Recall that Jews have nothing to do with Samaritans" (John 4:9). The point is clear. All of us are contaminated by evil (leprosy—sin), but redeemed from evil by faith sealed by baptism. Salvation from evil is given not only to us, but to all nations. And converts are often more appreciative and grateful than those of the household of faith. Ingratitude is a common human failing. We should be grateful for God's saving presence to us. "Let us give thanks to the Lord our God. It is right to give him thanks and praise" *(Introductory dialogue to the Preface).*

SCRIPTURE READING —

On his journey to Jerusalem [Jesus] passed along the borders of Samaria and Galilee. As he was entering a village, ten lepers met him. Keeping their distance, they raised their voices and said, "Jesus, Master, have pity on us!" When he saw them, he responded, "Go and show yourselves to the priests." On their way there they were cured. One of them, realizing that he had been cured, came back praising God in a loud voice. He threw himself on his face at the feet of Jesus and spoke his praises. This man was a Samaritan.

Jesus took the occasion to say, "Were not all ten made whole? Where are the other nine? Was there no one to return and give thanks to God except this foreigner?" He said to the man, "Stand up and go your way; your faith has been your salvation." (Luke 17:11-19)

September 2

"All Scripture is inspired by God"

THROUGH the media we have contact with people. Since association with people helps make us the kind of persons we are, we should be selective. Youngsters whose parents do not care with whom they are associated through the media (television, movies, books) inevitably hurt themselves. The books you read and the shows you watch reveal a great deal about yourself. There is an unsurpassed best-seller, known not as "a book" but as "The Book," the Bible. It is best-sold though probably not best-read, and certainly not best-understood.

As believers, we know that through this medium, the Bible, we associate with God. But we should realize that the Bible is first man's word, which was written in a time and culture alien to us. Hence it requires some exertion on our part to be understood. Is it worthwhile to put out the effort? Yes! Because through man's word in the Bible, we discover God's word. God inspired and guided the sacred writers! In reading the Bible, we associate with God, if we do it as it should be done, namely, prayerfully and meditatively. Reading the Bible makes you a different person.

Paul insists that preachers should know the Bible and use it as the source of the wisdom they preach. With Scripture the man of God (priest-preacher) is well-equipped for his job. This implies that we should listen with faith when the Bible is explained in church. But why did Paul not recommend Bible reading by all? Simply because Bibles were not printed in his day and the vast majority of the faithful were illiterates. In our literate age with Bibles available, we should read prayerfully for ourselves.

SCRIPTURE READING —

You, for your part, must remain faithful to what you have learned and believed, because you know who your teachers were. Likewise, from your infancy you have known the sacred Scriptures, the source of the wisdom which through faith in Jesus Christ leads to salvation. All Scripture is inspired of God and is useful for teaching—for reproof, correction, and training in holiness so that the man of God may be fully competent and equipped for every good work.

In the presence of God and of Christ Jesus, who is coming to judge the living and the dead, and by his appearing and his kingly power, I charge you to preach the word, to stay with this task whether convenient or inconvenient—correcting, reproving, appealing—constantly teaching and never losing patience. (2 Timothy 3:14—4:2)

"O God, be merciful to me, a sinner"

THERE is no doubt that "how to pray" is a problem for many Christians. To begin with, one must get rid of the secret suspicion that prayer is nothing else but a good psychological means of comfort by talking persuasively to oneself, as it is for the person who cannot see God transcending creation as an Absolute You. Following the inspired experience of the Hebrews and especially Jesus' example in faith, we know that the ground of our being, the Ultimate Reality, God, is a "You," really related to us as a person.

In the eyes of his contemporaries, the Pharisee of this passage was a righteous man and the tax collector the traditional crook. Yet Jesus points to the latter as the just! Why? The Pharisee was wrong because he trusted in his righteousness and thought that God owed him something for it. God does not owe us a thing. The tax collector knew this. He had no merits to set before God. He could only plead for mercy. Prayer is encounter between you and God. Meeting the Most High God, we should humbly realize who we are.

The great philosopher and devout Jew, Martin Buber, has said: "All real life is meeting." When you meet a good person and become his friend, your meeting him will enrich your life. Whenever you experience person-to-person contact, a dialogue, you live more fully. This is very evident in the encounter of two persons in love. "Prayer" is that encounter or meeting between you and God. Prayer is a dialogue between you and the "Absolute You," Almighty God. You speak and you listen when you meet God in your Bible, in a good sermon, in the Eucharistic celebration, in any good person, in any event of your life.

SCRIPTURE READING —

[Jesus] spoke this parable addressed to those who believed in their own self-righteousness while holding everyone else in contempt: "Two men went up to the temple to pray; one was a Pharisee, the other a tax collector. The Pharisee with head unbowed prayed in this fashion: 'I give you thanks, O God, that I am not like the rest of men—grasping, crooked, adulterous—or even like this tax collector. I fast twice a week. I pay tithes on all I possess.' The other man, however, kept his distance, not even daring to raise his eyes to heaven. All he did was beat his breast and say, 'O God, be merciful to me, a sinner.' Believe me, this man went home from the temple justified but the other did not." (Luke 18:9-14)

"I mean to stay at your house today"

"PRODUCE or perish" is a rule in the business world. Applied to university professors, it reads: "Publish or perish!" The guiding principle behind these sayings is that managers should produce. If they fail, they are ruthlessly pushed aside. When they get older and their productivity decreases, they face the same fate, if they have not protected themselves somehow. Big business, capitalism, is often as ruthless and ugly as communism. The person is like a machine which either operates or is dumped on a trash heap. This is what we often make of God's wonderful world!

How does the maker of the universe look at his creation? He has designed human beings as his co-workers. In a sacred partnership, called covenant, they must work on a better society together with God. They are God's managers on this planet. But how does God look at those who ostensibly fail: the dope addicts, hobos, prostitutes, criminals, dropouts of society? If he regarded them as "good for nothing," why would he not get rid of them! Today's Scripture reading deals with this issue.

The tax collectors were the quislings of Jesus' society. They collaborated with the Roman occupation forces by collecting the taxes for them. Tax collectors were hated and shunned by genuine Jews and regarded as "sinners." Zacchaeus' good will is clear. But Jesus takes the initiative. He shows concern for this apparent "failure" in his society. How do we handle "failures" in our community? Do we exhaust all means to help them?

SCRIPTURE READING —

Entering Jericho, [Jesus] passed through the city. There was a man there named Zacchaeus, the chief tax collector and a wealthy man. He was trying to see what Jesus was like, but being small of stature, was unable to do so because of the crowd. He first ran on in front, then climbed a sycamore tree which was along Jesus' route, in order to see him.

When Jesus came to the spot he looked up and said, "Zacchaeus, hurry down. I mean to stay at your house today." He quickly descended, and welcomed him with delight. When this was observed, everyone began to murmur, "He has gone to a sinner's house as a guest." Zacchaeus stood his ground and said to the Lord: "I give half my belongings, Lord, to the poor. If I have defrauded anyone in the least, I pay him back fourfold." Jesus said to them: "Today salvation has come to this house, for this is what it means to be a son of Abraham. The Son of Man has come to search out and save what was lost." (Luke 19:1-10)

"Sons of the resurrection, they are sons of God"

HOW tenacious is that inborn instinct in all of us to go on living even after this time comes to an end. Parents want to live on in their children. A father wants at least one of his sons to continue the business which he has founded. Ex-presidents and former prime ministers found memorial libraries and write memoirs. We do not want oblivion. How do we survive? In the memory of my beloved ones, I will live on as the person they have known. In God, I will live on as the person I am. For God there are no hidden aspects of my character, as there possibly could have been for those who loved me.

"Moses prescribed . . .": the Sadducees refer to Deuteronomy 25:5-10, the law of the "Levirate" marriage. The reasons for this law were to provide for the widow, the family name, and the inheritance. But Jesus' opponents are not interested in the legality of this law as such; they simply want to ridicule Jesus' teaching concerning the resurrection and life everlasting.

Jesus shows himself master of the situation. Those in the hereafter do not marry because they are no longer liable to death. The Sadducees did not believe in the resurrection because they could not find anything about it in the Books of Moses. That is why Jesus refers to Exodus (3:6) which was one of the Books of Moses. The God of the living cares also for you.

SCRIPTURE READING —

Some Sadducees came forward (the ones who claim there is no resurrection) to pose this problem to [Jesus]: "Master, Moses prescribed that if a man's brother dies leaving a wife and no child, the brother should marry the widow and raise posterity to his brother. Now there were seven brothers. The first one married and died childless. Next, the second brother married the widow, then the third, and so on. All seven died without leaving her any children. Finally the widow herself died. At the resurrection, whose wife will she be? Remember, seven married her."

Jesus said to them: "The children of this age marry and are given in marriage, but those judged worthy of a place in the age to come and of resurrection from the dead do not. They become like angels and are no longer liable to death. Sons of the resurrection, they are sons of God. Moses in the passage about the bush showed that the dead rise again when he called the Lord the God of Abraham, and the God of Isaac, and the God of Jacob. God is not the God of the dead but of the living. All are alive for him." (Luke 20:27-38)

"The day will come . . ."

ANY time we read that our armed forces are in a state of alert somewhere in the world, we know that there is a threat to our security. Alertness is good and necessary. When the Internal Revenue Service is about to check our files, we are alert and check first! Quite a few disasters, explosions, and fires could have been prevented if those in charge would have been as alert as they should have. Persons chosen to high office must submit themselves to scrutiny. If they have been honest, they can open their books fearlessly. Such persons have been on the alert all their lives, and they have no need to fear the day of scrutiny.

A concept, found in the Bible time and again, is that of "Day of the Lord," often called "The Day" or "That Day." It is a day of darkness and fear, a day of wrath and destruction. God will intervene in favor of the righteous, and punish the wicked. Gradually, "That Day" in the perspective of the prophets is delayed to the end-time. In the New Testament "That Day" is connected with Jesus Christ's second coming to judge the living and the dead.

Jesus had certainly predicted the destruction of the temple in Jerusalem, for this prediction was used against him during his final trial before the Sanhedrin. Later, however, the sayings of our Lord were expanded. As this passage now stands in Luke, it is an example of apocalyptic literature. The author interprets a present crisis (persecution, calamity, war, suffering of the innocent) with the use of symbolical language (fearful omens and great signs!). Have courage, soon God will definitely intervene! Notice again: "The day will come. . . . The time is at hand." It is a timeless message for all of us. Be on the alert. Be honest!

SCRIPTURE READING —

Some were speaking of how the temple was adorned with precious stones and votive offerings. [Jesus] said, "These things you are contemplating—the day will come when not one stone will be left on another, but it will all be torn down." They asked him, "When will this be, Teacher? And what will be the sign that it is going to happen?" He said, "Take care not to be misled. Many will come in my name saying, 'I am he' and 'The time is at hand.' Do not follow them. Neither must you be perturbed when you hear of wars and insurrections. These things are bound to happen first, but the end does not follow immediately."

(Luke 21:5-9)

"This is the king of the Jews"

IT IS vital for any organization to have capable leadership. We experience it on the parish level, and on the local and national level as well. That is why we test candidates on their leadership capabilities. We listen to their speeches. Their past is checked. And only if they are honest people and do a good job, do we elect and re-elect them.

Since Jesus of Nazareth is the man in whom God dwells in such a way that he is called the "Son of God" and even simply "God," we do not have to worry about his honesty and capability. "He [Jesus] is the image of the invisible God" (Colossians 1:15). Jesus now living and "sitting at God's right hand" (Hebrew idiom for "sharing power with God") is the leader of all who try to realize the reign of God in themselves and their fellow human beings.

Meditating on the Christ event, the New Testament writers described our Lord after the image they had of their great King David, who was God's vicegerent ruling "the kingdom of God" on earth. In Jesus they saw all Hebrew aspirations fulfilled: the kingdom (reign) of God established in our history. "The Lord God will give him the throne of David his father" (Luke 1:32).

Jesus is King. But his kingship is something different: Jesus is reigning from a cross. Apparent defeat is actual victory in the resurrection. We Christians must learn to see through the paradox of cross and suffering. Do you see the Lord Jesus as capable of giving direction to your life?

SCRIPTURE READING —

The people stood there watching, and the leaders kept jeering at [Jesus], saying, "He saved others; let him save himself if he is the Messiah of God, the chosen one." The soldiers also made fun of him, coming forward to offer him their sour wine and saying, "If you are the king of the Jews, save yourself." There was an inscription over the head:

"THIS IS THE KING OF THE JEWS."

One of the criminals hanging in crucifixion blasphemed him: "Aren't you the Messiah? Then save yourself and us." But the other one rebuked him: "Have you no fear of God, seeing you are under the same sentence? We deserve it, after all. We are only paying the price for what we've done, but this man has done nothing wrong." He then said, "Jesus, remember me when you enter upon your reign." And Jesus replied, "I assure you: this day you will be with me in paradise." (Luke 23:35-43)

September 8

"So glorify God in your body"

AS A Catholic priest, I have not taken part in the process of physical reproduction. Hence, I have no children to exhibit with pride. However, in dealing with people, I have learned a few things over the years. One thing I find amusing is that people, especially women, when you meet them for the first time, start telling you right away about their children. This is natural, of course. Only, I wonder at times whether there is not some wishful thinking in these motherly reports. Their children are portrayed most of the time as such excellent creatures and doing so extremely well that at least some exaggeration must be in the picture. Motherly love colors it brighter than it really is.

We are God's "handiwork," and, following Jesus of Nazareth in faith, we call him Father. Hence, we are his children. Can God be proud of you? He can only if we live up to what he rightly expects us to be. God loves us more than a proud mother can, but he looks at us realistically and is not blinded by wishful thinking. "Glorify God in your body!" Notice that in Paul's language "body" stands for the whole person. Therefore, glorify God by trying to become ever more the person he intends you to be.

We should live an ethically responsible life. The great absolute for ethically right behavior is the sublime law of love of God and neighbor. All other laws are just ramifications of this law. These ramifications can be complicated and in order to do the right thing we should form our consciences by observing what fellow Christians have done over the centuries. We find their decisions in the Bible and the guidance of the Church. Though your own conscience must make the final decision on "what is the loving thing to do" right now, you should not lightly deviate from what Bible and Church see as the loving thing in any particular situation. With this in mind, read today's Scripture prayerfully.

SCRIPTURE READING—

Do you not see that your bodies are members of Christ? Would you have me take Christ's members and make them the members of a prostitute? God forbid! But whoever is joined to the Lord becomes one spirit with him. Shun lewd conduct. You must know that your body is a temple of the Holy Spirit, who is within—the Spirit you have received from God. You are not your own. You have been purchased, and at a price. So glorify God in your body. (1 Corinthians 6:15, 17-20)

"They have been written as a warning for us"

THERE is a general complaint that our young people cannot read anymore, hence are not interested in books. Something seems to be wrong with quite a few schools, and a call on the part of some for returning to the basics of reading, writing, and arithmetic seems to be justified. Others blame lack of education in our homes, that have been infected by the electronic media, as the cause of the evil of semi-illiteracy. Yet the fact that many bookstores are still in business gives me hope.

I love to walk into a well stocked bookstore, peruse books of authors I know, and invariably walk out with some books, if my meager pocketbook permits me to do so. I love books. They are the silent friends that surround me. They are patient and can wait till I have time to read them. When I have a lost moment, I use it to stand in front of those bookshelves, and rearrange books, putting them where they belong: philosophy, theology, exegesis, catechetics, and literature.

A very good friend is my Bible. It is a library of books which requires some effort to be enjoyed, and cannot be adequately read by a semi-illiterate, who had to take remedial reading classes in college! But if the effort is made, one discovers therein a wealth of wisdom and beauty. In today's Scripture, Paul gives a hint for intelligent and faithful Bible reading. He reminds us that we should not read the biblical stories just for information's sake. That would be boring! The stories were written to teach us God's word, in this case to warn us. The lesson of a story is open-ended. Hence, the story (historically true, semi-true or entirely fictitious) contains unfailing riches to be discovered by prayerful meditation. For this Scripture, reading Exodus 13:21-22; 16:4-36; 17:1-7 may be useful.

SCRIPTURE READING —

Brothers, I want you to remember this: our fathers were all under the cloud and all passed through the sea; by the cloud and the sea all of them were baptized into Moses. All ate the same spiritual food. All drank the same spiritual drink (they drank from the spiritual rock that was following them, and the rock was Christ), yet we know that God was not pleased with most of them, for "they were struck down in the desert."

The things that happened to them serve as an example. They have been written as a warning to us, upon whom the end of the ages has come. (1 Corinthians 10:1-5, 11)

"I am ruined if I do not preach it"

AS A chaplain in a large penitentiary, years ago, I often shivered when I listened to hard-core criminals such as the man who told in detail how he had strangled a fellow human being. How is it possible for a man to be possessed by so much evil inclination that he is driven to hate and commit the most horrible cruelties? Sometimes there is pathological reason; most of the time an unfortunate past is the cause. Conversely, people can also be possessed by an irresistible urge to do good.

In the Christian tradition, we see the Spirit of God who seems to take over the natural potentials of people, making them do astounding things. I consider it a great privilege when I meet such persons. Among many, I remember a religious brother who was one of the first missionaries to penetrate into central New Guinea at the risk of his life. (Several of the missionaries were killed by the arrows of the hostile natives.) Such people make me realize my own pettiness and inspire me to do at least something worthwhile.

The apostle Paul seems to have been this type of person: "I am under compulsion and have no choice." He was fascinated by the person of Jesus Christ, whom he had encountered in a vision (Acts 9), and whose Spirit was spurring him forward from that moment on. We cannot accomplish the spectacular work which Paul did during his lifetime. But we can learn from him an unselfish dedication to a task in life—which should consist not in merely avoiding evil but in doing a great deal of good. You may feel incompetent. But then you should pray: "Come, Holy Spirit, fill the hearts of your faithful and kindle in them the fire of your love."

SCRIPTURE READING —

Preaching the gospel is not the subject of a boast; I am under compulsion and have no choice. I am ruined if I do not preach it! If I do it willingly, I have my recompense; if unwillingly, I am nonetheless entrusted with a charge. And this recompense of mine? It is simply this, that when preaching I offer the gospel free of charge and do not make full use of the authority the gospel gives me.

Although I am not bound to anyone, I made myself the slave of all so as to win over as many as possible.

To the weak I became a weak person with a view to winning the weak. I have made myself all things to all men in order to save at least some of them. In fact, I do all that I do for the sake of the gospel in the hope of having a share in its blessings. (1 Corinthians 9:16-19, 22-23)

"Give no offense to Jew or Greek"

HAVE you ever felt unhappy? I did when I sprained my ankle, fell flat on the street, bruised lip, arms, and knees badly, and all of this in the busy crowded centrum of Amsterdam right in front of the KLM (Royal Dutch Airlines) main office. I could get up and walk with a limp to a streetcar to go to the suburb, where I had parked my little car. But that streetcar was overcrowded. I had to stand. With one hand in a strap I stood swinging on the leg that was not hurt just opposite a hippie-type bearded young man. His hair untidy, shirt open, in torn blue jeans and shoeless, he sat talking with a similarly clad young lady. Then he saw my situation and with an intensely kind smile he stood up and offered me his seat. That was very considerate. I thanked him, and his girl friend advised me to wrap my ankle with an elastic bandage, which a doctor's nurse later did.

Consideration, thoughtful and sympathetic regard, is not practiced very much in public life, and there are many who fail to think of it even in dealing with friends. In today's Scripture Paul reminds us of its importance. He encourages us to imitate the Lord Jesus who was considerate and thoughtful. The problem in the congregation of Corinth was that of eating meat sacrificed to the pagan gods which was available at the market. Informed Christians knew that such gods did not exist and thus could eat this meat without thinking anything more about it. Paul himself sees no harm in eating sacrificed meat, but he knows that such an action might well scandalize less instructed fellow Christians (perhaps those of Jewish background). Hence, Paul's advice, "Give no offense to Jew or Greek," in other words, do not eat sacrificed meat for that reason.

Hence, God's message is: Be considerate! Do not hurt the feelings of others! Both "progressives" and "conservatives" should heed this message in the renewal of Church and religious life.

SCRIPTURE READING —

The fact is that whether you eat or drink—whatever you do—you should do all for the glory of God. Give no offense to Jew or Greek or to the church of God, just as I try to please all in any way I can by seeking, not my own advantage, but that of the many, that they may be saved. Imitate me as I imitate Christ. (1 Corinthians 10:31—11:1

"Whatever promises God has made have been fulfilled in him [Jesus Christ]"

A WELL-known finding of contemporary psychiatry is that the presence of anxiety in an interpersonal field severely inhibits effective communication and the development of intimacy. When people are anxious, they are not fully aware of what is taking place between themselves and others. Anxiety is related to lack of trust. Can I fully trust the other person? Will he/she be faithful to his/her promises? Our world is wounded and torn apart by promises made and not kept. Tears are shed by brokenhearted spouses, double-crossed boy- and girl-friends, and frustrated friends, who thought that they could trust the other on his/her word. This is one of the reasons for our insistence that serious promises be put in writing. No great honor for the human species!

The fact that God is absolutely trustworthy, that he keeps his word under all circumstances, is the reason that the believer (the word is akin to "beloved—lover") can be intimate with the One who both transcends reality and is simultaneously immanent in all of creation, you and me included. The believer does not have to be anxious lest God abandon him. In Jesus Christ, he has given us a pledge of his fidelity, and therefore it is through him that we address our Amen ("So be it") to God when we worship together.

Regardless of how wrong and unfaithful we have been, God is faithful. Once people have committed a crime, their police record will follow them wherever they go. But this is not the case before God. Once forgiven of our sins, we have no more record. Intimacy with God is, as far as we are concerned, a growing thing. A prayerful meditation on today's Scripture should contribute to this growth.

SCRIPTURE READING —

As God keeps his word, I declare that my word to you is not "yes" one minute and "no" the next. Jesus Christ, whom Silvanus, Timothy, and I preached to you as Son of God, was not alternately "yes" and "no"; he was never anything but "yes." Whatever promises God has made have been fulfilled in him; therefore it is through him that we address our Amen to God when we worship together. God is the one who firmly establishes us along with you in Christ; it is he who anointed us and has sealed us, thereby depositing the first payment, the Spirit, in our hearts.

(2 Corinthians 1:18-22)

"The written law kills, but the Spirit gives life"

AS PASTOR and educator, I am asked quite often for letters of recommendation. Alumni of our school apply for a job somewhere in the country and mention my name. I get a questionnaire in the mail and am asked to testify whether or not the person involved is reliable, emotionally balanced, and easy to get along with. Answering these questions often presents problems. I love my former students and want the best for them in life, but on the other hand I have to be truthful. A letter of recommendation must stand for a reality, otherwise it is a void document.

The same must be said about the documents which we call laws. For two centuries, we have had one of the most beautiful constitutions ever written. "All men are created equal . . . endowed with inalienable rights." Does this mean that such a sublime law has changed the hearts of all Americans? When I came to this country in 1960, I served for some months in a conservative county in southern Louisiana. During that time there were elections, and I found out that Blacks could not vote. In my innocence, I asked a wealthy white parishioner: "How come? This is the greatest democracy in the world!" I got a condescending and compassionate smile for an answer.

"The written law kills, but the Spirit gives life." The voting laws are now enforced, but have they changed the hearts of many racists? I was deeply involved in the civil rights movement of our troubled sixties in the Southland *(see May 31)*, but more than ever I am convinced that laws as such do not change people's minds. And only a change of mind can solve the problems of interpersonal relationships. In today's Scripture, Paul hints in the same direction.

SCRIPTURE READING —

Am I beginning to speak well of myself again? Or do I need letters of recommendation to you or from you as others might? You are my letter, known and read by all men, written on your hearts. Clearly you are a letter of Christ which I have delivered, a letter written not with ink but by the Spirit of the living God, not on tablets of stone but on tablets of flesh in the heart.

This great confidence in God is ours, through Christ. It is not that we are entitled of ourselves to take credit for anything. Our sole credit is from God, who has made us qualified ministers of a new covenant, a covenant not of a written law but of spirit. The written law kills, but the Spirit gives life. (2 Corinthians 3:1-6)

". . . that we in turn might make known the glory of God shining on the face of Christ"

I DID not have the opportunity to attend the Eucharistic Congress in Philadelphia (August, 1976) and had to be content with whatever I could watch on my television set. In particular, the closing ceremonies were a brilliant show. The rich pageantry of Church dignitaries, resplendent in scarlet silk, the massive choir, the colorful dances, the throng of faithful singing our common Creed, Pope and President of the United States speaking—all this must have given thousands what may be called that "cathedral experience," which boosts the feeling of belonging to a worldwide organization of believers. I am not alone with my faith! We should not forget, however, that such an occasional spectacle is just one way of "making known the glory of God shining on the face of Christ."

In today's Scripture, Paul shows himself critical toward any "triumphalism" in the Church. He is disappointed that his converts blame him for failing to be spectacular. Paul states that God's revelation was indeed given to him—but as a treasure in an earthen vessel. The Corinthians should look to the treasure, God's light, as shining on the face of Christ, and understand that the real Gospel is not the spectacular, but Christ crucified.

A prayerful meditation on this Scripture should help us to keep our balance in a Church which as an institution seems to be in trouble. Isn't it remarkable that the Church of Poland which is harassed daily has more vocations to the priesthood and religious life than ever, and even helps sister Churches in sending priests and nuns abroad? This too is "making known the glory of God shining on the face of Christ."

SCRIPTURE READING —

For God, who said, "Let light shine out of darkness," has shone in our hearts, that we in turn might make known the glory of God shining on the face of Christ. This treasure we possess in earthen vessels to make it clear that its surpassing power comes from God and not from us. We are afflicted in every way possible, but we are not crushed; full of doubts, we never despair. We are persecuted but never abandoned; we are struck down but never destroyed. Continually we carry about in our bodies the dying of Jesus, so that in our bodies the life of Jesus may also be revealed. (2 Corinthians 4:6-10)

"The power that has conquered the world is this faith of ours"

THE Dutch are proud of the "Nightwatch" by Rembrandt, the the French of their "Mona Lisa" in the Louvre, and the Italians of their "Pietà" by Michelangelo. Similarly, the Russians are proud of their "Troitsa—Trinity," one of the most beautiful icons ever painted (in 1411) by the devout monk and great artist Andrei Rublyov. Faithful to the tradition of the Russian Orthodox Church, the theme of the bucolic legend of Abraham and his three visitors found in Genesis 18 is used to depict the life of God in himself. The three angel images relate to one another in a sublime love which shines from their faces and is skillfully symbolized by the interplay of their eyes, the gestures of their hands, and the lines of their clothing. Standing in front of this moving picture and realizing that the heart of atheistic communism, the Kremlin, was only at walking distance compelled me to pray and meditate on God, who is love.

It is faith in a God who is love in himself that must keep us going in the valley of darkness which is the human condition. It is faith in such a God that makes us conquer the world of pseudo-sophistication and moral decay all around us. The Bible reading speaks of God as Father, Son, and Holy Spirit. From this God, who is love in himself, we are begotten. All human effort to reflect God's love is necessarily imperfect. This is true of Rublyov's "Trinity" as well as of our lives which are imperfect images of God, who is love. But with the power of our faith we should never give up.

The Church is seemingly losing ground in the selfish world of today. Why? What about your faith in a loving God? Is it still a power? Is it still very much alive?

SCRIPTURE READING —

The love of God consists in this:
that we keep his commandments—
and his commandments are not burdensome.
Everyone begotten of God conquers the world,
and the power that has conquered the world
is this faith of ours.
Who, then, is conqueror of the world?
The one who believes that Jesus is the Son of God.
Jesus Christ it is who came through water and blood—
not in water only,
but in water and in blood.
It is the Spirit who testifies to this,
and the Spirit is truth.

(1 John 5:3-6)

"The love of God . . . made perfect in him"

THERE is a difference between knowing *about* your marriage partner and knowing him/her. It is remarkable that in biblical language the word "knowing" is also used for the intimate knowing of two spouses, namely, knowing through sexual intercourse. Read 1 Kings 1:1-4. Both the *New American Bible* and the *Jerusalem Bible* translate verse 4 in this vein: "but the king did not have relations with her"/"the king had no intercourse with her." The *King James Bible*, however, translates literally: "but the king knew her not," since at the time when this translation appeared the word "know" was commonly used to refer to intercourse.

Knowing a great deal about God and religion does not make one necessarily a good Christian. The greatest theologians were not always the greatest saints! The author of John states that knowing God is a religious experience in which you are involved. Love has very much to do with it! "The way we can be sure of our knowledge of him [Christ-God] is to keep his commandments," in other words, to do what he wants us to do. This kind of knowledge is acquired not only by study but also and much more by prayer!

Does your Bible reading result in a more intimate "knowing" of God in Jesus Christ? If a Christian reads his Bible only to gather information, he misses the boat. Such an inquisitive kind of Bible reading gets boring quite soon. That is why Bible reading should always be prayerful meditation.

SCRIPTURE READING —

My little ones,
I am writing this to keep you from sin.
But if anyone should sin,
we have, in the presence of the Father,
Jesus Christ, an intercessor who is just.
He is an offering for our sins,
and not for our sins only,
but for those of the whole world.
The way we can be sure of our knowledge of him
is to keep his commandments,
The man who claims, "I have known him,"
without keeping his commandments,
is a liar; in such a one there is no truth.
But whoever keeps his word,
truly has the love of God been made perfect in him.

(1 John 2:1-5)

"See what love the Father has bestowed on us"

BALI, one of the 3,000 islands of the Indonesian archipelago, is considered a genuinely tropical paradise. Its luscious nature, dazzling temples, artwork, religious processions, cremations, and beautiful women make it a hideaway for artists and others who are fed up with the abysmal state of the human condition and are rich enough to settle down in one of the hotels. During my stay of two months on this island I came across some of these remarkable people.

More than once I visited the home of a Belgian artist. He had built a Balinese house on the seashore, married a Balinese beauty, and painted her in all postures possible on the walls of his home. From his house I had a brilliant view of the "Gunung Agung," the mountain of the gods, at the other side of the bay. A paradise! Walking on the beach, I thought of these people. What were they looking for? Many have tried to escape our overcivilized world. Gauguin the French impressionist went to Tahiti, and Marlon Brando the star of *The Godfather* spends half of his life on the Polynesian island of Tetiaroa. Is it the human longing for a utopia?

Today's Scripture tells us about the human condition as "already—and not yet." Both "see" and "we shall see" are used. We are already children of God, but we have to accept it on faith. God loves me. This is wonderful, but this same God seems quite often so absent and far away. And only later we will see him as he is. We Christians must live with this tension. Looking for paradise on earth, whether on Bali or Tahiti, does not make sense. We take our human limitations with us wherever we go. Prayerful reflection should help you to be happy with the "already" and to wait hopefully for the perfect bliss to come.

SCRIPTURE READING—

See what love the Father has bestowed on us
in letting us be called children of God!
Yet that is what we are.
The reason the world does not recognize us
is that it never recognized the Son.

Dearly beloved,
we are God's children now;
what we shall later be has not yet come to light.
We know that when it comes to light
we shall be like him,
for we shall see him as he is.

(1 John 3:1-2)

"Let us love in deed and in truth and not merely talk about it"

AT A workshop on prayer groups (Bible study groups, charismatic gatherings, little floating parishes, basic groups) the speaker, a professional sociologist specializing in the phenomenon Religion, gave us a well-informed introduction to these groups in the United States, Northern Europe and Latin America. There are similarities and dissimilarities. Similarities are that all have the fervor of a first love. The Spirit of God is very much alive in them. No formalism, which often makes organized religion so stale, has as yet got hold of them.

Dissimilarities are that Latin American groups are very much concerned about the liberation of the poor masses abused by the few rich. "The Theology of Liberation" comes from Latin America! The Northern Europeans are indeed sharing their experience in reading the Bible. They pray and sing together, but do not get very emotional; moreover they are very much socially involved. As for North American groups, the picture was that they are often elite groups of middle- or upper middle-class Christians who very frequently become emotional (mutual confession of sin, prayer over each other, speaking in tongues), but show little concern for suffering fellow human beings. Their approach is a cosy "getting high on Jesus," and being very lovable to members of the group, but seldom does the group as such get involved in social projects.

With Paul (1 Corinthians 12:1-11; 14:1-5, 39-40) we should observe that the gifts of the Spirit are different, and we should not easily criticize one another. Being different does not mean being more, neither does it mean being less. Whether or not you are a charismatic, and whether or not the qualification of this country's prayer groups is entirely true, heed today's Scripture, especially the sacred author's statement that we must love in deed and in truth and not merely talk about it.

SCRIPTURE READING —

Little children,
let us love in deed and in truth
and not merely talk about it.
[God's] commandment is this:
we are to believe in the name of his Son, Jesus Christ,
and are to love one another as he commanded us.
Those who keep his commandments remain in him
and he in them.
And this is how we know that he remains in us:
from the Spirit that he gave us.

(1 John 3:18, 23-24)

"We do not lose heart, because our inner being is renewed each day"

AT LEAST ever since Cicero (106-43 B.C.) wrote his booklet *De Senectute (On Old Age),* the human species has been involved in Gerontology, the study of old age. Every so often the mass media pay attention to it. Either they report that thousands of senior citizens of this richest country on earth are starving and living their last years in substandard conditions, or they give advice on how to make the best of old age. It is said to be a state of mind; old people should watch their eating habits, exercise and keep creatively busy.

In today's Bible reading, Paul makes a few statements which may encourage those of us who are getting on in years. He says: "We do not lose heart, because our inner being is renewed each day even though our body is being destroyed at the same time." Though we are aging, we can continue to grow into even more beautiful persons, in spite of the fact that the agility and physical functions of our body decay. "You," the person you make of yourself now, will live forever.

And even if you are still young, your condition too is subject to the same process of physical decay which is so clear in old age. Apply God's word to your own condition! Perhaps you could visit some old people and console them with this God-inspired insight.

In my Bible, I have underlined the words, "our inner being is renewed each day" and "we have a dwelling provided for us by God," and focused my reflective prayer on those thoughts.

SCRIPTURE READING —

We do not lose heart, because our inner being is renewed each day even though our body is being destroyed at the same time. The present burden of our trial is light enough, and earns for us an eternal weight of glory beyond all comparison. We do not fix our gaze on what is seen but on what is unseen. What is seen is transitory; what is unseen lasts forever.

Indeed, we know that when the earthly tent in which we dwell is destroyed we have a dwelling provided for us by God, a dwelling in the heavens, not made by hands but to last forever.

(2 Corinthians 4:16—5:1)

"We walk by faith, not by sight"

KNOWING everything would mean condoning everything! Being impatient and too rash in judgment usually does a lot of harm. Seldom do we know all the reasons why a fellow pilgrim ("we walk . . . ," Paul states) acts or reacts in a certain way. Personally, I tend to be rather hasty in my judgment about others, though over the years I have learned at least not to verbalize my opinions so quickly anymore. This cautiousness has kept me out of trouble and has prevented hard feelings as well.

I remember some harsh remarks I made to a high school senior who was mentally absent in class and apparently not interested. Then I found out to my regret that his brother had very recently been killed on the street in Chicago. Small wonder that the fellow worried! I had been away myself and should have been made aware of that fact by the principal or the other students. But whatever the case, I should have been more careful!

"We walk by faith, not by sight." We must have patience both with ourselves and our fellow Christians. Not all members of our parish, family, or religious community do things our way. Do not blame them! "You'd better be a progressive as I am, or you are a fool!" In our Church in transition, this kind of utterance is heard quite often. If we would walk "by sight," perhaps it would be easy to say how religion should be organized. But all of us are groping in the semidarkness of faith.

Our bishops don't have all the answers, and neither does the social worker in a ghetto have them ready on a platter. To a certain extent we are all myopic, since we see things from our own limited viewpoint. Admitting this would result in patience with one another. And indeed there will be some surprises when "the lives of all of us are . . . revealed before the tribunal of Christ."

SCRIPTURE READING —

Therefore we continue to be confident. We know that while we dwell in the body we are away from the Lord. We walk by faith, not by sight. I repeat, we are full of confidence and would much rather be away from the body and at home with the Lord. This being so, we make it our aim to please him whether we are with him or away from him. The lives of all of us are to be revealed before the tribunal of Christ so that each one may receive his recompense, good or bad, according to his life in the body. (2 Corinthians 5:6-10)

"He saved others"

DURING a visit to my native Netherlands, I went to see an exhibition of icons in the coastal town of Noordwijk. Like all art exhibitions its purpose was to sell paintings, and the dealer tried to do so when he saw me standing in profound meditation before a beautiful icon with a price tag of $2,000. I could not buy the painting, but it was a work of exceptional beauty, depicting Christ on the cross with scenes of his life pictured around him in minute detail. What struck me most was the artistic way in which the painter had symbolized the meritorious effect of our Lord's suffering and death: Blood was streaming down from his crucified body on a skull, and that skull was Adam, and in him all mankind.

We of the twentieth century may see this as a primitive and perhaps childlike way of teaching religious truth, telling the onlooker that through Christ's blood our sins were washed away. But the ancient masterpieces have done their job well. Illiterate people learned their faith by simply looking to these paintings time and again. And we can still experience their message, brought out so skillfully, if we are willing to step back in history and meditatively admire their beauty.

We should look at Christ as the one who "died for all and was raised up," and as such inaugurated the new age. "Anyone in Christ is a new creation" (2 Corinthians 5:17). "It is in Christ and through his blood that we have been redeemed and our sins forgiven, so immeasurably generous is God's favor to us" (Ephesians 1:7). Gratefully make this a contemplation of love!

SCRIPTURE READING —

The chief priests and the scribes also joined in and jeered: "He saved others but he cannot save himself! Let the 'Messiah,' the 'King of Israel,' come down from that cross here and now so that we can see it and believe in him!" The men who had been crucified with him likewise kept taunting him.

When noon came, darkness fell on the whole countryside and lasted until midafternoon. At that time Jesus cried in a loud voice, "Eloi, Eloi, lama sabachthani?" **which means, "My God, my God, why have you forsaken me?" A few of the bystanders who heard it remarked "Listen! He is calling on Elijah!" Someone ran off, and soaking a sponge in sour wine, stuck it on a reed to try to make him drink. The man said, "Now let's see whether Elijah comes to take him down."**

Then Jesus, uttering a loud cry, breathed his last. (Mark 15:31-37)

"The relief of others ought not to impoverish you"

AS THE oldest of ten I had the opportunity to observe a few things that may have escaped the attention of my younger brothers and sisters. Though the means to plan a family were known (neighbors raised families of two and three), in a thoroughly Catholic family of those days children were accepted as God sent them, and they were raised with love and care. My parents were not rich but not poor either. We were well fed and dressed and could enjoy the little niceties of life.

My mother never worked for others. Old-country pride dictated that a man took care of his wife and children. This does not mean that my mother did not work hard. It was the time before washing machines, vacuum cleaners, and other household appliances were available. After a day of washing, ironing, cooking, cleaning, wiping our noses, settling our conflicts, and soothing our little pains caused by a broken toy or a lost fight with Johnny next door, my mother sewed our clothes and at night darned the family stockings.

But there is one thing I will never forget—my mother always had time for others. Whenever there was trouble in the neighborhood, a lady who suddenly had to be taken to the hospital or a mother crying over a child who was deathly sick or injured, my mother was there. Women with two or three children were too busy but my mother had time without neglecting her own duties, since in our home the older ones were trained to take care of the little ones whenever necessary.

"The relief of others ought not to impoverish you." Why did my mother always have "plenty"? I think, because she loved! Works of charity, sharing whatever you have, do not make you poor. This may be God's word to you for today!

SCRIPTURE READING—

You are well acquainted with the favor shown you by our Lord Jesus Christ: how for your sake he made himself poor though he was rich, so that you might become rich by his poverty.

The relief of others ought not to impoverish you; there should be a certain equality. Your plenty at the present time should supply their need so that their surplus may one day supply your need, with equality as a result. It is written, "He who gathered much had no excess and he who gathered little had no lack." (2 Corinthians 8:9, 13-15)

"For in weakness power reaches perfection"

AS A little altar boy I overheard a conversation of one of the assistant priests and the sacristan. It was in the sacristy before Mass. The topic was the pastor, who was an asthma patient and had little patience both with himself and those who perchance crossed his path whenever his ailment was bothering him. The assistant, who apparently had had a run-in with the pastor a few moments earlier, said: "The man cannot handle himself." Maybe he was right.

The pastor was a tall grayish man, six feet high and way over two hundred pounds. It was with a sacred fear that we served his Mass. Ringing the altar bell too loud or at the wrong moment of the Latin Mass, pouring too little or too much water over his fingers at the "Lavabo," could earn you the instant epithet of "stupid," "ignorant," or "no good." And we boys said: "His asthma is bothering him." However, "Mijnheer Pastoor" ("Mr Pastor") had many excellent qualities and was above all a capable administrator. He had remodeled and enlarged our parish nursing home where no old person, no matter how poor, was ever refused lodging. And he financed it. The parishioners loved the pastor for his good qualities. And that was right. Being impatient and not always being able to handle your own limitations is so human!

A capable man like Paul had a similar problem. "False preachers" had confused the congregation of Corinth. They had bragged about supposedly extraordinary revelations received from God. Paul, on the contrary, would not boast. His physical situation was miserable and apparently he was not a flamboyant preacher. His sermons were too long and often too learned for his audience (see Acts 20:9 and 2 Peter 3:15-16). Other preachers were more spectacular. Read how Paul handled his limitations and check your own.

SCRIPTURE READING —

I refrain, lest anyone think more of me than what he sees in me or hears from my lips. As to the extraordinary revelations, in order that I might not become conceited I was given a thorn in the flesh, an angel of Satan to beat me and keep me from getting proud. Three times I begged the Lord that this might leave me. He said to me, "My grace is enough for you, for in weakness power reaches perfection." And so I willingly boast of my weaknesses instead, that the power of Christ may rest upon me. (2 Corinthians 12:7-9)

"God chose us in him [Christ] before the world began"

IN WATCHING the annual pageantry of choosing Miss America (I don't have time and patience to sit through the whole show but catch snatches of it), I am getting some philosophical thoughts of my own. The young lady finally chosen is lucky. A year of free traveling, a scholarship, interesting and very educational contacts —they are all hers. The girl has been blessed with a beautiful body, a charming personality, good talent, and excellent educators. Being chosen is first of all a gift. Why was she chosen rather than somebody else? But it is not only a gift. She has also worked hard to make of herself the talented good-looking person who will be Miss America for the next year.

In today's Bible reading Paul outlines a beautiful picture of who we are as Christians. Being chosen is a gift of God. And we should realize that it is *only* a gift for which we should be grateful. Unlike the efforts of Miss America, which contributed substantially to her success, we should realize that our efforts have not contributed to our election. God chose us in Christ before the world began. Our good works make sense, but we should keep our motivation to do them in the right perspective.

Quite a few Catholics have not always done this. We cannot buy our election and salvation by our own efforts. Gratitude and appreciation should motivate us to do good more than the gain of "graces." Theologians try to explain the tension between "God only" and "I too." Leave it up to them! This reading could be a starting point for a grateful contemplation of love. See Preface on meditation and contemplation!

SCRIPTURE READING —

Praised be the God and Father of our Lord Jesus Christ, who has bestowed on us in Christ every spiritual blessing in the heavens! God chose us in him before the world began, to be holy and blameless in his sight, to be full of love; he likewise predestined us through Christ Jesus to be his adopted sons—such was his will and pleasure—that all might praise the glorious favor he has bestowed on us in his beloved.

It is in Christ and through his blood that we have been redeemed and our sins forgiven, so immeasurably generous is God's favor to us. God has given us the wisdom to understand fully the mystery, the plan he was pleased to decree in Christ, to be carried out in the fullness of time: namely, to bring all things in the heavens and on earth into one under Christ's headship. (Ephesians 1:3-10)

"Through him we both have access in one Spirit to the Father"

I REMEMBER a cartoon in a newspaper depicting two young couples, one black and the other white. With a broad and beautiful smile the black lady introduces herself and her husband: "We are your new neighbors and members of St. Jude's." The expression on the white couple's faces is both startled and sour-sweet! Can our common faith overcome ethnic barriers? Guided by God, Paul states that it can and should be done. Christ broke down the barrier of hostility that kept Jews and Christians apart.

When I went to Israel I visited the sister of one of my Jewish friends in this country. She and her family were settlers from Germany. In their little car they showed me the area close to the Gaza strip, where the desert had been changed into miles of orange groves. During the conversation in the car, the lady asked me: "Have you observed our youngsters?" At first, I did not understand the import of her remark. Then I realized she was alluding to the traditional submissively smiling Jews of the old country and rightly contrasting them with the proud self-confident young Jews who were building up a new homeland.

Through two thousand years of ignoring Christ's teaching (today's Scripture) and harassing the Jews, Christians had made them the cautious and submissively smiling people that we knew before the war in Europe. These proud young Jews, working on tractors, building roads and irrigation systems, and the young women in impeccable army uniforms behaving like ladies were the evident proof to me that all people, regardless of race or ethnic background, can be beautiful persons, if only we give them a fair chance to be and develop themselves. What can you do?

SCRIPTURE READING —

But now in Christ Jesus you who once were far off have been brought near through the blood of Christ. It is he who is our peace, and who made the two of us one by breaking down the barrier of hostility that kept us apart. In his own flesh he abolished the law with its commands and precepts, to create in himself one new man from us who had been two and to make peace, reconciling both of us to God in one body through his cross, which put that enmity to death. He came and "announced the good news of peace to you who were far off, and to those who were near"; through him we both have access in one Spirit to the Father. (Ephesians 2:13-18)

September 26

"Unity which has the Spirit as its origin and peace as its binding force"

UNLIKE some other countries of Europe during the German occupation of World War II, The Netherlands was put under direct Nazi rule. Hitler had deemed this necessary to keep the unruly Dutch in line. One of those unruly Dutch was the archbishop of Utrecht. The Nazis tried to destroy the Catholic school system and to make the Church preach cooperation with the Germans. One injustice followed another, and one pastoral letter after another was read in the churches, exhorting Catholics to stick together in their resistance.

The German governor, a Nazi and fallen-away Catholic (later executed as a war criminal), went himself to the archbishop. He tried to convince him to cooperate by threatening him with reprisals. But he failed. His comment was: "With that man you can't talk!" The archbishop preached unity and during the war Catholics followed his advice. Years later, I heard the same archbishop, then a Cardinal, deliver his retirement speech over the radio, again pleading for unity. The disruptive forces that have done and are still doing so much harm to the (sometimes notorious) Church of the Netherlands, were already at work. Catholics did not listen.

From prison Paul exhorts the congregation of Ephesus to preserve unity. We symbolize our oneness as a congregation when we celebrate the Eucharist. "Make every effort to preserve [that] unity." All should heed this plea: grown-ups and young people, progressives and conservatives, charismatics and those who favor a less emotional way of living the message! "May all of us who share in the body and blood of Christ be brought together in unity by the Holy Spirit" (Eucharistic Prayer II).

SCRIPTURE READING —

I plead with you, then, as a prisoner for the Lord, to live a life worthy of the calling you have received, with perfect humility, meekness, and patience, bearing with one another lovingly. Make every effort to preserve the unity which has the Spirit as its origin and peace as its binding force. There is but one body and one Spirit, just as there is but one hope given all of you by your call. There is one Lord, one faith, one baptism; one God and Father of all, who is over all, and works through all, and is in all. (Ephesians 4:1-6)

"When you learned Christ . . ."

September 27

THE Rublev museum in Moscow, a former monastery, contains one of the most precious icon collections in Russia. These ancient paintings reflect the living faith of many Russian generations. Like the "Bible of the Poor" (the murals) in the cathedrals of Western Europe, they have been teaching Christ, his mother, and the Saints of heaven to Russian illiterates of bygone centuries. The communist regime has preserved these icons, since many of them are masterpieces of art. Natasha, a very intelligent young lady and representative of Intourist, the Russian travel agency, guided us through the collection.

In impeccable German and with great skill she could explain every detail of an icon, displaying a solid knowledge of Christ and his life. Yet Natasha was an unbeliever. A Communist through and through, voluntarily she had worked in Siberia for three years. She had studied German literature and as a tourist guide she was supposed to foster goodwill for the Communist system. In taking a course in Russian art, Natasha had learned a great deal about Christ and could explain the icons but she did so with the skill of a benign outsider. (Atheistic Communists in Russia see Jesus not as a historical person but as a myth. Hence, Christian art—icons—can be appreciated the way we appreciate Greek art, which is inspired by Greek mythology.)

"That is what you learned when you learned Christ." Notice that Paul does not say: "When you learned *about* Christ." No, you learned Christ, whom you accepted as a person in faith, with all the values he stands for. Christianity is not primarily a doctrine to go by; it is a person-to-person relationship with our Lord. The danger exists that daily Bible reading will become merely a learning about Christ. Check yourself! Does your Bible reading result in an ever more intimate encounter with our Lord? That is why your reading should always result in a prayerful response.

SCRIPTURE READING —

That is not what you learned when you learned Christ! I am supposing, of course, that he has been preached and taught to you in accord with the truth that is in Jesus: namely, that you must lay aside your former way of life and the old self which deteriorates through illusion and desire, and acquire a fresh, spiritual way of thinking. You must put on that new man created in God's image, whose justice and holiness are born of truth. (Ephesians 4:20-24)

"Follow the way of love, even as Christ loved you"

PASTORAL counseling is one of the most satisfying aspects of my priestly occupation. By keeping up with the literature in this field and attentively listening to people, I think that I have gathered some insights over the years. Possibly this is evidence of a paternal instinct of wishing to share my little wisdom of the Gospel. In any case, I like counseling more than doing the administration of school and church, though both are important.

Since counseling entails a good deal of listening, I constantly learn from it. I remember a divorced mother of a large family, whom I had been helping off and on, saying that she had spent a relatively large amount of money on the Christmas presents for her children. She saw me frowning. Perhaps it was the thrifty Dutchman in me. I asked: "Are Christmas presents that important?" She answered with the look that only mothers have: "To me they are!" I told myself: "John, you are a celibate priest and have never raised little kids of your own; you ought to be ashamed of yourself!" What is more and what is less important? We speak of a hierarchy (graded order) of values.

As Christians we agree that the most important value is love of God and neighbor. Paul words it today: "Follow the way of love." And, if you want to know how to do it, look at Jesus Christ! However, when we go into the ramifications of love, finding out what the most loving thing to do is in any particular situation, we may differ in opinion and should patiently respect those different insights. And we should learn from one another! Paul offers a few hints on what a loving person should do and not do. Learn from him, since his wisdom is Divinely inspired.

SCRIPTURE READING —

Do nothing to sadden the Holy Spirit with whom you were sealed against the day of redemption. Get rid of all bitterness, all passion and anger, harsh words, slander, and malice of every kind. In place of these, be kind to one another, compassionate, and mutually forgiving, just as God has forgiven you in Christ.

Be imitators of God as his dear children. Follow the way of love, even as Christ loved you. He gave himself for us as an offering to God, a gift of pleasing fragrance. (Ephesians 4:30—5:2)

"Sing praise to the Lord with all your hearts"

IN *Contemplation in a World of Action* (Doubleday, Image Books), Thomas Merton, one of the best known American contemplatives of our time, refutes the idea that the contemplative institution is an anachronism which has no point in the modern world. Even Catholics have strange ideas about the life of monks and cloistered nuns. Merton mentions that the mailbag of the monastery is daily full of letters, requesting prayers on the eve of a serious operation, on the occasion of a lawsuit, in sickness, and for personal and family problems. The prayers and sacrifices of nuns and monks are supposed to produce "graces" and in some way to "cause" Divine interventions.

Merton observes that it is right to believe God hears and answers prayers of petition, but that it is a distortion of the contemplative life to treat it as if the contemplative concentrates all his efforts on getting graces and favors from God for others and for self. Thomas Merton stresses the real purpose of meditation/contemplation—the exploration and discovery of new dimensions in freedom, illumination, and love, in deepening our awareness of our life in Christ. The monk's meditation and prayer are a celebration of love. Gradually with the help of God, he comes to an inner awareness of God's loving presence and this tends to alter his perspective. Moreover, we should observe that contemplatives spend much time on praying and singing together.

Paul states that a person who ignores the transcendental dimension of life is a fool. Not all of us can become monks and cloistered nuns; nonetheless, we must constantly grow in awareness of God's loving presence and sing praise to the Lord with all our hearts. We must take time for both private meditation and communal worship service.

SCRIPTURE READING —

Keep careful watch over your conduct. Do not act like fools, but like thoughtful men. Make the most of the present opportunity, for these are evil days. Do not continue in ignorance, but try to discern the will of the Lord. Avoid getting drunk on wine; that leads to debauchery. Be filled with the Spirit, addressing one another in psalms and hymns and inspired songs. Sing praise to the Lord with all your hearts. Give thanks to God the Father always and for everything in the name of our Lord Jesus Christ.

(Ephesians 5:15-20)

"As Christ cares for the Church . . ."

AN UNFORGETTABLE experience during my visit to Russia was my attendance at the High Mass in the cathedral of the monastery in Zagorsk. We had arrived by bus from Moscow, a seventy-two kilometer ride, passing by little red-painted log cabins and collective farms with rows of people chopping, as could be seen on the Southern plantations before the time of crop dusting by plane. The monastery itself is a medieval fortress, surrounded by a wall that protected monks and tenants against rampaging Tartars. When we arrived, the Mass had started, but "as a matter of fact" the guide ushered us to a little museum full of insignificant junk. I followed her for a few minutes, then sneaked away from the group to attend the High Mass.

What I want to refer to is the moment of Holy Communion. In the Russian Orthodox tradition, the Eucharist proper is celebrated behind the iconostasis *(see October 10)*. The sanctuary symbolizes heaven, where Christ and all the Saints worship the Father. At Holy Communion, the doors of the iconostasis were opened, and solemnly four priests, bedecked with gold vestments, walked out with the Blessed Sacrament. The plentiful incense, and the actions of the faithful bowing deeply, crossing themselves, and singing a melancholic song imparted a sense of awe. The heavenly Tsar, the Pantocrator (almighty ruler), Jesus Christ came down from his throne to take care of his people.

This is the way Russian Christians celebrate Christ's care for his Church, which is constantly harassed and persecuted. Russian Christians, defying subtle harassments, go on responding to Jesus' loving care. How do you, married or celibate, do it?

SCRIPTURE READING —

Wives should be submissive to their husbands as if to the Lord because the husband is head of his wife just as Christ is head of his body the church, as well as its savior. As the church submits to Christ, so wives should submit to their husbands in everything.

Husbands, love your wives, as Christ loved the church. He gave himself up for her to make her holy, purifying her in the bath of water by the power of the word, to present to him a glorious church, holy and immaculate without stain or wrinkle or anything of that sort. Husbands should love their wives as they do their own bodies. He who loves his wife loves himself. Observe that no one ever hates his own flesh; no, he nourishes it and takes care of it as Christ cares for the church—for we are members of his body. (Ephesians 5:22-30)

"Act on this word"

A FRIEND of mine, a charismatic, told me enthusiastically about the prayer group he had started and about an Evangelical he had invited to come and talk on Romans, the letter in which Paul stresses so strongly our justification by faith rather than by observance of the law. I asked him whether he had also invited an Evangelical to come and talk on James, who states so clearly that without works faith is idle. He laughed and retorted: "Once you have faith, action follows automatically."

For centuries, theologians have been writing on how to reconcile these two apparently contradictory approaches. On the one hand, we cannot do a thing without God, and on the other we must cooperate with God's grace in us. Luther, spellbound by Romans, preached his doctrine of "grace alone," firmly reacting against the abuse of Indulgences' sales in the Church of his day. He did not like James and claimed that the latter's emphasis on good works does not agree with Paul's doctrine of justification by faith. We should keep in mind that for Paul faith is a commitment to Christ —hence it implies "doing"; for James, faith is the acceptance of a doctrine as well as the doing of it—hence the second part, "doing," could be overlooked.

In the first part of today's Scripture, James is very much in line with Romans. It is God who calls before we are even able to think of him. And only after James has brought this out clearly, does he emphasize the necessity of acting on this word, saying explicitly what Paul in Romans and my friend, the charismatic, suppose to be a matter of fact. In this Scripture, find God's word to you, and prayerfully ponder it in your heart.

SCRIPTURE READING —

Every worthwhile gift, every genuine benefit comes from above, descending from the Father of the heavenly luminaries, who cannot change and who is never shadowed over. He wills to bring us to birth with a word spoken in truth so that we may be a kind of first fruits of his creatures.

Strip away all that is filthy, every vicious excess. Humbly welcome the word that has taken root in you, with its power to save you. Act on this word. If all you do is listen to it, you are deceiving yourselves.

Looking after orphans and widows in their distress and keeping oneself unspotted by the world make for pure worship without stain before our God and Father. (James 1:17-18, 21-22, 27)

"Did not God choose those who are poor?"

POVERTY is something one should not only have seen in pictures, but have touched and smelled as well. A visit to one of the big cities of the Far East can give you that experience. I have seen and touched and smelled my poor, starving, sick, and destitute fellow human beings in the streets of Djakarta. They sleep on a dirty mat on the sidewalk, their only home. They beg or roam the garbage cans for the leftovers to eat. They bathe and take care of their needs in the dirty water of the canals.

I have not seen Calcutta where things seem to be even worse. There it is that Mother Teresa and her sisters go into the streets every day to help these people, share with them the little food they have, dress their wounds, take them to a hospital if possible, and bury their emaciated bones. Is it because Mother Teresa spoke from experience that her speech at the Eucharistic Congress in Philadelphia (1976) was a highlight? She spoke of the many faces of poverty, not only the hungry in Calcutta, but the unloved children in affluent families, and the forgotten residents of posh nursing homes. She spoke of the poor whose diseased bodies were to be touched with the reverence owed to the body of Christ (see 1 Corinthians 12:27 and Matthew 25:31-46), and even acknowledged with a wry smile that she is sometimes criticized for "spoiling the poor." But is it not permissible to have one community of sisters that spoils the poor, she asked, when everyone else spoils the rich?

With this in mind, read today's Scripture meditatively and apply it to your own situation. Think of the many faces of poverty which Mother Teresa mentioned, and the respect we owe to the poor, since they are the body of Christ.

SCRIPTURE READING —

My brothers, your faith in our glorious Lord Jesus Christ must not allow of favoritism. Suppose there should come into your assembly a man fashionably dressed, with gold rings on his fingers, and at the same time a poor man in shabby clothes. Suppose further that you were to take notice of the well-dressed man and say, "Sit right here, please," whereas you were to say to the poor man, "You can stand!" or "Sit over there by my footrest." Have you not in a case like this discriminated in your hearts? Have you not set yourselves up as judges handing down corrupt decisions?

Listen, dear brothers. Did not God choose those who are poor in the eyes of the world to be rich in faith and heirs of the kingdom he promised to those who love him? (James 2:1-5)

"I will show you the faith that underlies my works"

IT WAS a tragic coincidence that two of their children, both in their late teens, died of an overdose of barbiturates in less than three weeks. They were such a nice family, upper middle-class, well respected both in town and in the Church. The children did not lack anything; they possessed cars, money, freedom. What else do you want? And yet this tragedy, which was the topic of guessing for many a day! Why did this happen? When the funerals were over, however, and the incidents forgotten by townfolks, the father made a remarkable confession. He admitted that he had not spent enough time with his children. Indeed, he was gone all the time and his wife as well, leaving the children to be cared for by a maid, as is done quite often in wealthy Southern homes. The parents have the faith, and the children starve for love! "So it is with the faith that does nothing in practice."

James is hitting hard in this Bible passage. Faith without works is idle, but works without faith are just as idle, for faith should underlie my works. Mrs. McLean (not her real name) was estranged from the Church for many years. Of course, the Church was wrong. Mrs. McLean had been a member of the parish council, as soon as councils came into being after Vatican II. She was very active, took many initiatives, worked hard. But Mrs. McLean was a very domineering lady, to say the least. The parish council had to do it her way or no way. There were bitter fights, which finally resulted in Mrs. McLean's resignation from council and Church on the same day. Did faith underlie Mrs. McLean's hard work?

James' remarks should make us check both our faith and our works, and see whether they are in line with God's plan as known to us in Scripture.

SCRIPTURE READING —

My brothers, what good is it to profess faith without practicing it? Such faith has no power to save one, has it? If a brother or sister has nothing to wear and no food for the day, and you say to them, "Good-bye and good luck! Keep warm and well fed," but do not meet their bodily needs, what good is that? So it is with the faith that does nothing in practice. It is thoroughly lifeless.

To such a person one might say, "You have faith and I have works— is that it?" Show me your faith without works, and I will show you the faith that underlies my works! (James 2:14-18)

277-7

"Is it not your inner cravings that make war within your members?"

EVER since human beings have been writing, they have displayed wisdom which implied observation of the self and fellow human creatures. For centuries, philosophy comprised all human wisdom. But gradually human wisdom grew to such an extent that one mind could not master all of it any longer. Philosophy had to branch off into ever more specializations even to such a degree that seemingly there is nothing left over for philosophy proper, and some state that it should go out of business. One of the specialties, sprung off from philosophy, is psychology, the science which deals with the mind.

In reading James' remarks on wisdom and the human psyche, we should keep the above observations in mind. James lived in a prescientific era. The question of whether a person's aggressiveness is innate or a side-effect of poor education was not yet a point of discussion. Psychology, as we know it, had still to be developed. Wisdom, however, existed. The Greeks had their "know yourself" (Socrates), and the Hebrews their rather extensive wisdom literature (see the table of contents in your Bible).

James' observations in today's reading are inspired by this Hebrew literature. They are the remarks of a down-to-earth man, gifted with a keen eye for the human condition. Moreover, James' observations are inspired (guided) by God. Hence, Christians find it worthwhile to take note of them, regardless of the label "prescientific" that characterizes them. We still agree that human wisdom (what we make of life) and wisdom coming from God are often strange bedfellows, and that we are a queer mixture of good and evil. Take this reading as a starting point for having a prayerful look at yourself!

SCRIPTURE READING —

Where there are jealousy and strife, there also are inconstancy and all kinds of vile behavior. Wisdom from above, by contrast, is first of all innocent. It is also peaceable, lenient, docile, rich in sympathy and the kindly deeds that are its fruits, impartial and sincere. The harvest of justice is sown in peace for those who cultivate peace.

Where do the conflicts and disputes among you originate? Is it not your inner cravings that make war within your members? What you desire you do not obtain, and so you resort to murder. You envy and you cannot acquire, so you quarrel and fight. (James 3:16—4:2)

"You fattened yourselves for the day of slaughter"

WHEN visiting the Hermitage in Leningrad, so majestically located on the banks of the river Neva, and admiringly gazing not only at the treasures of art exhibited in this largest museum of the Soviet Union but also at its excessively rich architecture, one wonders how it has been possible that all of this was built for one royal family. The Hermitage was the winter palace of the Russian Tsars. They built one palace after another, decorated them luxuriously, and filled them up with the most expensive treasures of art, all for themselves, while the people of Russia were starving. First humbly and respectfully, carrying their icons to the winter palace, the Russians asked for reforms (1905); then there were firm attempts to change the system, as the nations of Western Europe had done—but the answer was gunfire.

The Tsars and the nobility of Russia were Christians and attended their churches. I wonder whether their popes (Orthodox parish priests) ever preached on today's Scripture. If they did, the rich of those days did not listen, and one can understand why the revolution of 1917 had to occur. Of course, one injustice does not justify another one. Read Aleksandr Solzhenitsyn's *The Gulag Archipelago* *(see November 8)*. But, honestly, one may state with James: "They have fattened themselves for the day of slaughter."

Yet, the lesson has not been learned. A handful of corrupt rich families is still playing a similar game in many a country of Latin America! And, in a different way, many rich in our own United States do the same either individually or corporately by owning stocks in corrupt multinational corporations. When you employ people, own stock, or go to the polls to vote, know what you are doing and keep James' severe words of warning in mind.

SCRIPTURE READING —

As for you, you rich, weep and wail over your impending miseries. Your wealth has rotted, your fine wardrobe has grown moth-eaten, your gold and silver have corroded, and their corrosion shall be a testimony against you; it will devour your flesh like a fire. See what you have stored up for yourselves against the last days. Here, crying aloud, are the wages you withheld from the farmhands who harvested your fields. The cries of the harvesters have reached the ears of the Lord of hosts. You lived in wanton luxury on the earth; you fattened yourselves for the day of slaughter. You condemned, even killed, the just man; he does not resist you. (James 5:1-6)

"It was fitting that God . . . should make their leader . . . perfect through suffering"

RECENTLY, I read a booklet *Jesus Superstar or Savior?* (St. Anthony Messenger Press). As for me, I have an aversion against alternatives. Something is seldom either-or. Rather it is "yes, but" or "no, however." The rock-opera *Jesus Christ, Superstar* is today's idiom set to today's music. With *Godspell* it is perhaps the best known product of the Jesus movement in our seventies. However, the idea to answer Jesus' own question: "Who do *you* say that I am?" (Matthew 16:15) in contemporary concepts is not new. Christians in the Byzantine-Russian tradition saw and still see Jesus as the Pantocrator (almighty emperor, Caesar, tsar). For two centuries, Christians of the West have been spellbound by Jesus, the Sacred Heart. Later Jesus as "Christ the King" became popular. In our day it may be "Jesus Christ Superstar" for some and/or "The Man for Others," that captivates the interest.

An attempt to approach the Christ mystery in an idiom adapted to a certain group in a certain time and culture is found in the Epistle to the Hebrews, from which we will offer a few selections. The author writes for Christians of a Jewish background. That is why he refers to many details of Jewish worship (e.g., the Jewish high priest officiating in the Jerusalem temple), with which his readers are familiar. One may question: "Why should we learn to see Jesus as a High Priest, since Jewish high priests are past history and not part of our culture?" I would agree, if this Epistle were not part of Scripture and as such inspired by God. Whatever images of Christ we favor *(see March 5)*, we must always test them against the Bible, lest we deviate from the true person Jesus is.

This Bible passage describes what Jesus has done for us by using the images "leader-savior-brother." God made our leader (Jesus Christ) "in the work of salvation perfect" (i.e., he made him achieve his goal to save us) through his suffering on the cross.

SCRIPTURE READING —

But we do see Jesus crowned with glory and honor because he suffered death: Jesus, who was made for a little while lower than thc angels, that through God's gracious will he might taste death for the sake of all men. Indeed, it was fitting that when bringing many sons to glory, God, for whom and through whom all things exist, should make their leader in the work of salvation perfect through suffering. (Hebrews 2:9-10)

"God's word is living and effective"

THE St. Bavo cathedral in Haarlem, The Netherlands, may rightly boast of its organ, which is one of the most precious ones of Western Europe. While sitting in the nave of this majestic Gothic building and gazing up at the organ with its 500 pipes, I listened to Bach, Vivaldi, and other grandmasters. I let my thoughts go. The St. Bavo is impressive. Its ribs high up like hands in prayer, its pointed windows, archings and vaulting—all are one gracious invitation to lift up the mind to the transcendent. Nevertheless, something is missing.

St. Bavo's, like so many cathedrals which our brethren of the Reformation took over during the iconoclastic turmoil of the sixteenth century, is like a beautiful woman, robbed of her jewelry and colorful robe. There are no statues, no altars, and no stained glass windows in this cathedral. All were demolished and the walls, so richly painted by the greatest artists of the time, are covered with a coat of white chalk. Our brethren, however, admit that their ancestors in holy fury overreacted. They are restoring St. Bavo's. They peel off the chalk and artists are redoing the wall paintings, so that those noble scenes of the Bible which are of such august dignity can be seen again.

God's word is living and effective, not only as it is printed in the Bible and accepted in a good sermon or communal prayer, but also as celebrated in sacred signs. Liturgy, expressing itself in gestural speech and symbolic action, adds an important dimension to the living expression of faith beyond that which is found in preaching (Bible reading) and common prayer. The fact that, at some time in history, liturgy became an accumulation of void and meaningless symbols does not mean that we should ignore it. Intelligent Christians open up to God's penetrating word in Bible reading, prayer, and good liturgy. What do you contribute to meaningful liturgy in your congregation? It is a medium through which God's word penetrates your joints and marrow.

SCRIPTURE READING —

Indeed, God's word is living and effective, sharper than any two-edged sword. It penetrates and divides soul and spirit, joints and marrow; it judges the reflections and thoughts of the heart. Nothing is concealed from him; all lies bare and exposed to the eyes of him to whom we must render an account. (Hebrews 4:12-13)

"Let us confidently approach . . . to find help in time of need"

THE French statesman, Francois de Calliers, writes about eighteenth century France: "One may see often men who have never left their own country, who have never applied themselves to the study of public affairs, being of meager intelligence, appointed so to speak overnight to important embassies in countries of which they know neither the interests, the laws, the customs, the language, nor even the geographical situation." A new president of the United States owes much to those who have campaigned for him. He does not reward them with the command of a tank division or an aircraft carrier, but quite often he gives them an important embassy post abroad. In 1974, 82 foreign embassy chiefs were professionals, but 39 were politicos. Small wonder that there are voices who want a halt to this questionable practice.

An ambassador has to look after our interests abroad. He must be a skilled person who knows about human relations and how to act in highly sensitive situations. Presidents may make decisions on war or peace partly at least following the ambassador's judgment. Abroad I have seen dozens of hippie-type young Americans hanging around the American Express offices. Often they are ushered to a United States consul (ambassador). When in trouble (caught with dope, lost money or passport), they need a concerned mediator, somebody who takes care.

The Hebrews saw their high priest in the Jerusalem temple as their ambassador with the king of heaven and earth, almighty God. He had to intercede for them by prayer and the offering of sacrifice. The author of Hebrews uses this concept, well-known to his readers, to describe the risen Christ and what he is doing for us in the sanctuary of heaven. And our high priest is not just a politico but a very capable person who sympathizes with us "abroad" whenever we are in trouble even through our own fault.

SCRIPTURE READING —

Since, then, we have a great high priest who has passed through the heavens, Jesus, the Son of God, let us hold fast to our profession of faith. For we do not have a high priest who is unable to sympathize with our weakness, but one who was tempted in every way that we are, yet never sinned. So let us confidently approach the throne of grace to receive mercy and favor and to find help in time of need.

(Hebrews 4:14-16)

"He is able to deal patiently with erring sinners"

MY LONG stay in the tropics taught me a few unusual habits which have remained with me. One of these habits is taking a daily siesta. On the remote island in the Indian Ocean where I worked as a missionary, at two o'clock in the afternoon the streets became deserted. Offices and shops were closed. It was too hot to work. There was no electricity, hence no fans or air conditioning. Everyone took a nap, and only after four o'clock did life slowly return to the streets. I did the same as everyone else, and find myself still doing it. I need half an hour after lunch in order to get ready for the next round.

However, I have a telephone. Often nobody calls for hours, but the very moment I doze off that phone starts ringing. A lady from somewhere in the country wants me to subscribe to a magazine or a salesman is telling me that he will come by to sell candles for the sanctuary. I need every natural and supernatural motivation at my command to be patient, to be kind, to answer with a pleasant voice. And then I think of our Lord. Women with children came when he may have been taking his siesta, hence was not able to notice them! The disciples told the women to be quiet, scolding them. But Jesus was patient. "Let the children come to me" (Mark 10:14).

Jesus was patient most of all with his hard-headed and uneducated disciples. (Read Mark 9:33-37.) The Gospels give many examples of Jesus' patience with sinners and poor wayfarers. The writer of today's Scripture must have had all of this in mind when he wrote that every high priest (hence also the heavenly high priest, Jesus Christ) is able to deal patiently with erring sinners, all of us. If you feel "erring, weak or depressed," do not hesitate to turn to our Mediator (ambassador) before God's throne.

SCRIPTURE READING —

Every high priest is taken from among men and made their representative before God, to offer gifts and sacrifices for sins. He is able to deal patiently with erring sinners, for he himself is beset by weakness and so must make sin offerings for himself as well as for the people. One does not take this honor on his own initiative, but only when called by God as Aaron was. Even Christ did not glorify himself with the office of high priest; he received it from the One who said to him,

"You are a priest forever,
according to the order of Melchizedek." (Hebrews 5:1-6)

October 10

"Jesus has a priesthood which does not pass away"

IT WAS a lady in Moscow who told me that the most precious icons were not to be found in the Rublev museum, which is entirely dedicated to the art of the icons, but in the museum of Russian art. It was there that I should go and see *The Christ* of Andrei Rublyov, the grandmaster of Russian icon painting. The museum was within walking distance of my hotel, and after a few repeated requests for information I found the two rooms with the icon collection. On a huge wooden panel I saw the head of Christ, and what is unique about it, only his head. The rest of the icon was so badly damaged that everywhere the wood was visible.

This icon, painted about the year 1400, served as the centerpane for the iconostasis[1] in the church of the Dormition in Zvengorod. Later it was moved to the St. Sabbas monastery in the same city and finally found a place in this museum. I imagined this Christ icon, undamaged, back in its original setting. From the other world, the heavenly sanctuary, Jesus Christ (Pantocrator, almighty heavenly Tsar) looks down upon the earthly worshipers with those big serious eyes which have that penetrating personal fascination.

I stood meditating and praying in front of this icon for a long time—Christ, his surroundings, the Russian people, badly damaged and deeply wounded yet staring with that fixed gaze of infinite wisdom, understanding, and love. Jesus Christ forever making intercession also for those who in blind fanaticism have closed his churches. Apply this Scripture to your situation! In my Bible, I have underlined "he forever lives to make intercession for them," and concentrated my meditation on this thought.

1 The partition with doors, adorned with icons, which separates the sanctuary from the nave. In Russian-Byzantine tradition, the sanctuary of a church represents heaven where our high priest, Jesus Christ, intercedes for us. Christ's heavenly worship to the Father is made present in the Eucharist, in which the faithful in church may participate.

SCRIPTURE READING —

Under the old covenant there were many priests because they were prevented by death from remaining in office; but Jesus, because he remains forever, has a priesthood which does not pass away. Therefore he is always able to save those who approach God through him, since he forever lives to make intercession for them.

It was fitting that we should have such a high priest: holy, innocent, undefiled, separated from sinners, higher than the heavens.

(Hebrews 7:23-27)

"He entered heaven itself that he might appear before God now on our behalf"

TWICE that day, the *nakoda* (captain of a ship) had told me: "Sir, the sea is too high." Crossing the Strait of Timor from Kupang to the island of Roti would expose us to the open Indian Ocean. With a small government steamer, the captain could not take chances. But now I saw the shore line of Roti rising on the horizon. I watched two *ikan bilalang* (flying fish) playing on the white-crested waves. The sea was still rough. But approaching the pier of Baa, Roti, it got quiet and I saw the district commissioner and his wife waiting. Indonesia was still the Netherlands East Indies. As the only Dutch family on this lonely little island, they insisted on being my hosts whenever I came to say Mass for the few Catholics there, most of them native soldiers and police officers.

We exchanged some pleasant remarks, I mentioned the rough crossing, we drank tea, I took a bath, and then the commissioner proposed a short ride in his jeep over the island, since before it got dark at 6:00 p.m., I would not find my parishioners at home anyway. Up in the hills, we stopped to look at a *kebun djagung* (corn field), and there I saw some rocks, clearly a small altar, with some corn and grains of rice on it. The commissioner did not know its meaning. I had to tell him that the pagans offer rice, corn, chickens, and sometimes even water buffalos in sacrifice to their gods to ask them for favors or placate their anger.

The Jews offered daily sacrifices in the temple of Jerusalem to Yahweh, their God. Small wonder, then, that the Jewish writers of the New Testament have used this well-known symbolism to explain the redemptive act of Jesus' suffering and death on the cross. Respond in prayerful meditation!

SCRIPTURE READING —

Christ did not enter into a sanctuary made by hands, a mere copy of the true one; he entered heaven itself that he might appear before God now on our behalf. Not that he might offer himself there again and again, as the high priest enters year after year into the sanctuary with blood that is not his own; if that were so, he would have had to suffer death over and over from the creation of the world. But now he has appeared at the end of the ages to take away sins once for all by his sacrifice. (Hebrews 9:24-26)

"But Jesus offered one sacrifice for sins"

AMONG the many treasures which came from ancient Egypt and are found in the British Museum, I member best the throne of Tutankhamen (c. 1358 B.C.), the pharaoh of the 18th dynasty, whose tomb was discovered by Howard Carter in 1922. It was mainly the footstool that drew my attention, since it bears a representation (inlaid with cedar, ivory, and gold) of the nine traditional enemies of Egypt. It reminded me of Psalm 110, 1: "The Lord said to my Lord: 'Sit at my right hand till I make your enemies your footstool.'" The symbol of total victory was that the king, sitting on his royal throne, put his feet on the necks of defeated enemies.

Following the teachings of our Lord and the apostles, Catholic tradition has constantly interpreted Psalm 110 as referring to Christ, the Messianic king who defeated his enemies (i.e., all evil) through his death and resurrection. "Sitting at the right hand of the king" is a Hebraism for "sharing power with," which our Lord does with God the Father, because of his meritorious death; and "waiting until his enemies (evil) are placed beneath his feet" follows the language of Psalm 110.

We see here how much the concepts of God, Jesus Christ, and our redemption are conditioned by the sacred author's time and cultural background. We should keep this necessity of thinking in certain concepts well in mind also when we reflect on our own thinking about the Divine mysteries. Many a young person and even grown-up intellectuals with a one-sided secular education foster naive infantile concepts of the transcendent. They are assailed by doubts simply because they overlook the fact that all human thinking on the Divine is conditioned by our frail capacities and hence constitutes merely a weak approach to reality. Believing "the heart of the matter" which is found in this Scripture should give us hope in our often confused human condition.

SCRIPTURE READING —

Every other priest stands ministering day by day, and offering again and again those same sacrifices which can never take away sins. But Jesus offered one sacrifice for sins and took his seat forever at the right hand of God; now he waits until his enemies are placed beneath his feet. By one offering he has forever perfected those who are being sanctified. (Hebrews 10:11-14)

"Now the body is not one member, it is many"

A GREEK maxim declares: "Philosophy is the steersman of life." With respect to today's Scripture, I would like to refer briefly to two philosophical systems which greatly "steer" life on this planet in our day, namely, Communism and Capitalism.

Communism, as conceived by Marx and developed by Lenin in Russia, stresses socialized ownership. It speaks of the proletariat, i.e., proletarians collectively. Only after the rights and duties of the collectivity (the people as a body) are well established, does one look for concessions to the individual. There is some private ownership in Russia, but it is limited. *Capitalism,* on the other hand, starts thinking from the other pole. It stresses first of all the rights of the individual to gain the goods of the earth and to enlarge his private ownership by work, trade, and investment. Only with these individual rights in mind, can one think of duties to the collectivity, people as a whole, and make provision for those who for one reason or another cannot keep up with the process of gaining their share in the goods of the earth (various welfare programs).

We have optioned for Capitalism, and see this philosophy as the source of our economic greatness. But as Christians we should never forget that we are responsible for one another. Though collective thinking is not our cup of tea, we must keep in mind that collectively we are the body of Christ. Through their collective approach to the issue of ownership, the Communists have done away with poverty, but at the cost of man's freedom and responsibility for his own well-being. We see private ownership as an impetus to keep on working. I am all for it, but as Christians, both privately and together through our voting power, we must see to it that all members of Christ's body can get their share in the goods of the earth. If possible, read the whole passage (1 Corinthians 12:12-30) in your Bible!

SCRIPTURE READING —

The body is one and has many members, but all the members, many though they are, are one body; and so it is with Christ. It was in one Spirit that all of us, whether Jew or Greek, slave or free, were baptized into one body. All of us have been given to drink of the one Spirit. Now the body is not one member, it is many.

You, then, are the body of Christ. Every one of you is a member of it.

(1 Corinthians 12:12-14, 27)

"Love never fails"

AS AN educator, I am interested in how my former students are doing in life. I remember faces, but I am weak on names. Walking downtown, I hear quite often: "Hi, Father!" It is usually a former student: "Oh, Father, you don't remember my name anymore." Especially young ladies can look so disappointed. There are names I do remember, however. They are often those students I had some trouble with, the restless, the recalcitrant, the lazy, the "sassy" ones.

Some time ago, I met a young lady in this category and though she had graduated already eight years previously, I hit upon her name right away. And, what I had least expected, she had a Master's degree in special education and was teaching retarded children: "I love them, Father!" Then jokingly she quipped: "What is the loving thing to do? You always told us!" Walking on, I mused: In school a difficult child, hard to handle, tongue well-oiled, and after eight years, how beautiful! "I love them—retarded children!" I thanked God that I am able to be an instrument in his hands to help young people find their way in life!

In the restaurant where I eat my warm meal daily, I see quite often an elderly couple coming in with a retarded son of about thirty. As an outsider, it is difficult for me to understand how parents handle this for a lifetime. I admire them. One must have the love of a parent to deal with retarded persons lovingly and patiently. Above all, one must be motivated by a genuine love which has all the qualities Paul describes in today's Bible reading.

SCRIPTURE READING —

Love is patient; love is kind. Love is not jealous, it does not put on airs, it is not snobbish. Love is never rude, it is not self-seeking, it is not prone to anger; neither does it brood over injuries. Love does not rejoice in what is wrong but rejoices with the truth. There is no limit to love's forbearance, to its trust, its hope, its power to endure.

Love never fails. Prophecies will cease, tongues will be silent, knowledge will pass away. Our knowledge is imperfect and our prophesying is imperfect. When the perfect comes, the imperfect will pass away. When I was a child I used to talk like a child, think like a child, reason like a child. When I became a man I put childish ways aside. Now we see indistinctly, as in a mirror; then we shall see face to face. My knowledge is imperfect now; then I shall know even as I am known. There are in the end three things that last; faith, hope, and love, and the greatest of these is love.

(1 Corinthians 13:4-13)

"Last of all he was seen by me, as one born out of the normal course"

HIS name was John Bernadone (nicknamed Francesco, the Frenchman). His family, upper middle class, owned a department store in Assisi, Italy, and they were on the "party circuit," either preparing/having a party or going to one with other wealthy families. Francis was fed up with this kind of life and became a hippie. Blue jeans were not yet on the market, but some sackcloth that resembled the brown garb of a present-day friar of St. Francis, was available. This was his outfit, very showy indeed! A fellow giving away his own magnificent armor and clothing to a poverty-stricken gentleman, following "visions," and doing strange things like kissing the hand of a leper, visiting the sick, and with some other fellows, equally strange, living in a commune, a shabby building just outside of town—what a shame for his very respectable family! Francis related his conversion to a religious experience which overwhelmed him when he was reading Matthew 10:7-10.

Paul tells about his religious experience to his newly founded congregation in Corinth. "Last of all he [the Lord Jesus] was seen by me." (See Acts 9:1-19.) Paul's reason for a life of dedication to Jesus Christ was the Lord's death and resurrection as witnessed by the early disciples. But many had heard all of this, yet were not converted. Decisive for Paul was his experience on the road to Damascus.

In Christian circles of this country there is much talk nowadays about "religious experience." Some speak of "baptism of the Holy Spirit," which changes their lives completely. Others make the much in vogue personally-directed 30-day retreat (based on the Ignatian exercises), which often results in a similar experience. Whatever the name, pray for that inner light of faith which should change your life ever more.

SCRIPTURE READING —

I handed on to you first of all what I myself received, that Christ died for our sins in accordance with the Scriptures; that he was buried and, in accordance with the Scriptures, rose on the third day; that he was seen by Cephas, then by the Twelve. After that he was seen by five hundred brothers at once, most of whom are still alive, although some have fallen asleep. Next he was seen by James; then by all the apostles. Last of all he was seen by me, as one born out of the normal course. (1 Corinthians 15:3-8)

"If our hopes in Christ are limited to this life only, we are the most pitiable of men"

A FAMILIAR sight on the Red Square in Moscow is a long throng of people, patiently waiting for hours to have the experience of their lifetimes, namely, a look at the body of Lenin, lying in state in his mausoleum close to the wall of the Kremlin. The masterminds behind the Russian revolution have understood well that the ideals of Communism should be embodied in a person, if ever they were to have a lasting appeal on the people. Artists like Serov, Savitsky, and Brodsky have painted Lenin as a benevolent figure, like Christ the Pantocrator *(see October 10)*. In China we see the same phenomenon around the person of Mao Tse-tung.

The master mind of God, which originated a movement for a better world, the kingdom of God, had a similar vision. In fact, the Communists may have learned from God, who embodied his ideas for a happy life in the person of Jesus Christ. Christianity is not primarily a set of truths to be believed; even less is it a list of laws to go by in order not to miss the boat to heaven. Christianity is a firm commitment to the person of our Lord. Faith in Jesus Christ and in all he stands for makes the genuine Christian.

Watching those people on the Red Square, I thought of very dedicated Communists I have met, and of so many lukewarm Christians I know as well. How come? St. Basil's Cathedral still stands on that same Red Square, but as a fairy-tale castle, illuminated at night. It is not a church any longer but a museum. Isn't Christianity a similar fossilized relic of the past for many a Catholic?

Check your own motivation for a Christian way of life, and notice that in today's Scripture Paul does not speak of dogmas and rules but of Christ our pledge of life everlasting. Dedicated Communists could put many a Christian to shame!

SCRIPTURE READING —

Tell me, if Christ is preached as raised from the dead, how is it that some of you say there is no resurrection of the dead?

Why? Because if the dead are not raised, then Christ was not raised; and if Christ was not raised, your faith is worthless. You are still in your sins, and those who have fallen asleep in Christ are the deadest of the dead. If our hopes in Christ are limited to this life only, we are the most pitiable of men. (1 Corinthians 15:12, 16-19)

"So shall we bear the likeness of the man from heaven"

ON ONE occasion an adviser to President Lincoln recommended a candidate for his cabinet. Lincoln declined, and his reason was: "I don't like the man's face." The adviser was shocked: "But the poor fellow is not responsible for his face." "He is," Lincoln replied; "every man over forty is responsible for his face," and the subject was dropped. Lincoln did not state that we are responsible for scars or disfigurements caused by accidents or birth defects. What he meant is that forty years of living put a great deal into a face.

Your face portrays you as you are. You can't fool those who are usually around you for very long. Observe people when their defenses are down and they let themselves go: a woman who is jealous, a man who is angry or vain, a miser, a drunkard. Your face tells whether or not you are a mature person, intelligent, loving. Great portrait painters like Frans Halls and Rembrandt had the gift to analyze faces and the talent to paint a person as he/she was. That is why after centuries we still admire their paintings.

In today's Bible reading, Paul speaks about whom we resemble right now and what we will look like later. Right now we are human beings and our faces should reflect the best of humanness in us. The image of God, immanent in creation, should come through the more we mature. I remember the face of my aged mother, so human, understanding, loving! "First came the natural and after that the spiritual." In the risen Christ, we believers see how after the metamorphosis of death a more brilliant beauty will be ours. We will bear then the likeness of the man of heaven. During our lifetime now we should constantly grow into the likeness of Christ and in him into the likeness of God, immanent in creation.

SCRIPTURE READING —

Scripture has it that Adam, the first man, became a living soul; the last Adam has become a life-giving spirit. Take note, the spiritual was not first; first came the natural and after that the spiritual. The first man was of earth, formed from dust, the second is from heaven. Earthly men are like the man of earth, heavenly men are like the man of heaven. Just as we resemble the man from earth, so shall we bear the likeness of the man from heaven. (1 Corinthians 15:45-49)

"Fully engaged in the work of the Lord"

ALTHOUGH lack of time makes me a poor television viewer, I loved to watch Jack Benny. Whether he chatted with Johnny Carson, Bob Hope or anyone else, he stole the show with his witty down-to-earth little jokes. But as all human beings must, Jack Benny has gone on the journey from which there is no return. Recently I read that Jack Benny was extremely afraid of dying. I agree that leaving all and everything you cherish is not pleasant and I don't know how I will handle it when my time to go arrives. I hope that the Lord may have mercy on me! At least Jack Benny had reached an advanced age and could look back on a well spent life, in which he had made fellow wayfarers laugh a lot and forget the pressures and pains of life for a while. Isn't that wonderful?

Benny's valet told an interviewer: "Jack had a terrible fear of death. He would become melancholic and deeply depressed whenever he heard of friends dying or even being ill. He feared death because, as he used to say, there was nothing after death—no family, no friends, no laughs, and no audiences . . . just a great big black void." And then the valet went on to say that on his deathbed a former vaudeville partner appeared to Jack, assuring him that he was going to help him through into a beautiful hereafter. I hope and pray that almighty God may reward Jack Benny for all the good humor he shared with us.

However, we Christians have a few more reasons not to fear death so much. Following Jesus of Nazareth in faith, we see death as a metamorphosis which leads us to a beautiful life with God. "Being fully engaged in the work of the Lord" should help us. Our toil is not in vain so long as it is done in the Lord.

SCRIPTURE READING —

When the corruptible frame takes on incorruptibility and the mortal immortality, then will the saying of Scripture be fulfilled: "Death is swallowed up in victory." "O death, where is your victory? O death, where is your sting?" The sting of death is sin, and sin gets its power from the law. But thanks be to God who has given us the victory through our Lord Jesus Christ. Be steadfast and persevering, my beloved brothers, fully engaged in the work of the Lord. You know that your toil is not in vain when it is done in the Lord. (1 Corinthians 15:54-58)

"Some who wish to alter the Gospel of Christ must have confused you"

I KNOW Archbishop Marcel Lebebvre only from a few articles in the press. He spent thirty years as a missionary in Africa, and must have been doing a good job there for the Holy See made him archbishop of Dakar. Rome does a good deal of screening and inquiry before it appoints a priest as bishop! Back in his home country, France, the Holy Ghost Fathers elected him as their General Superior. Fellow priests have a keen eye as to their peers. They don't elect you for such a position if you are not fully qualified.

Nevertheless, the archbishop must be a confused person at this point and he is confusing quite a few fellow Christians. He does not agree with most of the renewals of Vatican Council II, and shows his discontent by leading a counter movement. He is establishing "a Church independent of Rome" with the Tridentine Latin Mass[1] and a few more customs as we had them before Vatican II.

At the early beginnings of the Church, Paul had to face a problem similar to the one presented by this archbishop. He had to cope with "some who wish to alter the gospel of Christ" and were confusing the faithful. They were Jewish-Christian preachers who tried to impose the Law of Moses (circumcision, abstinence from pork) on Gentiles who had joined the Church.

Be guided by the Gospel of our Lord as it is made available to you in your Bible and in the explanations of the Church. Be open-minded, recognize and acknowledge good wherever you experience it, but do not let others confuse you.

[1] Mass as authorized by the Council of Trent. It is the Tridentine rite that is forbidden, not Latin as such. There are Latin Masses in St. Peter's in Rome every so often.

SCRIPTURE READING —

Paul, an apostle sent, not by men or by any man, but by Jesus Christ and God his Father who raised him from the dead—I and my brothers who are with me send greetings to the churches in Galatia.

I am amazed that you are so soon deserting him who called you in accord with his gracious design in Christ, and are going over to another gospel. But there is no other. Some who wish to alter the gospel of Christ must have confused you. For even if we, or an angel from heaven, should preach to you a gospel not in accord with the one we delivered to you, let a curse be upon him! (Galatians 1:1-2, 6-8)

October 20

"No mere human invention"

WHILE walking through the main streets of Leningrad and Moscow, I was puzzling over what was different. There is a certain monotony which makes Nesky Prospekt in Leningrad different from Times Square in New York. I think that the absence of consumer advertisements in the Communist cities has something to do with it. Ads and commercials try to brainwash us to consume ever more, and to gradually consider ever more items as necessary for decent living, although we can do without them. Communist ideology disagrees with creating needs artificially as Capitalism does. Advertising flows necessarily from the Capitalist ideology *(see October 13);* hence whenever we watch television, the commercials will be with us, and consequently we should be careful that they don't change our set of values without our even being aware of it.

As Christians, we have opted for the values of the Gospel, which is no mere human invention as ads and commercials are. Paul was a stubborn Jew and not converted overnight. But once he was convinced by his "religious experience" *(see October 15),* he did not waver anymore. His dedication to the Gospel of Jesus Christ was a total and unconditional one.

Every so often are you checking your values against those of the Gospel? Especially, if you are a religious or a priest, do you foster needs for things you could do without? There was a time when we were happy with an efficient public transportation system, and a car was a luxury. The ads have changed this. Most Americans own a car; consequently public transportation is often in a state of decay, and the car is a necessity. But must it be a luxury car for a priest? Check your needs on their more or less artificiality, and perhaps you could spend some more money on works of charity!

SCRIPTURE READING —

I assure you, brothers, the gospel I proclaimed to you is no mere human invention. I did not receive it from any man, nor was I schooled in it. It came by revelation from Jesus Christ. You have heard, I know, the story of my former way of life in Judaism. You know that I went to extremes in persecuting the Church of God and tried to destroy it; I made progress in Jewish observance far beyond most of my contemporaries, in my excess of zeal to live out all the traditions of my ancestors.

(Galatians 1:11-14)

"Christ is living in me"

October 21

SCIENCE, art, trade, and professions have their own jargon or technical vocabulary. The latest addition to special jargons is that of C.B. (citizens' band radio) people. In a similar way, people who are in love have a special vocabulary. It is the language of love, which is rich in metaphors and often quite romantic. In the same vein we must see the language used by those faithful who are really in love/faith with God and write about their experiences. The following is one stanza of *The Spiritual Canticle* by St. John of the Cross, who is perhaps the best known mystic in the Catholic tradition. "The Soul" (i.e., John of the Cross) recites this poem:

Where have you [God] hidden,
Beloved, and left me moaning?
You fled like a stag
After wounding me;
I went out calling you, and you were gone.

St. John himself comments: "In this first stanza, the soul enamored of the Word, her Bridegroom, the Son of God, longs for union with him through clear and essential vision. She records her longings of love and complains to him of his absence, especially since his love wounds her." (As a theologian of his time, St. John sees soul and body almost as two separate entities, and treats "soul" as feminine. The biblical concept of soul is never entirely without body; it is close to our concept of "person.") Being in faith/love with God is not an everlasting honeymoon. Great believers have experienced God as absent.

All of this is language of love/faith, quite metaphorical, hence something to be learned. With this in mind, read the great mystic Paul, who has inspired many mystics of later centuries. (Exegetical note: "It was through the law *of faith* that I died to the law *of Moses*": by this mystic death, the Christian now lives with the life of God; "crucified with Christ": identified with the phases of Christ's passion, death, and resurrection.)

SCRIPTURE READING —

It was through the law that I died to the law, to live for God. I have been crucified with Christ, and the life I live now is not my own; Christ is living in me. I still live my human life, but it is a life of faith in the Son of God, who loved me and gave himself for me. I will not treat God's gracious gift as pointless. If justice is available through the law, then Christ died to no purpose! (Galatians 2:19-21)

October 22

"All are one in Christ Jesus"

DURING the bicentennial Americans did quite a bit of mutual shoulder patting. America is beautiful. Collectively, we are proud of our ancestors and of ourselves, who have built and are building this greatest country on earth. But the idea that "we are the greatest" (during Hitler's regime it was "Germany above all!") entails a danger. The fact that America is great does not mean that I am that great as well. It may be that I am very mediocre, insignificant, or even crooked!

We should be wary of respect paid to collectivity. In the early sixties, I was driving from El Paso to Dallas. The speed limit in Texas was 60 miles per hour in those days before the energy crisis, and I drove 70. No living soul in that wide empty wasteland! But over a hill, the highway patrol stopped me: "Sir, you came through our radar screen driving 70." I showed my driver's license, and the officer saw my Roman collar next to me on the front seat: "Are you a Catholic priest?" "Yes, I am." The officer got very kind all of a sudden: "Well, Father John, don't drive so fast. Be careful!" I was lucky. It saved me a few dollars. But later on my way, I felt shabby. Would the officer have been that kind and respectful if he had not seen my Roman collar? His respect was paid to collectivity —not to me as a person, but to me as a member of the clergy.

It can happen that a minority group, which has been harassed and discriminated against, collectively needs a boost. If praising the group as a whole helps to foster its self-respect and build up its identity with the final result of equal rights for all, I am in favor of it. Probably, the Christian congregation of Galatia, which was very heterogeneous and practicing discrimination, needed such a boost. Paul tells them: All of you are great, because of your common baptism in Christ. And that is why we too are great, should be grateful for our election, and never look down on any member of Christ's body. On the other hand, we should remember the French saying: "*Noblesse oblige*—nobility obliges."

SCRIPTURE READING —

Each one of you is a son of God because of your faith in Christ Jesus. All of you who have been baptized into Christ have clothed yourselves with him. There does not exist among you Jew or Greek, slave or freeman, male or female. All are one in Christ Jesus. Furthermore, if you belong to Christ you are the descendants of Abraham, which means you inherit all that was promised. (Galatians 3:26-29)

October 23

"You have been called to live in freedom"

AFTER a lovely drive with friends along the scenic Adriatic of Yugoslavia, we ended up in historic Dubrovnik, surrounded by walls, full of impressive churches, monuments, and bell towers. With Venice, medieval Dubrovnik once was the most important and rich trade center of the area. It was a wonderful evening, not too warm, not too cool. We took an after dinner walk through the city's main street. There were hundreds of young people in the streets, just walking up and down, doing some window shopping, talking, laughing. We were told that as members of the Communist youth organization, they were having their collective vacation in some youth hostels on the beach.

What I was amazed about is that there was no shouting, no littering of beer cans, no noisy showing off with motor bikes and cars, no mugging, no whistling when a girl passed by, some courting, though, but all in a civilized way. Years later, I experienced the same thing when walking at night in the main streets of Leningrad and Moscow. Is this typically European? No. The whole gamut of delinquencies is plaguing Amsterdam as much as it does any city of the United States. Is it typical of any Communist country? I told a friend about this experience after vandals had broken into his car and stolen his C.B. radio. He retorted: "But over there, they chop'm the head off." Perhaps he is right. It raises the question, though: How much freedom can average young persons handle without hurting themselves or impeding the constitutional freedom of fellow citizens?

Paul states that a Christian is free, but he hastens to qualify Christian freedom. It is a freedom for love. One may ask: Do we need the ramifications of love and its applications to life situations known as laws? Yes. Laws are needed, but their observance should always be guided by love.

SCRIPTURE READING —

It was for liberty that Christ freed us. So stand firm, and do not take on yourselves the yoke of slavery a second time!

My brothers, remember that you have been called to live in freedom—but not a freedom that gives free rein to the flesh. Out of love, place yourselves at one another's service. The whole law has found its fulfillment in this one saying: "You shall love your neighbor as yourself." If you go on biting and tearing one another to pieces, take care! You will end up in mutual destruction! (Galatians 5:1, 13-15)

"All that matters is that one is created anew"

EVER since Darwin (theory of evolution), Einstein (theory of relativity), Whitehead (his metaphysics) and Teilhard de Chardin (his evolutionary vision), we are inclined to see reality as a process, in a constant state of process or becoming. However, process philosophy is not new. Theravada (Buddhist) affirmed the primacy of becoming and interrelatedness. Heraclitus (535-475 B.C.) stated that all things are in flux. But he was overshadowed by the mainstream of Greek philosophy which since the time of Parmenides affirmed the primacy of being over becoming. Since Paul was part and parcel of Greek culture, we understand that his theological reflections on the deposit of faith are greatly influenced by this static way of thinking. And consequently, we Christians of the West still live with a tension between being (what I am) and becoming (what I am going to be).

In reading today's Scripture, we should keep Paul's static worldview—which as such is not part of Divine revelation—well in mind. "The world has been crucified to me and I to the world." In Paul's vocabulary "world" denotes all that stands in enmity with God. I am through with it! But *was* Paul as a human being, and *are* we, even after long years of ascetic disciplineship, really through with it? Evil will be in and around us till we breathe our last. Crucifying it is a lifetime process; hence, something we will have to work on constantly. This is the negative side of the process. The positive side is that as Christians we are created anew.

But even this new creation is not a static entity. There will be constant tension between what I am as a Christian (a new creature) and what I should be. The moment we stop moving (becoming), we will be stale and vapid. Be grateful for what you are through "the cross of our Lord Jesus Christ" and ask his Spirit to keep moving.

SCRIPTURE READING —

May I never boast of anything but the cross of our Lord Jesus Christ! Through it, the world has been crucified to me and I to the world. It means nothing whether one is circumcised or not. All that matters is that one is created anew. Peace and mercy on all who follow this rule of life, and on the Israel of God.

Henceforth, let no man trouble me, for I bear the brand marks of Jesus in my body.

Brothers, may the favor of our Lord Jesus Christ be with your spirit. Amen. (Galatians 6:14-18)

"Christ is the image of the invisible God"

IT IS a well-known fact that great people don't always get the appreciation they deserve. Often they are too great for their environment. "Who does he think he is?" Often they are ahead of their time, and only slowly and gradually are they acknowledged as great in the perspective of history. An artist like Vincent van Gogh lived and died as a poor man, and only later were his paintings sold for thousands of dollars. The new Van Gogh Museum in Amsterdam, exclusively dedicated to his work, is an impressive monument for a man whose greatness was discovered only decades after his death.

Something similar has happened to the great Jew of Galilee. In his native town, they asked: "Is this not the carpenter?" (Mark 6:3). "His own did not accept him" (John 1:11). He was not understood and was done away with as a criminal. It took the early Church decades to become fully aware of who he was. Study Jesus' portrait in the Synoptics, the Acts, John, and the Bible reading for today. You will see a growing awareness through theological reflection, guided by God's Spirit.

Today's poetic text from Paul is a beautiful synthesis of what the early Church thought of Christ, as man, Son of God, king and judge of the world. In reading, we must keep in mind that no clear distinction is made between the preexistent and the incarnate Christ. As wisdom (pronounced "Word"), Christ exists from all eternity in God, and Divine Wisdom is the pure emanation of the Almighty (see Wisdom 7:25-26). In Christ, God contemplated the plan of the universe. Hence, the universe owes its cohesiveness to Christ, God's wisdom (word). Contemplate God, visible to us in Christ Jesus.

SCRIPTURE READING —

He is the image of the invisible God, the firstborn of all creatures. In him everything in heaven and on earth was created, things visible and invisible, whether thrones or dominations, principalities or powers; all were created through him, and for him. He is before all else that is. In him everything continues in being. It is he who is head of the body, the church; he who is the beginning, the first-born of the dead, so that primacy may be his in everything. It pleased God to make absolute fullness reside in him and, by means of him, to reconcile everything in his person, both on earth and in the heavens, making peace through the blood of his cross. (Colossians 1:15-20)

"The mystery of Christ in you, your hope of glory"

IT SEEMS to be fashionable to join the "consciousness revolution" nowadays. Western psychotherapy and the disciplines of Eastern religions converge to help people become aware of themselves. They advertise transactional analysis, primal scream, bioenergetics, yoga, guided fantasy, gestalt therapy, psychosynthesis, or you name it. "Modest fees" go with it! The self should be released from the domination of the ego. Emotions are liberated in encounter groups. Most employ some form of meditation or breathing exercises as a means of conditioning the nervous system and expanding consciousness.

It is a remarkable fact that this phenomenon is doing best where there is widespread loss of faith in family, church, and government. The encounter group offers instant intimacy and an experience of the sacred, which many hunger for after giving up organized religion. Thousands of Americans are searching their identity ("Who am I?") and turn to this movement, a religion without a creed.

The quest for self-consciousness is good. And some of the techniques, which come from the East, can be used in Christian search for self as well. Meditation is as old as Christianity itself (see Preface). Today's Scripture invites you to be aware of who you are, not just as another human being but as a Christian, "'the mystery of Christ in you, your hope of glory." Christians, if mentally sick, may turn to a reliable psychiatrist. In meditating, some of the techniques of the East may be helpful. As for the rest of the above-mentioned movement, our own tradition offers something that is more solid. For us the answer is Christ!

SCRIPTURE READING—

Even now I find my joy in the suffering I endure for you. In my own flesh I fill up what is lacking in the sufferings of Christ for the sake of his body, the church. I became a minister of this church through the commission God gave me to preach among you his word in its fullness, that mystery hidden from ages and generations past but now revealed to his holy ones. God has willed to make known to them the glory beyond price which this mystery brings to the Gentiles—the mystery of Christ in you, your hope of glory. This is the Christ we proclaim while we admonish all men and teach them in the full measure of wisdom, hoping to make every man complete in Christ. (Colossians 1:24-28)

"New life in company with Christ"

INTRODUCE me to your company, people with whom you socialize, and I will tell you a few things about yourself. That is the reason why intelligent parents are selective about the company and friendships frequented by their children. One of my sisters-in-law told me about a clash she had with her parents long ago, when as a teenager she was dating a ne'er-do-well. Finally, she gave him up. But when she came home with my brother, her parents regarded everything as okay right away, because they knew that there was a priest in the family. The fact that I am a priest does not guarantee, of course, that all six of my brothers are fine fellows. However, the episode shows that those parents were concerned about what kind of company their daughter would keep the rest of her life.

Company may be books, movies, television shows. A woman who turns out to be addicted to the soap operas, a man who will not miss a single ball game during the season, a teenager who watches all the violent TV shows night after night and never reads a good book—they all tell about the kind of company they like, hence tell something about themselves. Company may change your life, even result in a new life. The single person who chooses a person of the opposite sex as company for life starts a new life and even receives a new name, husband/wife.

Today's Bible reading speaks about your new life in company with Christ. Those in company with Christ even carry a special name, Christians. We should be careful, however, not to see our company with Christ as a static situation *(see October 24)*. Husband and wife, in company with one another all the time, should try to keep their married life exciting. As a Christian in company with Christ, you should do the same. Company is alive and exciting only if it grows.

SCRIPTURE READING —

In baptism you were not only buried with him but also raised to life with him because you believed in the power of God who raised him from the dead. Even when you were dead in sin and your flesh was uncircumcised, God gave you new life in company with Christ. He pardoned all our sins. He canceled the bond that stood against us with all its claims, snatching it up and nailing it to the cross.

(Colossians 2:12-14)

"Put on a new man"

IN THE jungle of Southeast Asia, I have seen large-sized apes in their natural habitat. They are shy, but when you keep quiet you can observe them. As often as I see the same-sized apes in a zoo, I think of the jungle where I saw them free and I feel sorry for them. Why? Perhaps because they are so close to us human beings. However, I realize that there is no alternative. In the zoo, an ape must be kept behind bars, even when his name is "orangutan, man of the woods," since he is not a man.

I feel really sad when I see members of my own species, that supposedly has outgrown the jungle, being kept behind bars. It is depressing to see there long rows of double deck beds, each for a person to whom the Maker gave "dominion over all things that move on the earth" (Genesis 1:28). These people did not know how to handle their God-given freedom; hence, it had to be taken away. A person behind the bars of a state penitentiary is a pitiful being.

But the most degrading bars are those of man's vices. Man can be the sorry victim of his own depravity. Whether we think of craving for persons, which we call lust, or craving for things, which is called greed, when not under control these vices enslave us. Buddhist monks try to kill unruly desires by meditation. Great Christian mystics have done the same by reflective prayer in which they asked God to help them. Francis de Sales could say: "I have hardly any desires." He had reached a great conformity with the will of God. Paul speaks of putting on a new man, growing into conformity with the image of the Creator. Only when Christ will be everything in me will I be fully free.

SCRIPTURE READING —

Put to death whatever in your nature is rooted in earth: fornication, uncleanness, passion, evil desires, and that lust which is idolatry. These are the sins which provoke God's wrath. Your own conduct was once of this sort, when these sins were your very life. You must put that aside now: all the anger and quick temper, the malice, the insults, the foul language. Stop lying to one another. What you have done is put aside your old self with its past deeds and put on a new man, one who grows in knowledge as he is formed anew in the image of his Creator. There is no Greek or Jew here, circumcised or uncircumcised, foreigner, Scythian, slave, or freeman. Rather, Christ is everything in all of you.

(Colossians 3:5-11)

"We were the slaves of our passions"

TURNING away in distaste from what we dislike is called aversion, and forms of it are envy, jealousy, hatred, and similar vices. For a great man like Dr. Martin Luther King, who had dedicated his life to the dream of freedom and human dignity for the downtrodden, it would have been natural to submit himself to the natural inclination of aversion. There was so much that displeased him. He fought it, but always with nonviolent means. His very words show this: "There will be no permanent solution to the race problem until oppressed men develop the capacity to love their enemies." Dr. King felt more free than ever when he was jailed in Birmingham.

Just as delusion and craving do, so also will aversion enslave us to a certain extent. Zen masters advise us to withdraw from it every so often in contemplative meditation. We should empty our minds of delusion, craving *(see October 28),* and aversion. Only then can we attain pure awareness or intuition of the transcendent, which gives us freedom and peace of mind. Thought, including evil thought, creates duality in us—subject versus object. We should pursue a state of nonduality, intuitive awareness, mystic (direct) experience of "the over and beyond."

We Christians might well heed this advice. We should withdraw often and empty our minds in contemplative meditation, which is always "prayerful" for a Christian. Contemplation as such cannot set us free. It must be combined with prayer to the transcendent God whom I experience as in and around me, surrounding me with love, since he is love, and who saved me not because of my righteous deeds but because of his mercy (Titus 3:4-5). Meditate on today's Scripture with this in mind.

SCRIPTURE READING —

We ourselves were once foolish, disobedient, and far from true faith; we were the slaves of our passions and of pleasures of various kinds. We went our way in malice and envy, hateful ourselves and hating one another. But when the kindness and love of God our Savior appeared, he saved us; not because of any righteous deeds we had done, but because of his mercy. He saved us through baptism of new birth and renewal by the Holy Spirit. (Titus 3:3-5)

"As a result of this faith . . ."

I MET him on the train from Paris, France, to Lourdes, the famous shrine of our Lady. Apparently, he was a Chinese priest. I started a conversation first in French, then in English. And while I watched the endless vineyards of Bordeaux sliding by our window, he told me his story. He was a North Vietnamese, editor of the diocesan newspaper in Hanoi. He wrote anti-Communist articles. The French had left the country in the early fifties. A Red administration was in the process of taking over. Soldiers raided his church during Mass one Sunday, and his parishioners ushered him away through a back door. For weeks he was in mortal danger and promised Mary to make a pilgrimage to her shrine in Lourdes if he came out alive. At the present time he was studying more journalism at the Sorbonne (University of Paris), had a few days' vacation, and was now on his way to Lourdes to fulfill his promise.

The Imitation of Christ states somewhere: "Often I made a pilgrimage, seldom did I return holier." Apparently already in the Middle Ages shrines were pleasant tourist attractions, where churchy people had a good time. Did my pilgrimage to Lourdes make me holier?

By necessity we had to share a hotel room. How this man prayed! Obviously as he was used to, he knelt down before his bed every night and prayed a long time. He prayed at the shrine with his arms outstretched. I envied his faith, and it strengthened my weak belief. I prayed: "God, give me the faith of that man!" Can the faith of fellow believers strengthen ours? My pilgrimage to Lourdes, for one, proved the famous statement of *The Imitation of Christ* to be false. I returned holier, that is to say, with more faith.

The author of Hebrews invites you to watch the faith of men of old (see Genesis 12ff) and doing so should strengthen your faith.

SCRIPTURE READING —

By faith Abraham obeyed when he was called, and went forth to the place he was to receive as a heritage; he went forth, moreover, not knowing where he was going. By faith he sojourned in the promised land as in a foreign country, dwelling in tents with Isaac and Jacob, heirs of the same promise. As a result of this faith, there came forth from one man, who was himself as good as dead, descendants as numerous as the stars in the sky and the sands of the seashore. (Hebrews 11:8-9, 12)

October 31

"Persevere in running the race which lies ahead"

WHEN I skim the sports section of my newspaper, I love to read the statements of the coach whose team fared so poorly that weekend. He wishes, of course, that his team would have done better. But how to convince the players that next time they surely will do better? A Japanese saying goes: "Defeat shows that victory is possible." Life is a game that knows its defeats and victories daily. We all experience it in our own selves. The coach has something to do with it when the local "Tigers—Colts—Panthers" win or lose. When his team loses too often, he may even lose his job.

What about Jesus Christ as our coach in the game of life? It could sound blasphemous to those Christians whose mental picture of Christ resembles only and exclusively that of the traditional Sacred Heart. The writer of Hebrews introduces Jesus as coach in today's Scripture. Football, baseball, and basketball were unknown to the ancient Romans. But they loved their own games. When you visit cities around the Mediterranean, you find the ruins of amphitheaters all over. Not only the Christian lay people went there, but their pastors as well. Both Paul and the author of Hebrews seem to be well-acquainted with what was going on in the stadium.

In today's Bible reading, life is the arena of the local amphitheater. A cloud of witnesses/spectators watches us. Sins are hindering clothes. Take them off when you are running. Keep your eyes fixed on Jesus. As a good coach, he inspires and perfects your faith and self-confidence. And he gives the reason for your efforts, namely, the joy of heaven. He himself gave the example and endured the opposition of sinners. Do not abandon the struggle!

SCRIPTURE READING —

Therefore, since we for our part are surrounded by this cloud of witnesses, let us lay aside every encumbrance of sin which clings to us and persevere in running the race which lies ahead; let us keep our eyes fixed on Jesus, who inspires and perfects our faith. For the sake of the joy which lay before him he endured the cross, heedless of its shame. He has taken his seat at the right of the throne of God. Remember how he endured the opposition of sinners; hence do not grow despondent or abandon the struggle. In your fight against sin you have not yet resisted to the point of shedding blood. (Hebrews 12:1-4)

"After this I saw before me a huge crowd"

WE ARE acquainted with the Negro spiritual that goes: "When the saints go marchin' in . . . , I want to be in their number." The song reflects popular piety but it is to the point. So often we see human values out of perspective. Does the constant glittering of neon lights make us myopic? Christians are supposed to go by the light of faith. Why should we hurt ourselves by moving about in darkness when the real light is available? Christ tells us where to put priorities.

Many great Christians, unsung heroes of outstanding love and dedication to their commitment in life, have gone before us. Let us follow them, rather than those who are successful in sports, beauty, or money-making!

Using visionary language, the author of today's reading encourages Christians who are suffering persecution. "An angel coming from the east" [the source of light, rising Sun, place of paradise, Genesis 2:8] holds "the seal of the living God": Just as Oriental kings customarily impressed their seal on their belongings, so all who are "marked" by the seal of God belong to him and are saved. The number of 144,000 is symbolic (12 x 12 x 1000—12 is the symbol of perfection!). "The throne and the Lamb": Jesus Christ, the Lamb of God. This Bible word, God's word, should also encourage us, who still walk in the valley of darkness and go perhaps through a period of real trial and hardship.

SCRIPTURE READING —

I saw another angel come up from the east holding the seal of the living God. He cried out at the top of his voice to the four angels who were given power to ravage the land and the sea, "Do no harm to the land or the sea or the trees until we imprint this seal on the foreheads of the servants of our God." I heard the number of those who were so marked—one hundred and forty-four thousand from every tribe of Israel.

After this I saw before me a huge crowd which no one could count from every nation and race, people and tongue. They stood before the throne and the Lamb, dressed in long white robes and holding palm branches in their hands.

Then one of the elders asked me, "Who are these people all dressed in white? And where have they come from?" I said to him, "Sir, you should know better than I." He then told me, "These are the ones who have survived the great period of trial; they have washed their robes and made them white in the blood of the Lamb."

(Revelation 7:2-4, 9, 13-14)

"Whom I myself shall see"

NOTHING is more sure than that all of us are born to die. We have to face death first quite often, when it strikes our beloved ones, and finally when we ourselves are involved. We have to leave everything behind us. We may try not to think of it. Some consider death as an absurdity. Others learn to handle this reality as an integral part of our condition. Am I, who came into being and grew into a person through my relationship with fellow human beings, doomed to break for always the very ties that made me the person I am? Am I, who believe that God called me to live with him in a sacred partnership (covenant), rewarded with mere nothingness the moment I breathe my last?

We Christians are aware in faith that beyond death we will be with God. We are also aware that at the moment of death, we are not always the kind of persons we should be for all eternity; hence, that a process of purification follows death before we will share life with God, as promised. On this awareness Christians base their ancient custom of praying for the deceased, that God may grant them the vision of his glory. All Souls Day is a special day of prayer for all our brothers who have gone ahead of us.

If you are not familiar with the Book of Job, you should read Job 1—2:13 and 42:7-17. It is a folktale used by the author as a framework for a series of speeches or dialogues dealing with the problem of human suffering. Why do I have to suffer and ultimately die? In this passage, we have a beautiful specimen of God-inspired Hebrew insight. It should help us, when we have to face suffering and death.

SCRIPTURE READING —

Job answered and said:
Oh, would that my words were written down!
Would that they were inscribed in a record:
That with an iron chisel and with lead
they were cut in the rock forever!
But as for me, I know that my Vindicator lives,
and that he will at last stand forth upon the dust;
Whom I myself shall see:
my own eyes, not another's, shall behold him,
And from my flesh I shall see God;
my inmost being is consumed with longing. (Job 19:1, 23-27)

"As the discipline of God . . ."

OVER the centuries, not all cultures have handled the education of children in the same way. They developed philosophies of education. Some civilizations advocate a strict education, in which a strong father image, respect (filial love!), requirements and punishment in case of failure play an important role. Others want a more lenient and flexible approach in both family and school. The child should develop himself into a free and loving creature; hence, he is left free as much as possible in order to determine his own course in life.

We mentioned the youth in Communist countries *(October 23),* and we see with our own eyes what is going on in our families and schools under the guidance of contemporary psychology. Of course, "by their fruits you shall know them" (Matthew 7:20).

Today's Scripture deals with education. The English text uses the word "discipline" which can be misleading. The Greek word is *paideia,* which my dictionary translates first of all as: "the rearing of a child, teaching, education," and only then as "discipline, correction." Since the Vulgate translated "paideia" by "disciplina," it ended up as "discipline" in our translation. In this context (Hebrews 12:1-4, *October 21),* the author sees life as a contest. If you want to be in the game, you must submit yourself to rigorous training. Hence, quite a few commentators suggest translating "paideia" here by "training." The *Jerusalem Bible* does so, and *The Living New Testament* (a paraphrased edition) also uses the word "training." And isn't paideia-education (an ongoing process!) supposed to train a person for the arena of life?

SCRIPTURE READING —

"My sons, do not disdain the discipline of the Lord
nor lose heart when he reproves you;
For whom the Lord loves, he disciplines;
he scourges every son he receives."

Endure your trials as the discipline of God, who deals with you as sons. For what son is there whom his father does not discipline?

At the time it is administered, all discipline seems a cause for grief and not for joy, but later it brings forth the fruit of peace and justice to those who are trained in its school. So strengthen your drooping hands and your weak knees. Make straight the paths you walk on, that your halting limbs may not be dislocated but healed.

(Hebrews 12:5-7, 11-13)

"You have drawn near to Mount Zion and the city of the living God"

SOME time ago, I watched a television series on child abuse. It was depressing. I saw children cruelly maltreated by their parents. Children told what mom and dad had done to them. Repentent parents bore witness to their crime, and one wonders whether it was lack of love or prudence, or maybe both, that made them make those mistakes. There is no simple solution for this phenomenon. Education is a complicated process. It requires much wisdom, patience, determination, and most of all love.

Quite often the Bible uses the parent-model to describe God in his relationship to human beings. Often he is experienced as an angry God, smashing those who do not obey him. "You shall rule them with an iron rod; you shall shatter them like an earthen dish" (Psalm 2:9; Revelation 2:27). That is what the Messiah is supposed to do in God's name. It sounds very much like child abuse!

Today's Bible reading refers to Exodus 19:16-25, which depicts God in his frightening greatness. The biblical imagery of clouds, fire, storm, angels blasting trumpets, thunder and lightning is used to bring this out. The author compares the manifestation of God on Sinai with the theophany on Mount Zion, located in heaven, where we will see God without trembling and fear. Both Exodus 19:16-25 and today's Scripture contain a Divine message. As a reaction to the hell-and-brimstone sermons during missions in the pre-Vatican II Church, it seems to be only "love—sweet love" and a "relaxed way" of living the Christian message that one hears nowadays from the pulpit. We should not swing to either extreme, but try to assimilate the whole message.

SCRIPTURE READING—

You have not drawn near to an untouchable mountain and a blazing fire, nor gloomy darkness and storm and trumpet blast, nor a voice speaking words such that those who heard begged that they be not addressed to them.

No, you have drawn near to Mount Zion and the city of the living God, the heavenly Jerusalem, to myriads of angels in festal gathering, to the assembly of the first-born enrolled in heaven, to God the judge of all, to the spirits of just men made perfect, to Jesus, the mediator of a new covenant, and to the sprinkled blood which speaks more eloquently than that of Abel. (Hebrews 12:18-19, 22-24)

November 5

"Paul, ambassador of Christ and now a prisoner for him"

BORN in Germany and educated in the seminary very solidly and ascetically, two young foreign missionaries had arrived in Djakarta a few days earlier. They were our guests in the rectory, waiting for transportation to the remote island in the Timor Sea where they were going to dedicate their lives to God and suffering fellow human beings. It was their first experience with the Far East. And the Javanese are such beautiful people, so gentle, so kind, and many of them so poor *(see October 2)*. Indeed, it touches the heart of every compassionate European or American who riding from the airport to the terminal downtown sees the endless shanty towns made of bamboo, straw, and corrugated iron.

Yes, compassionate they were, these two young Germans! But they wanted to explore the city and see more of these gentle people. We warned them to be careful and beware of pickpockets. They smiled their superior smile of understanding: "They will respect our white cassocks." And certainly these gentle people had done so, when both returned, tired and soaked wet from perspiration, but without wallets. They were very disappointed: "And you leave your home country to come and help these people." I could not help laughing. It is, of course wonderful to leave your comfortable homeland to share a life of poverty and deprivation with these people, but it is quite naive to expect them to wait for you at the airport and sing: "Here comes our savior."

We Christians should minister to one another, but we should not expect appreciation from those whom we serve. If you receive it once in a while, be grateful! But don't break down if you don't get it! Our Lord came with the best intentions in the world, and they nailed him on a cross. Paul had preached the Gospel tirelessly year after year, and in today's Scripture we see him in jail.

SCRIPTURE READING —

I prefer to appeal in the name of love. Yes, I, Paul, ambassador of Christ and now a prisoner for him, appeal to you for my child, whom I have begotten during my imprisonment. It is he I am sending back to you—and that means I am sending my heart!

I had wanted to keep him with me, that he might serve me in your place while I am in prison for the gospel; but I did not want to do anything without your consent, that kindness might not be forced on you but might be freely bestowed. (Philemon 9-10, 12-14)

"I have been treated mercifully"

IT WAS in Old Mexico that I visited a remarkable museum, namely a former convent of cloistered nuns which was closed by the revolutionary government in the twenties. As a male, you don't get the opportunity to penetrate into a cloistered nuns' sanctuary so long as it is in operation, and even less do you receive first-hand information of what they are really doing. This Mexican convent must have been a very medieval one. I saw all kinds of scourges, switches, and other strange implements the sisters had been using to chastise their sinful (?) bodies. I suppose that Vatican Council II has done away with these peculiar customs.

Over the centuries, Christian practices to handle that remarkable being who is "simultaneously just and sinful" have varied widely. The Bible reflects peaks of holiness and dark pits of evildoing. Penance is mentioned on almost every page, and its beautiful prayers of remorse may still inspire you and me whenever we must admit that we have failed. Until recently we had our frequent Confessions—I still remember those days before Easter and Christmas which kept me ten or more hours in the confessional!—and now, as an alternative to a "quicky" before Mass, we have the new Rite of Penance "face to face with prayerful dialogue" and a revived public confession of sins in many a prayer group.

Practices of asceticism, confession, and penance have changed every so often, but the basics—confession of guilt (at least to yourself and God), conversion, penance, and total dependence on the mercy of God—are inalienable values in the Christian outlook on the human condition. Paul gives an example for us to think about: "I have been treated mercifully" (1 Timothy 1:13).

SCRIPTURE READING —

I thank Christ Jesus our Lord, who has strengthened me, that he has made me his servant and judged me faithful. I was once a blasphemer, a persecutor, a man filled with arrogance; but because I did not know what I was doing in my unbelief, I have been treated mercifully, and the grace of our Lord has been granted me in overflowing measure, along with the faith and love which are in Christ Jesus.

You can depend on this as worthy of full acceptance: that Christ Jesus came into the world to save sinners. Of these, I myself am the worst. But on that very account I was dealt with mercifully.

(1 Timothy 1:12-16)

November 7

"Petitions, prayers, intercessions, and thanksgiving . . .for all"

THOUGH not overly pious, my parents were devout Catholics. In our home, religion was practiced not only on the horizontal level (a no-nonsense and down-to-earth education, with plenty of love though!), but also vertically, i.e., God as transcending his creation got his due every day. Blessing and grace at table, morning and family night prayers were part of the daily routine. I remember the night prayers best. After supper, before the table was cleared, we all got on our knees, and my father started the rosary. My mother took the Litany of Mary (she knew it by heart!), and then we were only half finished.

We had plenty of dead members in the family, and for all of them individually "petitions, prayers, intercessions" had to be offered. Uncle Bill, Aunt Cora, Grandpa Ted and Grandpa John, no one was overlooked. All got their "Our Father," "Hail Mary," and "Eternal rest grant to them. . . ." Although once in a while one of the children asked to be excused, went to the restroom, and came out only after everything was over, for the most part we all stayed put and prayed. We were a happy crowd, although we had to clear the table, wash the dishes, and only then could go our way.

I don't recommend to my congregation this extensive way of interceding. As far as family night prayers are concerned, I find a short Bible reading, discussion, and responsorial prayer more meaningful. But petitions and prayerful intercessions are part of our Christian tradition. We partake in the Prayer of the Faithful in church, hence even privately we should pray for one another and not hesitate to ask God for favors. "Prayer of this kind is good," but don't overlook "thanksgiving." Evidently, Paul wants a balance.

SCRIPTURE READING —

First of all, I urge that petitions, prayers, intercessions, and thanksgiving be offered for all men, especially for kings and those in authority, that we may be able to lead undisturbed and tranquil lives in perfect piety and dignity. Prayer of this kind is good, and God our savior is pleased with it, for he wants all men to be saved and come to know the truth.

This truth was attested at the fitting time. I have been made its herald and apostle (believe me, I am not lying but speaking the truth), the teacher of the nations in the true faith.

It is my wish, then, that in every place the men shall offer prayers with blameless hands held aloft, and be free from anger and dissension.

(1 Timothy 2:1-4, 8)

"You made your noble profession of faith"

IN HIS book, *The Gulag Archipelago,* Aleksandr Solzhenitsyn describes Moscow and Petrograd (now Leningrad) church trials in 1922. Both the Patriarch of Moscow and the Metropolitan of Petrograd did not object to surrendering church valuables to feed the starving Volga peasants. The Archpriest A. N. Zaozersky had surrendered all the valuables of his own church, but he defended in principle the Patriarch's appeal regarding *forced* requisition as sacrilege. Patriarch Tikhon, summoned to the tribunal on May 5, 1922, took upon himself the entire blame for writing and disseminating a pastoral letter in which he protested against *forced* requisition of church goods.

Most of these churchmen, who made their "noble profession of faith," paid for it with their lives. It was stated that the Patriarch wanted to overthrow the Soviet government. This was proved as follows: "Propaganda is an attempt to prepare a mood preliminary to preparing a revolt in the future." All of this happened in our enlightened twentieth century.

In today's Scripture, Paul reminds Timothy of Jesus Christ "who bearing witness made his noble profession before Pontius Pilate." There was a mock trial and a death sentence. And over the centuries history repeats itself. Paul encourages his co-worker to be faithful to his baptismal vows, when "in the presence of many witnesses" he made his noble profession of faith.

We renew our profession of faith every year at Easter and as often as we are godparents at a baptism. We also do so every Sunday. Make it meaningful! Your baptismal vows qualify your freedom. Do you stand up for what you believe to be right?

SCRIPTURE READING —

Man of God that you are, flee from all this. Instead, seek after integrity, piety, faith, love, steadfastness and a gentle spirit. Fight the good fight of faith. Take firm hold on the everlasting life to which you were called when, in the presence of many witnesses, you made your noble profession of faith. Before God, who gives life to all, and before Christ Jesus, who in bearing witness made his noble profession before Pontius Pilate, I charge you to keep God's command without blame or reproach until our Lord Jesus Christ shall appear. This appearance God will bring to pass at his chosen time. (1 Timothy 6:11-15)

"Stir into flame the gift of God"

FROM the burning bush in Moses' desert experience (Exodus 3: 1-3) to the perpetual flame on J. F. Kennedy's graveside, the flame of fire is perhaps the most widely used metaphor to describe the mystery of the love/faith commitment, dedication, and similar aspirations. The flame of the Olympic games is simultaneously ancient and modern. The fiery flames of Pentecost and the Sacred Heart in homes and churches tell about God's unquenchable love for human beings. St. John of the Cross wrote a touching poem, *The Living Flame of Love,* with an extensive commentary at the request of Dona Ana de Penalosa *(see November 26),* and at Christmas, the feast of God's love made man, we have candlelight on the dinner table and sit around the open fireplace, if possible, rather than letting the heating system do its job.

Paul, himself in jail, reminds Timothy of his ordination to the ministry. There are dark days of persecution ahead. Leadership in such a situation requires courage and faith. "Stir into flame the gift of God bestowed when my hands were laid on you." Whether ordained to the ministerial priesthood, consecrated by taking vows, religious or marital, or just committed to God by the vows of baptism, we should stir into flame the gift of God.

Since it is more than a few years that I have inhabited the earth, I find myself quite often wrestling not only with time but also with energy. I wonder sometimes! When I don't have the stamina to work, am I really running out of steam or is my dedication (love/faith) just a smoldering wick that should be stirred into flame? Isaiah (42:3) tells me that the Messiah, for me the Lord Jesus, will not quench that smoldering wick of mine, but it is not very valuable either! Possibly I should pray oftener: "Come, Holy Spirit, kindle in me the fire of your love!" and then keep going with the help of the Holy Spirit who dwells in me.

SCRIPTURE READING —

I remind you to stir into flame the gift of God bestowed when my hands were laid on you. The Spirit God has given us is no cowardly spirit, but rather one that makes us strong, loving, and wise. Therefore, never be ashamed of your testimony to our Lord, nor of me, a prisoner for his sake; but with the strength which comes from God bear your share of the hardship which the gospel entails. (2 Timothy 1:6-8)

"But there is no chaining the word of God"

A COLLEAGUE, pastor in one of the most dilapidated areas of a big city, loves to work in the streets. He has programs going for youngsters who have been in and out of jail, who are addicted to dope, alcohol, or other vices. But in doing so with remarkable dedication, he does not see tangible results. He wants the poor to join the Church; but, seemingly, they are more interested in hamburgers and popcorn than in the bread of life, which he serves in church.

At a clergy meeting this churchman said that he found it difficult to talk about God in the street. He had put two dozen modern catechisms on the table. None of them appealed sufficiently. Would a new catechism for the poor be the solution? Among all those catechisms, however, I missed one about which all should agree. I did not see the Bible on the table. But does the Bible have all the answers. I think it does. Not explicitly, of course, but basically everything that the poor should know is in it. Perhaps we make Catholicism too complicated. The audience of the man of Galilee was so simple, so poor, and often so human, the woman caught in adultery included. Do we want these kinds of people in church? Yes, since the Lord wants them. "There is no chaining the word of God."

Driving home, I thought this over in the car. It is wonderful to have a church full of faithful on Sunday. But our Lord talked about God in the street, spoke with the woman at the well of Jacob, blessed screaming babies, discussed the kingdom with Nicodemus alone, and told Mary Magdalene to try to keep her needs under control. Paul suffered like a criminal but went on preaching. The results were not always very tangible *(see November 5)*. Can all of us who are concerned about the good news preached to the poor follow these great men in faith?

SCRIPTURE READING —

Remember that Jesus Christ, a descendant of David, was raised from the dead. This is the gospel I preach; in preaching it I suffer as a criminal, even to the point of being thrown into chains—but there is no chaining the word of God! Therefore I bear with all of this for the sake of those whom God has chosen, in order that they may obtain the salvation to be found in Christ Jesus and with it eternal glory.

(2 Timothy 2:8-10)

"In fact, everyone abandoned me"

FATHER Mike was a fine young priest, handsome, charming, dedicated to God and fellow human beings, serving with all the ardor that only prime love can bring forth. His favorite apostolate was the CYO (Catholic Youth Organization). He loved the youngsters, inspired them to pursue values in which he believed, and was loved by them. But one day I talked with an entirely different Father Mike. He was down in the dumps. Imagine what had happened. A young fellow he had spent so much time with, whom he had tutored and dragged through his high school finals, had married in a Protestant church. It seemed that Father Mike's world had collapsed.

This kind of disappointment is human. Paul was in jail, and where were the people to whom he had dedicated his life? But Paul knew how to handle this kind of situation. Priests, sisters, and all who dedicate time and energy to the apostolate may feel like Father Mike, when success fails to come around. It is so human to expect visible results from our efforts. Time and culture compel us to do so. Planning, calculation, budgeting, and reports show that the results are part and parcel of our corporate society.

As a pastor, I have to send the annual "Status animarum" ("State of souls") to the bishop. "U.S. Catholic Church, Inc." needs this information for the next edition of *The Official Catholic Directory*. How many converts, how many mixed and Catholic marriages? I don't deny the usefulness of statistics. Those in charge of the Institution must have something to go by. And I agree that lack of tangible success should not be a pretense for taking it easy! But we who work in the direct apostolate should keep our desire for visible success in its right perspective. When depressed, meditate on today's Scripture! *(See also November 5 and 10.)*

SCRIPTURE READING —

At the first hearing of my case in court, no one took my part. In fact, everyone abandoned me. May it not be held against them! But the Lord stood by my side and gave me strength, so that through me the preaching task might be completed and all the nations might hear the gospel. That is how I was saved from the lion's jaws. The Lord will continue to rescue me from all attempts to do me harm and will bring me safe to his heavenly kingdom. To him be glory forever and ever. Amen.

(2 Timothy 4:16-18)

"Our God may make you worthy of his call"

IN STUDYING Church history in the seminary, we had to analyze the many heresies that plagued God's people over the centuries. What always struck me was that heretics were usually very dedicated and concerned people, and secondly that they had a point. What then was wrong with them? I think that they were myopic. They focused all their attention on that one point, usually a few lines in the Bible, and were blind to all other Biblical statements which would have balanced their opinions.

Take the Pelagians (Pelagius was a British monk of the early fifth century), who conceived of human freedom as complete autonomy which by itself can and must observe the law of God. The Epistle of James could be their favorite book of the Bible. Of course, we are free, and the Bible states time and again that we are fully responsible for what we do and fail to do, and moreover that we should do a few things in order to be saved. What the Pelegians overlook is the necessity of God's grace.

Quietism (in German Lutheranism, pietism) takes another tack. It holds that perfection is selfless love of God in the sense of purely passive inwardness and resignation, from which all activity and all concern for one's own salvation has been eliminated. The Epistle to the Romans will be their favorite, as it was for Luther. Both extremes have a point, but the orthodox view is the balance of both.

In meditating on today's Scripture, you should keep this in mind. A friend of mine, formerly very involved in the civil rights movement and an enthusiastic doer of the good thing, is now an ardent charismatic and fervent reader of Romans. "Let him [God] do it," he told me recently. Of course, we human beings, burdened with concupiscence and sin, are fully dependent on God's grace. By our surrendering to it, the Lord Jesus must be glorified in us. No shadow of doubt! As children, we must hold the hand of the heavenly Father but walk ourselves!

SCRIPTURE READING —

We pray for you always that our God may make you worthy of his call, and fulfill by his power every honest intention and work of faith. In this way the name of our Lord Jesus may be glorified in you and you in him, in accord with the gracious gift of our God and of the Lord Jesus Christ. (2 Thessalonians 1:11-12)

November 13

"Eternal consolation and hope"

WHENEVER you have the opportunity to take a trip to Europe, don't take one that permits you to stay only half a day in Amsterdam so that you can tell your folks at home that you have seen The Netherlands. Stay a few days and visit the East Polder, and have the experience of riding at the bottom of the sea. The East Polder was reclaimed from the sea only twenty years ago. I drove through it in a little DKW German car. Looking at the vast wheat fields for miles and miles, I could not help musing.

My hometown was only a few miles from the seashore. As a young lad, I saw those fishermen who made their living on the Zuider Zee come to town on their carts drawn by dogs on Thursday peddling their fish from door to door. Though themselves stern Calvinists, they knew where to find the Catholics, who were supposed to eat fish on Friday. My mother used to buy from them. But how many found their graves on the tricky Zuider Zee!

In the Polder museum I saw the most remarkable articrafts found in the mud: aircrafts of World War II and remnants of boats that had perished as far back as the time of the Romans. But when in ancient times fishermen were caught by a storm, they had a beacon to go by, a sign of hope, "The Tower of our Lady" (300 feet) in my hometown Amersfoort. When all were still Catholics, they came to town to thank our Lady. They marched in procession to the shrine, singing *O Star of the Sea*. Religion was a living thing in those days, and my home town had its own miraculous statue of Mary.

One of the beautiful elements in the Christian faith is *hope*. Appreciate it and keep it alive by prayerful meditation. Persevering in hope against hope in spite of being tossed on the waves of the human condition is good Christian wisdom of life.

SCRIPTURE READING —

May our Lord Jesus Christ himself, may God our Father who loved us and in his mercy gave us eternal consolation and hope, console your hearts and strengthen them for every good work and word.

For the rest, brothers, pray for us that the word of the Lord may make progress and be hailed by many others, even as it has been by you. Pray that we may be delivered from confused and evil men.

(2 Thessalonians 2:16—3:1-2, 5)

"Anyone who [will] not work should not eat"

SINCE I spent the first thirty years of my life in Western Europe, and have been back occasionally, I have had the opportunity to visit quite a few medieval monasteries, as they are still in operation in the Old Country. The ancient saying *"Ora et Labora"* ("Pray and Work") originated behind those walls that shelter a very particular world in itself. Indeed those monks pray! Some start already at the time when quite a few urbanites go to bed. I have participated in those prayers, called the *Divine Office,* but seldom in their entirety, since I am an impatient man. The foreign missions, in far-away countries, have excited my young imagination more than the sheltered life in a monastery.

Another occupation of monks is working in the fields. They keep a careful balance: Prayer and work! On visits, it was usually Father Abbot or a guest Father who explained that way of life to us priests or seminarians. Most of the time, however, I got the impression that the monks labored in the fields, indeed, but Father Abbot kept vigil in his well-furnished office. This is all right, of course. Somebody must take care of the administration, do the counseling, and some more mental work. I was so much the more impressed, therefore, when on a recent visit to a famous abbey in Belgium I was told that a particular Abbot of eighty monks goes daily with them to the fields, and was digging potatoes at the very moment of my visit.

In today's Scripture, we see that Paul had a few problems with his recent converts. Believeing that the "Day of the Lord" was impending, they had stopped working. If everything would soon be over, why should they exert themselves? We know that at the moment you least expect it the end may be there. The Father Abbot in Belgium lives with this knowledge very consciously, but he digs potatoes! Both prayer (meditation) and work should be well balanced parts of our lives.

SCRIPTURE READING —

You know how you ought to imitate us. We did not live lives of disorder when we were among you, nor depend on anyone for food. Rather, we worked day and night, laboring to the point of exhaustion so as not to impose on any of you. Not that we had no claim on you, but that we might present ourselves as an example for you to imitate. Indeed, when we were with you we used to lay down the rule that anyone who would not work should not eat. (2 Thessalonians 3:7-10)

"Realize that you were delivered from the futile way of life your fathers handed on to you"

THE bicentennial celebrations have heightened our awareness of what July 4, Independence Day, means to us. Celebrations are intended to heighten awareness and inculcate feelings of appreciation that result therefrom. More than ever we appreciate the freedoms which we possess under the Constitution, and more than ever we are determined to protect and safeguard them.

Passover is Jewish Independence Day. Jews attribute their freedom from bondage in Egypt and all evil expressly to Almighty God. Until the destruction of the Jewish temple in Jerusalem (70 A.D.), the celebration consisted of the Passover sacrifice (offering God a lamb as a symbol of appreciation) and a sacrificial repast (symbolizing communion with both God and fellow worshipers).

In meditating on our Lord's death on the cross, the early Church saw Jesus as a Jewish high priest offering the Passover sacrifice to God. This sacrifice, however, was not a lamb; it was his own body and blood, shed to set us free from the bondage of evil. Following this trend of thought, we understand Paul when he says: "Christ, our Passover, has been sacrificed" (1 Corinthians 5:7). Easter is Christian Independence Day. It is the memorial of our redemption from the bondage of evil. The celebration consists of the Eucharist, which is a Christianized passover sacrifice and meal. Christ is both the passover lamb, offered in sacrifice to God, and sacrificial repast.

We keep in mind, however, that freedom now is only partial. We are still on our "sojourn in a strange land." Complete freedom is given when we enter our home country, heaven. The celebration of the Eucharist at Easter and every Sunday should heighten our awareness of freedom and lead to an ever growing appreciation.

SCRIPTURE READING—

In prayer you call upon a Father who judges each one justly on the basis of his actions. Since this is so, conduct yourselves reverently during your sojourn in a strange land. Realize that you were delivered from the futile way of life your fathers handed on to you, not by any diminishable sum of silver or gold, but by Christ's blood beyond all price: the blood of a spotless, unblemished lamb chosen before the world's foundation and revealed for your sake in these last days.

(1 Peter 1:17-20)

"If you put up with suffering for doing what is right . . ."

DURING World War II, when a bomb was dropped on our college, there were screaming, dust, confusion, and wounded people *(see also February 17)*. We were about sixty people worshiping in our little chapel that Sunday morning in November. Wet snow was drizzling down, and I had just preached on Matthew 24, the calamities of the last days. We lived only ten miles from the river Rhine, where the two mightiest armies of the world were confronting each other. People were evacuating, away from the battle line, pushing old carts and bicycles through the snow. "Pray that you will not have to flee in winter" (Matthew 24:20).

What puzzled me most was why only Jan van Leeuwen's wife, a mother of eight children, had to die, and no others. A school brother was seriously wounded but survived. I myself was badly bruised but could walk again after a week. Yet Mrs. van Leeuwen died, lying on the floor, when I gave her the Anointing of the Sick. Why she? Van Leeuwen was such a hard-working man, operating his little dairy farm and selling the milk in the neighboring town. His wife and sons helped him. He needed his wife, and the children needed a mother. It is the ancient tantalizing mystery of suffering.

The author of today's Scripture sheds some light on the mystery of human suffering. We Christians don't have all the answers, but at least we have a ray of light which should guide us through the dark valley of the human condition at times so full of misery and pain. That Sunday morning in November, I held Jan van Leeuwen's hand. I could not suppress my tears. We prayed, but without words.

SCRIPTURE READING —

If you do wrong and get beaten for it, what credit can you claim? But if you put up with suffering for doing what is right, this is acceptable in God's eyes. It was for this you were called, since Christ suffered for you in just this way and left you an example, to have you follow in his footsteps.

He did no wrong; no deceit was found in his mouth. When he was insulted, he returned no insult. When he was made to suffer, he did not counter with threats. Instead, he delivered himself up to the One who judges justly. In his own body he brought your sins to the cross, so that all of us, dead to sin, could live in accord with God's will. By his wounds you were healed. (1 Peter 2:20-24)

"You, however, are a chosen race, a royal priesthood"

AS A pastor, I have to be concerned about the broken homes in my parish. Usually the children follow the mother, who must try to give them an education as best she can under the circumstances. Thinking of the many tragic situations I have encounted over the years, I am amazed at what a strong woman is able to do. A strong mother, who combines the sternness of a father with her own female tenderness, can keep a family together. I admire these women for their wisdom, patience, tender care, and firm determination to do alone a job which God has designed to be done by both father and mother. Indeed, children are kept together as a family more by a person whom they can love and admire than by rules and regulations.

God's family, that "chosen race, a people he claims for his own," follows this same rule of nature. Church law, preached with the threat of eternal damnation if not observed, does not keep God's children together. As today's Scripture brings out with the metaphor of the cornerstone, it is the person of our Lord who keeps together "the living stones, built as an edifice of spirit." (Notice that homes were built with roughly chapped chalk stones, and that a cornerstone kept two walls together.)

What does Christ mean to you, your congregation, your religious community? Is he, as far as you are concerned, a living reality, a strong image, that helps you overcome human antagonisms which are found wherever people try to build community?

SCRIPTURE READING —

Come to him, a living stone, rejected by men but approved, nonetheless, and precious in God's eyes. You too are living stones, built as an edifice of spirit, into a holy priesthood, offering spiritual sacrifices acceptable to God through Jesus Christ. For Scripture has it:

"See, I am laying a cornerstone in Zion,
an approved stone, and precious.
He who puts his faith in it shall not be shaken."

You, however are a chosen race, a royal priesthood, a holy nation, a people he claims for his own to proclaim the glorious works" of the One who called you from darkness into his marvelous light.

(1 Peter 2:4-6, 9)

"Rejoice . . . in the measure that you share Christ's sufferings"

WHEN I read about the enthusiasm of those early Christians, their outbursts of joy at moments in life when I would be depressed and asking: "Why me?" I think nostalgically of Schiller's lines: "O that the beautiful time of young and tender love would last forever!" The apostles were arrested and whipped, but they left the courthouse "full of joy that they had been judged worthy of ill-treatment for the sake of the name [Jesus]" (Acts 5:41). The Acts of the Apostles is full of this kind of testimony; it describes, as it were, the honeymoon of the Church with the Bridegroom, the Lord Jesus.

The author of today's Scripture exhorts God's people to keep that first love alive: "Rejoice . . . in the measure that you share Christ's sufferings." Why is it that love grows stale so easily? "Marriage Encounters" are organized to do something about it. Thousands of marriages break up every year in this country, and people drift away from the Churches. Their main reason seems to be lack of further interest.

The Churches attempt to kindle interest by revivals, missions, and programs of renewal. I still remember the time when the heavy accent of mission sermons was on that eternal hell fire where the devil was waiting to barbecue me. There was little talk about love. Perhaps that is why those missions did not result in a renewal of enthusiasm akin to the spontaneous excitement of the early Church. "Happy are you when you are insulted for the sake of Christ." The charismatic movement seems to stir up some of that ancient enthusiasm, though the test of "insult and suffering" must prove whether or not it is lasting and genuine. We are all different. Pray that the Spirit may help you keep your first love alive!

SCRIPTURE READING —

Rejoice, instead, in the measure that you share Christ's sufferings. When his glory is revealed, you will rejoice exultantly. Happy are you when you are insulted for the sake of Christ, for then God's Spirit in its glory has come to rest on you. See to it that none of you suffers for being a murderer, a thief, a malefactor, or a destroyer of another's rights. If anyone suffers for being a Christian, however, he ought not to be ashamed. He should rather glorify God in virtue of that name.

(1 Peter 4:13-16)

"There is nothing to fear"

AT THE moment of writing these lines, a friend of mine (in her early seventies) knows that soon she will die of cancer. She has been taking chemical therapy for quite a while, but she feels that she is fighting a losing battle. Her congregation—she is a Methodist—is very considerate. Daily, they send her a warm meal, since she is living alone and it gets increasingly difficult to cook for herself. Recently, she told me: "Father Kersten, I don't fear. I know that I was destined to die ever since I was born."

In reading today's Scripture, I thought of her words. "He touched me with his right hand and said: 'There is nothing to fear.' " Apocalyptic literature (the books of Revelation and Daniel, as well as parts of the Gospels) does not make for easy reading. The writers use very esoteric literary forms, and special pains are needed to uncover the true meaning underlying it. It is a sort of underground literature which the author uses to console and encourage his fellow faithful suffering persecution because of their religious convictions. He speaks in symbols, and utilizes allusions which are known to the insider but not understandable to the persecutor.

We must try to hear "God's word" also in this kind of "man's word." In it God wants to give hope for a brighter future to believers of all ages. In your situation, think of the message: "There is nothing to fear."

SCRIPTURE READING—

I, John, your brother, who share with you the distress and the kingly reign and the endurance we have in Jesus, found myself on the island called Patmos because I proclaimed God's word and bore witness to Jesus. On the Lord's day I was caught up in ecstasy, and I heard behind me a piercing voice like the sound of a trumpet, which said, "Write on a scroll what you now see and send it to the seven churches: to Ephesus, Smyrna, Pergamum, Thyatira, Sardis, Philadelphia, and Laodicea." I turned around to see whose voice it was that spoke to me. When I did so I saw seven lampstands of gold, and among the lampstands One like a Son of Man wearing an ankle-length robe, with a sash of gold about his breast.

When I caught sight of him I fell down at his feet as though dead. He touched me with his right hand and said: "There is nothing to fear. I am the First and the Last and the One who lives. Once I was dead but now I live—forever and ever. I hold the keys of death and the nether world. Write down, therefore, whatever you see in visions—what you see now and will see in time to come." (Revelation 1:9-13, 17-19)

"Worthy is the Lamb that was slain"

ABOUT Saints I read somewhere the following definition: "The Saint is like a window through which another world is glimpsed, a person through whom the light of God shines." That is why I, common earthling and not a Saint, try to look at them when I am depressed and things don't go my way. For years, I have had a little bottle of tranquilizers in my medicine cabinet, next to my tube of toothpaste. A few years ago a doctor prescribed them because I was tense, depressed, and could not sleep. However, I have never had to use that bottle. I have found that at least in my case there are other means for handling depression.

I walk, listen to music, visit the poor, who are less fortunate than I am, and do my meditation (see Preface!). I can't cross my legs like an Indian guru, but my blending of the Eastern and Western way of meditating results in calming me down and bringing peace of mind. And as for Saints, I think of my mother. I was not older than four when she received a telegram that her mother had died. She cried, and in the living room she knelt down and prayed. Spontaneously I did the same; I did not pray but cried also. I don't know why. My mother could handle her problems!

Whether or not the author of this Scripture had a disclosure experience of a transcendent reality is not clear. What is important is that he consoles Christians with our common faith that the Lord Jesus is alive and exalted with God. Be consoled! Whatever your problems are, the Lord Jesus is alive and powerful. Turn to him in faithful meditation!

SCRIPTURE READING —

As my vision continued, I heard the voices of many angels who surrounded the throne and the living creatures and the elders. They were countless in number, thousands and tens of thousands, and they all cried out:

"Worthy is the Lamb that was slain
to receive power and riches, wisdom and strength,
honor and glory and praise!"

Then I heard the voices of every creature in heaven and on earth and under the earth and in the sea; everything in the universe cried aloud:

"To the One seated on the throne and to the Lamb,
be praise and honor, glory and might,
forever and ever!" (Revelation 5:11-13)

277-8

"For the glory of God gave it light"

WHEN I get up after a good night's sleep, there is continuity between the tired man who went to bed and the man who woke up. But there is also renewal. When I come back from my annual retreat, I experience that same phenomenon of continuity and renewal. And when I study Church history, I see that same happening: decay and rebirth. Sometimes a great Saint brings the rebirth about (St. Francis of Assisi and his movement!); quite often it is a Church Council (Trent, Vatican II). Rebirth (renewal) entails birthpangs. In the post-Vatican II Church we are right in the middle of them.

Utilizing the language of vision, in today's reading the writer describes the splendor of the Church, seeing the earthly and the heavenly Church in one perspective. The language is highly symbolic. The Church has a particular brilliance, which is the Divine indwelling. In New Testament thinking, the Church is the "Israel of God," succeeding the "Israel of the flesh." Thus the author shows that the Church is a renewed Israel by referring to her as "Jerusalem," founded on "the twelve apostles of the Lamb," who succeeded the twelve patriarchs of the Israel of old. In so doing the writer clearly indicates that there is *continuity* between the old Israel and the Church as well as a distinct aspect of *renewal.*

Hence, in order to be faithful to its mission in the world the Church should renew itself constantly. And under the guidance of the Spirit, we should be part of that same ongoing process of continuity and renewal until we are the heavenly Church!

SCRIPTURE READING —

He carried me away in spirit to the top of a very high mountain and showed me the holy city Jerusalem coming down out of heaven from God. It gleamed with the splendor of God. The city had the radiance of a precious jewel that sparkled like a diamond. Its wall, massive and high, had twelve gates at which twelve angels were stationed. Twelve names were written on the gates, the names of the twelve tribes of Israel. There were three gates facing east, three north, three south, and three west. The wall of the city had twelve courses of stones as its foundation, on which were written the names of the twelve apostles of the Lamb.

I saw no temple in the city. The Lord, God the Almighty, is its temple—he and the Lamb. The city had no need of sun or moon, for the glory of God gave it light, and its lamp was the Lamb.

(Revelation 21:10-14, 22-23)

"I will judge every one of you according to his ways"

ON THE plane, I was sitting next to a man who was reading a book on double justice in America (I have forgotten the exact title). I was reading a theological magazine and was not wearing my Roman collar. Apparently, both of us were inquisitive. I glanced at his book and was curious, and I sensed that he felt the same in regard to my reading. Finally, he broke the silence: "Are you a preacher?" "Yes. I am a Catholic priest." This was quickly followed by my question: "Are you a lawyer?" "Yes, I am." He went on to start a conversation about double justice from his own experience as a lawyer who tried to help the poor, as he told me.

Indeed, the rich can afford to hire the best lawyers available which the poor can't—leading to the consequences familiar to all of us. A friend of mine, for example, who is wealthy and influential in his community, worried about his son who was caught with other fellows hunting on posted ground. The sheriff had told him over the phone: "If he were not a Jones [fictitious name] he would be in jail right now."

Ezekiel describes God as a judge. However, he is different from the judges we encounter. He has no favorites but combines determination to punish evil with infinite mercy. We should approach the mystery of God with *all* the metaphors used in the Bible. God is judge but also father. He is just but also merciful. We should try to be like God whenever we express an opinion about others. And we should repent in order that God can treat us mercifully.

SCRIPTURE READING—

And though I say to the wicked man that he shall surely die, if he turns away from his sin and does what is right and just, giving back pledges, restoring stolen goods, living by the statutes that bring life, and doing no wrong, he shall surely live, he shall not die. None of the sins he committed shall be held against him; he has done what is right and just, he shall surely live.

Yet your countrymen say, "The way of the Lord is not fair!"; but it is their way that is not fair. When a virtuous man turns away from what is right and does wrong, he shall die for it. But when a wicked man turns away from wickedness and does what is right and just, because of this he shall live. And still you say, "The way of the Lord is not fair!"? I will judge every one of you according to his ways, O house of Israel.

(Ezekiel 33:14-20)

"The worldly take more initiative than the other-worldly."

ON THE plane that was flying me from Djakarta to Amsterdam, I was sitting next to a Javanese. He was very well educated and told me in perfect Dutch that he was on his way to Moscow. I asked him curiously: "What in the world are you going to do there?" His reply: "I've got a job with the Russian government to teach the Indonesian language to future Russian diplomats."

As I found out, the Russian embassy in Djakarta was staffed with 120 Russians, all of them knowing Indonesian, which was certainly not the case with the employees of other foreign embassies. "The worldly take more initiative than the other-worldly." What time, energy, and money they invest to spread the ideals of atheistic Communism and make other countries share in what they consider a perfect society!

We believe in the kingdom of God, the reign of justice, love, and concern, which our Lord came to establish on earth. We Christians are supposed to be goodwill ambassadors of that kingdom. How much dedication do we invest to establish it in our own direct environment? Could we learn a few things from the wily manager of today's Scripture and the Communists?

SCRIPTURE READING —

[Jesus] said to his disciples: "A rich man had a manager who was reported to him for dissipating his property. He summoned him and said, 'What is this I hear about you? Give me an account of your service, for it is about to come to an end.' The manager thought to himself, 'What shall I do next? My employer is sure to dismiss me. I cannot dig ditches. I am ashamed to go begging. I have it! Here is a way to make sure that people will take me into their homes when I am let go.'

"So he called in each of his master's debtors, and said to the first, 'How much do you owe my master?' The man replied, 'A hundred jars of oil.' The manager said, 'Take your invoice, sit down quickly, and make it fifty.' Then he said to a second, 'How much do you owe?' The answer came, 'A hundred measures of wheat,' and the manager said, 'Take your invoice and make it eighty.'

"The owner then gave his devious employee credit for being enterprising! Why? Because the worldly take more initiative than the other-worldly when it comes to dealing with their own kind."

(Luke 16:1-8)

"To bear witness . . ."

AS A little boy, long before electronic music had invaded our homes, I loved to watch the street corner concerts of the Salvation Army. I was impressed by the navy blue uniforms the men were wearing, and I found the bonnets of the ladies, kept in place by red ribbons tied under chins, so unusual. Why tie them when there was no wind blowing? I admired the huge tubas. How could those men carry them and, even more, blow them? It must have been a hard job. I still see the little swollen blood vessels on the temples of one of the tuba blowers. I thought that they would explode at any moment.

But what I remember best is Sister so and so, usually a converted prostitute (as I realized later!), telling about her experience of finding Jesus as her personal Savior. I had only vague ideas of the terrible sins of the flesh which she had committed, but I thought that it was great to admit to being a sinner right there on the sidewalk, whereas we Catholic boys told Father about our bad thoughts only in the privacy of the confessional.

Witnessing, however, is part and parcel of Christianity. I wonder whether we Catholics are witnessing enough. The Acts of the Apostles is one ongoing report on Christian witness. "He commissioned us . . . to bear witness." Comparing the Church with those early congregations in Acts, I fear that all of us are getting middle-aged or even old. Isn't it true that those groups which walk out of the established Churches often show more enthusiasm, zeal, and courage to witness than do we somewhat spoiled children of the rich heavenly Father? Wherever I go, both word and behavior should witness to the fact that I am a Christian.

SCRIPTURE READING —

We are witnesses to all that he did in the land of the Jews and in Jerusalem. They killed him, finally, hanging him on a tree, only to have God raise him up on the third day and grant that he be seen, not by all, but only by such witnesses as had been chosen beforehand by God— by us who ate and drank with him after he rose from the dead. He commissioned us to preach to the people and to bear witness that he is the one set apart by God as judge of the living and the dead. To him all the prophets testify, saying that everyone who believes in him has forgiveness of sins through his name. (Acts 10:39-43)

"Whenever you pray, go to your room, close your door. . . ."

CHURCHES should be designed and built not just as functional meeting halls, but in such a way that the architecture inspires the faithful to prayer and worship. I think of the beautiful Cathedral of Chartres, France, with its precious blue glass windows, its pointed arches and vaulting, as well as many an artful modern church in my own environment—all designed to lift up the spirit and to invite to prayer.

We believe that through the visible architecture, paintings, and sculptures the mind is lifted up to the transcendental. That is why we have our pictures (Byzantine churches have their icon wall! *See October 10)*, crucifixes, and statues of the Sacred Heart and the Saints. And our Protestant brethren, who did away with all of the visible to concentrate on the Bible word alone, admit that they have made mistakes *(see October 7)*. We should use these means for both communal and private prayer.

However, St. John of the Cross, a grandmaster in mental prayer, gives the following advice: "To direct the spirit to God, we should keep in mind that for beginners it is permissible and even fitting to find some sensible gratification and satisfaction in the use of images, oratories, and other visible objects of devotion. But in order to advance, the spiritual person should divest himself of all these satisfactions and appetites, for the pure spirit is bound to none of these objects, but turns only to interior recollection and mental communion with God. One should choose that place which least hinders the elevation of sense and spirit to God" *(The Ascent of Mount Carmel)*. "[Jesus] often retired to deserted places and prayed" (Luke 5:16). With this in mind, read today's Scripture meditatively!

SCRIPTURE READING —

[Jesus said:] "When you are praying, do not behave like the hypocrites who love to stand and pray in synagogues or on street corners in order to be noticed. I give you my word, they are already repaid. Whenever you pray, go to your room, close your door, and pray to your Father in private. Then your Father, who sees what no man sees, will repay you. In your prayer do not rattle on like the pagans. They think they will win a hearing by the sheer multiplication of words. Do not imitate them. Your Father knows what you need before you ask him."

(Matthew 6:5-8)

ADVENT

IN THIS land of the free, we know about captivity only from television. POWs could tell us what it means to wait for freedom. Missionaries, nuns and priests, jailed and then expelled from some dictator-run country in Latin America or Africa, could tell as well what it means to wait for someone to come and say: "You are free."

Captivity for the sake of God's kingdom, be it social justice or civil rights, is a frequently used model to explain the human condition as such, which is in need of redemption. Collectively we wait for someone to come, a savior to save us from ourselves and the boredom of a meaningless existence.

Jesus Christ is the Savior and we wait for his coming ever more. Coming results in presence. Ever more coming results in an ever more intimate presence. Awareness in faith of being in need of redemption is a must for meaningful celebration of Advent (coming) and Christmas.

With Christians of all ages we pray: "O Radiant Dawn, come, shine on those who dwell in darkness and the shadow of death" (Liturgy of the Hours for Dec. 21). And Jesus says: "Yes, I am coming soon." (See Revelation 22:16-20.)

Come, Lord Jesus.

November 26

"Let me see you, let me hear your voice"

A FRIEND wrote me: "As far as I know, I have never loved God really. And without that affectionate love 'believing in God' becomes a sterile affair, and that may be the reason that I have lost my faith." These are painful words, especially when they are written by a very dear friend who is so honest that he cannot possibly pretend to be the person he is not. Our relationship with God must be one of affectionate love—an I-Thou relationship, an I really in love with the Divine Thou! The great mystics in the Catholic tradition have expressed it in words like:

"O living flame of love
That tenderly wounds my soul
In its deepest center! Since
Now you are not oppressive,
Now consummate! if it be your will:
Tear through the veil of this sweet encounter!"

(St. John of the Cross, *The Living Flame of Love*)

The author has written a beautiful commentary on this stanza: "The soul feels that she is all inflamed in the divine union. [*See October 21* for "soul."] God's love wounds and stirs you so deeply as to make you dissolve in love. . . . Consummate the spiritual marriage with me perfectly by means of the beatific vision . . . tear the veil of the sensitive life and let me come to this 'sweet encounter' with you."

The Song of Songs is a love song in which young shepherds praise each other's beauty. Both the Jewish and the Christian traditions give this song a religious interpretation. Read this passage as such meditatively and respond in love as St. John of the Cross does.

SCRIPTURE READING—

My lover speaks; he says to me,
"Arise, my beloved, my beautiful one,
and come!

"For see, the winter is past,
the rains are over and gone.
The flowers appear on the earth,
the time of pruning the vines has come,
and the song of the dove is heard in our land.

"O my dove in the clefts of the rock,
in the secret recesses of the cliff,
Let me see you,
let me hear your voice,
For your voice is sweet,
and you are lovely."

(Song of Songs 2:10-12, 14)

"So strip away everything vicious, everything deceitful"

IN A didactic poem, *The Stranger within Ourself* (found in *The Birthday of the World*, p. 33), Moshe Davis and Victor Ratner ask:

Have you ever found yourself
fighting someone whom you love?
We do not often think of it as prejudice
when we fight with those we love.
Yet it almost always is.
It is prejudice to deny those
who are closest to us
their right to be different.

Then the authors refer to a wife who insists that her husband live up to her family's ways rather than his own; a father who tries to force his son into a career of his (the father's) choosing; a teacher who tries to press a student into his mold rather than to encourage him to discover his best potential.

If we demand that he live up to our image
of what he should be, rather than the best in himself,
we then bring him prejudice instead of love.

The Bible stresses the great command of love time and time again. Peter addresses recent converts. We derive our rebirth as Christians from Christ, the indestructible seed which effects a new and lasting existence in us. As new creatures, clothed with Christ, we cannot but be guided and motivated by love. But there are hidden sins against love. The authors of the above poem expose some of them. Check your own relations with your loved ones—your partner in marriage, your children/parents, your fellow religious, students, parishioners—and meditate prayerfully on God's word to you in Scripture.

SCRIPTURE READING —

By obedience to the truth you have purified yourselves for a genuine love of your brothers; therefore, love one another constantly from the heart. Your rebirth has come, not from a destructible but from an indestructible seed, through the living and enduring word of God.

So strip away everything vicious, everything deceitful; pretenses, jealousies, and disparaging remarks of any kind. Be as eager for milk as newborn babies—pure milk of the spirit to make you grow unto salvation, now that you have tasted that the Lord is good.

(1 Peter 1:22-23; 2:1-3)

"You must wash each other's feet"

A CHAINSTORE advertises in our newspaper: "Serving the area for more than thirty years," and making millions in the process, of course. From the service station, where I buy my gasoline, up to the Internal Revenue Service, all service is offered with strings attached. And when our public servants go abroad to offer aid to developing countries or the service of mediation in local conflicts, it is service for which we expect raw materials or political favors in return. In both the political and the business arena, it seems mandatory for service to be offered only "under certain conditions."

The service which the Lord Jesus wants Christians to offer one another is precisely a service with no strings attached. Christian service to God and fellow human beings is not the service of self-interest; it is the service of love. Perhaps we will not be as rude as the priest and the levite who passed by the poor man in the Parable of the Good Samaritan, obviously for no reason at all (Luke 10:30-32). But we are well inclined to find reasons for excuse: "The poor should learn to help themselves"; "Welfare programs make people lazy"; "He asked for it when he started taking dope." We are loath to admit collective guilt as to less privileged fellow human beings who suffer from lack of education, poor family background, and thousands of imponderables which we can judge (and condone!) only by close contact with their condition.

In this country of ours, there is no city which does not have a neighborhood where the poor have to flock together in substandard living conditions. What both economically and mentally poor people need is caring! Do you have contact with the poor and do you care?

SCRIPTURE READING —

After he had washed their feet, he put his cloak back on and reclined at table once more. He said to them:
"Do you understand what I just did for you?
You address me as 'Teacher' and 'Lord,'
and fittingly enough,
for that is what I am.
But if I washed your feet—
I who am Teacher and Lord—
then you must wash each other's feet.
What I just did was to give you an example:
as I have done, so you must do."

(John 13:12-15)

"I am not the one to condemn him"

ONCE a week, they gather together into his clinic, the wed and unwed welfare expectant mothers of the area. Many of them are very young. I can understand that it is irritating. A doctor has to listen to the same stories and treat the same old cases time and again. Furthermore, he finds little consolation in the remark by a priest-friend that the girls who come to his office at least don't go to the abortionist, and that he is the benefactor of as many babies as there are pregnant women, wed and unwed. Yet we Christians should try to understand.

In meditating on the Lord's preaching, the author of John offers a summary, the salient features of Jesus' discourses on belief, light, judgment, and life. By word and example Jesus came to offer light to those who live in darkness. But he does not condemn! The scribes and the Pharisees wanted him to condemn the woman who had been caught in adultery. (Read the story in John 8:1-11.) Jesus did not do so. Does this mean that the Lord condones evil? No! He told the woman: "From now on, avoid this sin" (John 8:11). In a similar vein, he spoke to the Samaritan woman whom he met at Jacob's well (John 4:17-18). Indeed, the Lord could hit hard as to social injustice, but then he always addressed groups of people (*the* rich, *the* Pharisees), not individuals, hence, condemning not the sinner but sin (e.g., see Luke 11:42). And that is exactly what a Christian should try to do.

A twofold meditation can be made on today's Scripture. Either, as a Christian, you identify with Jesus who states that he did not come to condemn the world but to save it, or you focus your attention on your own responsibility to accept the light.

SCRIPTURE READING —

Jesus proclaimed aloud:
"Whoever puts faith in me
believes not so much in me
as in him who sent me;
and whoever looks on me
is seeing him who sent me.
I have come to the world as its light,
to keep anyone who believes in me
from remaining in the dark.
If anyone hears my words and does not keep them,
I am not the one to condemn him,
for I did not come to condemn the world
but to save it." (John 12:44-47)

November 30

"Unless he is begotten from above"

THE Mennonites, named after Menno, a Dutch priest who left the Church and joined the Anabaptist (re-baptizer) movement, are plain people, shunning the newer conventions of dress, all jewelry, make-up and modern hairstyles for women. In my part of the country, the men wear beards and the ladies a black bonnet. They are kind people, though a little clannish. They believe that the more formal education people are exposed to, the greater the danger that they are going to fall for the temptation and want to conform to "the world" (all evil).

In today's Scripture, Nicodemus represents the imperfect faith of a sincere, cautious intellectual. Can intellectuals, highly trained in the best schools of the country, be sincere believers?

A highly educated couple will "love" one another differently from a couple without formal education. But in both cases, love can be equally sincere and tender. In the same way, a highly educated person is apt to ask more questions, and has perhaps more doubts (neither love nor faith is without occasional doubts!), but his faith can be as sincere and tender as that of a child! What about your faith? Pray for an increase of faith!

SCRIPTURE READING —

A certain Pharisee named Nicodemus, a member of the Jewish Sanhedrin, came to [Jesus] at night. "Rabbi," he said, "we know you are a teacher come from God, for no man can perform signs and wonders such as you perform unless God is with him." Jesus gave him this answer:

"I solemnly assure you.
no one can see the reign of God
unless he is begotten from above."

"How can a man be born again once he is old?" retorted Nicodemus. "Can he return to his mother's womb and be born over again?" Jesus replied:

"I solemnly assure you,
no one can enter into God's kingdom
without being begotten of water and Spirit.
Flesh begets flesh,
Spirit begets spirit.
Do not be surprised that I tell you
you must all be begotten from above." (John 3:1-7)

"You must be prepared"

THE word "Advent" (Coming) indicates how Christians view the four-week period preceding the Nativity of our Lord. It is a time of preparation for an ever more intimate coming of the Lord to you and all of us.

When I come to visit a friend, I am present to him. Coming results in presence. Of course, the Lord is already present to his people. Therefore, his coming at Christmas should result in a more intimate presence. People (friends, lovers) who get to know and love one another better are becoming more intimately, more personally, present to one another. It is a question of opening up and sharing one another's personality. Our preparation for Christ's coming should consist in an ever more opening up to him who wants to share our human condition in loving care.

By preparing for the Lord's coming time and again at Christmas, Christians prepare for his final coming, which will be decisive for you and all human beings. "Now we watch for the day hoping that the salvation promised us will be ours when Christ our Lord will come again in his glory" (Preface of Advent).

The coming of the Lord requires a decision. It is "either-or"! Matthew the evangelist is quite serious about this. It should be a decision of "conversion" to Jesus right now, as you are preparing for his coming at Christmas. Again, be watchful! The moment you least expect it could be the final coming of the Lord to you. Do not become so engrossed in the daily routine of life that you forget that the Day of the Son of Man may come at any time.

SCRIPTURE READING —

[Jesus said:] "The coming of the Son of Man will repeat what happened in Noah's time. In the days before the flood people were eating and drinking, marrying and being married, right up to the day Noah entered the ark. They were totally unconcerned until the flood came and destroyed them. So will it be at the coming of the Son of Man. Two men will be out in the field; one will be taken and one will be left. Two women will be grinding meal; one will be taken and one will be left. Stay awake, therefore! You cannot know the day your Lord is coming.

"Be sure of this: if the owner of the house knew when the thief was coming he would keep a watchful eye and not allow his house to be broken into. You must be prepared in the same way. The Son of Man is coming at the time you least expect." (Matthew 24:37-44)

December 2

"Nor shall they train for war again"

WITH God revealing himself in the Lord Jesus, we Christians believe that there is a future for man. Life is not an absurdity. Death is not "a transition from being into nothingness," as some contemporary "sages" allege. Life has meaning. In the confusion of daily life, the Lord Jesus comes to save us from apparent absurdity, from dangerous inertia and the numbness which the sedatives of modern life can bring about. The only prerequisite is that we be watchful and open up to him and his message found in the Scriptures. "When he [the Lord Jesus] comes may he find us watching in prayer, our hearts filled with wonder and praise" (Preface of Advent).

Inspired by God, the prophet Isaiah sees a bright future in the Messianic era—the time when God will appear in his Messiah, his anointed vicegerent on earth. The setting is Zion, the holy mountain of Jerusalem with the temple, God's dwelling place. "They shall beat their swords into plowshares . . . nor shall they ever train for war again." Wishful thinking? We Christians see Isaiah's vision fulfilled in Jesus, God's anointed one, the Christ. Therefore, "O house of Jacob [God's people], come, let us walk in the light of the Lord."

With God, present in Christ Jesus, we should keep working for this seemingly impossible dream. Start in your family, in your religious community, at your job, making them places of Shalom —peace.

SCRIPTURE READING—

Many peoples shall come and say:
say:
"Come, let us climb the Lord's mountain,
to the house of the God of Jacob,
That he may instruct us in his ways,
and we may walk in his paths."
For from Zion shall go forth instruction,
and the word of the Lord from Jerusalem.
He shall judge between the nations,
and impose terms on many peoples.
They shall beat their swords into plowshares
and their spears into pruning hooks;
One nation shall not raise the sword against another,
nor shall they train for war again.
O house of Jacob, come,
let us walk in the light of the Lord! (Isaiah 2:3-5)

December 3

"His winnowing-fan is in his hand"

CHRIST is the answer to the frightening questions of life. When the leaders of a nation are corrupt, its people usually suffer. The human family on this planet is afflicted with many maladies resulting from lack of leadership. The Hebrews of Isaiah's time (800 B.C.) yearned for a leader, an ideal king, who would be capable of restoring the nation and endowing it once again with the peace and prosperity of King David's time. Jesus Christ is the God-given Leader, who came to establish God's kingdom on earth, "a kingdom of truth and life, a kingdom of justice, love, and peace" (Preface of Christ the King).

Are you accepting Jesus Christ and the outlines he gives for a better society? We know that the ideal society as envisioned by Jesus will never be fully realized on this planet. Neither do we state that the Bible has all the answers. But society would be much better if all would heed the guiding principles of Jesus of Nazareth. Let us Christians give the example!

Preparing for the Lord's coming and fully accepting him may require a change in life-style. John the Baptizer speaks clear language not just to the Jews of his time but to all of us. You should not delay a decision. "His [Jesus Christ's] winnowing-fan is in his hand. He will clear his threshing floor." Make sure you do not end up with the chaff that will be burned up "in unquenchable fire."

SCRIPTURE READING —

When [John the Baptizer] saw that many of the Pharisees and Sadducees were stepping forward for this bath, he said to them: "You brood of vipers! Who told you to flee from the wrath to come? Give some evidence that you mean to reform. Do not pride yourselves on the claim, 'Abraham is our father.' I tell you, God can raise up children to Abraham from these very stones. Even now the ax is laid to the root of the tree. Every tree that is not fruitful will be cut down and thrown into the fire. I baptize you in water for the sake of reform, but the one who will follow me is more powerful than I. I am not even fit to carry his sandals. He it is who will baptize you in the Holy Spirit and fire. His winnowing-fan is in his hand. He will clear the threshing floor and gather his grain into the barn, but the chaff he will burn in unquenchable fire."

(Matthew 3:7-12)

"Say to those whose hearts are frightened: Be strong, fear not!"

TODAY'S Bible reading tells us again about a bright future, seemingly a utopia. "Joyful in hope" is a Christian's theme of life. Christian hope opposes despair, which often results in suicide or just "copping out." It opposes escaping from reality through the use of drugs, abuse of alcohol, or excessive addiction to the pleasures of modern life. Christian hope knows how to handle depression: You get on your knees, knowing that God loves you. What would you tell a friend who knows that he is a terminal cancer patient? A man without faith or hope might say: "Face it! We all have to, sooner or later!" What would you say? A Christian knows about "More to come. Stay tuned in!"

Today's beautiful poem is attributed to the so-called "Second Isaiah," a prophet who stayed with the Hebrews in the Babylonian exile. "Say to those whose hearts are frightened: Be strong, fear not!" Christians apply this vision to the future brought about by Jesus, the Messiah, God's Anointed One. "Then will the eyes of the blind be opened." This is our Christmas theme of joyful hope: Our Lord, who comes to be a light to the world. The lights of Christmas symbolize this idea.

How would this poem apply to your situation and what would be your prayerful response?

SCRIPTURE READING —

The desert and the parched land will exult;
the steppe will rejoice and bloom.
They will bloom with abundant flowers,
and rejoice with joyful song.
The glory of Lebanon will be given to them,
the splendor of Carmel and Sharon;
They will see the glory of the Lord,
the splendor of our God.
Strengthen the hands that are feeble,
make firm the knees that are weak,
Say to those whose hearts are frightened:
Be strong, fear not!
Here is your God,
he comes with vindication;
With divine recompense
he comes to save you.
Then will the eyes of the blind be opened,
the ears of the deaf be cleared;
Then will the lame leap like a stag,
then the tongue of the dumb will sing. (Isaiah 35:1-6)

"Do not let him come suddenly and catch you asleep"

WE CAN imagine the following embarrassing situation: A young baby sitter falling asleep or just stepping out for a short while, the children running all over the house, and the parents coming home from a party at midnight—a little bit earlier than anticipated! A soldier caught asleep on guard duty is court-martialed severely—and rightly so, for if the guards are sleeping, who can feel safe?

We Christians believe that "he [Jesus] will come again in glory to judge the living and the dead." According to the Bible, we are related to God in a sacred partnership (covenant). We are his co-workers in making this planet a better place to live for all. The moment you least expect it, the Lord may call you in. Hopefully, it is not going to be an embarrassing situation for you! "Be constantly on the watch" (Mark 13:33).

The meaning of the parable in today's reading is clear. Our Lord is "abroad." He ascended to heaven, but he will come back. Are we doing our job? Indeed, we are the "now" generation. The young want to enjoy everything they can right now. They are like high school dropouts who lack the energy to work first so as to enjoy a more beautiful life later! Grown-ups may get drowsy, drift away from God, as can happen to partners in marriage. God said to the Church of Ephesus: "I hold this against you: You have turned aside from your early love" (Revelation 2:4). "Be on guard! You do not know when the appointed time will come." Respond to God's word in reflective prayer!

SCRIPTURE READING —

[Jesus said:] "Be constantly on the watch! Stay awake! You do not know when the appointed time will come. It is like a man traveling abroad. He leaves home and places his servants in charge, each with his own task; and he orders the man at the gate to watch with a sharp eye. Look around you! You do not know when the master of the house is coming, whether at dusk, at midnight, when the cock crows, or at early dawn. Do not let him come suddenly and catch you asleep. What I say to you, I say to all: Be on guard!" (Mark 13:33-37)

"Give comfort to my people, says your God"

WAITING can be a tantalizing experience. Biding your time in a waiting room till the physician calls you in to hear the result of an X-ray of one of your beloved ones, you ask yourself questions: "Will it be a tumor? Is it malignant?" Waiting can take place with reference to the mail—a letter from a fiancée, for example, bearing good news or bad news! We had an unpleasant misunderstanding which culminated in an emotional outburst. On the way home we are waiting. How will it be straightened out?

In waiting, the question comes up as to how we will react to the outcome. Are we ready to accept all the consequences? What do we expect from life? Today's Bible reading sheds some light on our often dim and hopeless situations. It is God's light shining upon us in the waiting room of life! Read and listen prayerfully with a great faith.

In beautiful poetic language, the prophet tells the exiles in Babylon who were desperately waiting for freedom: "Have hope!" God will step in and lead you out of this hopeless situation back home! Notice God's tender love: "Like a shepherd he feeds his flock." What do we learn as God's word from this ancient piece of poetry? It could be: God cares! "Your guilt is expiated. Here comes with power the Lord God." Whatever your problems in life may be you can have a happy Christmas and celebrate "Emmanuel—God with us." Make Psalm 85:8 *your* prayer of today: "Lord, let us see your kindness and grant us your salvation."

SCRIPTURE READING —

Comfort, give comfort to my people,
says your God.
Speak tenderly to Jerusalem, and proclaim to her
that her service is at an end,
her guilt is expiated;
Indeed, she has received from the hand of the Lord
double for all her sins.
A voice cries out:
In the desert prepare the way of the Lord!
Make straight in the wasteland a highway for our God!
Every valley shall be filled in,
every mountain and hill shall be made low;
The rugged land shall be made a plain,
the rough country, a broad valley.
Then the glory of the Lord shall be revealed,
and all mankind shall see it together;
for the mouth of the Lord has spoken. (Isaiah 40:1-5)

"He has sent me . . . to heal the brokenhearted"

THE better the hostess has prepared for a party, scrutinizing all the details, checking the guest list and making sure that nobody has been overlooked, the more likely her party will be a success. The better we plan a vacation, the more guarantee we have that it will be a great one. It is a joy to prepare well for the visit of friends and to know that they have enjoyed it. Many people, however, want instant joy. They do not want to plan, to prepare, and sacrifice. Moreover, they do not have the insight or the faith that service to others can be a source of joy!

One of the great contributions of Christianity is that it has brought "joy to the world." This is even a well-known Christmas hymn! Today's Scripture reading deals with this joy. It is a joy which cannot be obtained overnight. It is a joy which is found in service. Christianity does not have the answer for all questions. But if you are yearning for real joy, happiness, and peace of mind, you should prayerfully go over today's reading.

The prophet describes his mission as service to his people. He announces glad tidings to the captives back from exile in Babylon. This poem greatly influenced our Lord's understanding of his mission of service. In describing his mission, he refers twice to it (Luke 4:16-22; Mark 11:2-6). God's word through this tradition could be that there is joy in service. The joy of service is not instant joy. It is a kind of happiness which must be obtained and safeguarded time and again with faith and patience.

SCRIPTURE READING —

The spirit of the Lord God is upon me,
because the Lord has anointed me;
He has sent me to bring glad tidings to the lowly,
to heal the brokenhearted,
To claim liberty to the captives
and release to the prisoners,
To announce a year of favor from the Lord
and a day of vindication by our God,
to comfort all who mourn;
To place on those who mourn in Zion
a diadem instead of ashes,
To give them oil of gladness in place of mourning,
a glorious mantle instead of a listless spirit.
They will be called oaks of justice,
planted by the Lord to show his glory. (Isaiah 61:1-3)

"I will put enmity between you and the woman"

A CHILD born and reared in an irreligious family of evildoers and thieves is seriously handicapped in becoming and remaining a good person. Similar to this is the human condition into which we are born. In the human race we experience a mysterious collectivity in evil which we cannot understand completely. Evil will always be obscure. And one thing is sure: it would require a special favor of God for us not to be infected by evil in and around us.

Adam ("Everyman") and Eve (the "Woman") have sinned and remain entangled in sin, since they do not show even the slightest sign of repentance. The man projects his guilt onto the woman, and the woman onto the serpent. The writer of Genesis, though a keen observer of the omnipresence of evil, believes in God's mercy! God must give a way out. "I will put enmity between you [the evil one] and the woman, and between your offspring and hers."

Later revelation will confirm this optimism and tell how victory over evil is attained. The woman's offspring then is primarily Christ. With the words of the psalmist we may praise God for overcoming evil through a woman (Mary) and her son: "Sing to the Lord a new song, for he has done marvelous deeds" (Psalm 98:1).

SCRIPTURE READING —

The Lord God . . . called to the man and asked him, "Where are you?" He answered, "I heard you in the garden; but I was afraid, because I was naked, so I hid myself." Then he asked, "Who told you that you were naked? You have eaten, then, from the tree of which I had forbidden you to eat!" The man replied, "The woman whom you put here with me—she gave me fruit from the tree, and so I ate it." The Lord God then asked the woman, "Why did you do such a thing?" The woman answered, "The serpent tricked me into it, so I ate it."

Then the Lord God said to the serpent:
"Because you have done this, you shall be banned
from all the animals
and from all the wild creatures;
On your belly shall you crawl,
and dirt shall you eat
all the days of your life.
I will put enmity between you and the woman,
and between your offspring and hers;
He will strike at your head,
while you strike at his heel."

(Genesis 3:9-15)

"The days are coming . . . when I will fulfill the promise"

THE virtue of patience is not as a rule one of the strong points of our contemporaries. They want things to be done quickly and efficiently. Promises and appointments should be kept as accurately as they were made; otherwise an outburst of impatience may follow. We have all experienced the impatient and compulsive driver behind us who takes unreasonable chances and causes disaster quite often. Patients in a hospital or nursing home obviously must practice the virtue of patience. They have to wait for recovery patiently and when they are old or sick for a long time they often have to wait for company or friends with even more patience.

Advent is a time of waiting for the coming of Christ. Promises have been made to us about a way out of our distress. Salvation will come, but when? We pray, but does God listen? The Bible reading deals with this problem. Waiting for somebody to come, i.e., Jesus Christ, supposes patience. We must accept the human condition of "not yet" with the patient hope for better things to come.

"I will raise up for David a just shoot." King David's dynasty came to a fall with the destruction of Jerusalem by the Babylonians in 586 B.C. It was like a stump. But from that stump God will cause a shoot to grow—a new Davidic king will be on the throne of Israel. Meanwhile, the Hebrews were in exile in Babylon. They knew God's promises, but were tempted to lose patience when time dragged on. Christians see this promise fulfilled with the coming of Jesus Christ. Then Judah, Jerusalem, God's people, received lasting salvation. But this salvation is only initiated in all of us. Full salvation from all evil and perfect bliss with God will be ours with Christ's final coming for you and me. When, depressed by life's tribulations, you are tempted to lose patience, make Psalm 25:5 your prayer! "God, for you I wait all the day."

SCRIPTURE READING —

The days are coming, says the Lord, when I will fulfill the promise I made to the house of Israel and Judah. In those days, in that time, I will raise up for David a just shoot; he shall do what is right and just in the land. In those days Judah shall be safe and Jerusalem shall dwell secure; this is what they shall call her: "The Lord our justice."

(Jeremiah 33:14-16)

"Proclaiming a baptism of repentance . . ."

IN our computerized society each necessity for change is carefully calculated. One wants to avoid mere chance. Every step in a new direction should be pondered on its pros and cons first. Hence, one is suspicious of any prophetic enthusiasm. Prophets see the necessity for change in a society, but, according to the calculators, they are motivated too much by intuition and great visions of a better future. Nevertheless, in order to have things done, we need the prophetic element. We need men like St. Francis of Assisi, who did not calculate but by a life of poverty effected a change in the Church back to evangelical simplicity. We need women like St. Catherine of Siena, who counseled the Pope on evangelical values and was heeded.

The society of Jesus' time was waiting for a change. John the Baptizer initiated Jesus' mission. Both were assassinated! But we need the prophets' intuition, their enthusiasm and dedication to a better future. Share it! The moment you start thinking: "It will last for my time," you are old and stale!

Luke relates John the Baptizer's call to be a prophet, i.e., God's spokesman. In God's name, he is to deliver a message of repentance. Change in attitude is necessary to make ready the way of the Lord. Later, Jesus himself will inaugurate his mission with a call for repentance (Mark 1:15). John was committed to his task. He did not preach only what people wanted to hear. He openly rebuked King Herod for wrongfully living with his brother's wife and this zeal for God's law cost his life (Mark 6:14ff). Calculators would say: "He should have been more careful!" But people like John with their great visions and enthusiastic commitment have changed the world!

Do you regard "commitment" as a value? It does not mean that you should give up planning. We need both the calculations of the computer and the commitment of the prophets!

SCRIPTURE READING —

In the fifteenth year of the rule of Tiberius Caesar, when Pontius Pilate was procurator of Judea, Herod tetrarch of Galilee, Philip his brother tetrarch of the region of Ituraea and Trachonitis, and Lysanias tetrarch of Abilene, during the high-priesthood of Annas and Caiaphas, the word of God was spoken to John son of Zechariah in the desert. He went about the entire region of the Jordan proclaiming a baptism of repentance which led to the forgiveness of sins. (Luke 3:1-3)

"The people were full of anticipation"

LIFE could be compared with a doctor's waiting room where people tell one another about their ailments. It could be the emergency room of a hospital where a mother waits with a sick child. She shares her anxiety with others whom perhaps she does not even know. This is the instinctive need for concern. Everyone hopes that the doctor can help and take away fear and anxiety.

Life is a waiting room, and Christians make themselves more aware of this during the time of Advent. All of us have our ailments and anxieties, like the rich people (having "two coats"), the tax collectors, and the soldiers of today's reading. We wait for Christ's coming into our lives. Hope for salvation is an integral part of the Christian life-style. And this hope is founded on our firm faith that somebody is concerned!

We see by this reading that there were people who reacted to John the Baptizer's sermons: "What ought we to do?" In searching for meaning in life, we ask this question too. It all depends whether or not we are "full of anticipation." Do we look at a future? Do we believe in Jesus to come, who will baptize us (immerse us) in the Holy Spirit and fire? There are wheat and chaff also in our lives. With our doubts, problems, and anxieties, we should turn to the Lord Jesus. He is concerned. Immersed in the Holy Spirit, we should come to new life! Christmas could be a new start for us.

SCRIPTURE READING —

The crowds asked [John the Baptizer], "What ought we to do?" In reply he said, "Let the man with two coats give to him who has none. The man who has food should do the same."

Tax collectors also came to be baptized, and they said to him, "Teacher, what are we to do?" He answered them, "Exact nothing over and above your fixed amount."

Soldiers likewise asked him, "What about us?" He told them, "Don't bully anyone. Denounce no one falsely. Be content with your pay."

The people were full of anticipation, wondering in their hearts whether John might be the Messiah. John answered them all by saying: "I am baptizing you in water, but there is one to come who is mightier than I. I am not fit to loosen his sandal strap. He will baptize you in the Holy Spirit and in fire. His winnowing-fan is in his hand to clear his threshing floor and gather the wheat into his granary; but the chaff he will burn in unquenchable fire." Using exhortations of this sort, he preached the good news to the people. (Luke 3:10-18)

"Let us live honorably as in daylight"

AS ONE gets on in years, one comes to realize that by the age of sixty most human beings have slept for twenty years of their lives. These many years of unconsciousness are necessary to make forty years of creative life possible. Small wonder that for the ancients the night was a symbol of gloom, evil, and unproductivity. Electricity, after all, is a blessing that is not yet a century old, and only a few acres of the planet enjoy an abundance of it in the manner of Times Square in New York City. Jesus has said: "The night comes on when no one can work" (John 9:4).

Visiting senior citizens can be an edifying experience but quite often a depressing one as well. I know old people that I like to be with. Serenity and peace, wit and wisdom are visibly beaming from their faces. They look back on a well-spent life. They are at peace with themselves and God. And why is it that all of us also know old grumblers whom all shun? They are usually the ones who regret their missed chances.

May you and I grow old as lovable people! Meanwhile, however, our years go on, one season following another! Hence, be watchful! Wake up! Carousing, drunkenness, sexual excess, lust, quarreling and jealousy are part of the human condition. The deeds of darkness can make us numb and insensitive to the beauty of life. "Put on the Lord Jesus," i.e., be ever more intimately united to him and what he stands for, and a bright future of Shalom —peace—will be yours.

SCRIPTURE READING —

Take care to do all these things, for you know the time in which we are living. It is now the hour for you to wake from sleep, for our salvation is closer than when we first accepted the faith. The night is far spent; the day draws near. Let us cast off deeds of darkness and put on the armor of light. Let us live honorably as in daylight; not in carousing and drunkenness, not in sexual excess and lust, not in quarreling and jealousy. Rather, put on the Lord Jesus Christ and make no provision for the desires of the flesh. (Romans 13:11-14)

"That we might derive hope from . . . the words of encouragement in the Scriptures"

WHILE lecturing on the Bible, I have been asked often: "What about *The Living Bible* [as developed by the editors of Campus Life Magazine, Youth for Christ International]?" It is not a translation of the Bible but a paraphrase.[1] In the statement of the editors, I have marked the word "youth." And that may be the answer.

Quite a few people read only the funny papers and skip the front page and editorial section of their daily newspapers. They are picture readers! We have nowadays a good deal of youthful and not so youthful semi-illiterates in this country. However, since the ancient Phoenicians found the Egyptian picture writing/reading (called hieroglyphics) inadequate and replaced it with an alphabet, one may expect that an American with a high school education will desire and be able to read God's word in a translation as close as possible to the original. But to each his own taste!

Paul tells us that Scripture was written for our instruction, that we might derive hope from it. In Christ is the yearning of people fulfilled. Accept Jesus Christ as your leader, and heed his great commandment to accept one another! Like Christ, become one another's servants! Then you will be working toward the realization of that seemingly impossible dream of Isaiah and Jesus: a society where "the wolf is the guest of the lamb" (Isaiah 11:16).

[1] *The Way—The Living Bible,* published by Our Sunday Visitor. In the same category are: *New World* and *Winding Quest* by Alan T. Dale, published by Morehouse Barlow Co., N.Y.

SCRIPTURE READING —

Everything written before our time was written for our instruction, that we might derive hope from the lessons of patience and the words of encouragement in the Scriptures. May God, the source of all patience and encouragement, enable you to live in perfect harmony with one another according to the spirit of Christ Jesus, so that with one heart and voice you may glorify God, the Father of our Lord Jesus Christ.

(Romans 15:4-6)

"Be patient, my brothers, until the coming of the Lord"

LIKE the writer of these Introductions, James lived no doubt in a rural situation. He observed the farmers of his time who were even more subject to the whims of nature than their counterparts in our time of scientific farming. Farmers need to look forward patiently. They invest thousands of dollars in labor, fertilizer, chemicals, and equipment. They can control pests and weeds all right, but the weather remains the threatening X factor in all their endeavors. They start planning and working in the early spring and know the outcome only late in the fall of the year. And that is true of life as well: patiently waiting after we have done whatever we are supposed to do.

Patience relates to self, fellow beings, and situations. Accepting yourself as you are with your limitations, little successes but also failures, is not easy. As a student, I knew fellows who achieved more than I did. It irritated me. I was ambitious. Whatever our limitations may be, physical, emotional, or intellectual, we should accept ourselves as precious in the eyes of our Maker. And as for others—members of the family, co-religious, co-workers, or students we teach—what about accepting them as different?

James reminds us not to be overly optimistic. The bright future of the Messianic era will not be fully realized on this side of the grave. We must be patient! "But steady your hearts, because the coming of the Lord is at hand." The prophets should be our models. If you are suffering, this reading could be an inspiring starting point for a personal prayer to God!

SCRIPTURE READING—

Be patient, therefore, my brothers, until the coming of the Lord. See how the farmer awaits the precious yield of the soil. He looks forward to it patiently while the soil receives the winter and the spring rains. You, too, must be patient. Steady your hearts, because the coming of the Lord is at hand. Do not grumble against one another, my brothers, lest you be condemned. See! The judge stands at the gate. As your models in suffering hardships and in patience, brothers, take the prophets who spoke in the name of the Lord. (James 5:7-10)

December 15

"To bring to obedient faith all the Gentiles"

THE Act of Faith found in the *Baltimore Catechism* reflects well how for a couple of centuries Catholic theology has been infected by the sciences that were seen as its competitors. Faith was viewed as another form of knowing: "O my God, I firmly believe *that* Thou art one God. . . . I believe these and all *the truths* which the Holy Catholic Church teaches, because Thou hast revealed them." Faith is seen as accepting (knowing) a set of truths to live by on the authority of God.

One may ask: "What is wrong with that?" Nothing. But it is not the faith with which the Bible deals. Biblical faith is faith in a person and hence a commitment to him/her. It is a person-to-person relationship which is different from a more or less uninvolved way of knowing a few truths.

Paul explains who the Savior, Jesus Christ, is. He is fully man, a descendant of King David, but made Son of God in power. Paul's task is to bring to obedient faith all the Gentiles. It is through our "obedient faith" in the Lord Jesus, sent by God to enlighten all who go through the darkness of the human condition, that we will be saved.

In my Bible, I have underlined "obedient faith" and "called to belong to Jesus Christ" as a referral for meditation.

SCRIPTURE READING —

Greetings from Paul, a servant of Christ Jesus, called to be an apostle and set apart to proclaim the gospel of God which he promised long ago through his prophets, as the holy Scriptures record—the gospel concerning his Son, who was descended from David according to the flesh but was made Son of God in power according to the spirit of holiness, by his resurrection from the dead: Jesus Christ our Lord. Through him we have been favored with apostleship, that we may spread his name and bring to obedient faith all the Gentiles, among whom are you who have been called to belong to Jesus Christ.

To all in Rome, beloved of God and called to holiness, grace and peace from God our Father and the Lord Jesus Christ. (Romans 1:1-7)

"He [Jesus Christ] will strengthen you to the end"

IN FOLLOWING the political campaigns via the media I often admire the determination of the contenders. What time and energy they invest! Some bow out at an early stage of the game. Do they lack perseverance? Perhaps. Those who go on to the end, however, have it indeed. They look tired, their voices get bitter and harsh the more they are determined to win the race. And finally they wait for the outcome.

Paul sees the community of Corinth as waiting for the revelation of our Lord Jesus Christ. He thanks God for the favors bestowed on them in Christ Jesus: the gifts of speech and knowledge. Later in the Epistle, he will tell them to use these gifts well! Waiting and persevering to the end requires the strength of God, but they will succeed. "God is faithful."

Using interdependence in lower animal life (e.g., in a colony of ants) as a base, sociolobiologists try to demonstrate that human interdependence relates mainly to our genetic structure. Many other scientists do not attribute the same importance to our genes. They see human growth more related to environment. Whatever the case, interdependent we are, and we need "strength" from outside ourselves if we want to persevere. Our Maker gives it through co-humanity with our fellow humans and moreover through intimate contact with the Lord Jesus in meditative prayer.

In my Bible, I have underlined "God is faithful" and "called to fellowship with his Son" and concentrated my reflective prayer around these thoughts.

SCRIPTURE READING —

I continually thank my God for you because of the favor he has bestowed on you in Christ Jesus, in whom you have been richly endowed with every gift of speech and knowledge. Likewise, the witness I bore to Christ has been so confirmed among you that you lack no spiritual gift as you wait for the revelation of our Lord Jesus Christ. He will strengthen you to the end, so that you will be blameless on the day of our Lord Jesus [Christ]. God is faithful, and it was he who called you to fellowship with his Son, Jesus Christ our Lord.

(1 Corinthians 1:4-9)

"No one who believes in him will be put to shame"

IT IS humiliating when you must admit that a person in whom you have faith disappoints you. Whether it is a teenager who finds out that her boyfriend is two-timing her, or an educator who recommends a former student for a job on which he fails, one feels embarrassed. I know colleagues who turn cynical almost to the point of misanthropy. Can one trust anybody?

I am thinking of that "upright man" Joseph, a carpenter, who had all the reason in the world to be suspicious of his fiancée-spouse (see Matthew 1:18-21). This was no small matter, for he loved that girl and held her in great esteem as a virtuous, faithful, lovable person with whom it was worthwhile sharing his life. And then to find out that she was pregnant! For him everything worked out well. But what may we have to go through when we change our opinion of someone we thought we could trust and love!

I still believe in the basic goodness of my fellow human beings, although as I get older I am not amazed by failures anymore. All of us are so human! But I have unconditional faith in one human being, just because he is not only human but also divine. He is Jesus Christ, a human being, who is so intimately united with God that under divine guidance the authors of the Bible call him: Word, Light, Son of God, and even God.

In today's Scripture Paul testifies to his faith in Jesus Christ and is very much convinced that he will not be put to shame. Whenever human beings disappoint you and cause you to be depressed, turn to the one who will never put you to shame! Advent and Christmas is a time to do it more than ever.

SCRIPTURE READING —

What is it he does say? "The word is near you, on your lips and in your heart" (that is, the word of faith which we preach). For if you confess with your lips that Jesus is Lord, and believe in your heart that God raised him from the dead, you will be saved. Faith in the heart leads to justification, confession on the lips to salvation. Scripture says, "No one who believes in him will be put to shame." Here there is no difference between Jew and Greek; all have the same Lord, rich in mercy toward all who call upon him. "Everyone who calls on the name of the Lord will be saved." (Romans 10:8-13)

December 18

"Be on guard lest your spirits become bloated"

QUITE a few Friday night drivers end up in the hospital or even in the funeral home simply because they have not been careful. Be on guard! We teach our children to be careful in the street. Often parents permit Junior to buy that first motorcycle only with reluctance because they are afraid that he may hurt himself, and they stress time and again: "Be careful!" What about the deeper dimension of our lives, the personal that will live on for ever?

The core of this tradition comes from Jesus, but it has been embellished extensively by oral tradition and the editing by Luke, who adapted it to the needs of his congregations. As mentioned before, signs in the sun, moon, and stars, gathering clouds, and the shaking of powers in the heavens constitute the familiar imagery utilized by biblical writers to describe the awe-inspiring event of manifestation of the Divine. The early Christians expected the return of Christ to take place in their own lifetime. They were waiting, ran out of patience, and gave in to laxity (characterized by Luke as indulgence, drunkenness, and worldly cares).

What is God's word to us in this passage? It is true that we do not expect Christ's second coming right now. However, it is equally true that God can call you and me the moment we least expect it. That moment represents "the great day" for each of us. "Be on guard."

SCRIPTURE READING —

[Jesus said:] "There will be signs in the sun, the moon and the stars. On the earth, nations will be in anguish, distraught at the roaring of the sea and the waves. Men will die of fright in anticipation of what is coming upon the earth. The powers in the heavens will be shaken. After that, men will see the Son of Man coming on a cloud with great power and glory. When these things begin to happen, stand erect and hold your heads high, for your deliverance is near at hand."

"Be on guard lest your spirits become bloated with indulgence and drunkenness and worldly cares. The great day will suddenly close in on you like a trap. The day I speak of will come upon all who dwell on the face of the earth. So be on the watch. Pray constantly for the strength to escape whatever is in prospect, and to stand secure before the Son of Man." (Luke 21:25-28, 34-36)

"That . . . you may learn to value the things that matter"

IT IS in a conflict of duties that we learn about our priority of values. Our decision reflects whether we value the things that really matter or whether we are attached to less valuable things. Having company on Sunday morning, for example, could result in the conflicting duties of preparing breakfast and going to church. In order to make the right decision, one needs an abundance of understanding and a wealth of experience, both rooted in love.

Paul prays that God may give all of this to the people of Philippi. We should pray for the same gifts. Married people, confronted with all the options which science and modern life offer, should search for the loving thing that must be done. Religious live with the tension between horizontal and vertical piety. What is the loving thing to do in each situation—this should be your constant concern.

Paul writes about "the day of Christ Jesus." It is the day of Christ's coming. In waiting for his coming, Christians must "learn to value the things that really matter." What is the priority of your values? During Advent we prepare for the Lord's coming at Christmas and his final coming to each of us. Could you explain your priorities if the Lord were to call you right now?

SCRIPTURE READING—

I am sure of this much: that he who has begun the good work in you will carry it through to completion, right up to the day of Christ Jesus. It is only right that I should entertain such expectations in your regard since I hold all of you dear—you who, to a man, are sharers of my gracious lot when I lie in prison or am summoned to defend the solid grounds on which the gospel rests. God himself can testify how much I long for each of you with the affection of Christ Jesus! My prayer is that your love may more and more abound, both in understanding and wealth of experience, so that with a clear conscience and blameless conduct you may learn to value the things that really matter, up to the very day of Christ. It is my wish that you may be found rich in the harvest of justice which Jesus Christ has ripened in you, to the glory and praise of God. (Philippians 1:6-11)

"They shall call him Emmanuel"

IT IS faith in God, who approaches us in the Lord Jesus, that saves us from a meaningless existence. God is willing to step into the darkness of our confusion, if we "let the Lord enter" (Psalm 24:1) Loneliness is the greatest threat to happiness. A human being alone has no answers. A loner is an unhappy person, depressed, facing absurdity. "Emmanuel—God with us" in Jesus Christ saves us from ourselves. Time and again, Christmas reminds Christians that God came to share our human situation on this planet. Looked at in this way, Christmas will become a happy and meaningful day for us.

Matthew quotes an oracle of Isaiah (7:10-14). The virgin (young maiden) who will bear a son is probably Abi, the young wife of King Ahaz.

Both Matthew and the Church have seen in the birth of Christ from the virgin Mother the perfect fulfillment of Isaiah's prophecy. It is through Jesus Christ that God steps in to save us, who pass through the twilight of human existence. In the Lord Jesus, God is "Emmanuel—God with us." And this tremendous mystery ("God with us—you do not have to go it alone") is what we are going to celebrate at Christmas. "Let the Lord enter; he is the king of glory" (Psalm 24:1)

SCRIPTURE READING —

All this happened to fulfill what the Lord had said through the prophet:

"The virgin shall be with child
and give birth to a son,
and they shall call him Emmanuel,"
a name which means "God is with us."

When Joseph awoke he did as the angel of the Lord had directed him and received her into his home as his wife. He had no relations with her at any time before she bore a son, whom he named Jesus.

(Matthew 1:22-25)

"And his reign will be without end"

WHEN a mother is expecting a baby, in a way the whole family is expecting with her. There is joy in expecting a beautiful happening to come. There is excitement in expecting a vacation trip which is going to be an entirely new experience. We ask friends who have been there. Expecting keeps us young. We look to the future instead of to the past. There are always new and exciting aspects in life, if only we have the eye to see them and the gift of wonderment, which children possess and grown-ups should never lose.

Christmas is such an event to come. It is God revealing "a mystery, hidden for many ages" (Romans 16:25). He wants to be present to us. He wants to give us an image of himself in Jesus Christ, an image which we are able to perceive with our weak human senses. Christmas is great every year, but only for those who are expecting "Emmanuel—God with us" in faith and wonderment.

Let us admire God's way every year again during Advent and Christmas time, and accept Jesus Christ as Luke wants us to do.

SCRIPTURE READING —

In the sixth month, the angel Gabriel was sent from God to a town of Galilee named Nazareth, to a virgin betrothed to a man named Joseph, of the house of David. The virgin's name was Mary. Upon arriving, the angel said to her: "Rejoice, O highly favored daughter! The Lord is with you. Blessed are you among women." She was deeply troubled by his words, and wondered what his greeting meant. The angel went on to say to her: "Do not fear, Mary. You have found favor with God. You shall conceive and bear a son and give him the name Jesus. Great will be his dignity and he will be called Son of the Most High. The Lord God will give him the throne of David his father. He will rule over the house of Jacob forever and his reign will be without end."

Mary said to the angel, "How can this be since I do not know man?" The angel answered her: "The Holy Spirit will come upon you and the power of the Most High will overshadow you; hence, the holy offspring to be born will be called Son of God. Know that Elizabeth your kinswoman has conceived a son in her old age; she who was thought to be sterile is now in her sixth month, for nothing is impossible with God."

Mary said: "I am the servant of the Lord. Let it be done to me as you say." With that the angel left her. (Luke 1:26-38)

"Blest are you among women"

WHEN candidates for public office are campaigning, they often bring their wives and children into the picture. They expect that their family setting will tell the voters something about them as persons. And when they have been elected to office, they make their first public appearance with their wives. What we are as persons is greatly influenced by the human beings to whom we are related. Many great men admit that they forged their career through the inspiration of their wives.

The New Testament writers describe Jesus of Nazareth as a celibate. There was no wife who inspired him to greatness. But a woman is mentioned, namely, his mother Mary. Luke states: "[Jesus] was obedient to them [his parents]. . . . [He] progressed steadily in wisdom and grace before God and men" (Luke 2:51-52). It was Mary who reared the man Jesus. In preparing for the Lord's coming, we do not leave Mary out of the picture. It was her faith and obedience which made the incarnation of God's Son possible. Mary's faith and obedience should also inspire us to greatness as Christians.

Filled with the Holy Spirit, Elizabeth calls Mary "blessed," because of her faith and the obedience with which she bore her child. The Second Vatican Council's *Constitution on the Church* states: "Mary devoted herself totally as a handmaid of the Lord to the person and work of her Son." By her faith and obedience to God's design, Mary was the great woman behind Jesus. We learn from Mary to be faithful to our commitments.

SCRIPTURE READING —

Mary set out, proceeding in haste into the hill country to a town of Judah, where she entered Zechariah's house and greeted Elizabeth. When Elizabeth heard Mary's greeting, the baby leapt in her womb. Elizabeth was filled with the Holy Spirit and cried out in a loud voice: "Blest are you among women and blest is the fruit of your womb. But who am I that the mother of my Lord should come to me? The moment your greeting sounded in my ears, the baby leapt in my womb for joy. Blest is she who trusted that the Lord's words to her would be fulfilled."

(Luke 1:39-45)

December 23

"But a body you have prepared for me"

A WELL-KNOWN entertainer used to give away expensive cars. Why? Lonely grandparents may shower a grandchild with gifts all the time. Why? When besides paying the fee, a patient sends flowers to the physician who operated on her and saved her life, fee and flowers are given for different reasons, the latter one being appreciative. It was in this perspective that the ancients saw their gifts (sacrifices) offered to God or their gods, and it is in this same perspective that the author of Hebrews sees our Lord's human life of dedication resulting finally in a cruel death.

Figuratively he lets Jesus say the words of Psalm 40:7-9. But remember well, Jesus' self-sacrifice is a symbol of a total dedication of heart, mind, and body. The sacrifices of the Old Law are refuted in that routine had made them void and meaningless. This is a danger that threatens all religious symbols.

Christ took a body in order to be able to sacrifice himself in total obedience to God. This reminds us of the reason for the incarnation, which is closely related to our Lord's sacrifice of atonement on Golgotha. Bethlehem and Calvary cannot be separated. We learn what is most characteristic about Jesus: "I have come to do your will."

SCRIPTURE READING —

On coming into the world, Jesus said:
"Sacrifice and offering you did not desire,
but a body you have prepared for me;
Holocausts and sin offerings you took no delight in.
Then I said, 'As is written of me in the book,
I have come to do your will, O God.' "
First he says,
"Sacrifices and offerings, holocausts and sin offerings,
you neither desired nor delighted in."
(These are offered according to the prescriptions of the law.) Then he says,
"I have come to do your will."
In other words, he takes away the first covenant to establish the second.

By this "will," we have been sanctified through the offering of the body of Jesus Christ once for all. (Hebrews 10:5-10)

"As a bridegroom rejoices in his bride so shall your God rejoice in you"

TOURIST bureaus, which organize guided tours, usually show the better parts of the city. If you want to see the slums and misery of a large part of the population, you must explore a city on your own. Evil is something one wants to hide from visitors. But if you are honest, you cannot deny its existence. Evil exists in and around us. We feel that often we fail to be the kind of persons we should be.

There is even more evil around us, and it enslaves us more than we want to admit. We need redemption from selfishness, apathy, and complacency in the kind of happiness which the mass media and society are constantly imposing on us. "Tomorrow [Christmas, present to you!] the wickedness of the earth will be destroyed" (Gospel Acclamation for Vigil Mass of Christmas).

The unknown prophet, called "Third Isaiah," addresses the Jews who have returned from Babylonian exile. The reconstruction of their homeland is not working too well. There is widespread disappointment. The prophet encourages his fellow citizens: "Have hope! Better times are at hand. God cares." The writer uses the model of marital love to describe God's care for his people. Through the incarnation, becoming "one flesh" (Matthew 19:6) with the human race, God espouses you and me. He sets us free, and "as a bridegroom rejoices in his bride, so shall your God rejoice in you." Your response?

SCRIPTURE READING —

Nations shall behold your vindication,
and all kings your glory;
You shall be called by a new name
pronounced by the mouth of the Lord.
You shall be a glorious crown in the hand of the Lord,
a royal diadem held by your God.
No more shall men call you "Forsaken,"
or your land "Desolate,"
But you shall be called "My Delight,"
and your land "Espoused."
For the Lord delights in you,
and makes your land his spouse.
As a young man marries a virgin,
your Builder shall marry you;
And as a bridegroom rejoices in his bride
so shall your God rejoice in you.
(Isaiah 62:2-5)

CHRISTMAS

INCREASED knowledge of the universe has only made man more aware of how much this little planet depends upon the sun. Dwindling raw materials and an ever growing demand for energy make us turn to the sun as our last resource.

Prescientific man experienced that same feeling of dependence and celebrated it with magic rites. A feast of the Unconquered Sun after the winter solstice is just one sign of awareness of the sun as the source of life on earth. In the Nordic countries of Europe in particular, there was a proliferation of customs associated with celebration of the lengthening days. It spurred the popularization of Christmas in the Western world.

In the dark human condition, Jesus Christ is our light and source of energy. He is the Unconquered Sun, a Radiant Dawn, Splendor of eternal light, Sun of justice. And gratefully Christians celebrate, because we have been rescued from the power of darkness. Darkness that covered the earth has given way to the bright dawn of God's Word made flesh. God, make us people of this light! (Liturgy of the Hours for Christmas).

In Him we see our God made visible.

Preface of Christmas

"The people who walked in darkness have seen a great light"

IT HAS been said that a philosophy of science must be created in the near future, otherwise mankind is going to make this planet unhabitable for the next generations, the lifetime of our children and grandchildren. This philosophy must lay the foundation for ecology, the global use of the planet's resources, the function of money, international law, and the solution of other vital problems.

Emmanuel (God with us in the Lord Jesus) offers such a philosophy of science. "Upon us, who dwell in the land of gloom, a light has shone." Today, we should more than ever be aware of the wealth of our Christian heritage. And though we cannot claim to have ready-made answers for all the details, the Bible and the great social encyclicals of Popes John and Paul give outlines which the human race can safely follow.

The enthronement anthem that forms today's reading was accustomed to be sung when a new king ascended the throne and expresses faith in the new king. He will do better than his predecessors. "For a child is born to us" refers to the fact that the enthronement of the king was conceived as God's adoption of the king as his son. Christians have reinterpreted this. Now these words suggest the birth at Bethlehem and explain what the Lord Jesus means to all of us. Respond in reflective prayer!

SCRIPTURE READING —

The people who walked in darkness
have seen a great light;
Upon those who dwelt in the land of gloom
a light has shone.
You have brought them abundant joy
and great rejoicing,
As they rejoice before you as at the harvest,
as men make merry when dividing spoils.
For the yoke that burdened them,
the pole on their shoulder,
And the rod of their taskmaster
you have smashed, as on the day of Midian.
For every boot that tramped in battle,
every cloak rolled in blood,
will be burned as fuel for flames.
For a child is born to us, a son is given us;
upon his shoulder dominion rests.
They name him Wonder-Counselor, God-Hero,
Father-Forever, Prince of Peace.

(Isaiah 9:1-5)

"Mary treasured all these things and reflected on them in her heart"

ANCIENT man, living before the electronic age, feared darkness more than we do. Darkness stands for isolation, uncertainty, evil, and also ignorance. We still speak of actions that shun daylight, and of the dark Middle Ages, a time of ignorance and decay. Light, especially bright daylight, changes a dark situation.

This contrast of light and darkness is used to explain the mystery of Christmas. The birth of our Lord marks the dawn of the Christian era. Christianity—Christians, you and I, filled with the light of faith—should shed light on dark human situations in our words and actions. The lights of your Christmas tree should symbolize this Christian concern.

Luke associates Jesus with shepherds, poor people, members of a despised trade, just as he will do later with prostitutes and other kinds of sinners. These disadvantaged people have seen the light. "The glory of the Lord shone around them" (Luke 2:9). Hence their conclusion: "Let us go over and see!" Luke wants you and me to do the same today: go and see and try to understand what has been told to you concerning this child. Mary should be your example. "She treasured all these things and reflected on them in her heart."

SCRIPTURE READING —

When the angels had returned to heaven, the shepherds said to one another: "Let us go over to Bethlehem and see this event which the Lord has made known to us." They went in haste and found Mary and Joseph, and the baby lying in the manger; once they saw, they understood what had been told them concerning this child. All who heard of it were astonished at the report given them by the shepherds.

Mary treasured all these things and reflected on them in her heart. The shepherds returned, glorifying and praising God for all they had heard and seen, in accord with what had been told them. (Luke 2:15-20)

"The Word became flesh"

CHRISTIANS have sometimes stressed the uniqueness of God's revelation in Jesus Christ so much that often the impression was given that God did not reveal himself elsewhere as well. The Second Vatican Council has mentioned that there is "a ray of truth" also in other religions. Indeed, people can gain salvation also in other ways, but accepting the Lord Jesus is the ordinary path.

The author of today's reading may have adapted a Jewish song on God's wisdom as incarnated in the Law of Moses *(see January 31)* and applied it to God's Logos (word, wisdom, light, Son) "made flesh" in the Lord Jesus. But his faithful, most of them from Jewish background, were inclined to see Moses, John the Baptizer, and Jesus on the same level: all three of them prophets, bearers of the Divine Logos! That is why he interrupts his song several times. *(See your Bible*—John 1:1-18.) The author has the Baptizer testify and mentions Moses to show that God's wisdom is incarnated in them as well but we Christians believe it to be "made flesh" in a very unique way in Jesus.

The invisible God has chosen to speak to us in and through Jesus. He is "God's Word made flesh." Whatever God has to tell us has been made "flesh" in the words, actions, and loving personality of the Lord Jesus, born in Bethlehem, reared in Nazareth, and put to death in Jerusalem.

However, the light can shine in darkness and not overcome it. Open up and gratefully accept God's word as spoken to you in and through Jesus. Only then will your Christmas be real and your Christmas joy not be gone with your tree on the garbage heap!

SCRIPTURE READING —

In the beginning was the Word;
the Word was in God's presence,
and the Word was God.
He was present to God in the beginning.
Through him all things came into being,
and apart from him nothing came to be.
Whatever came to be in him, found life,
life for the light of men.
The light shines on in darkness,
a darkness that did not overcome it.
The Word became flesh
and made his dwelling among us,
and we have seen his glory:
The glory of an only Son coming from the Father,
filled with enduring love.

(John 1:1-5, 14)

"Let the word of Christ, rich as it is, dwell in you"

WE ARE witnessing a breakdown of the traditional family and its values—filial respect for authority, exercised responsibly by parents—and a rising juvenile delinquency. Hence, our society can learn a few things from today's Bible reading. Of course, there is no easy remedy available for today's family crisis. Also, the Christian family is part of a culture in which humans participate—neighborhood, school, television, friends, and recreation patterns. But in stormy weather a ship may get at least some guidance from a beacon! And though authority from the earliest infancy on should be exercised perhaps in a different way, it should not be eliminated completely. Parents could discuss this with their children. A substitute for sound family life has not yet been offered by any of the behavioral sciences.

The holy family, Jesus, Mary, Joseph, must have cherished the values brought out in this Bible passage. "Let the word of Christ . . . dwell in you." Why not try regular family Bible reading, with a discussion afterward and an improvised prayer by one member of the family at the end? And if you are a religious, what about your regular prayerful Bible reading?

SCRIPTURE READING —

Because you are God's chosen ones, holy and beloved, clothe yourselves with heartfelt mercy, with kindness, humility, meekness, and patience. Bear with one another; forgive whatever grievances you have against one another. Forgive as the Lord has forgiven you. Over all these virtues put on love, which binds the rest together and makes them perfect.

Christ's peace must reign in your hearts, since as members of the one body you have been called to that peace. Dedicate yourselves to thankfulness. Let the word of Christ, rich as it is, dwell in you. In wisdom made perfect, instruct and admonish one another. Sing gratefully to God from your hearts in psalms, hymns, and inspired songs. Whatever you do, whatever in speech or in action, do it in the name of the Lord Jesus. Give thanks to God the Father through him. (Colossians 3:12-17)

"May he enlighten your innermost vision"

EVERY serious person desires a meaningful life. Wanting to be a playboy implies wanting to be and remain a boy, i.e., immature! We need a philosophy of life. As Christians, we believe that the wisdom (word, light) of God was dwelling in Jesus Christ. We look to the philosophy of life of the Lord Jesus as an example to be followed. We study the values he stood for.

The Hebrew Bible, the Old Testament, knows various ways of God's dwelling with his creatures. A bright cloud is often a sign of God's mysterious presence. Divine wisdom dwells in Israel: "In Zion [the holy temple mountain] I fixed my abode. I [God's wisdom] have struck root among the glorious people" (Sirach 24:12). We Christians are grateful for the indwelling of God's spirit of wisdom and insight in all believers.

The latest in commercial meditation (TM: *see pp. 3-5,* and *October 26)* is getting wrapped up in the transcendent to such a degree that the trainee can fly around the room. He/she is led to the Siddhis, or supernatural powers, and taught full development of consciousness with flying as a by-product. Price tag—$5,000.

Continuous Christian meditation should result in greater awareness of God as both immanent and transcendent, with our "innermost vision" enlightened by his light, wisdom, and insight. Indeed, Christian mystics write about the prayer of rapture, or ecstasy to the accompaniment of levitation (see St. Teresa of Avila, *Life,* ch. 20, 1-4). But such phenomena (if they are to be understood literally) are attributed to God and not to mental training.

In my Bible, I have marked: "May he enlighten your innermost vision." I did not pray for levitation. Landings could be bumpy!

SCRIPTURE READING—

For my part, from the time I first heard of your faith in the Lord Jesus and your love for all the members of the church, I have never stopped thanking God for you and recommending you in my prayers.

May the God of our Lord Jesus Christ, the Father of glory, grant you a spirit of wisdom and insight to know him clearly. May he enlighten your innermost vision that you may know the great hope to which he has called you, the wealth of his glorious heritage to be distributed among the members of the church. (Ephesians 1:15-18)

"This is my beloved son"

THE "Marriage Encounter" movement is rapidly spreading all over the United States and even the world. I have met dozens of couples who said that they had experienced something like a second honeymoon. Those two days of dialogue, writing, talking, and praying had brought them closer together. They got to know one another better and discovered qualities in each other hitherto overlooked. Communication, which had become somewhat bleakish over the years, was restored.

Indeed, every time we discover a new aspect in the person we love, we stop in wonderment. "I did not know him/her as such!" And this deeper insight and sharing in a person's self results in greater appreciation, intimacy, and love. Today's Scripture describes the Lord's baptism by John in the Jordan. Matthew relates Jesus' baptism as another epiphany (manifestation), declaring that the Lord Jesus is the Servant (Son) of Yahweh. His call in life is that of the Servant as depicted in Isaiah 42:1-4.

This is an aspect of Jesus' personality which gives us a deeper insight into who our Lord is. He is "the man for others." He is there for you and me. Experiencing this in prayer, we should appreciate and love our Lord more for it.

Everyone has his own calling in life. We must respond to it in the framework of our personal capabilities and the circumstances of time and milieu. Serious and mature people understand that only a life of service is a meaningful life. What do you consider your main calling in life, and how do you fulfill it?

SCRIPTURE READING —

Jesus, coming from Galilee, appeared before John at the Jordan to be baptized by him. John tried to refuse him with the protest, "I should be baptized by you, yet you come to me!" Jesus answered: "Give in for now. We must do this if we would fulfill all of God's demands." So John gave in.

After Jesus was baptized, he came directly out of the water. Suddenly the sky opened and he saw the Spirit of God descend like a dove and hover over him. With that, a voice from the heavens said, "This is my beloved Son. My favor rests on him." (Matthew 3:13-17)

"A sign that will be opposed" December 31

SHOULD controversy be avoided at any cost? It seems impossible to do so if one wants to live by values that are not negotiable in good conscience. The person who tries to be "Mr. Nice Guy" all the time usually ends up losing friends and incurs the serious troubles associated with constant compromising. If we stand for values like love, justice, and truth, we are controversial and might even hurt feelings. Jesus Christ was in conflict with opponents all the time.

Luke describes Jesus' presentation in the temple as another manifestation of the Lord. Who is he? He is a revealing light to the Gentiles, the glory of God's people Israel, but also a sign that will be opposed. Luke's point is very clear. Like our Lord, we Christians are supposed to be a light in our dim confused human condition. But being honest in business and public office and advocating values like fidelity, justice, and truth must result in controversy every so often. We should have the courage to face it, and follow our conscience wherever it dictates action or requires an absolute "no."

Are you willing to accept our Lord as controversial? His values, do's and don'ts, are not always those of your friends and associates! Take a stand!

SCRIPTURE READING—

When the day came to purify them according to the law of Moses, the couple brought [Jesus] up to Jerusalem so that he could be presented to the Lord.

There lived in Jerusalem at the time a certain man named Simeon. He was just and pious, and awaited the consolation of Israel, and the Holy Spirit was upon him.

He came to the temple now, inspired by the Spirit, and when the parents brought in the child Jesus to perform for him the customary ritual of the law, he took him in his arms and blessed God.

The child's father and mother were marveling at what was being said about him. Simeon blessed them and said to Mary his mother: "This child is destined to be the downfall and the rise of many in Israel, a sign that will be opposed—and you yourself shall be pierced with a sword—so that the thoughts of many hearts may be laid bare."

(Luke 2:22, 25, 27-28, 33-35)

INDEX OF SCRIPTURE READINGS

SUBJECT INDEX